ASIAN AMERICAN FICTION AFTER 1965

Asian American Fiction After 1965

TRANSNATIONAL FANTASIES OF ECONOMIC MOBILITY

Christopher T. Fan

Columbia University Press
New York

Columbia University Press
Publishers Since 1893
New York   Chichester, West Sussex
cup.columbia.edu
Copyright © 2024 Columbia University Press
All rights reserved

Library of Congress Cataloging-in-Publication Data
Names: Fan, Christopher T., author.
Title: Asian American fiction after 1965 : transnational fantasies of economic mobility / Christopher T. Fan.
Description: New York : Columbia University Press, 2024. | Includes bibliographical references and index.
Identifiers: LCCN 2023049595 (print) | LCCN 2023049596 (ebook) | ISBN 9780231213226 (hardback) | ISBN 9780231213233 (trade paperback) | ISBN 9780231559782 (ebook)
Subjects: LCSH: American fiction—Asian American authors—History and criticism. | LCGFT: Literary criticism.
Classification: LCC PS153.A84 F36 2024 (print) | LCC PS153.A84 (ebook) | DDC 813.009/895—dc23/eng/20231024
LC record available at https://lccn.loc.gov/2023049595
LC ebook record available at https://lccn.loc.gov/2023049596

Cover design: Chang Jae Lee
Cover image: © Yu-Wen Wu 2023, Installation view, 2023 James and Audrey Foster Prize, Institute of Contemporary Art/Boston, 2023–2024. Photo by Mel Taing.

For my family

Don't make me laugh / stick to math, motherfucker.

—BOHAN PHOENIX, "YMF"

CONTENTS

Introduction: Miracle Fiction? 1

Chapter One
Deep Conditions of the World: Modernization Theory and Transimperiality 39

Chapter Two
Writing Like an Engineer: Postracial Form and Utopia 83

Chapter Three
Shakespeare Words: Professional Identity and Literary Style 117

Chapter Four
Genres of Deprofessionalization: Economic Subjectivity and Chinese American Women Writers 154

Chapter Five
Enough? Semiperipheral Structures of Feeling in the Taiwanese American Novel 179

Conclusion: Asian Fetish 214

ACKNOWLEDGMENTS 223
NOTES 227
BIBLIOGRAPHY 273
INDEX 295

INTRODUCTION

Miracle Fiction?

It is all a question of concrete correlations.
—LEON TROTSKY, HISTORY OF THE RUSSIAN REVOLUTION

"Something wonderful is happening right at this moment," Maxine Hong Kingston, the erstwhile engineer turned English major, once told the poet Marilyn Chin in an interview. She was referring to the year 1989: "Right now, just in the last few months, I mean. Amy Tan published *Joy Luck Club*, Hisaye Yamamoto published *Sixteen Syllables*; Frank Chin has a collection of short stories, and I think maybe [Ruthanne Lum McCunn] just came out with her book on Chinese families. Jessica Hagedorn's [novel *Dogeaters*] in the spring, and Bharati Mukherjee's [novel *Jasmine*] is in the fall. She won the National Book Critics Circle Award. Something great must be going on."[1] It wouldn't be long before "wonderful" and "great" would become *miraculous*. Adding to Kingston's excitement over 1989, the literary scholar Sau-ling Wong would single out 1991 as an "annus mirabilis" in Asian American literary history because it saw yet another impressive uptick in the number of novels published by Asian American authors, including Gish Jen's *Typical American* and Amy Tan's *The Kitchen God's Wife*, as well as high-profile recognition of authors like Karen Tei Yamashita, whose *Through the Arc of the Rainforest* received the American Book Award.[2] The uptick didn't stop there, and it would be an understatement to describe what has happened since as a boom. Reflecting on Wong's observation two decades later, Min Hyoung Song wrote: "If 1991 was indeed a year of miracles, what makes it doubly miraculous is how its accomplishments have been dwarfed by the productivity and success of . . . the decades that followed."[3] Yet another decade has passed, and the boom shows no signs of subsiding.[4]

The same year that Wong offered her observation, 1993, the World Bank announced another miracle in its report *The East Asian Miracle: Economic Growth and Public Policy*. Since 1960, the authors wrote, "high-performing Asian economies"—Hong Kong, South Korea, Singapore, and Taiwan, also known as the "Four Tigers"—"have grown more than twice as fast as the rest of East Asia [which includes China, Thailand, and Southeast Asia], roughly three times as fast as Latin America and South Asia, and five times faster than Sub-Saharan Africa. They also significantly outperformed the industrial economies and the oil-rich Middle East–North Africa region."[5] For friendly readers of the bank's report, the miracles in East Asia were proof-positive of the power of free markets and that the governments there had been attentive students of U.S. capitalism. But for the Asian American authors bursting onto the literary scene in the 1990s, those so-called "miracles" were, in a way, of little concern. They were Asian *American* authors, after all, and the falling emphasis of that identity was being reinforced with every publication, every award. These authors were keenly aware that the "textual coalition" that they and their fiction comprised extended beyond the cultural realm. As Wong would argue, literary representation, mediated by a professional literary critical establishment, amounted to political representation.[6] However, the miracles abroad would soon become impossible to ignore because they were changing the very meanings of "Asia" and "America." In Asian American studies and beyond, people were talking about the end of the "American Century" and the beginning of the "Asian Century."[7] It wasn't just an American identity that was at stake for Asian American authors anymore. The horizon—for identity, for the representation of reality itself—was growing broader, more global. It was becoming more urgent to understand what it meant to be *Asian* American.[8]

As it turns out, there was nothing at all miraculous about any of these "miracles." Despite the free market fairytale that the World Bank was crafting, the East Asian "miracle" economies were the result of authoritarian state interventions, legacies of Japanese colonialism, and anticommunist U.S. military and economic intervention.[9] "What the World Bank deigned to call the 'East Asian miracle,'" writes the geographer Jim Glassman, "was dialectically connected to what we might call the 'East Asian massacres'"; the war in Vietnam played a particularly important role in this process.[10] Meanwhile, the literary boom of the 1990s was just one outcome of the 1965 Hart-Celler Immigration and Nationality Act's liberalization of immigration policy. As a direct result of the act, the Asian American population has increased by a factor of nearly *thirty*, making it the fastest growing ethnic group in the United States.[11] Miraculous as this cohort may seem, and as wonderful and great as their fiction certainly is, their emergence was in fact just as predictable as it was singular.[12] In Song's estimation the cohort of authors behind the Asian American boom—he calls them "the children of 1965"—is "the largest and most celebrated cohort of American authors of Asian ancestry ever to exist."[13]

The transformations behind the two miracles I have just described have more to do with each other than might be immediately apparent. Tracking very closely alongside the growth of the miracle economies has been a concomitant growth in the foreign-born populations in high-income countries such as the United States. Asian America's explosive population growth and economic success have been fueled by selective immigration policies. In the 1990s, more than 70 percent of the Asian American population was foreign-born, and at no point since the 1960s has the foreign-born proportion dropped below half. As Frédéric Docquier and Hillel Rapoport observe, "these immigrants are increasingly skilled: while migration to [high-income countries] increased at the same rate as trade [since 1960], high-skill migration (or brain drain) from developing to developed countries rose at a much faster pace and can certainly be regarded as one of the major aspects of globalization."[14] Moreover, middle-income countries like the Four Tigers featured the highest emigration rates, because people there had "both the incentives and the means to emigrate."[15] In the case of Asian America, a combination of mediating factors—ranging from the economic priorities of immigration policy and the social reproduction of family reunification, to the "success frame" of model minoritization—have shaped high-skilled migration into a process that sociologists and demographers call "occupational concentration."

Referring to the overrepresentation of Asian Americans in professional-managerial careers, especially in science, technology, engineering, and math (STEM) fields, occupational concentration is the national form of a *global* process. When we examine its determining factors more closely, what we find is a state-sponsored fantasy about the role that a certain class of Asian subjects would play in a global narrative of (so-called) modernization and economic growth. Despite the high proportion of STEM-focused Asian immigrants arriving in the United States after 1965, their professional trajectory was not a foregone conclusion in their sending countries. In Taiwan and South Korea, for instance, cultural and social attitudes made it difficult for each country's governments to align educational policy with the STEM human capital needs of rapid industrialization. STEM occupational concentration was in fact initially the result of authoritarian impositions of vocational and technical education policies that lacked public support and would not find broad acceptance until the 1970s.[16] The immigrants who went to the United States therefore tended not only to be preselected among their peers, but "hyper-selected," to use Jennifer Lee and Min Zhou's term.[17] The state-level fantasy behind such policies, when brought to the United States as the internalized fantasies of STEM-oriented immigrants, results in what Jini Kim Watson calls "the uneasy intersection between [Asian] industrialization and first world post-Fordism."[18] One of the most prevalent tropes in Asian American fiction after 1965 (hereafter "post-65") is a voicing of this uneasiness: a reaction to STEM-oriented trajectories and occupational concentration that, to borrow from the British author-cum-scientist C. P. Snow, is often expressed as a "two-cultures conflict" between the arts and sciences.[19]

When we find art taken up as a theme in post-65 Asian American fiction—its production, consumption, and aura—a two-cultures conflict signals how art is formulated dialectically with an ideology of science and its role in industrial expansion. It is often evoked in conflict with the sciences, which stand in for much more than a scientific worldview and STEM professional identity. The two cultures are always at the same time a figure for intergenerational conflict, the ambivalences of racial identity, and national belonging. When we encounter characters trapped between two seemingly irreconcilable cultures—a trope as trite as it is true to life—we often find the arts and sciences in tension with each other. And when a parent's devotion to a scientific worldview and the safety that a STEM professional identity supposedly offers come into conflict with a child's penchant for doing anything besides, you have rather explosive material on your hands indeed. The two-cultures conflict attunes us to the historical lineaments of what Wong once called the "extravagance" of taking up art as an

Asian American.[20] In Kingston's work of autofiction *The Woman Warrior: A Memoir of a Girlhood Among Ghosts* (1976), the protagonist Maxine threatens her mother with something quite drastic: "I could be a scientist or a mathematician if I want" (201). What her mother wants is for her to marry an undesirable man. She sees no point in Maxine going to college. After all, her own medical degree, which she earned back in China, didn't save her from an undesirable fate working long hours in her husband's laundry in Stockton, California. Maxine's threat therefore targets parental control and a Chinese "feminine" identity that, in her eyes, devalues women and girls. Maxine considers using other professions as threats, like "lumberjack and newspaper reporter," but "science" and "mathematics," with their glint of modernity, are her sharpest weapons. She has no interest in pursuing these fields, in fact, but her white "Teacher Ghosts" direct her toward them, promising an escape from not only Chinese "feminine" identity but its American counterpart as well. As it turns out, despite the many advantages of a STEM career, and despite earning multiple scholarships for an engineering major, in Kingston's sophomore year at Berkeley, she herself ultimately threw it all away for a major in English.[21] As I will argue more fully in chapter 4, the "postmodern," autopoetic style that *Woman Warrior* is credited for pioneering translates into literary form the ambivalences of the two-cultures conflict that Kingston had to pass through in order to become an author in the first place.[22] As Maxine reflects on her independence, the limits of "feminine" identity, and her future, the world that comes into focus before her is a *science fictional* one that replays in miniature, in a scene of intensely personal conflict with her mother, a longer history of modernization projects directing Asian subjects toward a future of economic integration via industrial development. As David Ekbladh writes, while America's postwar modernization projects were formulated and promoted by politicians, academics, and nongovernmental organizations that had their own ideas about Asia and the developing world, and how the West might lead them, "Individuals, as part of this larger process, had to incorporate modern outlooks on intimate levels for the process to proceed and succeed."[23] It was this "modern outlook" that was instilled in Maxine's mother during her medical school orientation in Hong Kong, when she and her classmates were instructed to "bring science to the villages."[24] This fantasy and the realities of modernization from which it arose and to which it responded are what I call *science fictionality*.[25]

Kingston would soon be joined by a deluge of post-65 Asian immigrants arriving in the United States in hot pursuit of the STEM future that she and her avatar Maxine rejected. We might find in subjects like these newer arrivals a tendency to develop what Istvan Csicsery-Ronay describes as "a mode of response that frames and tests experiences as if they were aspects of a work of science fiction"—a mode analogous to how Maxine's doctor mother "tested [her children's] strength to establish realities."[26] According to Csicsery-Ronay this orientation to the "science fictionality" of the world is characteristic of modernity at large, and the precondition for the literary genre of science fiction (SF). While this book tracks a conjuncture not quite as expansive as modernity, it will be very interested in how, in Yoon Sun Lee's words, "for Asian American writers, modernity is not a settled question, or something that belongs to the past. It is still an open question, belonging to the present, and even more to the future."[27] Key to this "open question" is how one fits into modernity, and where one finds the confidence to interpret reality as science fictional. Reflecting on how "science" was brought to him and his generation in martial law–era Taiwan, the activist, modernist writer, and UC Berkeley PhD dropout Guo Songfen argued that "objectivity . . . was in every way a bourgeois, subjective state of mind."[28] Being objective and viewing the world as science fictional was not only an imposition of the authoritarian state, it was also an expression of class desire. Touted as national heroes, students on STEM trajectories were narrated into proximity to what Jim Glassman calls the "Pacific ruling class," a "transnationalised set of elite actors" whose "elite" status did not greet the majority of post-65 STEM human capital when they arrived in the United States.[29]

The Taiwanese American author Charles Yu's 2010 novel *How to Live Safely in a Science Fictional Universe* captures how science fictionality structures the inner lives of post-65 Asian Americans, not least in its title, which reminds us of Maxine's demonstration that science fictionality is a strategy for negotiating the "uneasy intersections" (to use Watson's phrase again) that grate at Asian American identity. Yu's novel, and his fiction more broadly, explores the hopes and disappointments of immigrants who enjoyed some success after arriving in the United States, but not enough, and for whom the science fictional universe is not an abstraction but a project to which they and their STEM skillsets have directly contributed. The science fictional universe that, in Yu's novel, is an enterprise (owned and operated by Time Warner Time, subsidiary of Google) that expands infinitely into time and space in search of profit fixes, provides us with an allegory for the global capitalism that post-65 Asian American STEM professionals have played a special role in constructing. In the novel it is the protagonist's father, a Taiwanese American immigrant, who develops the physics behind the industries that create the novel's science fictional universe, offering the thinnest of allegories for the major role that East Asian immigrant entrepreneurs—whom economic historian AnnaLee Saxenian calls the "new Argonauts"—have played in developing the technical expertise and supply chains that made possible Silicon Valley's ascendancy since the 1970s: indeed, the putatively science fictional universe that we live in now.[30] His ambition, which multiple universes cannot contain, exaggerates the class aspirations of his generation of Taiwanese STEM professionals.

This is just a small slice of the larger story that I want to tell in this book. In the post-65 period, when Asian Americans authors reflect on their world and their place in it, the space in which they find themselves is a science fictional universe that is increasingly oriented to Asia rather than the United States alone. And what unfolds before them in time is a totality spanning U.S.-Asia relations from the inception of Japan's colonial projects in Korea and Taiwan at the turn of the twentieth century to the morphing of Japan's Greater East-Asian Co-Prosperity Sphere into the U.S.-led Northeast Asian political economy, and then on to the present in which China has both intensified and displaced those earlier formations. This *transimperial* science fictional universe, whether or not it is explicitly depicted or cognized, has defined the arena and set the ideological terms through which Asian human capital has struggled to valorize itself, and in which post-65 Asian American authors have attempted to locate themselves and their fiction.

This book's central question might therefore be posed like this: What's *Asian* about post-65 Asian American fiction? Over the past half-century of Asian American critique, this question has been framed predominantly in terms of race and racialization. In the 1960s and 1970s, the Asian American movement rejected this question on anti-orientalist grounds, insisting instead on political and cultural claims to American citizenship and identity on the one hand and racial identification with the Third World (rather than Asia exclusively) on the other.[31] Feminist and poststructuralist interventions in the 1980s and 1990s shifted focus to the legacies of wars in Asia and ongoing U.S.-Asia geopolitical entanglement while also preserving the strategic essentialism of Asian American cultural politics.[32] In the transnational turn that has unfolded since then, the Cold War has become a preeminent category because of how it brings into focus the importance of Asian racialization to the project of U.S. empire.[33] As Jodi Kim argues, "the relative 'inclusion' of Asians [in U.S. society] in the Cold War era ... [is not an act of] progressive, liberal democratic correction or reversal of a previously racist era, but an imperial governmentality whose logic is one of *expulsion* (out of Asia)."[34] Over time, however, "America" has morphed from a scene of political contestation into a "wounded attachment" to a political project whose terrain of contestation has totally transformed.[35] I thus take advisement from Yogita Goyal, who writes of the transnational turn, "Rather than viewing the charge of the field as either resisting or celebrating globalization, unveiling latent truths about militarism and empire or simply describing their historical formation, or moving away from such concerns towards surface or data, it is more helpful to reach for a more supple analysis of history and literature, to map itineraries that neither simply follow the reach of capital or the military, nor ignore it."[36] Among the best ways to pursue such a dialectically rich program, I would argue, is to focus on the typicality of the subjects who concretize economies and social forms.

What is *Asian* about post-65 Asian American fiction is the post-65 Asian American author itself—but the author here is not to be understood as the bearer of a racial, cultural, or even national essence. Rather, this book offers a *political economic* account of the Asian American author as a class formation. While I will be very interested in the racial forms that constitute this class, I stop short of reifying a correspondence between author and racial identity (e.g., the variously ascriptive and voluntarist racialization of the ethnographic imperative).[37] Instead, I consider race alongside a number of other factors relevant to an author's biographical connection to Asia and Asian America.[38] In Asian American historiography, the dates 1968 and 1965 symbolize two poles that have shaped Asian American life: 1968's race and identity and 1965's class and totality.[39] This book presumes that each pole presupposes the other, and brings into relief the dynamic that mediates between them: typicality.[40] As Kevin Floyd, Jen Hedler Phillis, and Sarika Chandra write, "Identity politics in its post-sixties form is a historical product, a side effect, of a specific, limited form of universalism: the point-of-production aspiration toward totality, the universalizing anti-capitalist standpoint that has traditionally taken the form of a worker standpoint.... What the term 'identity politics' describes has always been a problem of totality."⁴¹ Asian American identity is an "aspiration toward totality"—a phrase that Floyd, Phillis, and Chandra borrow from Georg Lukács's *History and Class Consciousness*—that proceeds from the historical figure of the Asian American subject. Asian Americans come into self-knowledge *as* Asian Americans when they understand themselves as both subjects and objects of the material relations linking Asia to America.

The model minority status against which Asian American political identity has traditionally defined itself is also the sign of its typicality within global capitalism.⁴² Yoon Sun Lee identifies an aspiration toward totality in Asian American literary realism, offering this explanation of how Lukács theorizes the relation between totality and typicality:⁴³

> Realist typicality, as [Lukács] describes it, is a different way of thinking about the relation between the individual and scalar possibility. The typical character, detail, or event stands for something larger and more real than its own particularity. The type is the opposite of a singular, isolated instance. But it cannot stand arbitrarily for any idea or concept; it does not stand for an abstract universal. Instead of being "brought into a direct, if paradoxical connection with transcendence" and thereby remaining abstract, the type is achieved through a careful qualification, mediation, or placement that links it with other instances and gives it a social though not purely empirical generality.⁴⁴

Typicality names the relation between Asian American "particularity" and its "social" generality: what Lee calls the "structural characteristic" of Asian American life. In Lee's examination of works of pre-65 Asian American literature such as Jade Snow Wong's *Fifth Chinese Daughter* (1950) and Younghill Kang's *East Goes West* (1937), along with depictions of pre-65 life such as *Woman Warrior*, the structural characteristic she identifies is the "constitutive dislocation" that strongly defined the experience of emigration to the United States during that period, as well as the spatial segregation of these immigrants upon their arrival.⁴⁵ While *Fifth Chinese Daughter* is too early for the literary period that this book is tracking, a shift in analytical emphasis from identity to typicality reveals how texts like *Woman Warrior* are just as much about class anxiety as they are about the dislocations of Asian American identity.⁴⁶

An account of Asian American subjectivity as *typicality* might appear to stand in contrast with the account of *identity* that has grounded Asian American cultural politics and institutionalization since the term "Asian America" was invented in 1968, amid the Third Worldist, anti–Vietnam War student movements at UC Berkeley and San Francisco State University.[47] Subsequent arguments in left theory that have pitted race against class will no doubt cast this apparent contrast in even starker relief.[48] However, what Floyd, Phillis, and Chandra remind us is that an anticapitalist analysis that would emphasize typicality and universality emerges from the same fundamental aspiration that inspired identity politics to conceptualize totality through specific standpoints.[49] Indeed, from the very beginning of Asian American studies' institutionalization, Calvin Cheung-Miaw observes, "Asian Americanists [within the academy] constantly struggled with how to conceptualize the relationship between racial identity and class interests."[50] It was the diversity of class identities within Asian America, which exploded in the post-65 period, that would set the stage for Asian American studies' poststructuralist turn in the 1990s. For scholars like Lisa Lowe and Kandice Chuh, this class diversity shed light on what they saw as an array of heterogeneities that was ultimately intractable, and that undermined the referential capacity of Asian American identity.[51] As Colleen Lye observes, Chuh's verdict that Asian American studies is fundamentally a "subjectless discourse" is on one hand the logical completion of Lowe's intervention, which has led to an important "pluralizing" of Asian American knowledge production.[52] But on the other hand, "subjectlessness" has left "Asian America" open to any who would like to define it.[53]

Over the years, the field's political and intellectual commitment to strategic essentialism has waned in the wake of correctives offered by scholars like Lye, Mark Chiang, Yen Le Espiritu, Susan Koshy, Jinqi Ling, Viet Thanh Nguyen, and erin Khûe Ninh, who have argued forcefully that the poststructuralist celebration of difference as identity is not only politically constraining, and not only papers over material contradictions, but is at bottom a class tendency that reflects the investments of professional Asian American critics like themselves in an idealized conception of resistant racial identity.[54] For example, Ninh trenchantly argues that Asian American studies' traditional rejection of the model minority stereotype as a myth not only distracts from the model minority status of Asian Americanist academics themselves, but it is also possible only by "trotting out [Asian

INTRODUCTION

America's] sub-par Southeast Asians, whose material deprivation is [the] only too-scant argument for the falseness of the model minority myth, and on whose continued failure must rest the hopes of entire academic and political platforms."[55] Ninh's disambiguation, in my view, grows out of an aspiration toward totality that illuminates aspects of the model minority trope's conditions of emergence—here, its institutional reproduction as a red herring—and in doing so contributes to a dialectical understanding of Asian American reality. Indeed, regarding the model minority specifically, this book builds upon Ninh's work, which shows that if "Asian America" is to sustain a coherence that is not presupposed by an idealism, then that coherence is rooted in the community's material and psychic commitments to model minoritization.

In the post-65 period, Asian American authors have increasingly sought to depict what Yoon Sun Lee calls "a world single though far-flung, intimate and complete, materially and meaningfully connected."[56] What distinguishes the post-65 world from the one that preceded it is that Asian American authors find it ensconced in a science fictional universe. The world that emerges in their writing is so often a world that is viewed from the perspective of post-65 professionals who not only tend to perceive the world as science fictional but also have a propensity to reproduce that worldview in subsequent generations. These tendencies are poignantly captured in a scene in *How to Live Safely in a Science Fictional Universe*. The protagonist recalls a memory of his father reading to him when he is three years old: "This is what I remember: (i) the little pocket of space he creates for me, (ii) how it is enough, (iii) the sound of his voice, (iv) the way those spaceships look, shot through from behind with light, so that every stitch in the fabric of the surface is a hole and a source, a point and an absence, a coordinate in the ship's celestial navigation, (v) how the bed feels like a little spaceship itself."[57] The scene is bathed in "the soft yellow light of my lamp, which has a cloth lamp shade, light blue, covered by an alternating pattern of robots and spaceships." While the protagonist remembers nothing about the book, the scientific accoutrements of the scene (space, spaceships, coordinates, celestial navigation, robots) and its precision ("it is enough"; the schematization of the memory's elements), convey how the propensity to transmit professional identity from one post-65 generation to the next is as much about the inheritance of an all-encompassing worldview as it is about a career trajectory. Narratives of intergenerational occupational concentration are not always this tender, however, as many of my readers can confirm.

This book pursues an account of a specific yet typical category of Asian American professionals: authors, mostly novelists, whose fiction depicts Asian American subjects coming into self-knowledge as *Northeast* Asian Americans. While this identity is almost never expressed explicitly as "*Northeast* Asian American"—"East Asian" is more common, if not historically apt (more on this in chapter 1)—it takes shape as these authors explore how economic integration connects their narratives and characters to a Northeast Asian regional formation. My focus on professionals is not especially intended to account for what Viet Thanh Nguyen calls the ideological diversity of Asian America (thus aiming for a more complete, or additive, analysis of the Asian American community), nor to focus on what Christine So calls the equivalences of Asian America with normative American subject formation (and thus reveal the spiritual alignment of Asian Americans with the interests of capital).[58] Instead, I describe the material conditions of emergence subtending post-65 professional reproduction, which leads most often to STEM occupational concentration, but also exerts a profound force on the production of Asian American fiction. This book therefore understands the category of Asian America through concrete economic relations in order to show how historically specific routes of capital have corresponded to racial and literary forms.[59]

In the chapters that follow I will sometimes use "Asian American" as a shorthand for "Northeast Asian American," but I would emphasize that its referent is the dialectic joining the two terms. Not all Asian American genealogies are immediately commensurable, though they may seem so. For instance, the Filipinx American novelist Elaine Castillo has written: "the most realist mode for an immigrant is science-fiction. For this, I know now, is also science-fiction: the worlding of your body as hyper-meaningful to the point of allegory."[60] As apt as Castillo's reflection might be for this book's arguments, the crux of her distinction between Filipinx and Northeast Asian contexts is the "hyper-meaningful" body, which comes to Castillo, as her brilliant debut novel *America Is Not the Heart* (2018) details, through the tremendous influx of nurses, doctors, and other "foreign medical graduates" to the United States from the Philippines beginning in the 1960s and 1970s.[61] Like Hagedorn, Castillo's work is oriented to a different transimperial history (Spain–United States) than the one this book tracks.

INTRODUCTION

Whatever science fictionality makes its way into Southeast Asian American fiction—like the Cambodian American author Anthony Veasna So's short story "Human Development" (2021), the Vietnamese American author Kevin Nguyen's novel *New Waves* (2020), and the Thai American author Tony Tulathimutte's *Private Citizens: A Novel* (2016), all satires of Silicon Valley hustle—is generally confined to naturalistic details rather than posed as the affective and ideological horizon that each work strives to encompass. Similarly, even when South Asian American authors such as Hari Kunzru, Jhumpa Lahiri, and Bharati Mukherjee take up STEM professional characters, they are oriented to a genealogy of modernity shaped by British colonialism and the legacies of partition, which rarely manifests via a two-cultures conflict.

All that said, a focus on Northeast Asia that stalls at the too specific without making a move toward larger analytical units risks undermining itself. Bruce Cumings calls this the "fallacy of disaggregation": "if there has been a miracle in East Asia . . . it is misleading to assess the industrialization pattern in *any one* of these countries: such an approach misses, through a fallacy of disaggregation, the fundamental unity and integrity of the regional effort in this century."[62] Such an approach would fail to conceptualize the scope and coordination of U.S. empire, Japanese empire before it, and the recent reemergence of China's imperial motives. It would also fail to grasp how, in Christine So's words, "The threat of Asian capital and Asians as capital [has] morphed [at the turn of the millennium] into an overall anxiety about global capital in general."[63] The corollary of this fallacy in Asian American cultural politics is the additive concept of Asian America that seeks the articulation and inclusion of all possible Asian American subcategorizations. This book explores what unfolds when we take an inductive approach and proceed from the question of what it means for an American author to be *from Asia*. A nonreductive answer, which I hope to offer, will account for the specificities of Northeast Asia as a geopolitical space, and how its variability over time is a function of the modes of development that have produced post-65 Asian America and its fiction. Only through such an account can we learn what the post-65 formation of Asian America, Asian Americans, and Asian American fiction can tell us about the histories, subjects, and forms of global capitalism. It is along these lines that I see this book pursuing the aspiration toward totality at the very foundation of strategic essentialism's *strategic* aims.

My goal in this introduction is to begin describing the authorial mediation of science fictionality. The chapters that follow will provide a fuller accounting. After explaining in more detail the book's Northeast Asian American focus, I will situate the post-65 Asian American author within that context. The material and relational coordinates that emerge will provide a basis for understanding science fictionality's literary expressions in relation to SF—a literary genre that is certainly a privileged expression of science fictionality's political economic totality but is not its sole or even most prevalent expression.

NORTHEAST ASIAN AMERICA

The material relations structuring Asian racial form in the United States have been highly variable since the beginning of mass immigration from Asia in the mid-nineteenth century, which responded first to the Gold Rush and then to the call of industrialization. Lisa Lowe argues that the racialization of Chinese laborers has served a consistent function in the capital-labor relation: "If the nineteenth-century racialized and gendered formation of Chinese male immigrants as laborers sublated the contradictions between economic imperatives and the state, then these contradictions emerge in the demographic composition of the post-65 Asian migrant group, a group still racialized and exploited, yet complicated by class and gender stratification."[64] While I agree with Lowe's observation, I would also draw our attention to the vastness of its historical scope. The postwar period has seen rapid industrialization in Asia as well as deindustrialization in the United States, interdependency between the United States and Japan and the United States and China, and what some now call deglobalization and decoupling. The following chapters will explore these developments in detail. The stability of Asian racial form across these developments is a kind of hologram—to be sure, one with *very real* consequences, as the anti-Asian violence of the pandemic era has shown us—generated by the predominance and persistence of two stereotypes: the "model minority" and the "yellow peril." While it is foundational to Asian American critique that these stereotypes are two sides of the same coin (efficient laborers as reliable yet wage-depressing; straight-A students as praiseworthy yet supernumerary), we are better served, as Colleen Lye argues, when our attention is trained on their conditions of emergence at any particular moment.[65] Bewitched by their constant reappearance, we accept them as natural features of our racial reality.

The reproduction of these stereotypes is guaranteed by material processes going on behind our backs. At stake here, as the *Endnotes* collective explains, is our very understanding of the challenge we wish to pose to capital: "if the historical workers' movement is today alien to us, it is because the *form* of the capital-labour relation that sustained the workers' movement no longer obtains."[66] Lye offers what we could read as a reformulation of this challenge vis-à-vis the U.S.-Asia totality that science fictionality cathects:

> The increasingly *visible* shift of global capital accumulation to Asia over the last several decades has eroded the anti-imperialist aura of Asian American cultural politics so that the associations born of their 1968 genesis now seem to be but a distant memory. As much as this situation has helped feed a more general uncertainty as to whether there is such a thing as Asian American identity at all, the "rise of Asia" also provides intellectual opportunities for historicizing and theorizing Asian racialization anew. Thinking such a challenge would require asking whether an Asian racial form legible in today's context of trans-Pacific integration and contradiction requires a politics that goes beyond the moment of struggle for national self-determination or racial self-expression.[67]

Rather than describe stereotypes and other discursive formations, my goal in this book is to scrutinize interactions between the "visible" domain of discourse that they occupy and the hidden abode of material relations. Thus the transformation of the economic base underlying U.S.-Asia political economy indicates that our attention should be trained not so much on the *repetitions* of stereotypes and tropes, but instead on what has made them appear as repetitions when everything has changed in the interval. Lye goes on to ask, "if the exclusion of 'cheap Asian labor' was central to U.S. Fordism, and post-Fordism meanwhile has involved extensive reliance on offshore and onshore Asian labor, including skilled labor, to what extent has the shift from Fordism to post-Fordism also entailed *discontinuities* between the racialized norms of U.S. white-collar work and industrial work?"[68] This book will be centrally concerned with the postwar economic transition that

Lye narrates here, which is in many ways a story about Asian racial form in the age of deindustrialization.⁶⁹

Rather than ground my account of Asia in its most abstract and ideological forms, my focus will be exclusive to the concrete political economic formation of Northeast Asia: Japan, South Korea, Taiwan, and China. For Asian Americanist scholars, this will no doubt come off as a jarring move. For a discipline and cultural politics that have struggled to preserve a pan-ethnic claim to Asian America and projects of maximum inclusiveness, relinquishing strategic essentialism for a regional formation that encompasses what have been, in the post-65 period, among the most economically and socially privileged national origin groups, might additionally come off as politically suspect. More sympathetic readers might wonder why I am, in a way, saying the quiet part out loud when I might have gotten away with simply doing what Asian American literary studies has almost always done: tacitly accept Northeast Asia as emblematic of Asian America as a whole.⁷⁰ In Long Le-Khac and Kate Hao's survey of Asian Americanist literary scholarship from the early years of the field up to 2016, they identify an "East Asian American hegemony in the field: Chinese, Korean, and Japanese American literatures, in that order," and that "the conflation of Chinese American literature with Asian American literature as a whole has intensified."⁷¹ Moreover, in terms of national origin, Northeast Asia is overrepresented among Asian Americanist scholars.⁷² This is perhaps one of the unspoken reasons why Asian American literary studies has often been unapologetic about extending claims about Northeast Asian American authors and communities to Asian America more broadly, suggesting race-based equivalences between, say, an MFA-holding Chinese American author from an affluent background and a Cambodian American author from a poor background. Before we can even think about what undoing these tendencies might mean—institutionally, pedagogically, politically—we need to understand their material conditions of reproduction.

The Northeast Asian political economy has its origins in Japan's colonial projects, beginning in 1895 with the latter's possession and colonization of Taiwan, and in 1910 with its colonization of the Korean peninsula. Bruce Cumings offers this summary:

> In the past century Japan, Korea, and Taiwan have also moved fluidly through a classic product-cycle industrialization pattern, Korea and Taiwan

following in Japan's wake. Japan's industrialization has gone through three phases, the last of which is just beginning. The first phase began in the 1880s, with textiles the leading sector, and lasted through Japan's rise to world power. In the mid 1930s Japan began the second, heavy phase, based on steel, chemicals, armaments, and ultimately automobiles; it did not begin to end until the mid 1960s. The third phase emphasizes high-technology "knowledge" industries such as electronics, communications, computers, and silicon-chip microprocessors.[73]

The pattern that Cumings describes here is drawn from the Japanese economist Kaname Akamatsu, who famously proposed that "The countries of the world form a wild-geese-flying order from the advanced countries which have reached the stage of high-degree heavy and chemical industries to the less-advanced countries which are still in the stage of primary industries."[74] When Akamatsu coined the phrase "wild-geese flying" in 1935 (frequently shortened to "flying geese") Japan had already begun focusing its imperialist ambitions into a pan-Asianist vision that sought to assert its independence from the West as a regional formation that, in 1940, Foreign Minister Matsuoka Yōsuke introduced as the "Greater East-Asia Co-Prosperity Sphere." By the time of Japan's surrender in 1945, the Sphere included Korea, Taiwan, Manchuria, Thailand, Burma, the Philippines, and a handful of short-lived puppet states. Its colonies in Korea and Taiwan, however, were by far its most significant possessions. While Japanese empire was in many ways envisioned as a racial and ideological revolt against what Matsuoka called "the white race bloc," the Sphere also aimed to consolidate a decades-old flying-geese formation.[75] After the war, the formation continued under the aegis of the United States, which, as Chris Suh has detailed, had been collaborating with Japan on the strategies and rhetoric of "progressive empire" since the turn of the twentieth century.[76] Post-65 Asian American fiction is a repository of transimperial continuity at least as much as it is of Cold War U.S. militarism. For instance, the strong modal tendencies of Taiwanese American and South Korean American fiction—toward comedy and tragedy, respectively—are to some extent a legacy of differential colonial experiences under Japan. While Taiwan was treated as a "model" colony, Korea suffered brutal repression.

To this snapshot of the Northeast Asian political economy at the height of "miracle discourse" in the 1990s, Ho-fung Hung helps us to understand the significance of China, which began directing its economic reform and opening toward capitalism in 1978. Rather than take China's rapid economic rise as the isolated achievement of an authoritarian single-party state, Hung argues that it would not have been possible without the "tiger economies." Which is to say, China's own miracle would not have been possible without the provocation of the anticommunist ideological and military project of U.S. empire: "China's capitalist boom," Hung writes, "is tantamount to an explosion ignited by the mixing of the Maoist legacies and East Asian capitalism, each developed separately on opposing sides of the Cold War in Asia."[77] The flames of this "explosion" were fanned by financial and human capital from the miracle economies as well as the United States, linking China to the Northeast Asian political economy. It is on this basis that this book focuses on authors who trace their national origins to China, South Korea, Taiwan, and Japan—not to the exclusion of any other national origin group, but rather out of a commitment to tracking a specific transimperial history and its outsized influence on post-65 Asian American fiction.

SEMIPERIPHERAL INVERSIONS

While occupational concentration in STEM fields has impacted nearly every segment of Asian America, it has impacted Asian Americans who become authors in a particular way. It is the coalescence of occupational concentration into an aggregate *type* of the post-65 Asian American author that Chang-rae Lee describes in a 2017 interview: "A lot of Asian American writers, mostly of my generation and a little younger . . . and without exception, I mean really without exception, you know, at a writer's conference maybe 20 of us sitting around, every single one of them started out in a very professional, very respectable gig before they threw it all away to become a writer."[78] As one of the most commercially and critically successful authors of his generation, and as a professional who has spent almost all of his fiction-writing career administrating and teaching in prestigious creative writing departments (CUNY, Princeton, Stanford), Lee certainly didn't throw it all away. Part of what Lee is describing is not particular to Asian American authors and is in fact a longstanding feature of creative writing in the United States. As Mark McGurl has shown, university-housed creative writing programs have dominated the production of American fiction

INTRODUCTION

in the postwar period, all but completely wiping out the distinction between professional and author. But the detail that Lee adds—that his Asian American colleagues "started out" as professionals *before* throwing it all away—hints at the particularity of the post-65 Asian American author, who has been subjected to a kind of *double professionalization*.[79] Generally hailing from professional-managerial class (PMC) backgrounds, most of these authors pursued a PMC career trajectory before turning to creative writing.

In this book the figure of the Asian American author will never only refer to individual authors.[80] Even when I focus on individual authors, my goal will be to account for their typicality. As Yoon Sun Lee elegantly explains, Lukács's *type* is distinct from the *stereotype*: the "type embodies the contradictions of a historical moment rather than a reified social or demographic category."[81] I approach the Asian American author as a *class formation* that is certainly racialized, but that can be understood in more depth if we approach it as an instance of a transnational PMC. Defined by John and Barbara Ehrenreich in an influential 1977 article, the PMC consists of "salaried mental workers who do not own the means of production and whose major function in the social division of labor may be described broadly as the reproduction of capitalist culture and capitalist class relations."[82] The emergence of this "new class" in the United States—perhaps better known as "white-collar" workers—has famously been documented by midcentury scholars such as C. Wright Mills, William Whyte, and David Riesman.[83] In the postwar period, the numbers of white-collar workers exploded, and in 1956 they finally outnumbered blue-collar workers.[84] The awkward position of the PMC—its dependence on the wage aligning it materially with the proletariat, even as its managerial role brings it into identification with the interests of capital—describes an important dimension of the relationship between many professional authors and the institutions from which they often seek employment. In the "program era," creative writing departments turn "writers into salaried writing professors and students into tuition-paying apprentices."[85] Consequently, McGurl argues, "the overriding problem for postwar American fiction has been how to adapt modernist principles of writing, developed in the late nineteenth and early twentieth centuries well outside the academy, to a literary field increasingly dominated by bureaucratic institutions of higher education."[86] For post-65 Asian American authors, double professionalization brings an additional resonance of racialization into the tension between institutionalization and aesthetic freedom: the PMC's awkward class position resonates with the awkward racialization of Asian Americans, and additionally with the even more awkward racialization of post-65 Asian Americans as institutional creatures, of the university above all. Resisting this association with the university is among the impetuses behind a recent spate of novels featuring college and grad school dropouts, such as Elysha Chang's *A Quitter's Paradise* (2023), Elaine Hsieh Chou's *Disorientation* (2022), Jean Chen Ho's *Fiona and Jane* (2022), Grace D. Li's *Portrait of a Thief* (2022), Lisa Ko's *The Leavers* (2017), Celeste Ng's *Everything I Never Told You* (2014), Kathy Wang's *Family Trust* (2018), and Weike Wang's *Chemistry* (2017). A more ambivalent approach to the university as site of capitalist excess and moral proving ground might be tracked into Silicon Valley novels, which exchange the college campus for the tech campus. This theme is especially pronounced in Charles Yu's *How to Live Safely in a Science Fictional Universe* (2010), Anna Yen's *Sophia of Silicon Valley* (2018), and Kathy Wang's *Impostor Syndrome* (2021).[87]

Underlying this tight association with the campus and, more generally, institutions, is a unique dynamic that arises from the awkwardness of the PMC's class alignments. As Yoonmee Chang puts it, "The linear relationship between race and class inequity, that being racially different has negative class effects, is derailed for Asian Americans. For Asian Americans, the conventional relationship between race and class inequality is *inverted*."[88] This inversion certainly has not always been the case in Asian American history. It would not be going too far to argue that what distinguishes *post-65* Asiatic racial form from its *pre-65* regime is precisely this inversion. Indeed, a desire to explore periods of Asian American history in which this inversion was *not* dominant—that is, when class did not interfere with the straightforward abjection of Asian bodies—offers one explanation for the recent mini-boom of Asian American historical fiction set during the exclusion era, which include what Julia H. Lee calls "neo-frontier" narratives: C Pam Zhang's *How Much of These Hills Is Gold* (2020), Jenny Tinghui Zhang's *Four Treasures of the Sky* (2022), Hanya Yanagihara's *To Paradise* (2022), Tom Lin's *The Thousand Crimes of Ming Tsu* (2021), Brian Leung's *Take Me Home* (2010), and Peter Ho Davies's *The Fortunes* (2016).[89] The pedagogical impulse behind this historical shift also helps to explain why this mini-boom has been especially pronounced in children's and young adult fiction, such as George Takei's *They Called Us Enemy* (2019), Allen Say's *Home of*

INTRODUCTION

the Brave (2002), Linda Sue Park's *Prairie Lotus* (2020), Amy Lee-Tai's *A Place Where Sunflowers Grow* (2006), Shing Yin Khor's *The Legend of Auntie Po* (2021), Cynthia Kadohata's *Weedflower* (2006), and Martha Brockenbrough, Grace Lin, and Julia Kuo's *I Am an American: The Wong Kim Ark Story* (2021). In other words, the "past" operates not so much as a temporal category in these works but as an ideological framing of Asian American life that has not been "inverted." And as disparate as the ethnic and national backgrounds of these authors might be, what they hold in common are MFAs—if not also, as Chang-rae Lee put it, a "very professional, very respectable gig."

It is difficult to locate where to begin the story of occupational concentration, but in medias res is as good a place as any. On or about October 3, 1965, the character of Asian America changed. That was the day that Lyndon B. Johnson signed into law the Hart-Celler Immigration and Nationality Act. Seated at a desk on Ellis Island, darkened by the shadow of the Statue of Liberty, he declared that the Act "corrects a cruel and enduring wrong in the conduct of the American nation."[90] Johnson was referring to the longstanding system of exclusion based on country of origin and eugenic racial science that the 1965 act finally brought to an end; Hart-Celler replaced 1920s-legislated restrictions with an across-the-board quota on all sending countries as well as two main criteria for selection: family reunification and job skills. While the act did not go into effect until 1968, there was an overnight explosion of immigration from Asia when it did. Since then, Asian America has radically increased in kind (i.e., national origins) and in quantity (as we have already seen). Crucially, the act's skills-based labor provisions shifted the basis of U.S. immigration policy away from principles of exclusion to principles of economic selection. Madeline Hsu explains that this shift "turned immigration selection into an aspect of fiscal policy. The growing influence of such neoliberal principles has masked emerging forms of inequality in global migrations that privilege the mobility of educated elites, particularly for those concentrated in what are now labeled STEM, or science, technology, engineering, and mathematics, fields, and most prominently from Asia."[91] As a result of this shift, Jennifer Lee and Min Zhou argue, post-65 Asian America has become what they call a "hyperselected" population. Not only did the act already privilege educated and highly skilled immigrants, but as well, "Asian immigrants are . . . also more highly educated than the average American, despite the tremendous heterogeneity in their countries of origin."[92] The share of Asian immigrants who arrive in the United States with a bachelor's degree or higher has historically been the highest compared to other immigrant groups.[93]

A number of employment and job skills-related policies and legislation, most notably the 1990 Immigration Act, have subsequently extended the 1965 Act's provisions, thus intensifying hyper-selection. In 1964, Asian immigrants constituted only 14 percent of technical and scientific students and professionals arriving in the United States. In 1970, two years after the act went into effect, that percentage rose to a dizzying 62 percent.[94] Since 1970, trends have shown that Asian American men enter STEM fields at nearly four times the rate of white Americans; Asian American women enter STEM fields at lower rates than men but still almost three times the rate of white women.[95] The 1965 Act also established the H-1B visa program for highly skilled, predominantly technical, workers. Subsequent legislation, rule-making, and regional advantages have skewed the H-1B and similar programs heavily toward Asian applicants with technical backgrounds. In 2022, for instance, more than 81 percent of H-1B visas were granted for STEM professions, and over 85 percent of visas were granted to workers from India and China alone, with South Korea, the Philippines, Taiwan, and Pakistan also in the top-ten of visa approvals.[96] Because of these overwhelmingly uniform repetitions of economic subject formation, Pyong Gap Min and Sou Hyun Jang conclude that "Asian immigrants have fairly successfully transmitted their concentration in the STEM fields of study to their younger-generation . . . children."[97] Significantly, the trends of occupational concentration and academic achievement have increasingly been found in nonvoluntary Asian immigrant populations like Southeast Asian refugee communities, which have historically experienced high rates of poverty and have struggled academically and professionally. Lee and Zhou describe a phenomenon they call "second-generation convergence," in which the 1.5- and second-generation children of these immigrants begin to exhibit the academic and professional outcomes of more privileged Asian immigrants from East Asia and South Asia. This "achievement paradox" defies "expectations of the classic status attainment model, which privileges parental human and cultural capital. Rejecting the kinds of cultural explanations (e.g., Confucianism, patriarchal discipline) popular among ethnic essentialists Lee and Zhou attribute second-generation convergence to a cognitive model, which they call the "success frame," that

INTRODUCTION

permeates nearly all Asian American groups and that is grounded in a feedback loop of selected immigrants and the institutions and networks they have established: "The frame entails earning straight A's, graduating as the high school valedictorian, earning a degree from an elite university, attaining an advanced degree, and working in one of four high-status professional fields: medicine, law, engineering, or science."[98] As I suggested earlier, aside from the fiat of strategic essentialism, or a more vulgar racial essentialism, the sole empirical factor vouching for the coherence of pan-Asian American experience is the economic mobility envisioned by the "success frame." The proliferation of the "success frame," moreover, is a powerful indication that the science fictional fantasy of social integration via economic mobility has become fundamental to the social reproduction of post-65 Asian America.

Even as the 1965 Act aimed to rectify America's Cold War persona of moral superiority, it was also designed to address looming economic stagnation: in particular a global restructuring of economic relations that saw U.S. companies responding to falling profits by expanding their supply chains to countries offering cheaper labor. As the sociologists Paul Ong, Edna Bonacich, and Lucie Cheng put it, "capital [began] seeking out new recruits for industrial production around the globe."[99] The recruits they found were no miraculous free gifts of nature, however. They were the human capital products both of U.S. Cold War neoimperialism as it interacted with Northeast Asia's drive to industrialize rapidly and of the educational and economic legacies of Japanese colonialism.[100] Thanks to these transimperial developments, American corporations found workers that were literate, healthy, and tractable. Meanwhile, when panic over the Space Race provoked American policymakers to forecast shortages of technical and scientific expertise, Northeast Asian countries were able to offer up their surpluses. As a result, development economists began raising alarms about "brain drain," defined by Walter Adams as "human capital ... flowing out of economies where it can make the greatest contribution to human welfare, and into economies already well-supplied with trained, capable, scientific and administrative personnel."[101] In 1968, when Adams was writing, "The drain from Asian nations, particularly Taiwan and Korea, [was] most serious ... over 90 per cent of Asian students who arrive for training in the United States never return home."[102] Among the many reasons behind such migration, AnnaLee Saxenian observes, was that developing countries like Taiwan and South Korea "typically lacked the industrial base to employ the larger numbers of graduates who never left the country."[103] Moreover, as Alejandro Portes and Adrienne Celaya argue, "Countries at mid-levels of development," like Taiwan and South Korea at the time, were "particularly susceptible to this effect since they [were] the most motivated to 'catch up' with the advanced world and possess the resources to copy its educational practices."[104] Contrary to the brain drain narrative's implied one-way migration, Portes and Celaya go on to point out that, today—for our purposes, the post-65 period—the theory of "push-pull" migration, whose "theoretical cousin" is the classical theory of straight-line assimilation, fails to account for at least two phenomena: why only a small percentage of equivalently trained highly skilled human capital in a given country ends up migrating, and why so many highly skilled migrants end up returning to their country of origin or increasing their ties to it (e.g., political participation, investment).[105] An account of highly skilled emigration must therefore reject "invidious" comparisons between receiving countries—overwhelmingly this has been the United States—and the "relative deprivation" of sending countries and instead focus on "the *internal* conditions of the sending countries."[106] It is precisely such an account that this book aims to bring into conversation with Asian American literary studies, focusing on the conditions and vicissitudes of Northeast Asian human capital's "exposure to modern-scientific values."[107]

Today, post–economic miracle, what once appeared as expropriation from the periphery to the core has now taken on a different guise, as the Northeast Asian periphery has ascended to semiperipheral status. While brain drain certainly still continues—in 2021 Taiwan and Japan were the top two countries with the largest "talent deficits," with South Korea in seventh place—the countries that in the postwar period were most impacted by brain drain now benefit the most from the return of their human capital.[108] In recent years, China has entered this story of "brain circulation." Saxenian writes: "Migration is now a two-way street, and the circulation of skill, capital, and know-how between the United States and China has reached unprecedented levels. The overseas Chinese and Taiwanese professional and technical community that built the bridge linking Silicon Valley and Taiwan in the 1980s and 1990s is now extending its networks to the technology regions in mainland China."[109] Much of what this book explores are the stakes of Asian American authorship and fiction being drawn into the orbit of these human capital flows, and into a posture in the world-system that is as much subimperial as it is postcolonial.[110]

SCIENCE FICTIONALITY ≠ SF

Before the 1990s the act of writing as an Asian American was more likely to conflict with an identification with Asia. Now Asian American authors are more open to identifying with Asia and exploring Asia in fiction. We need not resort to guesses about psychological motivation to explain why, even though biographical detail and authorial intention might provide useful insights into any given author's typicality. The increased likelihood of identification with Asia is due in part to the spectacular development and visibility of Asian miracle economies, which have helped to render a "developed" Asia familiar to Asian Americans who had grown up far away from the "developing" world. This fundamentally economic familiarity, moreover, has hinted at potentially viable futures for Asian Americans entering professional life at the dusk of the "American Century." In contrast, Asian American literature (fiction and nonfiction) written within and set in the pre-65 period is largely about *dis*identification with Asia. As we will explore in the final chapter, which is on Taiwanese American return fiction, the viability of "return" to Asia has been increasingly taken up in fiction by Asian American authors, whereas return narratives have traditionally been confined to memoir and autobiography.[111]

As the horizon of those circumstances, the science fictional universe generates a proliferation of such contradictions. Occupational concentration, like post-65 Asian American fiction, is an expression of the material relations constituting science fictionality. The distinction between the two can also be understood as one of spatial scale: science fictionality as a U.S.-Asia form, and occupational concentration as a national form that results from the mediation of science fictionality through racial and economic institutions and discourses of subject formation that are specific to the United States. Just as an overrepresentation of Asian Americans in STEM fields is registered demographically as occupational concentration, science fictionality is registered aesthetically as a set of formal tendencies. Sometimes science fictionality appears in just the way we might expect: *as* SF. More often it doesn't. Science fictionality encompasses SF but is not reducible to it. It is not reducible to SF for the same reasons that we would never say that

U.S.-Asia political economy is reducible to the post-65 Asian American author.

We might usefully turn to a brief history of Asian American SF for a case study that will demonstrate the coarticulation of occupational concentration and post-65 Asian American fiction. In addition to the "miraculous" gains of 1991, that year is significant in Asian American literary history for at least one other reason. It was in 1991 that Ted Chiang became the first Asian American author to win a major SF award: the Nebula for his debut publication, the novelette *Tower of Babylon*. Chiang's award was significant because it marked the beginning of a period, still ongoing, of enormous productivity by Asian Americans in the genre of SF.[112] Since 1991 Asian American authors have been publishing in SF venues and winning awards at a steadily increasing pace (see figure 0.1). These years have seen the emergence of Asian American authors such as Aliette de Bodard, R. F. Kuang, Yoon Ha Lee, Ken Liu, Marjorie Liu, and E. Lily Yu, who are now among the most frequently nominated and awarded authors for the Hugo, Nebula, and Sturgeon—the most prestigious awards in American SF.

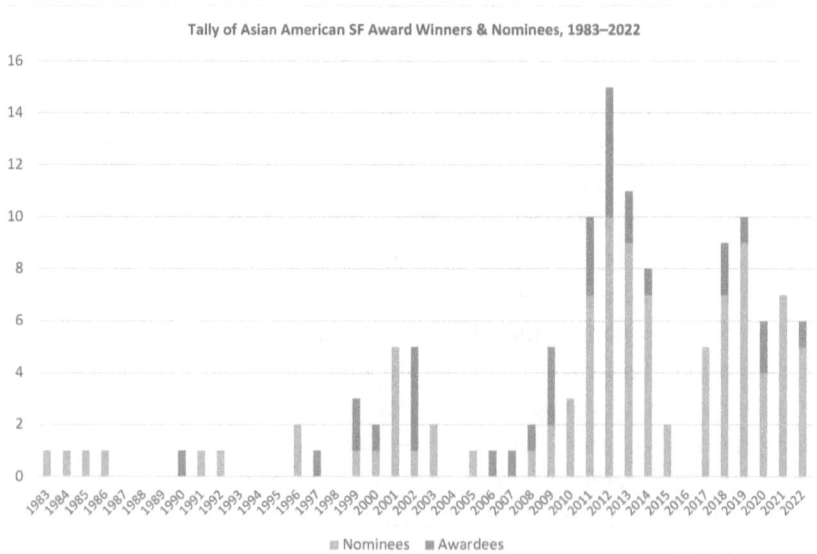

FIGURE 0.1. Tally of Asian American SF award winners and nominees, 1983–2022 (Hugo, Nebula, Sturgeon, World Fantasy). Graph and data collected by author.

INTRODUCTION

Outside of these award venues, this period has seen the appearance of Asian American authors who are now widely read and published in marquee SF imprints like Tor, Ace, Del Rey, and Small Beer, as well as magazines like *Asimov's*, *Fantasy & Science Fiction*, and *Analog* (the emergence of online venues like Tor.com and Lightspeed have also been significant factors in this boom, and not only for Asian American authors). These include authors like John Chu, S. L. Huang, Alice Sola Kim, and Alec Nevala-Lee. SF genre conventions have also more frequently found their way into the work of Asian American authors who are not typically associated with SF publishing venues, such as Sesshu Foster, Maggie Shen King, Claire Light/Jadie Jang, Cynthia Kadohata, Eugene Lim, Ling Ma, Xuan Juliana Wang, Karen Tei Yamashita, and Charles Yu. Alongside SF authors, a number of feature-length SF films have been written and directed by Asian American independent filmmakers: Greg Pak's *Robot Stories* (2003), Jennifer Phang's *Advantageous* (2015), Kogonada's *After Yang* (2021), and Daniel Kwan and Daniel Scheinert's *Everything Everywhere All at Once* (2022). Coincident with the "genre turn" of the 1990s and 2000s, Asian American authors known for their literary fiction have published works of SF: Ruth Ozeki's *A Tale for the Time Being* (2013) and Chang-rae Lee's *On Such a Full Sea* (2014) (about which I will have more to say in chapters 1 and 3, respectively), and Gish Jen's *The Resisters* (2020) being among the best-known examples. Meanwhile, the enormous and rapid growth of SF has extended to the contemporaneous explosion of young adult fiction as seen in the success of authors and graphic novelists such as Julie Kagawa, Kazu Kibuishi, Malinda Lo, Marjorie Liu, Cindy Pon, and Gene Luen Yang.[113] To put these booms into perspective, prior to the 1990s only a handful of Asian American authors had ever published SF in any venue, and while there have been substantial upticks of Asian American authors writing detective novels, SF has been the largest and fastest growing subfield of Asian American fiction.[114] Moreover, most had published only one or two pieces of short fiction; very had few generated a body of work, and even fewer had published novels.[115] There are only a handful of exceptions. In the 1970s and 1980s, Glenn Chang, Brenda W. Clough, and William F. Wu launched prolific careers—and Wu was the first Asian American to be nominated for a prestigious SF award, the Nebula, in 1983 for his short story, "Wong's Lost and Found Emporium."[116] It would still be years until other Asian American SF authors would join them in significant numbers.

It is worth repeating here that my claim is that "science fictionality" describes how the world appears to post-65 Northeast Asian American authors when they turn their attention to Asia. And to the extent that this perception shapes what we find written in the pages of post-65 Asian American fiction, it passes through a familiar set of mutually interacting standpoint dynamics like race, gender, sexuality, and dis/ability, *as well as* class dynamics pertaining to professional identity, economic subject formation, and the two cultures conflict. That said, the turn to Asia in this archive is of a piece with a more general turn to the self for source material: an "autopoetic" process in postwar American fiction that, McGurl writes, betrays "the fundamental non-naïveté of modern literary authorship, which as a product most broadly of reflexive modernity and, more specifically, of the school, cannot help seeing and knowingly announcing itself as authorship of one or another kind."[117] Like other kinds of authors, Asian Americans are perhaps also "condemned to individualization," as Ulrich Beck puts it, but I would argue that their path to condemnation is especially fraught.[118] If, as Dan Sinykin argues, the postwar trend of "inserting a version of oneself in one's novel reveals a desire for control and recognition and is evidence of anxiety about lacking the same," then Asian American authors, navigating the ethnographic imperative on one side and the two-cultures conflict on the other, have felt this anxiety even more keenly than others.[119] As McGurl observes of postwar ethnic American fiction, "a racial identity, no matter how realistically described, is a reflexive identity, and ethnic realism is perforce a reflexive realism (as W. E. B. Du Bois could have predicted)."[120] As these authors grasp for the autonomous freedoms of individual expression, they are hailed by stereotype and group identities that are never perfectly adequate because they are simultaneously elected and ascribed. For Asian American authors, this reflexivity is uniquely fraught compared to other minoritized groups.[121] One reason being the stereotype of the perpetual foreigner. As Lisa Lowe has famously argued, this stereotype not only vexes Asian Americans' relation to abstract and concrete regimes of citizenship and renders Asian American cultural production "at odds" with the U.S. nation-state, but it also tilts Asian American literary expression into the role of speaking ethnographic truth.[122] Another reason is, as Claire Jean Kim has shown, Asian Americans' relation to a dominant black-white schema of racial positions in post–civil rights era America, which compels Asian Americans to analogize their racial status—an analogy that she argues should be resisted by conceptualizing white-black-Asian racialization as a "triangulation" of different social meanings and material factors within a "field of racial positions."[123] In Patricia Chu's account, these factors result in the self-reflexivity and formal irony of the Asian American bildungsroman, a genre that Asian Americans rewrite by drawing from "a repertoire of representational conventions that purport to transcend . . . political differences while providing an idiom for addressing them indirectly."[124]

As we will see, the "repertoire of representational conventions" that post-65 Asian American authors draw from, especially the ones who hail directly from backgrounds of STEM occupational concentration (sometimes their parents', sometimes their own), is deeply structured by the two-cultures conflict between the arts and sciences. Even when the intergenerational allegory is absent (e.g., the culture of an older, Asia-born generation coming into conflict with a U.S.-born generation), the two-cultures trope reverberates with its intensity. The arts and sciences are obviously very different categories, but in post-65 Asian American fiction, they are for all intents and purposes libidinally identical: one is always pursued at the expense of the other. Whenever art is conjured, so is its shadow, science; and whenever science is conjured, art is right there beside it. In regard to the *production* of post-65 Asian American fiction, the two-cultures conflict worms its way into the confrontation between professional identity and authorship. The stereotype that results—of Asian parents prohibiting pursuit of the arts—is so familiar even to non–Asian Americans that it scarcely bears repeating. In the same way that genre fiction is frequently stereotyped as a deficient mode of literary fiction, literary authorship is, for post-65 Asian Americans always contradistinguished from more prestigious, STEM-related professional identities.

For all these reasons and more besides, the figure of the author in this book will not be understood as "an utterly free artistic being, with responsibilities only to posterity and eternal truth (or whatever)," but first and foremost as "a person constrained by circumstance—a person who needs money, and whose milieu influences the way she lives, reads, thinks, and writes. A person whose work is shaped by education and economy and a host of other pressures, large and small."[125] Because the Asian American author mediates an aesthetic relation to institutional subjectification—an ideology of professionalism, in other words—my account of post-65 Asian American fiction fits into broader accounts of postwar American literature. While it is important to reconcile these accounts, it is no less important to show how Asian American fiction has followed its own trajectory. Louis Menand and Thomas Strychacz associate the ideology of professionalism with the rise of the PMC at the turn of the twentieth century, identifying in it a modernist esoterism that shores the authority of the author against the commodification of the market.[126] For Andrew Hoberek postmodernism aligns with the dissipation of the PMC's entrepreneurial and anti-institutional ethos into middle-class salaried employment. And for critics like McGurl, Michael Szalay, and Sean McCann, American modernism and postmodernism developed as authors retreated into salaried employment in venues like the Works Progress Administration and the university, perches from which they no longer felt the pressure of catering to the tastes of a mass audience.[127] Even as their situation of relative security gave rise to striking new formal experimentations, these authors would soon feel constricted within their institutions. Aesthetic freedom then came to stand in for freedom from institutions and bureaucracy that resonated with the ressentiment festering among a proletarianized knowledge-worker class. In Audrey Wu-Clark's account, the modernist aesthetics of pre-65 Asian American authors such as Sui Sin Far and Carlos Bulosan inflected modernism's central concern with the alienations and ruptures of the self-other antinomy in this way: "If . . . the opaque 'thingness' of avant-garde objects represents the reified racialization of Asian Americans, then the Asian American avant-garde attempts to 'de-thing-ify' the foreign objects that problematically represent the Asian American and her work."[128] We might then say that Asian American postmodernism, in contrast, shifts focus from reification and representation, whose horizon is the U.S. nation-state, to the uncertainties of identifying with Asian economic futurity.

My use of genre categories in this book will be "heuristic," to use Phillip E. Wegner's term. I will not seek out checklists of aesthetic features or latch onto "postmodernism" any more than "SF," and will instead approach genre as something "created by a particular reader or critic in order to heighten the awareness of previously unacknowledged connections and continuities of a range of texts."[129] For instance, I am not so much interested in modernism or postmodernism as much as I am in how the

INTRODUCTION

distinction between them accords with a class standpoint that responds to contradictions between institutional rationality and an awkwardly class-situated PMC. As McCann argues, the postwar PMC's "central question becomes 'Who am I?' and more fundamentally still: 'Who owns my abilities, and how creative can I be in realizing on them?'"[130] The weight of these questions is doubled for post-65 Asian Americans, for whom employment and economic mobility are conflated with citizenship, and especially for post-65 Asian American authors who find themselves on the wrong side of occupational concentration's STEM normativity. In chapters 2 and 3, I explore how post-65 Asian American authors also find themselves beholden to the concrete institution of multiculturalism, to which they owe their entrée into the literary market. And as I show in the final chapter, an ambiguous "Asian" identity, amplified by Taiwan's ambiguous national sovereignty, makes possible the evasion of multiculturalism's discursive demands, often taking the form of the ideologically unreliable narrative voice that we find in Kathy Wang's and Charles Yu's fiction, as well as other post-65 Taiwanese American authors.[131]

The conditions underlying post-65 Asian American fiction differ from the above accounts of postmodernism in at least one more key detail. Postwar authors like Don DeLillo, Philip Roth, and Thomas Pynchon reacted to what Hoberek describes as "the expansion and ultimate proletarianization of mental labor."[132] Meanwhile, since the 1980s Asian American median household incomes have been consistently higher on average than non-Hispanic white incomes (figure 0.2). By no means exempt from the proletarianization of mental work, the Asian American experience of that more general process has overall been one of upward economic and social mobility, or at least middle-class stability and development, rather than a downward trend or stagnation. This inversion, to use once again Yoonmee Chang's term for the inverse relation between racial abjection and economic success in Asian American racial form, results in the illusion that Asian Americans in general are subject to different economic forces. For instance, one of the characters in Kathy Wang's *Family Trust* (2018) scoffs at white people's dismay that Asians are "just as adept at the form of capitalism they had invented."[133] This inversion is thematized in many of Chang-rae Lee's novels, where his white protagonists (e.g., Jerry Battle of *Aloft*, Hector Brennan of *The Surrendered*, Tiller Bardmon's father in *My Year Abroad*) struggle with economic downturn and career stagnation

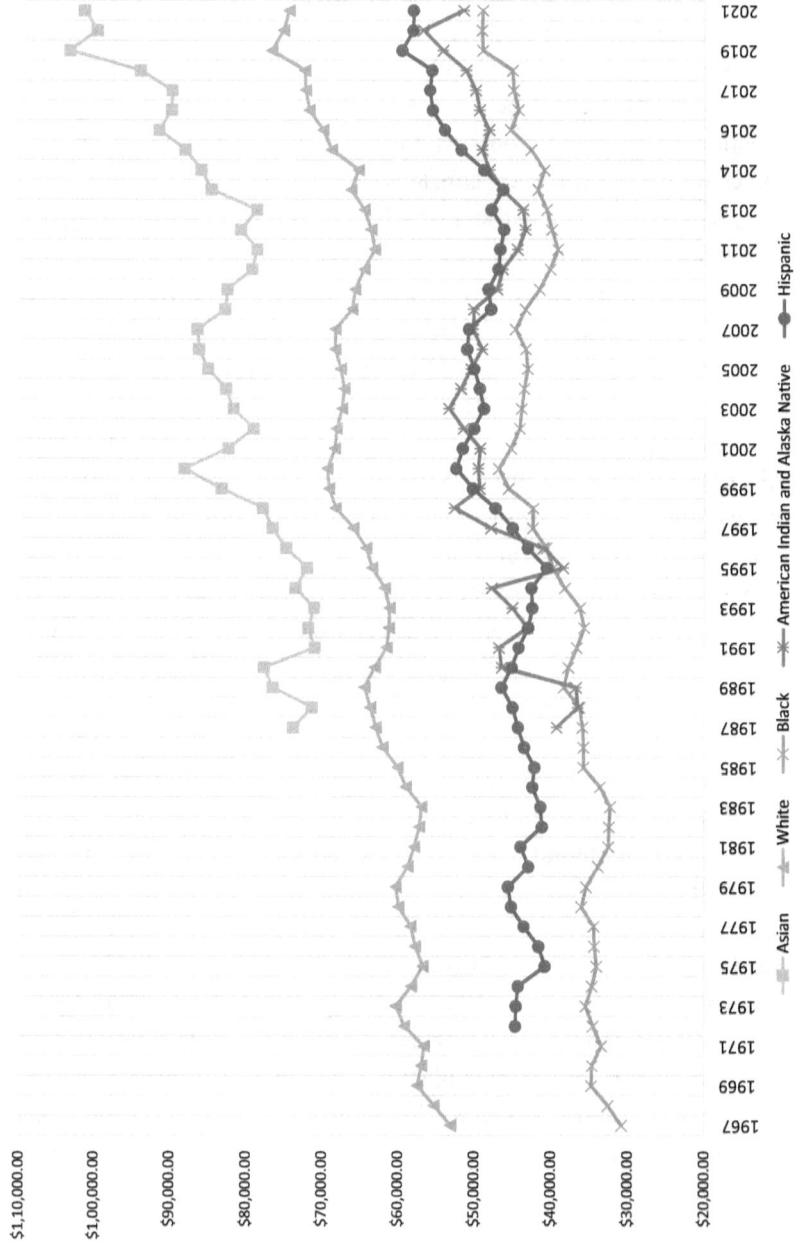

FIGURE 0.2. Median household income by race and Hispanic origin, 1967–2021. Graph by author. Data from U.S. Census Bureau, Current Population Survey, 1967 to 2021 Annual Social and Economic Supplements.

while the dramas surrounding his Asian characters pertain to the vicissitudes facing upwardly mobile immigrants whose economic mobility fails to translate to social integration. In Ling Ma's *Severance* a striking illustration of inversion occurs when an oil tycoon purchases a print from the protagonist's college honors art project: a collection of "color [photos] of decaying steel mills, Saturday nights at polka halls, bocce games in the back of Italian restaurants . . . [a] Rust Belt series [that] was supposed to be the first of several on declining industries in America."[134] What the tycoon shares with the protagonist, a 1.5-generation, middle-class Chinese American woman from a middle-class PMC background, is an *aesthetic* appreciation of blue-collar life. As I show in chapter 4, recent fiction by Chinese American authors worries quite a bit about this inversion, specifically through the class anxieties of its characters, who are mostly recent immigrants from China. For postwar American authors, McCann argues, "fiction [becomes] a means for the creative intellectual to emancipate himself from the threat of proletarianization."[135] Post-65 Asian American fiction diverges from this template in that, rather than translate this loss into the downward inflection of dispossession, we find the ballooning fantasy of social integration via economic mobility, which ventures beyond American identity in search for models of economic subject formation. Post-65 Asian American fiction also registers the upswing of the Asian American PMC through the trope of inversion: the good economic fortunes of post-65 Asian America compared to the bad fortunes of a deindustrializing economy's falling rate of profit.

When science fictionality isn't explicitly depicted in Asian American fiction, it is registered as a *gravitational pull* tugging at characterization, setting, diction, metaphor, and theme. As I will demonstrate in the chapters that follow, while it is still relatively easy to detect the pull of science fictionality via the literalism of conflicts generated by STEM occupational concentration, the broader trend in Anglophone fiction of blurring the distinction between "genre" fiction and conventional realism—often referred to as "the genre turn"—can make the pull more difficult to detect. As opposed, say, to Hoberek's prime example of a genre turn novel, Colson Whitehead's satirical zombie novel *Zone One* (2011), in which the world doesn't end so much as stubbornly refuse to end, science fictionality tends to produce an *upward inflection* that is the affective form of Chang's inversion.[136] That is, when the pain of racial abjection is subtracted from the pleasures of economic success, in the calculus of a science fictional universe, a surplus remains. But because the post-65 Asian American author is keenly aware of the moral valences of inversion, the "extravagance" of that surplus can never be freely enjoyed. In Hoberek's account the genre turn signals an aesthetic crisis at the end of history, insofar as it reacts to the capture of creativity by institution ("neoliberal capital itself obsessed with innovation") through an assertion of aesthetic autonomy ("genre reemerged as a kind of archive of conventions capable of providing a renewed backdrop for individual artistic expression").[137] No wonder, then, that the endings of its representative works so often feel dystopian and suffocated, like Whitehead's Mark Spitz under a crush of zombies, or the "completion" of Kazuo Ishiguro's clones at the end of *Never Let Me Go* (2005). While I would not deny that a novel like *Native Speaker* is also an inaugural instance of the "genre turn," as Hoberek claims, I would add that the difference between Lee's novel and Whitehead's is that Lee's ends on an upward inflection: a literal group hug that is as awkward as it is endearing. The science fictional elements of Lee's novel and of, say, a very genre turn-y novel like Ruth Ozeki's *A Tale for the Time Being* (2013) do not come close to rendering either text as instances of SF. Instead, the formal elements that announce their difference from conventional realism serve a kind of searching, heuristic role in which they might appear to be hunting down an emotional truth or undoing a psychological knot, but that instead leads into a sublation that isn't exactly optimism, not quite hope, and definitely not hopelessness. In Lee's novel it is the resolution of the two-cultures conflict via an embrace of neoliberal subjectivity. In Ozeki's novel it is the conflation of Japan and North America via a kind of transpacific ecological and geopolitical catastrophism. Science fictionality's material determinants are not ultimately mysterious. Indeed, its gravitational pull boils down to an ethos of science-led economic futurity that is foundational to the post-65 fantasy of social integration via economic mobility: an ethos that, in chapters 1 and 2, I will trace to midcentury modernization theory's fetishization of the engineer and its utopian end of history. As the arch modernization theorist Walt Rostow once argued, the falling rate of profit could not possibly hold true as long as scientific discovery was possible.[138] The fear of falling that for Ehrenreich so strongly characterizes the

PMC is neutralized away by the breezy, deterministic confidence of STEM occupational concentration.

When viewed from a slightly different angle, upward inflections present as disappointment, which is a major theme in post-65 Asian American fiction. This disappointment emerges not so much from the irreconcilability of abstract and concrete citizenship, the capriciousness of Asian inclusion and exclusion, or the awkwardness of Asian Americans' place in a binary racial hierarchy—structural and juridical complexities that more strongly determined the Asiatic racial form of an earlier era of industrialization. In the post-65 period, disappointment emerges even more from what greets STEM professionals upon their arrival in the United States, not to mention the reverberation of those disappointments down through the generations. As the immigrant parents in so much of post-65 Asian American fiction know painfully well, heroic training in STEM professions doesn't come close to translating to heroic status in the United States. What awaits instead is deprofessionalization, proletarianization, and, at best, middle management; and for their children, like the protagonist of *How to Live Safely*, watching one's parents, night after night, "jaw clenched at dinner . . . seeming to physically shrink with each professional defeat . . . finding new and deep places to hide it all."[139] If these are the emblems of relative economic success, then it's enough to make someone wonder if there might be more for them out there in the science fictional universe.

A question emerges here: Have I been conflating the first generation of post-65 STEM professionals with their children? Am I reading into the fiction of the "children of 1965" the hopes and anxieties of their parents? The answer is yes, I am. Mooting these questions, however, is the fact that all post-65 Asian American generations are dominated by the same racial form, and it is this racial form that mediates occupational concentration, science fictionality, and post-65 Asian American authorship. Trained to produce miraculous economic growth, post-65 Asian Americans have languished in deindustrializing America in a very particular way. These defeats and disappointments have been reason enough for Saxenian's "new Argonauts" to circulate back to their home countries, or at least imagine doing so. And they have been reason enough for the authors who emerge among post-65 Asian Americans to risk exchanging the compensations of Asian American identity for the science fictionality of a global, Asian economic futurity.

THE CHAPTERS

Each chapter in this book explores a science fictional mediation of transimperial U.S.-Asia political economy. Chapter 1, "Deep Conditions of the World: Modernization Theory and Transimperiality," engages the question of midcentury modernization theory's influence on Northeast Asian economic development, and how the link between scientific positivism and economic growth that it promoted helped to lay the groundwork for the production of surplus STEM human capital and the fantasy of economic integration. It outlines the historical links between modernization theory and Asian America through readings of work by Ruth Ozeki and Ken Liu, both of whom explicitly engage legacies of modernization and the continuities joining Japanese and U.S. imperialisms.

Chapter 2, "Writing Like an Engineer: Postracial Form and Utopia," traces "postracial aesthetics" into the racial discourses of Japan-U.S. transimperiality. Key to this genealogy is the elevation of the figure of the *engineer* during the postwar years as a kind of national hero in the developing world. The engineer bears not only national hopes of economic development and global integration, but also the worldview of modernization theory that believed itself to be ideologically and scientifically beyond race. The conviction that economic growth was available to all human societies, regardless of race and history, and that the only precondition for economic "takeoff" was taking the right steps through stages of development, projects a utopianism that is captured by an amplified version of "postracial" aesthetics. All of this is exemplified in the fiction of Ted Chiang, which not only brackets historical contingency but literary style itself. The result is a kind of technical writing that crystalizes an "expository impulse" that is a key formal register of science fictionality, and that can be tracked in post-65 Asian American fiction more broadly.

Chapter 3, "Shakespeare Words: Professional Identity and Literary Style," turns to the oeuvre of Chang-rae Lee, the prose-poet of the post-65 Asian American PMC. It focuses specifically on how the central concern over professional identity in Lee's work in some ways undermines the allegory of race and literary style that has informed so much Asian Americanist literary scholarship. Style is at once the most personal and the most typical aspect of an author's writing, and Lee's style in particular develops in response to the interrelation between Japan-U.S. transimperiality and the post-65 Asian American PMC's class anxieties: a response that is most powerfully registered in the trope of the two-cultures conflict, in which an excessive aestheticism compensates for the disappointments of occupational concentration and hyper-selection.

Chapter 4, "Genres of Deprofessionalization: Economic Subjectivity and Chinese American Women Writers," examines a generic continuity in Chinese American women's writing that contends, via autopoesis, with a distinctly post-65 struggle to reconcile interconnected conflicts pertaining to occupational concentration, normative femininity, and Asian economic futurity.[140] Beginning with a reading of the theme of deprofessionalization in Maxine Hong Kingston's *Woman Warrior* (1976), this chapter then makes a heuristic leap forward in time to a recent cluster of Chinese American women authors whose debut novels feature characters that, like Kingston's protagonist, resolve these conflicts by cathecting professional identity and an emerging U.S.-China economic subjectivity.

In the concluding chapter, "Enough? Semiperipheral Structures of Feeling in the Taiwanese American Novel," I show how in recent Taiwanese American novels the trope of the ideologically unreliable narrator who plays fast and loose with the mores of racial discourse is a convention that can be traced back to Taiwan's emergence into semiperipheral geopolitical status. Because Taiwan "exists in the between"—as a sovereign nation lacking international recognition, caught between two superpowers, and yet dominating the world's supply of advanced semiconductors—the stakes of racial discourse in this fiction are amplified not only by the act of return, but also by the semiperipheral ambiguities of Taiwanese identity.[141]

What will emerge in these chapters is an account of how post-65 Northeast Asian American fiction has responded formally to the shifting geopolitical relations between Northeast Asia and the United States. What I hope becomes apparent is how such an account depends on taking seriously the questions of what makes a text *Asian*, and what it means for an author to be *from Asia*. Through the geographical itineraries they trace, and the temporalities they evoke, the texts examined in these chapters, along with their authors, will bring into relief these material realities as well as their intimate, private dimensions. Conflicts between parents and children, contradictions of cultural identity, the fraught process of envisioning a future for oneself and one's community—these are not isolated events but dialectical aspects of a broader historical process in which one is implicated not only via race, but also class. Connecting Northeast Asia to post-65 Asian America helps us to understand the deep anxiety, also known as model minoritization, in which PMC status (whether STEM professional or author) will never be good enough. Not only because the "success frame" might assign higher material ambitions, but because the transimperial project of modernization was itself never good enough for the countries it guided, the region it cohered, or the people whose fantasies it shaped.

Chapter One

DEEP CONDITIONS OF THE WORLD

Modernization Theory and Transimperiality

> In that same nature whose destructive force was a cause of this pessimism, he sought peace for his soul.
>
> —MASAO WATANABE, *THE JAPANESE AND WESTERN SCIENCE*

In the introduction I sketched out the fantasy of science-led economic futurity that has strongly defined Northeast Asian American life since 1965. This chapter offers an account of that fantasy's origins in modernization projects spanning Japanese colonialism and U.S. neoimperialism, as well as how recent Asian American fiction has begun to engage with these histories. While the diverse intellectual and colonial histories of modernization discourse will be important in what follows, this chapter focuses on its manifestation in the mid-century American promulgation of modernization theory. From the 1930s through the 1970s, liberals sought to expand America's political and ideological reach across the globe via the putatively progressive framework of modernization, but as David Ekbladh observes, "Asia... would see the largest and most intense application of these ideas."[1] Policymakers and intellectuals looked to South Korea in particular as the "proving ground" for their ideas about economic and social progress, but would set their sights on all of Northeast Asia—China included—as their "laboratories."[2] Taiwan would become their model student, as it was for Japan. And Japan would be the regional linchpin to the whole scheme. At the ground level, however, as Ekbladh reminds us, "Individuals... had to incorporate modern outlooks on intimate levels for the [modernization] process to proceed and succeed."[3] These "modern outlooks," as I have already suggested, are *science fictional* not only because of their internalization of modernization's positivism and scientific universalism but also because of their implicit class aspirations. When the human capital surplus that postwar modernization created in Northeast Asian countries arrived in the United States, these individuals brought with them fantasies of economic mobility and social integration, as well as a class orientation to a "transnationalised set of elite actors that include capitalists, but also state planners, military leaders, and others who help set in motion policies and projects connected to industrialization."[4] What set many post-65 immigrants on a path to STEM occupational concentration in the first place was an identification with this "Pacific ruling class," to use Jim Glassman's term—an identification that was sometimes embraced, sometimes violently rejected, but in all cases strongly encouraged by their home countries' authoritarian governments, and linked to the kinds of STEM fields that would most benefit rapid industrialization.[5] U.S. modernization theory generated the economic, political, and intellectual conditions for the postwar formation of the Northeast Asian political economy that structures the political unconscious of post-65 Asian American literature.

U.S. modernization theory also provided the intellectual basis for the continuation of Japan's imperial project by U.S. Cold War neoimperialism. Transimperiality has not received adequate attention in Asian American studies due to the latter's focus on a critique of U.S. racism and empire.[6] Despite this aporia, post-65 Asian American fiction has often reflected on this history quite explicitly, as we will see when I turn to Ken Liu's and Ruth Ozeki's fiction in this chapter's final section. Far from being a fait accompli, modernization and its concomitants were, for Asian states and peoples, ambivalently figured as targets of resistance (sometimes violent) and embrace (sometimes fervent). The postwar struggle in northeast Asian countries to assert native control over paths of national economic development that "Western" capitalism sought to dominate was deeply ambivalent. The imposition of modernization theory on client states by the United States took place in an environment of hegemonic predominance and consent, mainly through the mechanisms of foreign aid and expert guidance. As Dipesh Chakrabarty has written, "The discourse and politics of decolonization in the nations that met in Bandung [in 1955] often displayed an uncritical emphasis on modernization. Sustaining this attitude was a clear and conscious desire to 'catch up' with the West."[7] Within this milieu, the technical and scientific professional arose as a hypercathected embodiment of national identities, center-periphery dynamics, civilizational ideologies, and aspirations to class mobility. In the U.S. context this embodiment would be expressed via the "model minority" stereotype. As scholars like Victor Bascara, Leo Ching, Takeshi Fujitani, and Robert G. Lee have shown, this stereotype, especially as it has been taken up in Asian American studies, has been quite narrowly conceived as a fiction arising from the crucible of U.S. racial dynamics rather than overdetermined by factors far beyond U.S. borders.[8]

This chapter has two aims. One is to provide an account of the historical links between modernization theory and post-65 Asian America: in short, to provide a prehistory of occupational concentration that explains why STEM human capital could be found in such abundance in Northeast Asia, why that human capital was willing to leave Asia behind, and what they expected to find on the other side. This account will deepen the correspondence between Northeast Asian transimperiality and Northeast Asian American fiction. Because the rest of this book will explore the implications of this account via occupational concentration and the figure of the Asian American author, this chapter's second aim swerves in a slightly different direction. It uses the discussion of modernization theory as an opportunity to describe and think through questions of literary form, and to emphasize the literary mediation of transimperiality. In the next section, I will describe in more detail the co-emergence of Asian American SF and the transnational turn in Asian American literary fiction mentioned above, alongside the emergence of a "techno-orientalist" aesthetics that is awkwardly situated in relation to Asian American literary production. In this chapter's final section I will examine how Ken Liu and Ruth Ozeki have engaged with histories of modernization and transimperiality in their work, and how their depiction of those histories works through a set of narrative problems pertaining to the nation form and temporality. As one of Liu's characters puts it in regard to the adjudication of war crimes committed by Japanese troops in World War II, "Our doctrines concerning the succession of states, developed under the Westphalian framework, simply cannot deal with ... questions" pertaining to historical justice.[9] When Liu and Ozeki reach for the tools of SF, they do so in order to bring forth historical continuities rather than conjure SF possibilities. This focus on continuity, moreover, leads each author's historical materialist commitments to temporal horizons far exceeding even transimperiality's longue durée—in Ozeki's case, far exceeding the human scale. As one of Ozeki's characters muses: "A wave is born from deep conditions of the ocean. A person is born from deep conditions of the world. A person pokes up from the world and rolls along like a wave, until it is time to sink down again. Up, down. Person, wave."[10] Liu's and Ozeki's fiction, we might say, emerges from the "deep conditions" of U.S.-Northeast Asia's science fictional totality.

TOOLS OF THE TRADE

It was only when the children of 1965 came of age in the 1990s that Asia would finally become *present* in their fiction. The allure of East Asian miracle economies, brightened by China's liberalization, raised anew the question of what it meant to be *from* Asia, as well as a new set of questions pertaining to what Asia now had to offer. Many Northeast Asian American authors responded by looking simultaneously into the past and the future: at histories that explained Asia's persistent material and imaginative presence in the United States and possibilities that promised entirely new worlds. What they found were justifications for imperial expansion (first Japan, then the United States, now China) constructed out of ideologies of modernization that accounted for their own presence in the United States and, to a great extent, their decision to write in the first place. When we examine the literary expressions of this Asia-directed gaze, what emerges out of their complex negotiations of geopolitical and libidinal dynamics is a science fictional horizon of reference within which a diverse array of aesthetic forms has emerged.

Until the late 1980s Asian American literature had been preoccupied with leaving Asia behind amid dramas of immigration and assimilation.[11] The reasons for Asia's absence in this archive are complex. For one, "Asia" was either politically unavailable or no longer existed. China, for instance, would not open its doors to American tourists until 1978, two years after *Woman Warrior* was published, thus leaving Maxine Hong Kingston empty-handed in her book's final pages: "Soon I want to go to China and find out who's lying," the Communists or her relatives.[12] But even if Asia were totally accessible, its direct representation could hinder a project of claiming and problematizing an American identity. It could constrain the aesthetic freedom of text and author, thrusting both into a minefield of demands for ethnic spokespersonship and authenticity that might drive an author to circumnavigate such dangers by simply embracing the presumption of literalism through memoir or autobiography. This period of "life writing" gave way to a transnational turn.[13] In novels like Susan Choi's *The Foreign Student* (1998), Ruth Ozeki's *My Year of Meats* (1998), and Chang-rae Lee's *A Gesture Life* (1999), as well as in short stories by authors like Lan Samantha Chang and David Wong Louie, readers were presented with narratives set in Asia, and in which Asia is an abiding presence, thanks to factors like war trauma and international commerce.[14]

If the uncanny shock of global capital provoked the transnational turn in literary fiction, for authors of SF it provided a raison d'être. In Min Hyoung Song's assessment, Yamashita's 1990 SF novel *Through the Arc of the Rainforest* inaugurated an especially vibrant period in which Asian American authors could "imagine otherwise" a "smooth space not striated by a global imaginary, an act of deterritorialization that imagines less an American globalism and more a planetary becoming."[15] This scope is strikingly registered in the novel's novum of the Matacão, a mysterious plasticine substance gathering under the Amazon rainforest that is the amalgamation of the "non-biodegradable material buried under virtually every populated part of the Earth" (202). Eventually revealed to be "the compressed regurgitation of First World waste," the Matacão, in Aimee Bahng's gloss, allegorizes "the by-product of the most powerful and productive economies."[16] This version of the transnational, in which the global is equated to a world-system of uneven and combined development, draws not only from Yamashita's own personal experience as a Japanese American who lived for many years in Brazil, but also from a corresponding trope in Anglophone SF, which was a dominant convention when Yamashita was writing, thanks primarily to the subgenre of cyberpunk. As Bruce Sterling puts it in the introduction to his landmark anthology *Mirrorshades* (1986), cyberpunk is a genre that "has little patience for borders" and champions the "tools of global integration—the satellite media net, the multinational corporation."[17] Emblematized by novels like William Gibson's *Neuromancer* (1984), films like Ridley Scott's *Blade Runner* (1982), and publications like *Wired* magazine (1993–present), it continues to enjoy considerable influence over mainstream SF, not least through constant revivals in films like *The Matrix* series (1999–2021), television series like *Altered Carbon* (2018–2020), and videogames like *Cyberpunk 2077* (2020).[18] David Morley and Kevin Robins famously associated cyberpunk's cultural logic of "techno-orientalism" with an ambivalent response to the "Japan Panic" of the 1970s and 1980s, in which the West anxiously observed the global advance of Japanese capital in quotidian manifestations like personal electronics, automobiles, and high-profile real estate acquisitions. Cyberpunk's premise was a syllogism proposing that "If the future is technological, and if technology has become 'Japanised,' then ... the future is now Japanese too."[19] So influential has cyberpunk been, and so deep-seated is techno-orientalism's cultural logic, that it is very likely that my use of "science fictional" has conjured for readers an array of high-tech and orientalist tropes: the multinational sublime of *Neuromancer*'s dynastic *zaibatsu*, the ramen vendor-lined streets of *Blade Runner*'s Tokyo-ized Los Angeles, a racially ambiguous (but vaguely Asian) Neo "downloading" kung-fu in *The Matrix*.

Asian Americanist critics have come to approach cyberpunk and other "techno-orientalist" aesthetics as either a set of vulgarities to be rejected or as an "opportunity for critical reappropriations in texts that self-referentially engage with Asian images."[20] What I would suggest is that representationally problematic as these tropes may be, they emerge from the same set of material relations as the transnational turn and the emergence of SF in Asian American fiction, and should be read as "flexible strategies" for engaging with global capitalism.[21] They are, to borrow Sterling's phrase, "tools of global integration": forms for grappling with a world increasingly defined by Asia, especially Northeast Asia, and by U.S.-Asia hegemonic transition. What Sterling says about the cyberpunk generation also applies to post-65 Northeast Asian American authors: "The cyberpunks are perhaps the first SF generation to grow up not only within the literary tradition of science fiction but in a truly science-fictional world. For them, the techniques of classical 'hard SF'—extrapolation, technological literacy—are not just literary tools but an aid to daily life. They are a means of understanding, and highly valued" (xi). An important difference, however, is that post-65 Northeast Asian Americans and the authors among them are not passive recipients and remixers of the "science-fictional world," as Sterling's cyberpunks appear to be, but in many ways its unsung creators.

We find this constructionist posture and its reproductive, pedagogical dimension efficiently captured in the title of Charles Yu's 2010 debut novel, *How to Live Safely in a Science Fictional Universe*. In that novel, the protagonist's father invents "chronodiegetics," the "branch of science fictional science focusing on the physical and metaphysical properties of time . . . within a narrative space" that gives rise to time travel technology and an entire industry of manufactured universes—although he never sees a penny of profit because another inventor beats him to market (33). The protagonist registers a note of complicity in how those inventions have produced persistent structures of inequality. In "NEW ANGELES/LOST TOKYO-2," the capital city of "Minor Universe 31," "successful transition into the SF zone remains difficult to achieve for many immigrant families, and even after decades of an earnest and often desperate striving for acceptance and assimilation, many remain in the lower-middle reaches of the zone, along the border between SF and 'reality'" (78). On a less cosmic scale, the character Haruki Yasutani ("Haruki #2") in Ruth Ozeki's 2013 novel *A Tale for the Time Being*, a computer scientist known in Silicon Valley as the "Pioneer of POV," protests his company's licensing of his technology to the U.S. military. He is subsequently fired, loses his work visa, and returns to his native Japan, where he falls into a deep depression, not only because he is jobless but also because of the knowledge that his technology is being used to sustain a project of militarized violence and transimperial continuity that his namesake, his uncle "Haruki #1," also protested as an unwilling kamikaze pilot for Japan in World War II.

The transnational becomes of interest for Northeast Asian American authors at a moment when "Asia" becomes not only a symbol and site of capitalist futurity but also a world that post-65 Northeast Asian Americans themselves have brought into existence. What awaits them there, however, is not the locus of cultural essence and fulfillment that Asia might have symbolized for an earlier generation of writers, but instead a tangle of complications and uncanny repetitions. As Yamashita, Yu, and Ozeki suggest to us, the "tools" of SF have become for Asian American writers particularly useful for grappling with the dangers of living in a science fictional universe. We even see Amy Tan reaching for them in *The Joy Luck Club*, where we fine a fanciful SF description of what "becoming Chinese" means: "I saw myself transforming like a werewolf, a mutant tag of DNA suddenly triggered, replicating itself insidiously into a *syndrome*" (304, original emphasis).

When William Gibson tells us that "the street finds its own uses for things"—a slogan of the cyberpunks drawn from his short story "Burning

Chrome," which coined the term "cyberspace"—the history of modernization theory reveals how these "uses" became science fictional and orientalized.[22] Tracking the itinerary of modernization in Northeast Asia helps us to see that the hyper-selected professionals who came after 1965, and whose children now produce the bulk of Asian American literature, themselves came of age in a milieu in which their scientific and technical career visions were anything but value-neutral and their professional identities anything but nonideological. These were people who felt their proximity to the Pacific ruling class, if they were not already members, and were told to return to their home countries one day to participate in reconstruction and nation-building. Some ignored or were unable to answer this call because they were escaping actual or potential political persecution, and many more simply ended up staying in the United States much longer than they had intended. If they returned, their home countries benefited tremendously from the expertise and networks they brought with them, and often enough it was at home where they would either realize dreams that were thwarted in the United States or pursue them to their tragic endings.

MANDARINS OF THE FUTURE

As Leo Ching has observed, modernization theory occupies an aporia in Asian American studies, and as such might be taken as a preeminent sign of the disciplinary divide between Asian studies and Asian American studies.[23] One obvious reason for this is that modernization theory was foreign policy, while Asian American studies arose out of a political claim to American citizenship and a cultural claim to American identity. Another reason has to do with the different institutional histories of Asian studies and Asian American studies. While the latter emerged from demands made by radical Third-Worldist student movements in the San Francisco Bay Area in the late-1960s, Asian studies traces its origins to the American state's demand for knowledge production during World War II and the expansion of those interests through nongovernmental organizations like the Ford Foundation and the Asia Foundation.[24] Writing from the vantage of Asian studies, Ching argues:

> Despite their common origins in the American Empire ... Asian studies and
> Asian American studies, until recently, have remained largely insulated from

each other. This disengagement, for example, has obscured the parallelism between modernization theory as applied to Japan and later other East Asian countries and the model minority myth that aimed to divide Asian Americans from other underrepresented populations.... Reading modernization theory and the model minority myth contrapuntally allows us to apprehend American imperial design as a dialectical process of expansion and domestication under the ideology of postwar liberalism.[25]

I would concur that the figure of the model minority could reveal at least as much as it obscures, if only we would resist the temptation of moralism and shift our focus to its economic function and historicity. Kandice Chuh's account of the "dialectical process" described by Ching brings attention to the model minority's role in the widening wealth and class stratification within Asian America: "The contemporary model minority," Chuh argues, is "a figure and lived subjectivity that emerges at the conjuncture of the rise of global capitalism and U.S. neoimperialism. Clearly, there is a homology between the modernization of Asia and the domestic figure of the model minority that emerges in and following the Second World War."[26] In the early 2000s, when the "sudden appearance of wealthy Asians" was just beginning to register for Americans, Viet Thanh Nguyen argued that this sharpening class stratification brought into relief how "Asian America is an often willing and enthusiastic participant in global capitalism, racial domination, and class stratification."[27] Echoing Nguyen's intervention, Chuh's methodological conclusion is that "there needs now to be a dismantling of the assumption that... the [Asian American] community... refers only or even primarily to groups living marginal lives."[28] Tracing the link between modernization theory and the model minority almost immediately necessitates disambiguating what is meant by "Asia," in regard not only to the vicissitudes of national and regional context but also to the mutual, U.S.-Asia cultivation of the Pacific ruling class.

Standard accounts of modernization theory follow a narrative of rise and fall, beginning with the emergence of postwar evangelists like Walt Rostow, Gabriel Almond, Lucian Pye, David Apter, Cyril Black, Bert Hoselitz, Myron Weiner, Karl Deutsch, and Daniel Lerner; routing through their influence among the "best and the brightest" in the Eisenhower and Kennedy administrations and in the development activities of the United Nations Educational, Scientific, and Cultural Organization (UNESCO); and finally ending with the theory's discrediting in the 1970s.[29] As Nils Gilman writes, modernization theory stands as "the most explicit and systematic blueprint ever created by Americans for reshaping foreign societies."[30] Rostow's career offers an efficient lens for tracking modernization theory's vicissitudes. Before the publication of his landmark 1960 book *The Stages of Economic Growth: A Non-Communist Manifesto*, Rostow and his theories were already influential in the Eisenhower administration. His book would later impress Kennedy with its schema of economic development, which proposed that societies passed through five phases: "traditional society, the preconditions for take-off, the take-off, the drive to maturity, and the age of high mass-consumption."[31] Rostow's framework was welcomed by a foreign policy community struggling to grapple with the postwar U.S. occupations in Asia, and especially decolonization in the Third World. The mission here was not only to transform the Third World into the image of the United States but also, in Michael E. Latham's words, "to alter the very environmental conditions in which they believed that radicalism grew and attempt to control the course of nationalist aspirations."[32] From his cabinet position in Kennedy's administration, Rostow became "America's Rasputin," and "during both the Kennedy and the Johnson years [symbolized] the aggressive, combative liberal nationalism of the era."[33] His devotion to setting "traditional" societies on track by any means necessary contributed to modernization theory's eventual discrediting in the tumult of the civil rights and antiwar movements, when it succumbed to challenges "on the left by arguments about the devastating effects of international capitalism, and on the right by a rising neoliberal chorus condemning attempts at social engineering and proclaiming the virtue of free markets."[34] Despite this declensionist narrative, it is now generally accepted that while the term "modernization" fell out of favor, as did its statism, its stagism has remained very much intact and has integrated into neoliberal common sense, not least via the "shock therapy" of structural adjustment and the "Washington Consensus" that consolidated in the 1990s.

Much of the challenge of attaching a literary history to an ideological framework like modernization theory, which was less a science or set of axioms than an earworm of a marketing campaign for U.S. geopolitical interests, is that the latter can be tracked backward and forward in history to the point of incoherence. Though the term "modernization," according to Michael Adas, was rarely used until after World War II, "American educators, missionaries, and engineers of the 1920s and 1930s advocated political, economic, and cultural transformations in China, the Philippines, and Latin America which were as fundamental and wide-ranging as those proposed by development specialists in the 1950s and 1960s."[35] As Gilman, Latham, and others have noted, modernization theory's antinomies have even deeper historical roots. According to one of its most prominent proponents, Lucian Pye, these roots are to be found in "that powerful tradition of Western social philosophy in which it is assumed that all societies can be classified according to a dichotomous scheme [traditional versus modern] and in which all significant social and cultural changes are seen as related to the movement of a society from one category to the other."[36] In Gilman's account, U.S. modernization theory can be traced back to Talcott Parsons, the giant of American sociology who elaborated Max Weber's concept of "rationalization," and, further, to Enlightenment and post-Enlightenment figures like Immanuel Kant, Adam Smith, Georg Wilhelm Friedrich Hegel, Karl Marx, and the Marquis de Condorcet.[37] C. P. Snow channeled this intellectual tradition into his narrative of the two-cultures conflict, in which he speculated that a "scientific revolution" in the United States and Soviet Union could bring an end to the Cold War by bringing the two powers together to solve social problems such as poverty.[38] The relevance of modernization theory to my account of post-65 Asian American literature builds upon its explicit manifestations in Cold War foreign policy, which had direct bearing on the eventual hyper-selection and occupational concentration of post-65 Asian America: it defined a narrative of economic development and national strengthening as led by applied science and technology, cultivated dependency on U.S. foreign aid and military protection, and shaped educational and human capital policies that would sustain and expand its worldview. Whether or not you agreed with modernization theory's worldview, as a Northeast Asian you had to contend with it.

The conception of Asia as incapable of capitalist development, and thus requiring external, namely European, intervention would become perhaps the most jealously guarded tenet of modernization theory–informed U.S. foreign policy. The "progressive, humanist ideology" shared by Enlightenment and post-Enlightenment philosophers of modernity deeply influenced not only colonial projects at the time but anticolonial, anticapitalist projects as well: a contradiction whose resolution is found in a shared orientalism. In one of the most infamous passages from his reporting for the *New York Herald Tribune*, Marx wrote that "Indian society has no history at all. . . . England has to fulfill a double mission in India: one destructive, the other regenerating—the annihilation of the old Asiatic society, and the laying of the material foundations of Western society in Asia."[39] This stereotype of backwardness—theoretically enshrined in the centrality of "oriental despotism" in Weber's work, and the "Asiatic mode of production" in Marx's—would find its way, notoriously, into the discourse of the "white man's burden" that shaped the cultures and policies of U.S. colonization of the Philippines. "The idea of a racially inflected destiny," Latham explains, led Americans to imagine "their conquest of the Philippines . . . as part of a broader process in which they were taking on the obligations of a great power to act as a civilizing force in the world."[40] Even as modernization theorists "eschewed the racism of earlier colonialist discourse," avowing the capacity of all societies to develop—sometimes quickly over the course of mere decades, sometimes more slowly—"it still defined modernity in contrast to an implicitly inferior 'traditional' other" whose content was, as its Weberian roots reveal, fundamentally orientalist.[41] The importance of "oriental despotism" for Weber and the "Asiatic mode of production" for Marx as paradigmatic civilizational others "in illustration of a theory," as Edward Said put it, was repressed in modernization theory's discursive expressions, which were couched in the bourgeois rhetoric of scientific universalism (Parson's "evolutionary universals" and social Darwinism).[42] As Gilman writes, "modernization theory would be Exhibit A in what [Noam Chomsky] called 'the double myth of the social sciences': the myth of political benevolence and the myth of scientific omniscience."[43] This longstanding traditional-modern antinomy is, moreover, the basis of techno-orientalism's "premodern-hypermodern dynamic" in which Asia and Asians are always temporally displaced, never present and available to the register of the mundane.[44] Asians were never themselves passive or naïve objects of modernization discourses, however. Indeed, the "double myth" itself was an important site of resistance against orientalist stereotypes and Western power: for instance, the Meiji restoration's adoption of Western science ("Japanese ethics, European science"), and the May Fourth movement's refurbishing of China's nineteenth century ethos of *zhōngtǐ xīyòng* ("Chinese learning as substance, Western learning for application") as "Mr. Science" and "Mr. Democracy."[45]

It is important to keep this orientalist project and its contestations in mind when reconstructing the ideology of scientific objectivity that informed the direction of East Asian industrialization, human capital development, and post-65 Asian America, especially its supposedly value-neutral relation to economic development.[46] Modernization at its core was an effort not only to "rationalize" U.S. imperialism but also to render human contingency scientific. It was, after a fashion, an epic SF narrative and sublation of the two-cultures conflict, albeit one with enormous consequences. As Adas writes, "The stress on the pivotal roles of applied science and technology in the modernizing process was repeatedly affirmed by the foremost champions of the paradigm in its mid-1960s heyday."[47] In the context of Taiwan, as Chih-ming Wang has written, the values of scientific "neutrality" instilled in Taiwanese students studying abroad in the United States were laden with ideological baggage. Moreover, the theoretical fungibility of "Third World countries"—what theorists termed their "functional equivalence"—was crucial to the project of modernization, and science and technology were to play a leading role in justifying "cross-cultural" comparisons.[48] "For Kennedy and his advisers," writes Odd Arne Westad, "the key to what America could do to help avoid breakdown in the Third World was held by its technological success. Money in itself could not do the job—only the diffusion of technology and the accompanying know-how could bring Third World countries swiftly across the period of uncertainty in which Communism threatened."[49] Not only did immutable scientific truth provide modernization's horizon of theoretical verification, but its pursuit would also be a libidinal heatsink for modernization's utopian desire.

TRANSIMPERIALITY: THE NORTHEAST ASIAN POLITICAL ECONOMY

Modernization theory played an outsized role in directing the economic miracles in Northeast Asia. My focus on these countries, as I explained in the introduction, is far from arbitrary. Not only are they points of origin for the majority of Asian American writers, but they also form a political economic totality whose coherence was underwritten by imperial projects of scientific knowledge production. These countries were thought of by modernization theorists as testing grounds for their social engineering and policy experiments. Far from being isolated cases, their space-times of development were determined by the dual hegemony of the United States and Japan, as well as their interrelations with each other. In 1930, the Japanese economist Kaname Akamatsu famously dubbed this the "wild-geese-flying" (frequently reconfigured in development literature as "flying geese formation") formation of development with Japan as the lead, "advanced" economy, and the "less-advanced" economies of Manchuria, Korea, and Taiwan serving as markets and low-value-added manufacturing.[50] With the exception of Manchuria, this formation would be recreated after the war, but under the auspices of the United States, as Bruce Cumings recounts in a well-known anecdote: "In September 1945, as U.S. occupation forces filtered into Japan, an American officer walked into a Mitsui office in Tokyo and introduced himself. A man in the office pointed to a map of the Greater East Asian Coprosperity Sphere and said, 'There it is. We tried. See what you can do with it!' "[51] Cumings also argues that, for historians of Asia, a nation-specific approach to understanding the development of the region would obscure far more than it would illuminate: "it is misleading," he writes, "to assess the industrialization pattern in any one of these countries: such an approach misses, through a fallacy of disaggregation, the fundamental unity and integrity of the regional effort in this century."[52] This fallacy, moreover, would render us "incapable of accounting for the remarkably similar trajectories of Korea and Taiwan" under Japanese colonialism and under U.S. neoimperial management.[53] As preeminent examples of what Immanuel Wallerstein called "development by invitation"—a kind of model minority status conferred to certain developing nations—the two countries were joined to Japan, which, as Cumings notes, "was chosen [too], if at a higher level in the system."[54] In the postwar years, the United States would recreate the "flying geese" formation in their policy prescriptions for South Korea and Taiwan, which positioned them as peripheries to Japan.[55] Importantly, this core-periphery hierarchy was deeply informed by a racial schema. Japan's modernization, beginning with the late nineteenth-century Meiji Restoration and its defeat of Russia, would make it an honorary European country, setting it at an even "higher level" than model minority. As Chris Suh has shown, Japan's embrace of this schema made it a welcome partner for the United States in refining the rhetoric and practice of a "progressive" imperialism that, in Japan's hands, justified its "civilizing" mission in Korea, and, in America's hands, justified its occupations of Cuba and the Philippines.[56]

Asia is more than just a point of origin, waypoint, or destination for return in the U.S. formation called Asian America. As David Eng argues, "any serious understanding of Asian American racial formation must be considered in relation to a comparative and internationalist model of subject formation and subjection beyond the real and imaginary borders of the U.S. nation-state."[57] To think of Asian America as the sum of its parts is to succumb to the "fallacy of disaggregation"—Susan Koshy calls this "catachresis"—and, more seriously, to risk reinscribing U.S. exceptionalism.[58] The transnational turn that Eng and others facilitated through their work in the late 1990s and early 2000s has certainly produced a rich and important body of scholarship, but one that primarily pursues a "disaggregated," nation-based approach that presumes the coherence of Asian America. What is less clear in this work is what the concrete basis of something larger in scope than a nation-specific account of transnationality might be, short of global capitalism itself. The materiality of Asian America can only be found in either idealist enunciations of "Asian America," or material histories like the "Northeast Asia" I am describing.

Modernization theory would enter postwar Asia through two main avenues, both paved by militarization: foreign aid and the marketplace of ideas.[59] Aid came in the form of enormous military and economic development outlays. As frontier nations containing communist China, the United States extended to Japan and South Korea an "ironclad commitment" to defense against communism. Toward Taiwan, which General Douglas MacArthur referred to as the "unsinkable aircraft carrier," the United States was more reserved, not wanting to encourage Chiang Kai-shek's revanchism through military commitments. Still, Taiwan and South Korea each received more military funding from the United States than the United States guaranteed to whole continents.[60] Even as official aid programs to both petered out in the early-1960s, the United States continued making significant military requisitions throughout the war in Vietnam (which in Korea came to be called "El Dorado").[61] The 1950s was a crucial period for shaping economic policy, especially in regard to land reform, which the United States underwrote in South Korea and Taiwan; the modernization theorists saw both as barreling toward economic "take-off" and salivated over their potential to "skip stages." From 1953–1958, the United States sent $270 million per year to South Korea for reconstruction.[62] During that same period, Taiwan received almost half of its public

FIGURE 1.1. Ox cart transporting an IBM punched card machine to the Council for United States Aid's new data processing center on Roosevelt Road in Taipei, Taiwan, 1963. Reprint courtesy of IBM Corporation © 1963.

infrastructure funding from the United States (figure 1.1).[63] Meanwhile, "Japan's economy was reinforced, while its political and military power (beyond its borders) was shorn."[64] This reinforcement, through the 1970s, in fact kept Japan on a very tight leash, with the United States controlling imports of oil and food, the last of which the United States provided upwards of 60 to 70 percent. As Japan weaned itself off of its dependency on the United States, it began to develop dependency in Taiwan and Korea, recreating the pre–World War II tripartite colonial structure. In the 1980s, this "flying geese" formation entailed Japan outsourcing its low-value-added production to Taiwan and South Korea. Cumings offers the example of "letting [Taiwan and South Korea] assemble color television sets while jealously guarding the technology necessary to make a color picture tube."[65] Beginning in the mid-1980s, with the Kuomintang (KMT)'s relaxing of travel and economic policy with China, the role that Taiwanese entrepreneurs (*táishāng*) played in jump-starting China's world-historically rapid economic development would resolutely shift Taiwan into the status of semiperipheral nation. In Shelley Rigger's phrase, the "tiger" would begin to lead the "dragon."[66]

While the dynamics of modernization's predominance and the consent it elicited are more easily observed in discursive contestations at the nation-specific level, clear regional patterns emerge. In the 1950s and 1960s, modernization theorists spent a lot of time in Japan and South Korea promoting their ideas in academic venues. While they often met receptive, even enthusiastic audiences, which often consisted of U.S.-trained technocrats, they were also at pains to scrub their message of all signs of "westernization," wary of the anti-U.S.-Japan Security Treaty opposition (the Anpo movement), and, in South Korea, the Minjung movement's anti-U.S. and anti-Western stance.[67] Brief accounts of two academic conferences will be illustrative.

The landmark 1965 "Conference on Modern Japan," hosted in the hot springs town of Hakone just outside of Tokyo, was organized by University of Michigan history professor John W. Hall and scheduled to coincide with the arrival in-country of the U.S. ambassador to Japan, historian Edwin O. Reischauer, and yet was touted as "the first truly international gathering in which Japanese served as the official language."[68] The unspoken but, for some, thinly veiled goal of the three-day event was to facilitate the indigenization of modernization theory, there discussed less as a set of policies than as an intellectual orientation. In Harry Harootunian's words, the conference sought to ensure that "America's Japan became Japan's Japan."[69] The strategy of the American contingent was a mix of flattery and condescension. While Japan was flattered for its honorary status as the only non-European country to have industrialized, the conference's intellectual division of labor betrayed an implicit hierarchy: "the papers prepared by US participants were to focus on the 'general principles,' [and] the Japanese participants were asked to 'direct their thought to the more specific problem of the modernization process in Japan.'"[70] Also in 1965, a similar effort was underway in South Korea at the "International Conference on the Problems of Modernization in Asia," which was attended by Pye and another prominent modernization theorist, Marion Levy (who also attended the Hakone conference). Levy would insist on framing modernization as a path with no alternative, encouraging the South Korean scholars and officials in his audience "to put aside what you would like [modernization] to be and examine with great care what it is likely to be."[71] Pye and Levy were in many ways preaching to a receptive choir, among whom modernization theory was already a "smash hit."[72] Rostow himself had just the year before been invited to speak at Seoul National University, and by 1964 his *Stages*, which had already gone through two printings, "was credited by visiting American economists with widely influencing their South Korean counterparts."[73] Moreover, the stagist and technocratic values foundational to modernization theory had long been overdetermined features of both societies, traceable back to what Chalmers Johnson called the Meiji "developmental state," and educational reforms and industrialization in colonial Korea (of which a more detailed account will be provided in chapter three, in regard to Chang-rae Lee's fiction).[74] In Japan the grounds for modernization theory's positive reception were similarly predetermined and continuous with prewar intellectual traditions. According to Sebastian Conrad, the "Hakone version of modernization theory essentially translated many of the earlier concerns of Weber-influenced scholarship into the context of the 1960s, and thus into high-growth Japan," while at the same time facilitating a historiographical detente between conservatives and Marxists. Thus, Harootunian's assessment that Japan "essentially incorporated a U.S. image of Japan and formulated it as a self-realization" perhaps glosses over the extent to which modernization theory was compatible with indigenous intellectual traditions and intentionally embraced by Japanese reformers, rather than naïvely imbibed.[75]

In concert with the intellectual importation of modernization theory, efforts were already underway at this time to transform educational policy to emphasize training in professions that would directly benefit industrialization.[76] Just before war, in 1950, the United States determined that South Korea had "a serious deficiency in technical and supervisory personnel."[77] The education policies promoted by the U.S. Military Government in Korea (USAMGIK) and other agencies like the UN Korea Reconstruction Agency and the U.S. Agency for International Development (USAID) sought to rectify these deficits by building "a training ground for professional personnel such as engineers, economists and managers."[78] These prescriptions were also resolutely anticommunist, which created uncomfortable contradictions with these agencies' putative commitment to democratization. Not only did the military government purge thousands of "leftists" and other suspected teachers soon after it assumed power, but it also "revise[d] textbooks so they emphasized anti-Communism and democracy."[79] After the cessation of hostilities in 1953, the United States began to direct significant funding toward the development of Korean higher education. In the 1955–59 period, 58 percent of U.S. higher education funding in South Korea went to technical and scientific fields, with engineering receiving 25 percent of the total share of funding.[80] When Park Chung-hee came to power in 1961, his administration continued these efforts, moving quickly to align educational policy with economic policy. The Korean public, however, remained skeptical, even hostile toward technical and vocational training. As Michael J. Seth notes, cultural prejudices against manual and technical labor meant that "Few Koreans wanted to be mere technicians. To push public sentiment in favor of such reforms, Park's first five-year plan drastically shifted emphasis away from university-bound academic education to technical and vocational fields, and subsequent reforms instituted vocational requirements for college entrance.[81] It wouldn't be until the 1970s that STEM education and professions would receive broad public support—an achievement of the authoritarian, developmental state.

In contrast to South Korea and Japan, modernization theory and indeed economic development itself were in some ways a much tougher sell in postwar Taiwan, even absent anxieties over Westernization and indigenization. As J. Megan Greene writes, "Although the KMT government was committed to promoting industrial science policy on the mainland, it lost interest in this area of development in the 1950s and 1960s in Taiwan."[82] During this period, Chiang Kai-shek and his inner circle were much more concerned with political stability and building the military capacity to retake mainland China. However, a rearguard effort led by Western-trained technocrats like K. Y. Yin and Lee Kuo-ting quietly advocated for modernization-style economic development. Yin, who trained as an electrical engineer and worked for Westinghouse for years, was a prime example of the STEM expertise that the KMT brought to Taiwan from the mainland. One of the two main architects of Taiwan's economic "miracle," along with his mentee Lee Kuo-ting, Yin "established a pattern of engineers, not professional economists, running the key economic planning agencies."[83] U.S. funding agencies, as well as the U.S. shadow government on the island, enthusiastically supported efforts by Yin and other modernizing free-market advocates in hopes of distracting Chiang from his reunificationist ambitions and simultaneously bolstering, via economic development, his regime's stability as a bulwark against China. The KMT responded by "implementing science education policies only to secure U.S. [military] funding but not, it seems, out of any sense of commitment to S&T as an essential feature of industrial development."[84]

In the early 1960s, as enthusiasm for retaking the mainland began to subside and direct U.S. aid programs ended, the Taiwanese state would begin to take tentative steps toward revamping its human capital production to focus on modernization.[85] Two important visits by U.S. experts and officials would help to clarify this new orientation. In 1962, at the urging of education minister Huang Chi-lu (who was himself urged by U.S. advisors), the Stanford Research Institute sent a team of experts to Taiwan for a three-month visit to evaluate manpower capacity and educational policy.[86] In response to the team's recommendations, Taiwan's newly established National Council for Scientific Development ("tailored to fit the requirements for U.S. aid") crafted a "Scientific Manpower Development Program" that recommended the creation of "a four-year program for strengthening the development of the scientific manpower which is urgently needed for social and economic development."[87] A Sputnik moment came between 1964 and 1966, when China tested nuclear bombs and guided missiles. It was at this point that military and economic interests in STEM finally converged, prompting "a low-level propaganda campaign" launched in 1967–68 "that would boost interest in S&T."[88] Following a May 1967 conversation between President Lyndon Johnson and premier C. K. Yen, Johnson's Science and Technology Policy advisor Donald Hornig was sent to Taiwan with his team, tasked to evaluate Taiwan's STEM academic and industrial capacities. The Hornig mission arrived that September, just two years after it visited South Korea for the same reasons. In fact, Taiwanese officials were specifically interested in creating a dedicated institute for applied science and technology modeled after Korea's Institute for Science and Technology, which was established in 1966 following Hornig's mission. Hornig's recommendations were "based on technological upgrading of existing industries like electronics, with greater dependence on spin-off technology from leading US (and other) multinationals."[89] These recommendations would have far-reaching consequences, setting the stage for Taiwan's embrace of semiconductor fabrication, which, with the creation of companies like Taiwanese Semiconductor Manufacturing Corporation in the mid-1980s, now form the "Silicon Shield" that guarantees Taiwan's economic and strategic survival in the midst of U.S.-China geopolitical tension. It would be a number of years before these recommendations would be clearly articulated through policy and bear fruit, however. Greene observes that even though "By the 1960s . . . development had become equated with command of scientific knowledge," it wasn't until 1979 that "S&T [science and technology] was . . . substantially empowered by the ROC state . . . and calls for S&T development became a hallmark of the state."[90] Until the mid-1960s, humanities and social sciences saw the highest enrollments among undergraduates and graduate students (similarly in South Korea); the social sciences would take the top spot until the mid-1970s, at which point engineering began to catch up.[91] From 1980 onward, engineering, scientific, and technical fields would definitively become the most popular fields, with the humanities and social sciences steadily falling in popularity.[92] This uptick indicated a successful reorientation of educational policy to STEM fields in the late 1960s and early 1970s: a key period in the history of post-65 Asian America. Because Taiwan's human capital supply and industrial demand lacked coordination, its colleges and universities responded to the new direction by pumping out more STEM graduates than the still industrializing economy could immediately absorb. Moreover, the lack of coordination was also due to policy indecision over whether scientific and technical research should focus on applied, industrial applications, or pure research. This lack of clarity contributed to an ethos among this generation that deepened and exaggerated a dichotomy between theory and economics (as SF writer Ted Chiang puts it in one of his stories, "pragmatism avails a savior far more than aestheticism").[93]

Among the major challenges Taiwan had to overcome at this time was the problem of "brain drain." According to a contemporaneous U.S. report, "Approximately 85 percent of the [Taiwanese] students sent to the United States for graduate work do not return."[94] U.S. advisors would recommend as a solution deeper cooperation with the United States and increased investment in new research centers. As it turns out, Taiwan's "scientific desert" was only one major factor in the brain drain.[95] The other was the KMT's repression of the Taiwanese population, and control of the elite spheres of government, academia, journalism, and banking, which forced Taiwanese into small business and to venture abroad. Despite this political persecution, as Chih-ming Wang writes, even those among Taiwanese students who came into political consciousness and activism against the KMT would not necessarily link that opposition to a critique of U.S. empire: "Chinese students in the United States were still mesmerized by such beliefs and tried to import them wholesale to Taiwan as gospel. American cultural colonization of Taiwan was thus facilitated and fortified by this historic bloc of 'comprador doctorates' who willingly enslaved themselves to perpetuate U.S. dominance."[96] These factors contributed to a future orientation among Taiwanese emigrants in which the United States, and the STEM careers they envisioned there, constituted their horizon of possibility; return to Taiwan either made no professional sense, was politically hazardous, or prohibited because of KMT blacklisting. This one-way futurity generated ancillary pressures on settlement patterns (i.e., suburban ethnic enclaves) and cultural assimilation that would have an enormous impact on Asian American life and especially the fiction that their children would write. Moreover, the different formations of nationalism in South Korea and Taiwan under Japanese colonialism, which would carry over into the U.S. neoimperial period, have contributed to a structure of feeling captured in Cuming's observation that "Taiwan produced a weak nationalist impulse, Korea an extraordinarily strong one."[97] As two sides of the same coin of Japanese colonialism and its reproduction in U.S. neoimperialism, these traditions are inextricably bound to one another.

While on one hand the success of modernization theory's assumptions in guiding Taiwan's economic development and cultivation of STEM human capital was the result of influential technocrats and the heavy hand of the U.S. foreign policy establishment, as it turns out, post-65 Taiwanese STEM professionals have paradoxically furnished proof of modernization's theoretical paucity. The World Bank's (in)famous 1993 white paper *The East Asian Miracle* provided the confirmation that the coalescing Washington Consensus needed at the time for its antistatist modernization narratives of economic development and political democratization. Korea and Taiwan are held up in the report as the shiniest of shining examples of the "miracle" of "market-friendly" approaches to industrialization.[98] In fact, Taiwan was even more impressive to neoliberal observers than South Korea because of the KMT dictatorship's relatively peaceful transition to free elections in 1987: proof-positive, apparently, of the democratizing influence of markets. Jim Glassman writes, "the growth and economic diversification that occurred on Taiwan during the 1950s and 1960s was eagerly seized on by

U.S. planners as vindication of Walt Rostow's theories of economic development."[99] As it turns out, the World Bank's "miracle" narrative was just the latest in a longer tradition of characterizing Taiwan as a model minority among East Asian model minority nations.[100] These neoliberal narratives comprise another kind of model minority myth.[101] Since the World Bank's report was published, an entire literature has emerged to debunk it. As Alice Amsden pointed out in her review of the report, the latter is schizophrenic and "ideological" insofar as it smooshes together two contradictory accounts: one from the Bank's "middle management ... of highly respected economists," and one from its "top management ... of political appointees." Despite a consensus among "highly respected" economists that economic growth has "no single explanation," the report argues that growth "is a fairly straightforward process."[102] Scholars like Amsden and Glassman have demonstrated the thinness of the neoliberals' core claim, that East Asia's miracles were the result of the state's nonintervention. While a single pathway to growth cannot be systematized, East Asian states enjoyed a high degree of coordination with the private sector, not least in the creation of industrial policy, but, in the case of Taiwan, especially the cultivation of human capital.[103]

China would seem to be an obvious outlier in the postwar Northeast Asian political economy, as the communist threat incarnate, but any account of the region would be incoherent without taking the measure of its influence. As Glassman emphasizes, "The 'first generation' of post-World War II industrialisers, Japan, Taiwan, and South Korea, developed in the 1950s and 1960s on the foundations laid by a geopolitical economic alliance of antagonism to the PRC. . . . the era of antagonism to China elevated military men the most, in alliance with military-industrialists (and supported by planners); the era of rapprochement with China elevated the planners, in alliance with various kinds of capitalists including military-industrial (and backed up by military men)."[104] While these Northeast Asian economies developed via America's "invitations" into global capitalism, when China began its liberalization process in the 1970s, an important factor in its development was how it extended its own invitations to prominent Western experts to shape domestic policy. As Julian Gewirtz shows, China "is not properly understood as a story of modernization theorists transplanting their norms on a developing country, but rather as a story of the developing country's outreach and interpretation of those ideas and norms."[105]

While figures like Milton Friedman and Alvin Toffler were invited to offer their recommendations, Chinese officials were committed to inflecting those recommendations "with Chinese characteristics." Rostow's work, in fact, was explicitly rejected. Ideas about "modernization" first came to China through the Japanese, a provenance underscored by the fact that the Chinese term for modernization, *xiàndàihuà*, is adapted from the (slightly different) Japanese term *kindai-ka*.[106] The Japanese term was itself an adaptation of concepts imported from Europe and America. While there is substantial overlap in the term's meaning across the three linguistic contexts, there are still significant differences between them: as a term and as a concept, "modernization" does not translate seamlessly. In contrast to its overall positive connotation in Japanese, Mao viewed modernization with suspicion as a form of class warfare ("poisonous weeds"). After his death, Deng Xiaoping's top priority was the pursuit of "socialist modernization," a precursor term to "socialism with Chinese characteristics" that was designed "to give ideological cover to the constantly changing patterns of experiment" with market reforms.[107] Under Deng, China drew selectively from the experiences of its neighbors with U.S.-led economic development, and also lured back its diaspora, who brought with them expertise and lessons learned from engaging with Western markets. As Ho-fung Hung argues, "China's capitalist boom is tantamount to an explosion ignited by the mixing of the Maoist legacies and East Asian capitalism, each developed separately on opposing sides of the Cold War in Asia."[108] Indeed, despite its ideological contradictions, the region continues to be coherent as a political economic totality.

NARRATING TRANSIMPERIALITY

If China is an awkward fit in our account of the Northeast Asian political economy, part of the reason is because it complicates modernization theory's narrative—indeed, its bildungsroman—of national economic development. For Northeast Asian American authors, holding focus on the dialectic through which these regional dynamics have replicated themselves brings forth the set of relations that I am calling science fictionality. When these regional dynamics are then folded into the experiences of the Northeast Asian diaspora in the United States, science fictionality tends to be heightened. At the dusk of the American century, Asian American authors have begun to weigh alternatives to their American identities. Turning to Asia often becomes an exercise in time travel that entails looking into both the personal and world-historical past. Sorting through these histories brings Asian American authors into encounters with the ideologies and desires of modernization. This section takes up the fiction of Ken Liu and Ruth Ozeki as case studies revealing that the arena in which post-65 authors grapple with the complexities of these histories is a science fictional universe.

Liu's and Ozeki's common goal of depicting transimperiality bumps up against at least three complications related to narrative form: one pertaining to historical justice, another to national identity, and the third to temporal scale. These authors contend with a nation form that is both unshakable and untenable as a narrative horizon, leaving them without a convenient antagonist and figure for negativity, and without a stable telos toward which to direct their characters' development. For Liu and Ozeki, the main factors undermining the nation form are what Lisa Yoneyama calls the "unredressable" crimes and violence committed on behalf of Japanese colonialism and their continuation by the United States, as well as by victims like China. Institutions of transitional justice, Yoneyama argues, tend to focus on negotiating a tricky terrain: "how to manage disturbing pasts and to secure the globalized system of liberal economy" (13). When these goals conflict, what is foregrounded is the unaccountability of these nations to their own citizens and the inadequacy of international institutions. In Liu's and Ozeki's fiction, what then comes to take the place of the nation form is the alternative temporal horizon of transimperiality. While Liu's fiction focuses primarily on depicting a U.S.–Northeast Asian science fictional totality, there are moments in which it reaches out toward a more distant horizon of geological time that is more prominent in Ozeki's fiction. Moreover, the short stories of Liu's that I will be examining engage in self-contained formal experiments, perhaps as a consequence of their status as short stories, whereas Ozeki's works are part of a sustained engagement with the Japanese *shishōsetsu* ("I-novel") genre. This raises questions about the relation between fiction and reality that Ozeki associates with transimperiality and resolves through a science fictional synthesis of Buddhist philosophy and quantum mechanics.

Liu's biography and career in many ways exemplify the relation between U.S.–Northeast Asian science fictional totality and occupational concentration that I am tracking in this book. Born in the northwestern Chinese city of Lanzhou, Liu was raised mostly by his grandparents ("science professors who were 'book hoarders'") while his mother and father pursued graduate training in chemistry and computer science, respectively. At age eleven he and his parents emigrated to Palo Alto, where "his mother worked as a pharmaceutical chemist and his father worked as a statistical analyst."[109] As an undergraduate at Harvard, he majored in English while studying computer science. Liu's interest in being "closer to the machines" would come in handy after graduation in 1998, when he went to work for Microsoft as a software engineer. He would soon leave that job for a stint at a tech startup, which came to a close with the bursting of the dot-com bubble. Looking for a change, Liu enrolled in Harvard's law school and after graduation went into corporate law. Eventually the long hours caught up with him, and he quit to hang a shingle as a litigation consultant for patent and technology cases. Amid these career changes Liu was all the while writing, publishing, and translating. His first short story, "Carthaginian Rose," appeared in Orson Scott Card and Keith Olexa's anthology *Empire of Dreams and Miracles* in 2002. His first translation, of Chinese SF writer Chen Qiufan's "The Fish of Lijiang," was published in *Clarkesworld* in 2011.

These two tracks—Liu's own fiction on one hand, his translations on the other—have been casually ascribed correspondences to his Chinese American and Chinese identities by the SF publishing world, critics, and readers. However, by the time he began translating Liu had long been publishing his own work at a ferocious pace. His star would rise to unprecedented heights with the publication of his 2011 short story, "The Paper Menagerie," which became the first work of fiction to win the three most prestigious awards in Anglophone SF: the Hugo, Nebula, and World Fantasy Award. In 2014 and 2015 even those heights would be surpassed with the publication of his translation of Chinese SF author Liu Cixin's novel *The Three-Body Problem*. The first volume of Chinese SF writer Liu Cixin's blockbuster trilogy, *Remembrance of Earth's Past*, the novel was already a global phenomenon before the likes of Mark Zuckerberg and Barack Obama touted it on their year's best lists. Despite Ken Liu's status as one of the most decorated and widely read SF writers of his generation, that reputation is now inextricable from his reputation as one of the preeminent translators of Chinese SF into English, and specifically as Liu Cixin's best-known

DEEP CONDITIONS OF THE WORLD

translator. It certainly hasn't helped that they share a surname. While the bifurcation of Ken Liu's career reveals a great deal about the limitations of identity categories like "Asian American," "Chinese American," and "Chinese," it is not purely a consequence of his publication history and commercial positioning. It is also a consequence of how his fiction undermines the national forms that make these categories coherent in the first place.

The science fictionality of Japan-U.S.-China modernization achieves a nearly literal depiction in Liu's 2013 short story "A Brief History of the Trans-Pacific Tunnel," which poses an alternate history in which World War II and the Great Depression are averted by Japan's plan to build a tunnel under the Pacific Ocean connecting Shanghai, Tokyo, and Seattle. With the Japanese Empire established in Korea, Manchuria, and Taiwan and making inroads into China, Western anxieties over Japan's ascendancy are exacerbated by the Great Depression. Rather than continue colonial expansion, "The brilliant Emperor Hirohito seized the opportunity and suggested to President Herbert Hoover his vision of the Trans-Pacific Tunnel as the solution to the worldwide economic crisis." During construction the bulk of the tunnel's seven million workers, called "Diggers," are supplied by Japan and the United States, but also include "Koreans, Formosans, Okinawans, Filipinos, Chinese."[110] Upon completion in 1938, the Diggers who survived, now richly compensated for their service and ruined bodies, settle in the underground metropolis of Midpoint City. Eventually the protagonist, Charlie, unearths a long-repressed memory of an incident from his days as a Digger in which a crew of shackled prisoners is sacrificed in order to seal off a chamber that suffered a catastrophic leak. His thoughts then turn to his own positionality in structures of domination operating closer to home. He reflects on his status as a Han Taiwanese who was "considered superior to the other races except the Japanese and Koreans" (358). As a technological yet fundamentally economic solution that imaginatively resolves geopolitical tensions between Japan and the United States and their refraction through racial forms, the tunnel offers a paradigmatic figure for the scope and expression of science fictionality.

Racked with guilt, Charlie heads to a monument commemorating the Diggers in Friendship Square at the center of Midpoint City, where he then proceeds to chisel his name off of its bronze plaque: "With each strike of the hammer, I feel as though I am chipping away the shell around me, the numbness, the silence. *Make the secret a bit harder to keep. That counts for something*" (362). Rather than an act of self-erasure or self-expression, Charlie inscribes one kind of marking—"three ovals interlinked, a chain"—over another kind of marking, his name, rendering the latter illegible and his political act legible: "These are the links that bound two continents and three great cities together, and these are the shackles that bound men whose voices were forever silenced, whose names were forgotten. There is beauty and wonder here, and also horror and death" (362). The ambivalent signification of the chain links, their "beauty and wonder," acknowledge the world-building capacity of economic and racial forms, as well as their deadly potentials. Charlie's carving collapses into a single mechanical figure the linkage between Japanese and U.S. imperialism and how it is sustained by racial hierarchies, political economy, and shared ideologies of modernity.

When Liu turns his focus to the more abstract question of the relation between imperialism and modernization's scientific will to knowledge, he leans much harder on SF conventions of cognitive estrangement. Liu's 2010 story "The Literomancer," for instance, introduces an element of magical realism into a story about the brutality of political repression in martial law–era Taiwan, and the collaboration between the CIA and the KMT to ferret out and exterminate clandestine Chinese communists in their midst. In "Good Hunting" (2012), the racism of British colonialism in Hong Kong is reconfigured as the steampunk mechanization of hybrid Chinese bodies that, tracking Hong Kong's historical industrialization and Westernization, become progressively more mechanical than human. And in "Maxwell's Demon" (2012), an interned Japanese American theoretical physicist and "no-no girl," Takako Yamashiro, is forced by a racist and misogynistic white American intelligence officer to repatriate to Japan and spy on their weapons research program in Okinawa, which is being conducted on the ghosts of Chinese, Korean, and Communist prisoners. Takako is killed in the Battle of Okinawa, shot by American marines before she can finish telling them that she's an American. The soldiers, also racist and misogynist, stand over her body ("What a pretty Jap," 45) as her final thoughts turn to her family, still interned at Tule Lake. The implication of sexual violence is meant to echo the actual sexual violence inflicted on Takako by a Japanese commander, which blurs the distinction between Japanese fascists and so-called American liberators and reveals the militaristic and libidinal drives behind scientific research itself.

DEEP CONDITIONS OF THE WORLD

Liu's most fully realized engagement with transimperiality and modernization's will to power appears in his 2011 novella *The Man Who Ended History: A Documentary*. The central narrative focuses on the mission of Dr. Evan Wei, a 1.5-generation Chinese American professor of Japanese history to find justice for the victims of Japan's Unit 731.[111] The unit's not at all fictional activities in Pingfang, Manchuria, from 1935 until the end of the war in 1945 are relatively unknown because they were covered up by Japan, China, and the United States. These activities included live medical experiments on Chinese and Allied prisoners, biological and chemical weapons tests, vivisections, and amputations: monstrous realizations of scientific knowledge's will to power. An estimated 3,000 prisoners were killed during the unit's operation, and an additional 200,000 to 500,000 Chinese civilians were killed by the weapons developed by Unit 731. The immediate result of the facility's shuttering—on which occasion an additional 400 prisoners were executed to ensure secrecy—was transimperial continuity. As the narrator of the story's titular documentary explains, "At the end of the War, General MacArthur, supreme commander of the Allied forces, granted all members of Unit 731 immunity from war crimes prosecution in order to get the data from their experiments and to keep the data away from the Soviet Union" (393).

For Wei and his wife Dr. Akemi Kirino, a Japanese American theoretical physicist, the key to historical justice is establishing the truth of Unit 731's crimes. To this end, Kirino has developed a technology that makes it possible for an observer to witness photons emitted by past events through an MRI-like machine, essentially sending them back in time. As Wei puts it, "what my wife and I have done is to take narrative away, and to give us all a chance to see the past with our own eyes" (433). A limitation of this technology, however, is that events can be rewitnessed only once. As soon as an event is rewitnessed, the particles captured by Kirino's machine become disentangled from the photons emitted from the original event. Those photons are lost forever, zooming away from their origin into the distant universe at the speed of light. Kirino and Wei's activism eventually begins to upset geopolitical relations between the United States, China, and Japan. Opting for economic stability over justice, even for their own citizens, the governments begin casting doubt on the truth of Unit 731's activities and demoting the experiences of descendants who have used Kirino's machine to the shaky evidentiary status of eyewitness testimony.[112] For

Kirino and Wei's movement, this unwillingness undermines the nation form itself and is further complicated by the question of jurisdiction: "As control over a territory shifts between sovereigns over time, which sovereign should have jurisdiction over that territory's past? ... Our doctrines concerning the succession of states, developed under the Westphalian framework, simply cannot deal with these questions raised by Dr. Wei's experiments" (399). History, now ended thanks to Kirino's machine, can no longer provide the basis for claims of sovereignty. This leads to an international crisis as other groups begin to use Kirino's machine for their own projects of truth and reconciliation, compelling governments to outlaw the technology altogether.

It is against the backdrop of a nation form obsolesced by juridical contradictions and technology that Kirino narrates her Japanese American identity. She dismisses her American side rather quickly as an impossible basis for a coherent Japanese American identity—a dismissal, by the way, that Northeast Asian American authors have shown increasing willingness to make, as we will see in later chapters. For Kirino Japanese identity in America means liking anime and karaoke, acting out "Oriental sex fantasies," and "leaving your past behind" (401). "American" serves as a marker not of national or cultural identity but of racial alienation and historical ignorance. Japanese national identity obviously raises similar problems for Kirino. She resolves these by severing Japanese identity from its national form (a gesture that we will also find in *A Tale for the Time Being*):

> Evan told the history of Japan to me not as a recitation of dates or myths, but as an illustration of scientific principles embedded in humanity.... Clearing away the superficial structure of the reigns of emperors and the dates of battles, there was the deeper rhythm of history's ebb and flow not as the deeds of great men, but as lives lived by ordinary men and women wading through the currents of the natural world around them: its geology, its seasons, its climate and ecology, the abundance and scarcity of the raw material for life. It was the kind of history that a physicist could love.
>
> Japan was at once universal and unique. Evan made me aware of the connection between me and the people who have called themselves Japanese for millennia. (402)

In her reinterpretation of Japaneseness as a dialectical materialist history from below, Kirino replaces national form with a narrative "that a physicist could love," in which past events, human and nonhuman, are related in proportions dictated by a scientific universalism not dissimilar to the vision for modernization theory that Rostow put forth when he wrote, "I believe the approach used in [*Stages of Growth*] is not only legitimate but fundamental to making the analysis of growth a useful biological science."[113] Couched in a story about the monstrous potential of scientific knowledge production and modernization's will to power, Kirino's narrative suggests that that monstrous potential is a characteristic of the "superficial structure" of "emperors" and "great men." Her narrative also privileges a temporality of "ebb and flow" over teleological forms like modernization and the bildungsroman—a temporality that, in the next chapter, we will see Ted Chiang take up in his SF experiments with temporality.

In Ruth Ozeki's work we can detect a similar ambivalence regarding the kinds of narratives and temporalities that science might produce. Ambivalence is implied in the title of Ozeki's 1995 film *Halving the Bones*. A metatextual work that explores the Japanese half of Ozeki's identity, the film traces Ozeki's family history from her great-grandfather's Meiji Japan to her maternal grandparents' Hawai'i and her mother's East Haven, Connecticut. The film begins with Ruth traveling from Brooklyn to her mother's house to deliver half of her recently deceased grandmother's bones, which were separated after her cremation in Japan in a ritual called *hone wake* (dividing of the bones). Besides delivering the bones, which were given to Ruth in a Tupperware container, her trip has an additional purpose: discovering the source of her mother's deep ambivalence about returning to Japan, and specifically why she chose not to attend her own mother's funeral and sent Ruth in her stead. Narrated by Ozeki and by her grandmother, it prefigures the contrapuntal structure of Ozeki's novels and their incorporation of the *shishōsetsu* convention of the confessional author-narrator.[114] While these double voicings are intended as a form for the autopoetic exploration of the "half"-ness of Ozeki's own biracial identity, they also open up space for the history of Japan-U.S. transimperiality to intervene. The film offers a metaphor for this history in Ruth's inheritance of her grandfather's "artistic and scientific disposition" ("people say I'm like him") and her maternal great-grandfather's fondness for "science and foreign places," which is framed as an outgrowth of Meiji nationalism. In the following analysis, we will see how Ozeki's association of her scientific predilection with Japan's modernization surfaces in her work as a Buddhist materialism and as a project of showing her audience "the way that the history of the military-industrial complex in both Japan and America impacts our moment-to-moment experience, here and now."[115]

Halving the Bones is divided into a thesis/antithesis/synthesis structure. The first section is narrated by Ruth's grandmother Matsuye (born in 1892), who reads from an autobiographical essay in voiceover as archival documents and family films are presented. She begins by describing her father, a Japanese nationalist who felt that "it was the duty of Japanese people to disseminate throughout the world." Her second brother was sent to São Paulo, while she was sent to Hawai'i as a picture bride. The husband awaiting her was a botanist who photographed Hawai'i's flora and a poet who became well known in Japan for his haiku. The film's second section reveals the first section as a fabrication constructed out of half-remembered stories and scattered documents.[116] Ruth confesses that she performed Matsuye's voiceover and played the role of Matsuye in the old family films, which she shot herself. As she explains, she performs these fabrications because she is left with only fragments. Her grandfather's films and other documents were confiscated by the U.S. military after the attack on Pearl Harbor, and her grandfather, who was interned at Fort Sam Houston, was unable to communicate with his wife and children in Japan. Indeed, at almost every turn in the film's narrative an aspect of U.S.-Japan conflict intervenes to shape the truth. In the process of reflecting on why she has become so fixated on her family's history to the point of fabricating it, Ruth launches into an extended meditation on her biracial identity, World War II anti-Japanese propaganda, and her father's naming her Ruth (a decision that disregarded how difficult it would be for native Japanese speakers to pronounce her name correctly, as well as the awkwardness of its homonym in Japanese, *rusu*, which means "not at home" or "absent"). In the third section the film turns to a conventional documentary format in which Ruth is at her mother's home asking her directly about the preceding facts that have been fictionally and racially mediated. While her mother offers some corrections and amendments, she stops short of offering a satisfactory answer to the question of why she never returned to Japan. The film's final section is an epilogue set at the Pearl Harbor National

Memorial, where Ruth notes the abundance of Japanese tourists, and ends up in the Shrine Room, where she finds someone with her surname, Lounsbury, etched on the wall along with the names of the other soldiers who died on the USS *Arizona*. Like much of the film, the confessional's disclosure of guilt and complicity operates in this scene unannounced. The film then ends abruptly with a story about how her father named her after Babe Ruth because—and these are the film's final words—"He wanted me to be an all-American kid."

Halving the Bones leaves viewers with the task of weighing its ambiguities, which are multiplied by Ruth's ambivalences about both sides of her identity. These unresolved resonances between identity, race, and Japan-U.S. transimperiality reemerge in Ozeki's first novel, *My Year of Meats*, which focuses on Jane Takagi-Little, a biracial Japanese American producer of the Japanese television show *My American Wife!* The show features a new locale each week as well as a new American wife who instructs the show's Japanese audience how to prepare dinner using American beef. As a marketing vehicle for an American beef lobbying syndicate seeking to take advantage of "consumerism" resulting from "Japan's 'economic miracle'" and the 1990 New Beef Agreement through which Japan was compelled to increase market share for U.S. producers, the show's aim is "to foster among Japanese housewives a proper understanding of the wholesomeness of U.S. meats" (13, 10). However, in the process of finding families and locales to feature in the show, Jane discovers the ugly underbelly of industrial agriculture's pharmaceutical arms race: "Profit's so small these days you gotta deal in volume, and without the drugs we'd be finished," a farmer explains to her. "The math just doesn't work out. I'm bringing more head to slaughter than [my father] ever did. If it weren't for the modernizing I accomplished around here" (263). (Ozeki's 2002 *All Over Creation*, which followed *My Year of Meats*, makes many of the same critiques via genetically modified monoculture but is more bounded to the United States.) These experiences open Jane's eyes to the connections between modernization, industrial agriculture, and the toxic legacies of U.S. militarized empire.[117]

In *My Year of Meats* the science fictional totality of Japan-U.S. transimperiality appears to us as a series of impressionistic moments: A 1902 textbook on "The Races of Men" that commends the Japanese for having "made more progress than any other branch of the race," and for being "eager to learn how the white men do all kinds of work" (150). Asides considering the 1992 murder of the Japanese exchange student Yoshihiro Hattori by Rodney Dwayne Peairs, who was employed as a butcher, when Hattori accidentally knocked on Peairs's door in search of a Halloween Party: "Guns, race, meat, and Manifest Destiny all collided in a single explosion of violent, dehumanized activity," Jane argues. "In the subsequent civil trial, evidence . . . was introduced, including Peairs's affiliation with the Ku Klux Klan" (89). In a conversation about her exposure to industrial hormones while producing the show, Jane's recalls that her father, a botanist with the U.S. Army, was sent to Hiroshima after the bomb was dropped: "They were kind of checking up on their handiwork . . . looking at people and monstrous plant mutations—to see if we should drop an A-bomb on Korea. Dad died of cancer and I've always wondered whether there's some connection" (235). In Fly, Oregon, just outside the Department of Energy's 580-square-mile Hanford Site, which produced the plutonium for "Fat Man," a waitress tells her that in the 1950s "the radioactive iodine had contaminated local dairy cattle, their milk, and all the children who drank it. As the incidence of thyroid cancer grew, the farmers in the surrounding areas—'downwinders,' they're called—began to wear turtlenecks to hide their scars. It was the fashion, the waitress told me" (246). Here Ozeki reprises the "deeply rooted conflation of sickness and race" that in *Halving the Bones* she confesses to having internalized. In the film Ruth explains that, as a child, she processed the anti-Asian racism she encountered by blaming her mother for making her sick with Japaneseness: an association she inherited from an old family story about how her grandmother discovered she was pregnant with Ruth's mother after being admitted to a Japanese hospital for a suspected tumor. In *My Year of Meats*, the race-sickness conflation is connected to U.S. militarization and its neoimperial relation to Japan.

If the conventional literary realism of *My Year of Meats* and the metatextual pastiche of *Halving the Bones* furnish Ozeki with the ambiguities and fragments of Japan-U.S. transimperiality, then *A Tale for the Time Being* sets as its central goal bringing this totality into focus.[118] A lot of this work is performed by the trope of twoness that we have been tracking and that is refurbished in *A Tale for the Time Being* as a trope of repetition that joins together multiple generations of the Yasutani family as well as Japanese and U.S. empire. For starters, the novel revolves around two historical foci: the Battle of Okinawa in 1945, and the 2011 magnitude 9.1 Tōhoku earthquake off Japan's northeastern coast, which caused a tsunami that claimed more than twenty thousand lives. The diegetic present belongs to the character Ruth, who shares a biography with Ozeki, and who lives in Whaletown, a small community located on a remote island in British Columbia. One day on the beach, Ruth discovers a tightly wrapped package containing the diary of Naoko "Nao" Yasutani, a teenage girl in Tokyo, which documents, among many other things, Nao's time with her great-grandmother Jiko, a 104-year-old Buddhist nun, at a temple overlooking the sea in Miyagi Prefecture.

The novel's central narrative tracks Ruth's reading of Nao's diary, Ruth's reactions to Nao's suicidal ideations and struggle to live with her father's own suicidal tendencies and attempts, and Ruth's urgent efforts to track down Nao and her father as well as to figure out how Nao's diary arrived in her corner of the Pacific in the first place. The novel's chapters alternate between Ruth's perspective, narrated in the third person, and entries from Nao's diary, which begin to disappear as Ruth nears the diary's end. The pairing of Ruth and Nao is echoed in the pairing of Nao's father Haruki #2 with his deceased uncle, Haruki #1, who was a young philosophy student with a penchant for French poetry at Tokyo University in the mid-1940s when he was conscripted. In training to become a pilot, he becomes the target of severe bullying and physical abuse (*ijime*). He recounts this to Jiko, his mother, in a secret diary written in French, as well as his encounters with extreme sadism in his witnessing of other soldiers being abused, and in stories told to him by veterans of the China Offensive (May 5–September 2, 1945): "These deeds they described as they'd performed them, with no shame. They were carrying out orders, they said, to teach the Chinese a lesson, performing these massacres in front of entire villages, while the victims' children and parents, neighbors and friends, looked on. And in their retelling, they were teaching us a lesson, too, to toughen us up and inure us for what was to come" (328). He eventually arrives at the understanding that these crimes are of a piece with the *ijime* directed at him, and that they fit into a broader national devotion to capitalism and imperialism. This leads him to a radical decision. On the eve of his kamikaze run he writes to Jiko: "Tomorrow morning I will wrap my head tightly in a band that bears the insignia of the Rising Sun and fly south to Okinawa, where I will give my life for my country. I have always believed that this war is wrong. I have always despised the capitalist greed and imperialist hubris that have motivated it. And now, knowing what I do about the depravity with which this war has been waged, I am determined to do my utmost to steer my plane away from my target and into the sea" (328). The act of wrapping himself in the Japanese flag in preparation to commit treason against the Japanese empire echoes the crisis of the nation form that is so central to Liu's transimperial fiction. It is also perhaps less a contradiction than a parting acknowledgment that the philosophy and French poetry that he loved were the flipside of the Meiji spirit of integrating Western thought with Japanese tradition, which was itself the wellspring of ressentiment out of which fascism and imperial ambition arose.

Nao becomes, in another repetition, the unfortunate legatee of the *ijime* to which Haruki #1 was subjected. Like Haruki #1, she becomes the victim of physical and sexual abuse, as well as extreme forms of ostracism. She is targeted at her junior high school because she had recently returned to Japan, where she was born, from Sunnyvale, where she had spent the bulk of a happy childhood. In Sunnyvale, her father, Haruki #2, was employed as a computer programmer making "tons of money" (43). As mentioned earlier, his work on human-computer interface attracts the interest of the U.S. military who wants to use the technology for semiautonomous weapon development. This new direction launches him into an ethical crisis, in which he finds himself in the same position as the "Japanese people [who] committed genocide and torture of the Chinese people" and who committed "atrocity like Manchu [sic]," except in this case he is in the service of the U.S. military: "A generation of young American pilots would use my interfaces to hunt and kill Afghani people and Iraqi people, too. This would be my fault.... American pilots would suffer, too" (388). Consequently, Haruki shifts the focus of his research to building a "conscience" into his interface design. He explains his goal to a psychology professor: "If my uncle's plane had a conscience, maybe he would not have done such a bombing. For the pilot of the Enola Gay, it is the same thing, and maybe there would not have been a Hiroshima and Nagasaki, too. Of course, technology was not so advanced then, so such a thing was not possible. Now it is possible" (309). Haruki's employer, however, had no interest in its possibility and fires him. Not long thereafter the dot-com bubble burst, and because Haruki was paid mostly in stock options he was left with nothing. He then moves his family back to Japan, where he struggles to find employment and inherits Haruki #1's fascination with suicide. The two struggles

DEEP CONDITIONS OF THE WORLD

are, unsurprisingly, connected, as he explains to the psychology professor some years later: "Nowadays in Japan, because of Economic Recession and downsizing, suicide is very popular, especially for middle-age salarymen like myself. They get downsized from their company and cannot support their family. Sometimes they have much debt. They cannot tell their wife, so they sit on the park bench everyday like gomi. Do you know gomi? It means garbage, the kind to throw away and not even to recycle. Men are scared and feel ashamed like gomi" (88). At this point in the novel, the reader has been made aware that the "deep conditions" of Haruki's fascination with suicide have to do with his guilt over how his technology was being used and how it draws him into the shame of his uncle's kamikaze. Haruki #2's suicide attempts are attempts at severing one small thread of Japan-U.S. transimperial continuity—analogous to Kirino's attempt at severing Japanese identity from its national forms. As Nao explains, "the big change happened on September 11 [2001]," when the events of that day drag Haruki #1 into an even deeper depression (266). Haruki #2 further explains to the professor that "in Japan, suicide was primarily an aesthetic, not a moral, act, triggered by a sense of honor or shame"—in other words, for Haruki, it is an act not only of personal desperation but of national identification (309). Importantly, it will be years before he reads the secret French diary and discovers the truth of Haruki #1's plan to crash his plane into the ocean—which means that the transimperial continuity he dreaded had in fact already been severed.

As Ruth becomes immersed in Nao's diary, she uncovers multiple lines connecting her to Nao that pertain to World War II, the longue durée of transimperiality, and the ecology of the Pacific Ocean. The moment in the novel that perhaps most efficiently brings these strands together, albeit somewhat elliptically, comes in an expository passage that echoes the scale and scope of Kirino's antinational narration of Japanese identity:

> Miyagi prefecture is located in the Tohoku region, in the northeastern part of Japan. This area was one of the last pieces of tribal land to be taken from the indigenous Emishi, descendants of the Jōmon people, who had lived there from prehistoric times until they were defeated by the Japanese Imperial Army in the eighth century. The Miyagi coastline was also one of the areas hardest hit by the 2011 earthquake and tsunami. Old Jiko's temple was located somewhere along this stretch of coastline.

Fukushima prefecture, located just south of Miyagi, was also part of the ancestral lands of the Emishi. Now Fukushima is the prefectural home to the Fukushima Daiichi Nuclear Power Station. The name Fukushima means "Happy Island." Before the tsunami caused the catastrophic meltdown of the nuclear power station, people believed Fukushima to be a happy place, and the banners stretched across the main streets of the nearby towns reflected this sense of optimism.

> **Nuclear power is energy for a brighter future!**
> **The correct understanding of nuclear power leads to a better life!**[119]

These passages appear in the midst of Ruth's attempt to determine how and when Nao's diary ended up in the ocean, suggesting the possibility that either Nao or her diary were washed out to sea by the tsunami. They are layered with references to transimperial histories spanning millennia, from "prehistoric times" to Japan's conquering of indigenous people and lands to the violent introduction of nuclear power by American empire: first via the bombs, and then, beginning in the 1950s, via a "vigorous offensive" and propaganda campaign, echoed by the banners, to convince the Japanese to adopt nuclear power.[120] Rather than reject or elide the "happy" trajectory of neoimperial modernization (in an act of what Kirino would call "leaving your past behind"), Ozeki returns it to a longue durée that in the very next paragraph evokes still more histories of empire: "The island where Ruth and Oliver lived was named for a famous Spanish conquistador, who overthrew the Aztec empire. Although he never made it up as far north as his eponymous isle, his men did, which is why the inlets and sounds of coastal British Columbia are scattered with the names of famous Spanish mass murderers" (141). This passage continues the pivot of modernity and antimodernity around the Japan-U.S. relation, which at this point in the novel has become so strongly fused to the figure of the Pacific Ocean that other national contexts like Ruth's location in Canada have dissolved into it. Where Ozeki departs from Kirino's human-scaled narrative vision is in how she pushes her temporal dilation to horizons that, while still scaled to the human in these passages, will ultimately dissolve the human scale. As I will discuss in a moment, this dilation betrays an ambivalence over temporality and the human capacity for action that Ozeki grapples with through the genre of the *shishōsetsu*.

DEEP CONDITIONS OF THE WORLD

Whaletown, located on Cortes Island, is characterized throughout the novel as antimodern, or at least unaccommodating to modernity and modernization: in addition to frequent power and internet outages, its extreme weather, untamable flora, and predatory fauna are constantly injuring, killing, or patiently engulfing its human and nonhuman inhabitants. Oliver, an environmental activist and artist, constantly evokes and is fixated on planetary timescales and dynamics. His latest artwork is a "botanical intervention" called the "Neo-Eocene," for which "He planted groves of ancient natives—metasequoia, giant sequoia, coast redwoods, Juglans, Ulmus, and ginkgo—species that had been indigenous to the area during the Eocene Thermal Maximum, some 55 million years ago" (60). A "collaboration with time and place," he takes solace in the fact that "neither he nor any of his contemporaries would ever live to witness" its outcome (61). He also introduces Ruth to the rhythm of the Pacific Ocean's currents, called gyres: "Each gyre orbits at its own speed ... And the length of an orbit is called a tone. Isn't that beautiful? Like the music of the spheres. ... The flotsam that rides the gyres is called drift. Drift that stays in the orbit of the gyre is considered to be part of the gyre memory" (13–14). Ruth theorizes that Nao's diary was sucked up and ejected by the gyres connecting them to Japan and the rest of the Pacific, rather than, say, tossed off a passing cruise ship. Corroborating this theory is the strange appearance at their house of a Japanese crow (*Corvus japonensis*). Adhy Kim notes that the novel's ambivalent stance toward nature and the human is personified via Ruth and Oliver's sometimes rocky relationship: "A tension runs through the novel between Oliver's aesthetic acceptance of future human extinction and Ruth's novelistic preference for 'human time and history.'"[121]

As a reader, Ruth is unable to determine the temporality of Nao's diary. Is it narrating a present urgency, cause to act *now*? Or are events so far in the past and removed from Ruth's reality that it should be treated as history or even fiction? This confusion provokes Ruth into constructing a desperate account of reality out of a synthesis of Buddhist philosophy and the quantum theory of multiple universes in which, like Schrödinger's cat, Nao and her father are both alive and dead.[122] As Ozeki explains in an interview, the novel "plays with Buddhist notions of self and no-self. ... Who is the self in this novel? ... Who is Ruth? ... Are these people real, or are they not real? What is reality? And here is where the quantum universes come in."[123] Here she refers to the "many worlds" interpretation of quantum physics that Hugh Everett developed in 1957 as a solution to the paradox that Schrödinger's famous thought experiment illustrated. Whereas the act of observing collapses the infinite possibilities of an event (its "superposition") into a single measurement—the cat being either dead or alive—Everett proposed (as Oliver explains to Ruth) that "the superposed quantum system persists, only, when it is observed, it branches. The cat isn't either dead or alive. It's both dead *and* alive, only now it exists as two cats in two different worlds" (397). For Ozeki, this theory offers a scientific basis for the Buddhist principle of nonduality, and it is, as Michelle N. Huang argues, of a piece with the novel's project of exploring the "nonpriority" of vastly different scales, from gyres and geological periods to the inheritances of a young girl in Tokyo.[124] Nonetheless, Ozeki also fidgets toward prioritizing the human scale: "I don't care about other worlds," Ruth barks at Oliver. "I care about this one" (400). It's this prioritization that Huang registers in her claim that novel's preeminent figure for negotiating scalar nonpriority is the Great Pacific Garbage Patch, which Oliver explains is actually two patches that are "enormous masses of garbage and debris floating in the oceans"—one the size of Texas, the other half the size of the continental United States (36). The Patch, in Huang's reading, gives figure to "networks of circulation that diffuse the boundaries of the human by foregrounding the relationships between us and the world with which we interact, including the environment" (98). To Huang's account we might add that Ozeki is interested in "garbage" circulating at the scale of gyres as well as the scale of human capital: the "gomi . . . garbage, the kind to throw away and not even to recycle" to which Haruki compares himself and other Japanese unemployed.

The tension between nonpriority/nonduality and the human scale registers a deep ambivalence on Ozeki's part pertaining to the uneasy fit between her writing and her Buddhist practice—in 2010 she was ordained as a Soto Zen priest—and that often manifests in her work as ambivalence over political action. The form that Ozeki uses to grapple with these ambivalences is *shishōsetsu*, often translated as "I-Novel," a genre that emerged in the late nineteenth century and reached the height of its popularity during the Taishō period (1912–1926).[125] A sublation of the liberal, Judeo-Christian tradition of the Western novel and an "indigenous [Japanese] intellectual tradition quite disparate from western individualism," *shishōsetsu*'s primary convention of a confessional and autobiographical yet fictionalized first-person narrator is a feature of *Halving the Bones*, and its resonances can be found in *My Year of Meats*' Jane Takagi-Little and *All Over Creation*'s Yummy Fuller.[126] If we take up *A Tale for the Time Being*'s invitation to read it as a *shishōsetsu*, then it is important to note how Ozeki aligns the novel with a feminist, anarcho-socialist tradition of the genre. This alignment is made explicit via the characterization of Jiko, who, before she took vows as a Zen Buddhist nun, was a pioneering *shishōsetsu* writer and an anarchist feminist deeply involved with Taishō-era radical left-wing movements—she even names her two daughters after the anarchists Emma Goldman and Kanno Sugako. Jiko herself appears to be modeled after the novelist and feminist historian Setouchi Harumi, who was also a pioneering *shishōsetsu* writer and, as Ozeki recounts, "at the age of fifty, [Setouchi] shaved her head, changed her name to Jakucho, and took Buddhist vows."[127] Jiko similarly takes vows later in life, after the execution of Prime Minister Tojo Hideki in 1948, and indeed her 104-year-long biography is offered to us as a counter-imperial continuity spanning Japan's colonial projects and their echo in post-9/11 U.S. imperialism.

Although Ozeki intentionally imagines a feminist tradition at the genre's origins, since it was not until the 1930s that feminists turned to the genre,[128] we might still read the "groundbreaking, energetic, and radical" modifications that Jiko allegedly contributed to the genre into Ozeki's previous work. Where, for instance, *Halving the Bones* introduces a poststructuralist inflection to *shishōsetsu* conventions by confessing epistemological as well as biographical truths, *A Tale for the Time Being* sets aside the confessional mode in order to maximize the genre's scalar range. This maximization, as we have seen, takes place in a nested structure of continuities in which the figure of the author-narrator is at the core and transimperiality provides a node that opens to geological temporalities and ultimately to multiple universes. More relevantly in regard to the origins of the genre, however, this maximization is a reflection of Ozeki's ambivalence over political action. As Edward Fowler explains, *shishōsetsu* was "primarily Buddhist in inspiration" insofar as it "provided [authors with] a rationale for their withdrawal from society and their embrace of the aesthetic instead of the political, the contemplative instead of the active."[129] As opposed to the bildungsroman's telos of integration with society, *shishōsetsu* writers rejected integration with Meiji and Taishō society. The genre's elevation of the author-narrator, according to Fowler, was "not an expression of 'self-validation' in a 'modern' society but rather a move . . . away from political and social integration promoted by Meiji bureaucratism and toward a quietist and separatist ideal of domestic exile that makes possible a peculiarly Japanese kind of selfhood: a nonparticipatory and nonconfrontational existence by which a Japanese, normally that most social of social animals, turns his back on society and loses himself in the aesthetic life and in nature."[130] It is, in other words, a genre that might have appealed to a sensitive student like Haruki #1, who longs for the "quiet, empty rooms of Dōgen," the Japanese Zen master (325).

A Tale for the Time Being arguably concludes with a similar gesture of withdrawal and quietism—the last sentence of the final chapter is "That's good enough" (401)—and even appears to retreat into the historical revisionism that the novel has argued against at length. Happily, Nao and Haruki both emerge from their depressions. Nao transfers to an international high school in Montreal, where she studies French, and Haruki becomes quite successful from developing software that scours "the Internets of many worlds" and deletes his client's traces by "switch[ing] possible pasts" (383). For Haruki and his new company, Taishō-era withdrawal is refashioned as Internet-era anonymity: "anonymity is the new celebrity," Nao tells him (383). Complicating this further is the specter of transimperiality: Haruki's software might end up being, like everything else, an echo of U.S. empire. As Ozeki explains in an appendix, Everett was ridiculed by an academic establishment fixated on Cold War research priorities. He eventually left the academy to develop weapons for the Pentagon, including the "software targeting cities and civilian population centers with atomic weapons, should the nuclear Cold War turn hot" (417). Ozeki suggests that Everett believed so deeply in his many worlds interpretation that it ruined his personal life and led to the nihilism that enabled him to write the nuclear targeting software. This ambivalence about the possibility of change versus being condemned to repetition is further amplified by Ozeki's own reflections on the conflict between her writing and her Buddhist practice. In an article for the Buddhist magazine *Lion's Roar* just ahead of *A Tale for the Time Being*'s publication, and with the *shishōsetsu*-inspired title "Confessions of a Zen Novelist," she writes:

> Ordination is a renunciation. . . . Fiction demands a total immersion in the fictional dream. This is not compatible with sitting *sesshin* [Zen meditation],

which demands total immersion in awakened reality. You can't do both at once.... And then there's the sticky problem of language. Linguistic representation is an unreliable and even dangerous business ... It's an occupational hazard, since language, the tool of my trade, is also a tool of discriminative thinking and is, by its nature, divisive: it exists in order to distinguish this from that.[131]

A Tale for the Time Being, Ozeki recounts, was in part the outcome of this spiritual struggle: she ultimately sides with the human scale of language, citing the founder of Soto Zen (and frequent intertextual presence in the novel) Dōgen Zenji, who argues that "we can escape the thrall of language only through language itself."[132] At the same time, the novel was also in part a reaction to "everything that has happened in the past decade [prior to 2013], personally as well as globally, in the post-9/11 period and since the turn of the millennium."[133] Indeed, despite Ozeki's spiritual desire to withdraw from the world and the novel's apparent quietism, it is *A Tale for the Time Being*'s feminism that finally anchors it to the human scale.

When feminists took up *shishōsetsu*, one of the key revisions that authors like Setouchi made was to reverse the hitherto male-dominated genre's vector of withdrawal from society and to valorize political radicalism and revolutionary action. In Ozeki's previous novels, political desire moves from hesitation to large-scale action: *My Year of Meats* ends with Jane's documentary exposé of the meat industry making waves in the media, and *All Over Creation*'s final image is a photograph of Yummi's teenage son smiling triumphantly behind a gas mask at the 1999 WTO protests in Seattle. While *A Tale for the Time Being* features no such large-scale action and is ultimately uncertain about the scale and strategy of political action in the face of the geopolitical, geological, and ecological threats depicted in its pages (the political consequences of its scalar nonpriority), the two actions that it leaves us with are the cultivation of solidarity between women and a refusal to end. Indeed, the novel's final words—"That's good enough"—are not in fact its final words. There is an epilogue in which Ruth writes to Nao that she would like to meet her someday. This is followed by six appendices whose paratextual status heightens the conflation of author-Ozeki and narrator-Ruth in their quasi-diegetic elaboration of details in the preceding text, whose author could very well have been Ruth rather than Ozeki.

Ozeki's refusal to end is of a piece with the *shishōsetsu*'s utopian vision of extending the radical openness between author and narrator to the reader. While neither she nor Ruth is a quantum physicist, their recourse to technical and scientific frameworks for elaborating this vision brings them in line with the tendencies of post-65 Northeast Asian American authors generally. In the next chapter we will explore just why this means that the fictions they jointly produce are fictions that an engineer could love.

Chapter Two

WRITING LIKE AN ENGINEER
Postracial Form and Utopia

> The engineer in our society is an individual of surprisingly varied talents.
> —JOHN OKADA, "TECHNOCRATS OF INDUSTRY"

For the historian of Asian American literature, what is perhaps striking about Asian American SF is that often it does not contain literal representations of racially marked Asians or Asian Americans. When such representations are present, their relevance as Asian American meanings is just as likely to be displaced, abstracted, or diminished as it is to be directly elaborated. Toward one end of this bell curve of racial representation and nonrepresentation we might find literal yet abstracted representations like the Japanese American *sansei* character Manzanar Murakami in Karen Tei Yamashita's novel *Tropic of Orange* (1997), whose orchestral conducting of Los Angeles traffic allegorizes the experience of Japanese internment and human migration across trade and political borders. Or we might have a short story like Claire Light's "Abducted by Aliens!" (2009), which is at once literally about the internment of Japanese Americans and yet contains an allegorical, irrealist narrative about the psychological experience of internment. Toward the other end of the curve are "postracial" texts that Yoonmee Chang would describe as "literature written by Asian American writers that does not contain Asian American characters or address Asian American experiences."[1] Here we would find work by Ted Chiang, Sesshu Foster, Charles Yu, and E. Lily Yu that operate along the lines of what Stephen Hong Sohn calls "racial asymmetry": a mode of narrative perspective in which "the author's ethnoracial status is not easily or directly mirrored within the fictional world."[2] What this rather variegated range of approaches to racial representation reveals is an anxiety on the part of Asian American authors over the implications of racial representation, and that Min Hyoung Song elegantly summarizes as the decision to write "as, or not as" an Asian American.[3]

In light of all of this we can understand how SF might be attractive to Asian American authors. Its unique synthesis of scientific positivism and the fantastic allows for a maximum of representational nuance when it comes to something as irrefutably material and intractably imaginary as race—and as awkward as Asian American racial formation. There is, however, a desire beneath these racial representations that exceeds a commitment to racial representation alone. Because racial representation is always of a piece with a projected worldview that contains a utopian claim and because, as I have been arguing, modernization is the political unconscious of post-65 Northeast Asian American literature, an additional reason why the genre of SF might exert a gravitational pull on that literature's authors is that SF is an especially conducive venue for coordinating the utopian claims of racial representation with the utopian claims of modernization. *Coordinating*, yet not necessarily *reconciling*. It is precisely the abiding contradictions between these utopian claims—racial representation's telos of democratic equality and modernization's stagism—that Asian American SF most powerfully translates into literary form. These contradictions, moreover, are doubled in regard to Asian American SF: they vex not only the literary text itself, but also the structural position of the post-65 author. The account that I began in the previous chapter, of Japan-U.S. transimperial modernization and mid-century modernization theory's impact on the post-65 ideological configuration of Asian American authorship, will be developed in this chapter into a set of arguments about how those factors relate to genre.

How might we think of post-65 Asian American literature as a genre? In the introduction, I was at pains to reject "SF" as the answer to this question, opting instead for "science fictional" to describe the space-time in which Asian Americans become authors and write what they know. In this chapter I offer a more detailed answer and in doing so build upon the best answer we have to this question, which is Yoon Sun Lee's account of Asian American literature as preoccupied with the temporal and spatial category of the "everyday." Asian American authors, according to Lee, critique the everyday as that which registers the "nonfulfillment of modernity's promises," and they have arrived at a set of formal strategies for doing so that include minimal narration and emplotment, repetition, parataxis, and lists.[4] That is to say, forms of disconnected "side-by-sideness" in which the everyday obfuscates the interconnectedness of capitalist relations.[5] These are formal features that strongly define some of the best-known and hypercanonized works of what Lee calls "Asian American realism," from Maxine Hong Kingston's *Woman Warrior* (1976) and Theresa Hak Kyung Cha's *DICTEE* (1982) to Chang-rae Lee's *Native Speaker* (1995) and Karen Tei Yamashita's *I-Hotel* (2010).[6] They are also the formal features that strongly characterize Asian American SF. As a worldbuilding genre concerned with efficiently depicting a "cognitively estranged"[7] and immersive everyday, SF's formal conventions include tropes like the "infodump," which relies on parataxis, as well as expository strategies like didacticism and repetition. While SF, broadly conceived, stereotypically pursues these tropes at the expense of narration, emplotment, and characterization, Asian American SF, as we saw in Liu's and Ozeki's fiction in the last chapter, tends not to sacrifice these formal elements. What distinguishes Asian American SF from a normative SF is the same thing that, to an extent, also distinguishes Asian American SF from Lee's account of Asian American realism, namely its post-65 positionality. The mimetic desires that drive post-65 Asian American authors toward either realistic depictions of social reality or immersive SF worldbuilding—and often both at the same time—are shaped by the temporal and racial forms of modernization's utopian vision. And central to modernization's vision in Northeast Asia was the mediating figure of the engineer, who, in Dipesh Chakrabarty's words, was "one of the most eroticized figures of the postcolonial developmentalist imagination."[8] The bearer of hopes at the scale of national and racial uplift, down to the most private desires for survival and social mobility, the Northeast Asian engineer was trained not only to execute but to embody modernization's developmental narrative. For instance, when Park Chung-hee was strong-arming South Korean society into embracing the engineering ethos in the 1960s, technical and vocational high schools appeared across the country, their buildings emblazoned with slogans like the one that greeted students entering the Busan Mechanical High School for Boys: "The Engineer Is Bearer of the Nation's Industrialization" (figure 2.1). This is the ideological

FIGURE 2.1. Banner reading "The Engineer Is Bearer of the Nation's Industrialization." Busan Mechanical High School for Boys, Busan, South Korea, 1975. Photo credit: Ko Moon-ok.

baggage that is bequeathed to the children of 1965 and that finds its way into the fiction they write.

Lee's account of Asian American realism is grounded in the historical perspective of Asian Americans' involvement in U.S. industrialization, which is to say a pre-65 framework in which the horizon of Asian American identification is inclusion in the United States via regimes of manufacturing and agricultural labor, and in which race strongly defines Asian American subject formation and everyday experience.[9] Despite Asian American realism's *formal* preoccupation with the minutiae of the everyday, these spatial, historical, and ideological constraints generate an outwardly directed excess: "a desire for a broader perspective, an inescapable and limiting sense of scale, though also a hope for something more."[10] Lee calls this desire "a potentially utopian dimension" that opens precisely when modernity fails and the everyday reveals itself; in her readings of Asian American literature, she accounts for it as a "structure of feeling" that falls short of explicit depiction.[11] Asian American SF contains the same "desire" and "structure of feeling," but in contrast to Asian American realism, it self-consciously attempts to depict totality and its utopian dimension. Asian American SF and my account of it thus pick up where Lee's account leaves off, which is on "matters of scale": "This means the tendency to see modernity not only in terms of stark contrasts of new and old, transitory and permanent, mechanical and organic, self and other, but in terms of measure: how big or how small something is, how close or how far things are, how many times something happens."[12] These are the contours of the transnational turn. In the last chapter, we examined how Liu's and Ozeki's fiction engaged with the Asian-ness of Asian American identity by grappling with Japan-U.S. transimperiality. In this chapter I draw out the desires and anxieties of those transimperial legacies to consider how they congeal as genre. After providing an account of the figure of the engineer and how it mediates between transimperial modernization and literary form, I turn my attention to the Taiwanese American SF writer Ted Chiang and his attempts to depict "matters of scale." The "modernity" structuring his stories' ideological forms, I argue, is a legacy of Northeast Asia's modernization as viewed from the standpoint of post-65 Taiwanese American human capital. Among these legacies is a contradictory relation between race and modernity that was nonetheless a centerpiece of modernization theory's intellectual justification and political promotion and that would subsequently inform the anxieties over racial representation for which racially asymmetric and "postracial" forms are solutions. Engineers were tasked with translating one racially inflected developmental context into another, receiving in return an enigmatic social status that from one angle appears as the model minority, but from another appears as the Pacific ruling class.

MODERN MINORITIES

Odd Arne Westad writes, "American modernization theory meant breaking away from past doubts—in part of a racial character—of whether 'development' was really available to all."[13] Breaking away would entail not so much an antiracism as a nonracism arrived at via modernization theory's strictly patrolled belief in its own scientific positivism. This belief in its own belief, as it were, contributed greatly to what Jodi Melamed, by way of Howard Winant, calls the postwar "racial break" in the United States, in which a white supremacist racial order was displaced by "a formally antiracist, liberal-capitalist modernity articulated under conditions of U.S. global ascendancy."[14] Even as modernization's promoters assumed, according to Michael Adas, "that all peoples and societies not only could but would 'develop' along the scientific-industrial lines pioneered by the West," the way they envisioned this process unfolding—both temporally and politically—smuggled in a racial hierarchy that replicated the "divide and conquer" strategies of European colonialism, and managed to operate beneath the register of visibility.[15] Modernization theorists saw their approach as fundamentally different from the "civilizing" interventions of European colonialism, going so far as to argue that, as Adas puts it, "modernization as it has been understood since World War II [by the modernizers themselves] would have been inconceivable in the colonial context."[16] Though figures like Walt Rostow, Marion Levy, and Lucian Pye "regarded American and European capital and technical assistance as vital to Third World development, they envisioned Africans and Asians—not Westerners—as the main agents of the transformation of underdeveloped societies."[17] It was this assumption that Pye voiced, for instance, at the 1965 "International Conference on the Problems of Modernization in Asia" in Seoul, where he insisted that "the problems of modernization of Asia will ultimately be resolved by Asians."[18] Such liberal appeals to racial equality were also aimed at cultivating class distinctions. By "Asians" Pye in fact meant (in Adas's words) a comprador class of "new elites who were to oversee the transition from tradition to modernity."[19] Elites like the ones in the conference's attendance occupied influential positions in business, academia, the arts, and government, and often lived quite transnational lives that would garner a rather different "racial character" than their less privileged compatriots at home. Jim Glassman refers to these elites as the "Pacific ruling class," attributing special prominence to military leaders who led industrialization policy from the end of World War II to the fall of Saigon.[20] Riffing on C. Wright Mills, Bruce Cumings calls this class a "transnational power elite" that is "intertwined in various networks and educated at top-rated American or British universities."[21] We could just as easily group them under the heading of model minorities.

Takeshi Fujitani has provided the most detailed and convincing account of the dialectic of modernization theory and Asian American racial formation.[22] In his account, there is not just a resonance but a "homology" joining the U.S. promotion of modernization theory to the Asian American racial form of the "model minority." The standard account of model minority discourse is a cultural one. It begins with the term's coinage by UC Berkeley sociologist William Petersen in a 1966 *New York Times* article titled "Success Story, Japanese-American Style," where he argued that Japanese Americans had bounced back economically and socially from internment because of essential features of Japanese culture, and, crucially, in spite of racism. In many ways Petersen merely codified a rhetorical maneuver used by other liberals at the time to dismiss racism as a cause of Black poverty and to shift focus to the alleged pathologies of the Black family, a case famously made by Daniel Patrick Moynihan in his 1965 report for Lyndon B. Johnson, "The Negro Family: The Case For National Action." Fujitani demonstrates how this potted narrative entirely glosses over the model minority's mutual articulation with Cold War policy, arguing that the model minority illustrates the space-time dialectic of U.S.-Japan political economy. He writes: "the logic of modernization theory and the 'model minority' ideal" both hinge on the proposition that "the unique quality of the nonwhite nation/race/culture is allowed to exist insofar as it does not upset the dominant position of the white nation/race/culture and in fact assists the subject in becoming the (white) Other."[23] More specifically, he shows that "Cold War modernization theory made the liberal gesture toward a common humanity by indicating that models for this process should be sought especially within the 'Asiatic countries,'" and by doing so "it betrayed the extreme attentiveness of strategies for U.S. hegemony in the region to the management of race."[24]

Modernization theory and model minority discourse both facilitate the dematerialization of race and racism by framing them as ultimately superficial cultural differences indicative of a regressive moment in society's stages of development. These discourses are progenitors, I want to argue, of what Ramon Saldívar calls "postracial" literary aesthetics. Critics like Saldívar, Sohn, Song, Yoonmee Chang, Patricia Chu, Elena Machado Saez, Raphael Dalleo, and Ken Warren have attempted, from various angles, to theorize the "post–civil rights" emergence of so-called postracial forms.[25] Rather than refer to an after of race or racism, "postracial" for these critics refers to a set of representational and social problems that have arisen as a result of the silences and deformations that have shaped U.S. racial discourse since at least the 1960s. In Saldívar's account, postracial aesthetics are symptomatic of "views [that] are changing from formerly held essentialist notions of biological races to more complex understandings of race as an element of human experience based on ancestral group characteristics, shaped by psychosocial patterns, and institutionalized into political and economic structures of inequality."[26] Postracial aesthetics are thus in part a belated, generational adjustment to the "racial break" and the cognitive dissonance of the postwar official antiracism for which modernization theory was a handmaiden. As Melamed puts it, this regime of antiracism followed "the massive production and dissemination of representations of black experience formulated in accord with the rubric of the Negro problem. In other words, the organizing terms of the Negro problem subtended the shift from white supremacy to a formally antiracist, liberal-capitalist modernity. According to these terms, U.S.-style democracy and capitalism would be redeemed through the full integration of African Americans into U.S. society."[27] Fujitani's account of the Japanese American model minority informs us how, domestically, Asiatic racial form articulated to the pathologization of Black Americans. What our focus brings into relief in Fujitani's account is the weighty, insidious materiality of what Melamed calls antiracism's formalism, and how, in Asia, modernization theory-informed race liberalism fused to Asiatic racial form a scientific and technical futurity that was, at the same time, ideologically anticommunist. The postracial aesthetic in Asian American fiction is therefore not only symptomatic of contestations with U.S.-based racial discourses but also a legacy of modernization theory's conflation of scientific progress, racial transcendence, economic development, and democratic nationalism.

Fujitani points out a kind of smoking gun in regard to the connection between modernization theory and the trope of the model minority: Petersen's citation of his Berkeley colleague, the sociologist of Japan and erstwhile modernization theorist Robert Bellah, as verification for his interpretation of Japanese American model minority culture.[28] In his first book, *Tokugawa Religion: The Cultural Roots of Modern Japan* (1957), Bellah argues that the core features of Weber's Protestant ethic could be found in the culture of Tokugawa Japan, offering the "theoretical possibility" of a "modern, secular, capitalist society that infused liberal values with shared social purpose...'capitalism with an ethical constraint.'"[29] In Fujitani's gloss of Bellah, "it was as if the Japanese people, possessed of an ethic of hard work and frugality, had already desired to be the same as (white) Americans and Western Europeans even before the West's arrival."[30] Racial hierarchy, which modernization theorists were constantly scrambling to euphemize to their Asian audiences, apparently disappears when racial difference is flattened into a continuum of whiteness. An official anti-racism was seen as a key rationale for U.S. occupation by officials like Ambassador Edwin O. Reischauer, who in a 1942 memo "presented a scheme by which the United States would win the peace in the region by establishing a 'puppet regime' in Tokyo and also by presenting itself as a nation that condemned racism."[31] This effort was inextricable from Reischauer's promotion of modernization theory. As Sebastian Conrad writes, "Just as [Reischauer's] father [August Karl] had participated in the State Department planning for the occupation of Japan, he was now plotting a second occupation—not physical, but of the minds of the Japanese elites."[32] Indeed, just as internment was justified by liberal antiracism, so was modernization theory's interventionism.[33]

These dynamics culminate in the racial form (i.e., character type *and* professional identity) of the engineer. As the embodiment of modernization's technological determinism, the engineer mediates between global North and South, furnishing racial proof of modernization's nonracism by enacting and embodying its scientific positivism. While Chakrabarty can recall from his own upbringing how "[his] generation of Indians could testify to the cult of engineering and management" that ascended even as Nehru resisted U.S. overtures of aid, engineers in the Third World also served "as willful or unwitting missionaries for a Euro-American, especially U.S., doctrine of progress through private industry and, hence, as agents for expanding networks of multi-national capitalism."[34] In other words, wrapped into the apparent objectivity of scientific positivism is the class anxiety of proximity to the Pacific ruling class. As the preeminent personification of post-65 Asian American racial form, projected most forcefully into the figure of the model minority, the engineer looms large over Asian American authors. It looms larger still over Asian American SF authors, whose work crosses the shortest distance between the worldview of the occupationally concentrated post-65 Asian American and that of the Northeast Asian engineer—the same distance, I argue, between the *literary* genre of SF and a *literal* genre of writing: technical writing. Between these two poles vibrates an inexorable force field shaping post-65 Northeast Asian American literature, literary realism included.

PROSE ENGINEERS

In the 1970s, Frank Chin, Lawson Inada, and Shawn Wong would associate the engineer with a kind of cultural nationalist masculinity. In Inada's introduction to the 1976 reprint of John Okada's novel *No-No Boy*, admiration is shown for Okada, the English major turned technical writer, for his work ethic, "power and stature," and being a "man with a *vision*" whose "*heart*" one could find "throbbing" on the page.[35] This ethos is reflected in Okada's antihero, Ichiro Yamada, whose education as an engineer is cut short by internment but who compares his slide rule to a "sword of learning" and muses that "to be a student in America studying engineering was a beautiful life."[36] Okada/Ichiro's resolution of the two-cultures conflict (the beauty of engineering) gives expression to the postracial ethos of modernization theory. Moreover, despite being a pre-65 figure, Okada reveals the continuities traversing that periodization. Chin himself majored in English at Berkeley and UC Santa Barbara, and grew up on the railroad tracks, where his father worked, and where he himself worked as a brakeman during college. The railroad and railroad workers appear frequently his texts. As Julia H. Lee demonstrates, the railroad—one of the engineer's native environments—has been, throughout Asian American history, a heavily cathected setting, both a "highly visible signifier of Chinese lives, communities, and experiences" and "the cause and sign of Chinese American erasure."[37] Indeed, one kind of erasure would take place between the lionization of Okada in the 1970s and when Sau-ling Wong in 1993 decried the "nerd syndrome" afflicting Asian Americans who opt for "'safe' fields like science, engineering, or medicine."[38] By "safe," Wong meant the self-effacement and quietism of the model minority. However, the engineers depicted in Asian American literature are figures of *ressentiment* who, like the father character in Charles Yu's *How to Live Safely in a Science Fictional Universe* (2010), might find themselves, "jaw clenched" at the kitchen table, unable to process the racism behind some workplace slight or career setback.[39] Or they are like Prof. Lee in Susan Choi's *A Person of Interest* (2008), whose general misanthropy is in fact an entirely apt behavioral reaction to the racist milieu in which he becomes a prime, and mistaken, suspect in a federal terrorism case. Or they are like the computer scientist father in Xuan Juliana Wang's 2019 short story "Algorithmic Problem-Solving for Father-Daughter Relationships," whose stubborn adherence to logical reasoning is a defense mechanism against the indignities of deprofessionalization that ends up driving his daughter away from him.

Indeed, the engineer in Asian American fiction, obscure and melancholy, has taken on a different cast than its longstanding form in American literature. In Cecelia Tichi's account, it was in the period between the 1890s and 1920s that the American engineer became "the representative man for the era, a symbol of efficiency, stability, functionalism, and power . . . a new hero who enacts the values of civilization."[40] In their characterization of Okada, Inada and others appear to have drawn from this tradition in American literary and popular culture an idea of the engineer as a "masculine figure in a male profession," which was in fact a reconfiguration of the cowboy, an archetype that, according to Allen Trachtenberg, "reflected the post–Civil War incorporation of America, becoming the guardian of the private property of the conservative ruling class."[41] Toward the end of Tichi's periodization, this class function came to be euphemized as the engineer/cowboy's "imperviousness to corruption," a crux of professional resistance to bureaucratic rationality that Edwin Layton famously described.[42] In regard to how the technocratic worldview of the rapidly increasing white-collar class related to literary form, Tichi shows how "engineering values entered the national literature" during this period "virtually as a matter of course, once the national landscape burgeoned with engineers' achievements."[43] In the work of preeminent modernist writers like John Dos Passos, William Carlos Williams, Ernest Hemingway, and Ezra Pound, "Fiction and poetry became recognizable as designed assemblies of component parts, including prefabricated parts.... The author's role in this technology was to design, even engineer, the arts of the written word."[44]

In addition to being a character type in Asian American fiction, the engineer is also a type of Asian American author. Asian American authors who were trained or practiced in STEM fields include canonical writers such as Okada and Chin, as well as Younghill Kang, Maxine Hong Kingston, Arthur Sze, and Amy Tan. As I explained in the introduction, a high proportion of post-65 Asian American writers are the children of STEM-trained immigrants. In SF, Asian American authors strongly tend to have a STEM background. Just among the top SF and fantasy award nominees and winners, these would include writers and artists like Aliette de Bodard, Ted Chiang, Vincent Chong, John Chu, Wesley Chu, S. L. Huang, Yoon Ha Lee, Ken Liu, and Frank Wu. Even Xuan Juliana Wang took a computer science course during her MFA at Columbia.[45] Not dissimilar from Tichi's account of American modernism, Ken Liu's description of his professional identity and literary style captures an engineer's worldview:

> As a programmer, a lawyer, and an author, I'm always writing, for machines and also for people. In each case, I'm constructing machines out of symbols that solve specific problems, and they do this by making use of rules in different systems.... In a contract or brief, these are the legal rules of the particular jurisdiction as well as the rules of interpretation and enforcement followed by authorities in that jurisdiction. In a story or novel, these are the set of grammars and interpretive frameworks, unique to every reading community, that readers deploy to bring the words on the page to life.[46]

For some readers Liu's highly technical, rules-based approach to writing fiction results in a kind of literalism—he calls it "didacticism."[47] As I will try to show in this chapter's final section, what comes into relief in statements like this is an *expository impulse* that arises from an engineering ethos shaped by modernization and transimperiality. Liu's explanation of his writing process helps us to see how the genre of Asian American SF reveals the two poles of SF and technical writing that structure post-65 Northeast Asian American fiction.

Via the trope of temporality, Ted Chiang's stories furthermore help us to see how the force field between these two poles is racially charged—how there is a deeper connection between Asian American SF and modernization theory's postracial imagination. Okada hints at this latter connection in his 1962 satirical article "The Technocrats of Industry," where he describes an unlikely figure that resembles Liu, as well as himself: "Occasionally, however, one finds 'passing' as a member of the select group [of engineers] a fleet-footed, high I.Q. English type who has had the unusually good fortune of having his B.A. in Eng. interpreted too hopefully by a desperate recruiter [of engineers]."[48] The scare-quoting of "passing" hints at a kind of racialization of the profession of engineering, which is what the rest of the article goes on to extrapolate, telling the story of "S. V.," a "nonengineering engineer." After a transitional stint as a technical writer, S. V. is finally "accepted as an engineer" by the military-industrial complex. In the article's final scene, S. V. recalls his "professional segregation," and boards a "bus" to go "demand equal rights."[49] What Okada ironizes, however absurdly, is a social process in which technical writing, as an especially fungible mode of mental work, facilitates professional, class, even racial mobility. For example, in regard to American Jews, who over the twentieth century began to migrate professionally into managerial and technical fields, Andrew Hoberek argues that "they became white . . . as they became white-collar."[50] This intersection of class, race, and professional identity came to shape post-65 Asian American racialization as well, rendering the model minority not merely a "racially triangulated" opposite of Black Americans but also, following Fujitani, a racial form of U.S.-Asia Cold War political economy. Reading for the residues of modernization theory in Chiang's postracial aesthetics allows us to perform an analytical shift similar to Fujitani's, in which the delimitations of U.S. racial discourse and forms are situated within a U.S.-Asia dialectic. These residues are traceable to the values and professional forms necessitated by, in Chiang's case, postwar Taiwan's development of human capital, especially engineers. Taiwan's modernization—specifically its emphasis on applied science and technology, in which scientific knowledge and national development are conflated—brought into relation the linguistic circulation of scientific knowledge and the freedom and expansion of agency promised by economic growth. The engineer thus became a preeminent repository for modernization's contradictory worldviews, a figure mediating between the utopian desires of technical writing and SF.

As I have suggested, a key linguistic mediation of our now transnationalized racial form of the engineer as model minority is *technical writing*. I stop short of equating technical writing's formal features with the fiction of Asian American SF writers and instead draw our attention to Liu's homological description of both modes: as "machines" designed to "solve specific problems" that are made out of "symbols" and "rules." Although some Asian American SF authors like Liu and (as we will see) Chiang have said that they think of their SF writing as a kind of technical writing, I am not, to be clear, making the strong claim that all Asian American writers, or even SF writers, think about their writing in the same way. Rather, my claim is that their writing is bounded by stylistic parameters—technical writing on one side, SF on the other—that differ from one another in that one side is literal while the other is robustly figurative, but both are oriented to a scientific positivism that is the legacy of transimperial modernization. In this way, post-65 "engineering values" enter Asian American literature.

Another way to slice this is to think of technical writing as a preeminent use of language in capitalism, and the production of technical writing as a site in which the abstractions of difference (e.g., racial and professional identity) can be valorized—in which a BA in Eng(lish) can be leveraged as a BS in Eng(ineering). As Bernadette Longo argues in her history of technical writing, "Scientific and technical knowledge is wealth made visible through the coinage of technical language."[51] Relatedly, Jasper Bernes argues, "There is no better figure for the subsumption of the writer and writing by capital and its compulsion to work than the technical writer, the writer of manuals, whose every sentence is both subject and object of the managerial hierarchies of postwar society."[52] My ultimate quarry is an account of how Asian American SF mediates an ideological position—the hyper-selected PMC—that, as this book has been arguing, has become central to the fictional depiction of Asian American character and narrative, and that I am now exploring vis-à-vis one of its especially salient manifestations, the engineer. The apparent formal differences between SF and literary realism, literary writing and technical writing, obscure more than they might reveal about the social relations constituting the post-65 Northeast Asian American PMC. Technical writing and SF, like the model minority, mediate the linguistic excesses of modernization's scientism, the institutions of human capital that enact its postracial fictions, and the class desires that modernization unleashed in order to propel Northeast Asian societies toward its utopian telos.

MELANCHOLY TRANSCENDENCE

Beginning with the publication of his first story, "Tower of Babylon," in 1990, Ted Chiang has produced one of the most impressive bodies of work of any SF writer of his generation. One of the most notable features of his career is the extremely high award-to-publication ratio he has achieved. As a member of a genre community whose most successful writers are maniacally prolific, it is somewhat surprising that Chiang has published only eighteen stories, most of which are collected in *Stories of Your Life and Others* (2002) and *Exhalation* (2019). Along the way Chiang has been awarded three of SF's most prestigious prizes—the Hugo, Nebula, and Locus—several times each. When Chiang began publishing his writing as a teenager in the early 1980s, however, it wasn't fiction but technical writing for periodicals dedicated to an early personal computer, the Kaypro, which had a cult following among PC hobbyists and was a favorite of writers like Arthur C. Clarke, Robert Sawyer, David Gerrold, Ben Fong-Torres, and Amy Tan (a self-described "geekette" who ran a Kaypro user group in San Francisco called "Bad Sector" and wrote her debut novel *The Joy Luck Club* on a Radio Shack TRS-80).[53] As an undergraduate at Brown University Chiang majored in computer science. Soon after graduation he went to work for Microsoft as a technical writer and also attended the Clarion Writer's Workshop, the prestigious multiweek bootcamp for aspiring SF writers.[54] Throughout his fiction writing career he has continued to work as a technical writer, eventually leaving Microsoft to become a contract employee and settling into a schedule in which he spends half the year on technical writing contracts that help to pay for the other half of the year, which he dedicates to writing fiction. Despite the temporal bifurcation of these two modes of writing, for many readers Chiang's fiction has taken on features of technical writing. Sherryl Vint sees in Chiang's work the pursuit of a "relentlessly logical extrapolation."[55] Reviewers often use the adjectives "meticulous," "methodical," and "precise" to describe Chiang's spare style—synonyms for whatever word one might use for the engineer's professional persona as, in Tichi's words, the "exponent of efficiency and the slayer of that dragon, waste."[56]

Chiang writes like an engineer—but not just any kind of engineer. He writes like a post-65 Asian American engineer armed with conceptual and aesthetic tools originating in Northeast Asia's industrialization. The residues of modernization appear at the very beginning of Chiang's fiction writing career in his 1991 story "Understand," which Chiang describes in his story notes (an expository genre that we will have more to say about later) as "the oldest" in his first collection, *Stories of Your Life and Others* (2002). Extending the intelligence-increasing premise of "Flowers for Algernon" (Daniel Keyes's 1958 SF short story), "Understand" imagines a life-or-death confrontation between two individuals whose intelligence is increased by orders of magnitude after an experimental hormone therapy. For the narrator, Leon, and his rival superintelligence, Reynolds, every aspect of material reality (from social patterns to stock market data) and phenomenal corporeal experience (pheromones and subaudible sounds) becomes knowable and manipulable as language that appears as poetic ("*Finnegans Wake* multiplied by Pound's *Cantos*").[57] When they finally encounter each other, their "ideological differences" are made "luminously clear," locking them into a verbal standoff through which the materiality of language results in Leon's death. While Leon's goal is to reorganize humanity and harness its collective cognitive capacity in his pursuit of "greater gestalts," Reynolds's goals are paternalistic ("He plans to save the world, to protect it from itself"), aimed at reorganizing humanity into a "planetary society" not unlike what modernization theorists envisioned. He devotes his intelligence to developing reformist measures: "bioengineered microorganisms for toxic waste disposal, inertial containment for practical fusion, and subliminal dissemination of information through societies of various structures" (62). In the story's final refrain—"Pragmatism avails a savior far more than aestheticism"—uttered just before Leon's annihilation, we hear the echo of C. P. Snow's two-cultures conflict and a number of variations on that conflict besides, from the stereotypical Asian immigrant parent's injunction against their children going into the arts to the financialization of the university that has resulted in the demotion of the humanities and hypertrophy of STEM fields.

The story's philosophical conflicts uncannily echo the terms of modernization theory's stagist developmentalism. We hear echoes of an ethos that would translate scientific and technical knowledge into what Longo calls "wealth made visible": an ethos that Taiwan's Premier Chiang Ching-kuo once voiced in the midst of a heated debate in the 1970s over the question of whether Taiwan should devote funds to basic research in semiconductors, or to applied research: "We should not spend our limited resources on basic research, but should focus on applied research for industrial purposes."[58] The plan for human capital and industrial development that followed from Chiang Ching-kuo's injunction—and that would lay the path for the creation of firms like Taiwan Semiconductor Manufacturing Corporation, which now underwrite the conflation of the semiconductor industry and Taiwan's national security—resembles very strongly Reynolds's plan "for establishing a global network of influence, to create world prosperity." To execute this plan, "he'll employ a number of people, some of whom he'll give simple heightened intelligence, some meta-self-awareness; a few of them will pose threats to him" (64–65). Here Reynolds is echoing not so much Chiang Ching-kuo as one of modernization theory's central problematics, posed most prominently by Max Weber, and, in the U.S. context, most influentially by Talcott Parsons: how individual agency and contingency result in social change, which, *pace* nineteenth-century determinisms, could not be reduced to impersonal forces. For Reynolds, Chiang Ching-kuo, and midcentury modernization theorists, a key factor in the "catch-up" process is the cultivation of a comprador class of intellectual elites, especially STEM professionals: "comprador doctorates," to use the Taiwanese author and political activist Guo Songfen's phrase.[59] The clarity of Chiang Ching-kuo's injunction (quite a departure from the Kuomintang's indecision on this issue) might have been welcomed by many (though not all) among the generation of Taiwanese students—Ted Chiang's father Fu-pen among their number—who had already emigrated to the United States for graduate study in STEM fields because industry and academia in Taiwan were unable to absorb them, and who entered their PhD programs uncertain about whether to focus on applied science or pure research.[60] Understood as a struggle for multiple and often contradictory forms of freedom—national, economic, professional, intellectual, personal, aesthetic—these vicissitudes of human capital development and migration are registered in "Understand" through the trope of agency, which Reynolds wants to gift to humanity through selective augmentations and Leon wants to elevate to sublime heights through his aesthetic pursuit of "gestalts."

The heightening of agency and intelligence in "Understand" is facilitated via a novum that poses language as a kind of technology for eliminating, rather than proliferating, mediation. As Leon and Reynolds bump up against the limits of their increasing intelligence, they invent new languages to make further progress. Eventually these languages exceed their representational and expressive functions to become pure speech acts: Reynolds kills Leon by uttering the word "understand," which triggers a string of memories and perceptions that ultimately destroys the most fundamental mediating register of all, the body itself. The story's final sentence—"I comprehend the Word, and the means by which it operates, and so I dissolve"—cleverly terminates Leon and the story in the same gesture (70). But what I want to draw our attention to is how the story's science fictionalization of language projects a fantasy of pure transmission whose asymptotic aspiration is not telepathy—the lossless transmission of data—but of a world-mind in which the distinctions between observer and observed, subject and object, are dissolved. This is the utopian vision underlying technical writing's emphasis on achieving "perspicuity": a "clearness" and "transparency" in writing that "never presents the reader with a word or construction that requires undue scrutiny or that creates confusion regarding what meaning is intended." According to Bernadette Longo, it is this devotion to "perspicuity" that directly links the profession of technical writing to nineteenth-century rhetorical theory and ultimately back to visions of scientific utopia like Francis Bacon's *New Atlantis* (1626).[61]

The naturalistic totality presumed by perspicuity and ordered by scientific positivism echoes the utopian vision of modernization theorists. In Michael Latham's summary, this was a vision of "the world as a seamless whole, fully integrated by new technologies that allowed threats and dangers to rapidly cross the barriers of time and space."[62] Whether or not Leon's and Reynolds's "ideological differences" cleanly schematize to communism versus free market positions, they certainly reproduce elements of each position's vision of the end of history, and converge upon the "secular, materialist utopia" that was so important to figures like Rostow.[63] This "seamless" totality constitutes the brute, material limit that appears in many of Chiang's stories, and that, for many readers, has become one of his stylistic signatures. Rather than an aesthetic form, however, I suggest we understand this aspect of Chiang's style as a historical form. We might therefore follow China Miéville's lead in his description of Chiang's writing as a "traditional" approach that somehow "never feels dated." Miéville explains: "Partly this is because the 'wonder' of these stories is a modern, melancholy transcendence, not the naïve 50s dreams of the genre's golden age."[64] The effect that Miéville calls "melancholy transcendence" is a transcendence that, in the words of one of Chiang's characters, is "not spiritual but rational" (55).[65] Even when science fictional and fantastic elements are introduced, they are treated with the mechanical coldness of positivism. In "Tower of Babylon," the mythical tower reaches the seemingly impenetrable firmament, but workers nonetheless breach it using the mining techniques of dynastic Egypt. "Hell Is the Absence of God" (2001) treats divine visitations with all the ordinariness of weather patterns. In "Liking What You See: A Documentary" (2002), a neurological treatment that disables one's ability to gauge the physical attractiveness of others offers a kind of liberation from the tyranny of the corporeal but falls short of its promise unless 100 percent of a population accepts the treatment. Attempts to transcend the brute facts of the empirical world inevitably return Chiang's characters to those brute facts. "Melancholy transcendence" will therefore be my name for that aspect of Chiang's style that *indicates and conceals* a positivist universal in the same gesture. I borrow this dynamic from "Tower of Babylon," Chiang's first published story, in which the protagonist Hillalum is the first of a team of miners to break through the cosmic firmament, up to which the mythical tower has been built. After climbing through the breach he is shocked to discover that he has emerged back on Earth, not far from the base of the tower. He thus realizes that the universe is in fact unrolled like a print made by a seal cylinder: "When rolled upon a tablet of soft clay, the carved cylinder left an imprint that formed a picture. Two figures might appear at opposite ends of the tablet, though they stood side by side on the surface of the cylinder" (28). This becomes a description of the empirical closure and spiritual foreclosure of the universe and one of the most efficient moments of melancholy transcendence in Chiang's oeuvre. It is a stylistic distillation of modernization theory's "secular, materialist utopia"—or, as Chiang's narrator puts it, "By this construction, Yahweh's work was indicated, and Yahweh's work was concealed. Thus would men know their place" (28).

Chiang describes his fiction as structured by the trope of "conceptual breakthrough," a term coined by John Clute and Peter Nicholls that describes the paradigm shifts produced by "scientific revolutions" and that is an aesthetic sign of "modern" SF (as opposed to Golden Age or earlier SF).[66] However, in Chiang's usage, as with Clute and Nicholls's, "conceptual breakthrough" is meant to demarcate a kind of rationalization quite separate from the implied Kuhnian framework of "scientific revolution" in which science is socially embedded. As Chiang has said, these narratives interest him "because they're a way of dramatizing the process of scientific discovery *without being limited by history.*"[67] Indeed, the unadorned, unaesthetic style that allegedly enables Chiang to focus "relentlessly" and "methodically" on "dramatizing" conceptual breakthrough is underwritten by a principle of selection that, as with other instances of a plain style, say Ernest Hemingway's "theory of omission," is in fact deeply aesthetic. It is not lost on us that in his description of Chiang's style Miéville finds so close to hand the stagist antinomy of "traditional" and "modern." The insulation of Chiang's fiction from history and negativity thus mirrors the modernization theorist's idea of traditional society as "inert" and "essentially fixed."[68]

For Chiang this devotion to perspicuity is a way to isolate his fiction from the intensely cathected category he calls "history." While Chiang never explicitly defines what he means by "history," his framing of it as a limitation sheds light on the function that race plays in his work—in particular, the force of its absent presence. When asked if "being Asian American had any influence or impact" on his writing, he is at a loss: "I can't point to any specific examples of how it has influenced me."[69] And when another interviewer asks about one of the few moments in his oeuvre when he explicitly addresses race, Chiang explains his view that race is not reducible to biology: "While I agree that race blindness is an interesting idea, I didn't think there was any way to make it even remotely plausible in neurological terms. Because there are just too many things that go into racism. It seems to me that to eliminate the perception of race at a neurological level, you'd have to rewrite the underpinnings of our social behavior."[70] As to the question of why he avoids race in his work, he offers two explanations. The first concerns control over the play of meaning in his texts: "I may address the topic of race at some point, but until I do, I'm hesitant about making my protagonists Asian Americans because I'm wary of readers trying to interpret my stories as being about race when they aren't."[71] The second has to do with the politics of publishing: "I think it's hard enough to write about issues of race and get published, even when you're working in respectable literary fiction. If you try to do it in genre, it'd be an even steeper uphill battle because there would be, I think, two axes of disenfranchisement to deal with."[72] Despite this systematic account of the aesthetic and institutional limitations posed by "history" and race, what will become clear in my reading of Chiang's 1998 novella "Story of Your Life" is how racial form exceeds any teleological or mimetic depiction of race, and, in Chiang's fiction, operates instead as narratives of "melancholy transcendence."[73] Our interest here is in the *typicality* of the dynamic between Chiang's biography and his fiction; how it is paradigmatic of post-65 Northeast Asian American fiction.

The absence of mimetic depictions of race in Chiang's work raises a different set of questions than those posed by "racially asymmetric" fiction like Chang-rae Lee's *Aloft* (2004) and Susan Choi's *Trust Exercise* (2019). Both of these novels are bereft of Asian American protagonists and narrated from the standpoint of non–Asian American characters, and yet they cannot *not* be read in light of each author's critical and market identities as successful Asian American writers whose previous novels have been installed in the Asian American literary canon.[74] The questions Chiang's work raises are different still from the ones posed by the intraethnic ressentiment expressed by writers like Tao Lin and Frank Chin.[75] Instead Chiang's work represents what Viet Thanh Nguyen has called a "flexible strategy" of either resisting or accommodating modes of identification; a strategy that does not fall into the normative, oppositional framework of Asian American literary studies in which a politics of resistance has become the predominant hermeneutic and criteria for canonization.[76] Unlike Lee and Choi, who sometimes write as Asian Americans and sometimes do not, Chiang indicates and conceals his Asian American identity in the same gesture. We might draw from this a more general observation about race and postrace discourse: namely, that it is impossible to think or write about race without reference to a material manifestation of it, whether that manifestation be the mimetic epidermal schema, or the immaterial but objective social relations that span the United States and Asia. The Asian American and postracial dimensions of Chiang's fiction therefore do not operate independently from each other. Every enunciation of the postracial is an enunciation of a specific racial relation. The post-65 model minority, for example, stabilizes a hierarchy of Japanese, white, and Black, and the postracial form of Chiang's melancholy transcendence references the stagism of modernization's scientism as Taiwanese engineers internalized it.

MODERNIZATION, TEMPORALITY, AND AESTHETIC FREEDOM

"Story of Your Life" proceeds contrapuntally, alternating between two storylines from the life of Louise Banks, a linguistics professor. Its characters are all racially unmarked. The first storyline recounts episodes from Louise's sometimes fraught relationship with her daughter, who we learn will die at age twenty-five in a rock climbing accident. These episodes are presented in no particular chronological order, which, as we will see, purposively defers to a nonhierarchical chronology. The second storyline focuses on Louise and her partner Gary, a physicist and eventually the father of her daughter, both of whom are commissioned by the U.S. military to learn the language of a race of aliens that Gary calls "heptapods" on account of their seven limbs. Upon arrival, the heptapods themselves remain in orbit and then deploy 112 wall-sized "looking glasses" to various sites on Earth—specifically, "in meadows"—to serve as two-way videoconferencing screens. Louise and Gary are based at a looking glass located "in a farmer's sun-scorched pasture," one of nine in the United States, alongside which the military has set up an encampment (95).[77] The troping of agrarian space as potentially modern rather than a romantic figure for traditional society is a direct legacy of modernization theory's focus on land reform in Asia as a crucial step within Rostow's stage of "preconditions for take-off," and that became key to the narrative of Taiwan in particular as a confirmation of modernization theory (as the most miraculous of the Asian "economic miracles"). The humming potentiality of agrarian space as a pivot between the traditional and modern resonates with the story's mood of looming transformation. As the story unfolds, tension mounts between the scientific and military interests, the latter not only paranoically assessing potential security threats, but also sniffing out opportunities for "trade negotiations" (128). While it might be tempting to read the military-developmental interests in contradiction to Louise and Gary's devotion to pure scientific research, this apparent contradiction is in fact entirely consistent with modernization theory's utopian temporality. Historically it was the realization of this temporality that justified modernization's hawkishness and interventionism. As Gilman puts it, "Rostow [and other modernizationists] hoped to make the social democratic welfare state the final outcome of world history, and [they] had the courage to recommend that the necessary sins be committed in order to bring it about."[78] Chiang's story captures not only these contradictions but their complex interaction with the racial hierarchies underlying modernization's ideology of temporality.

Louise and Gary begin holding virtual meetings with the heptapods, who are patient and cooperative in teaching them their spoken and written languages, which Louise designates as Heptapod A and B, respectively. These languages, Louise soon comes to realize, are completely separate: B is not "glottographic" like human writing, because it "conveys meaning without reference to speech" (108). Faced with the problem of how to categorize Heptapod B, Louise rejects the categories of logograms and ideograms, which appear to be obvious analogues. She disqualifies "logogram" because it implies a corresponding spoken word, and "ideogram" for the somewhat cryptic reason of "how it had been used in the past" (111). She settles on "semagrams," since the sentences of Heptapod B operate according to their own grammar and syntax. They look "almost like mandalas," she explains: the large, intricate, circular images representing the totality of the universe in Buddhist cosmology: "When a Heptapod B sentence grew fairly sizable, its visual impact was remarkable. If I wasn't trying to decipher it, the writing looked like fanciful praying mantids drawn in a cursive style, all clinging to each other to form an Escheresque lattice, each slightly different in its stance. And the biggest sentences had an effect similar to that of psychedelic posters: sometimes eye-watering, sometimes hypnotic" (112). Louise describes this use of space as a "two dimensional grammar," and then stumbles upon a crucial realization after asking a heptapod to demonstrate the stroke-order of a sentence. Its design is so intricate that "the heptapod had to know how the entire sentence would be laid out before it could write the very first stroke" (123). She finds an analogy in Arabic calligraphy, which in some forms features strokes "so interconnected that none could be removed without redesigning the entire sentence.... But those designs had required careful planning by expert calligraphers. No one could lay out such an intricate design at the speed needed for holding a conversation. At least, no human could" (123). Heptapod B, as it turns out, is a time-symmetrical language whose users possess a "simultaneous," as opposed to "sequential," consciousness that perceives all points in time at once, past, present, and future: a mode of consciousness appropriate to what philosophers of science call "block time" or the "block universe theory." The Time Traveler in H. G. Wells's *The Time Machine* presents a version of this theory: "Really this is what is meant by the Fourth Dimension, though some people who talk about the Fourth Dimension do not know they mean it. It is only another way of looking at Time. There is no difference between time and any of the three dimensions of Space except that our consciousness moves along it."[79]

The contrapuntal narratives in "Story of Your Life" are structured so as to provide a representation of Heptapod B's semagrams and their simultaneous temporality: an obviously impossible attempt at ekphrasis whose impossibility is designed to resonate diegetically with Louise's grief over her daughter's death, and extradiegetically/metafictionally with the linguistic mediation of her daughter's ontological existence. The affective force of this impossibility is amplified by the fact that her daughter is never named. For instance, it is never made explicit that Gary is the father of Louise's daughter until quite late in the story, yet clues are offered in what we might call interdependent narrations. Gary's impatience will reappear in his daughter in a subsequent section. At one point early on in their process of learning Heptapod B, Gary asks Louise, "So are we ready to start asking about their mathematics?" To which she responds, "We need a better grasp on this writing system before we begin anything else.... Patience, good sir" (110). In the next section, their daughter cannot wait to go to Hawaiʻi. "I wanna be in Hawaii now," she whines, and Louise tells her, "Sometimes it's good to wait... the anticipation makes it more fun when you get there" (111). At another moment in the story, after Louise realizes that Heptapod language is fundamentally performative, we are given a scene from her daughter's childhood that illustrates her realization. Tired of reciting the story of "Goldilocks and the Three Bears" for the umpteenth time, Louise decides to make a few changes. These her daughter rejects, insisting, "That's not how the story goes." Flabbergasted, Louise asks her why she wants to hear the story if she already knows it goes. She replies: "Cause I wanna hear it!" (138).

Chiang stages the interdependency of the story's two narratives visually as well. In one scene, Louise's fourteen-year-old daughter is pestering her for an answer to a homework question: "Mom, what do you call it when both sides can win?" In a subsequent scene, set chronologically before her daughter has been conceived, Gary groans sarcastically in response to something a U.S. diplomat says:

> "You mean it's a non-zero-sum game?" Gary said in mock incredulity. "Oh my gosh."
>
> "A non-zero-sum game."
> "What?" You'll reverse course, heading back from your bedroom.
> "When both sides can win: I just remembered, it's called a non-zero-sum game." (128)

Louise's daughter's statement, "a non-zero sum game," returns us to the homework scene from before, so it is as if Gary had answered her question more than fourteen years before she had asked it—or, as if the time elapsed makes no meaningful difference. The conceit of simultaneous time sets the ground for the story's central thought experiment, which considers how learning Heptapod B might affect a sequential human consciousness vis-à-vis the theory of linguistic relativity. Also known as the Sapir-Whorf hypothesis, this theory speculates that "the structure and lexicon of one's language influences how one perceives and conceptualizes the world, and they do so in a systematic way."[80] This takes up one of the prevailing interests in Chiang's fiction, the linguistic mediation of scientific reason and reality. In his story "The Evolution of Human Science" (2000), human scientists must decide how to interpret the impenetrable scientific research produced by superintelligent "metahumans," so they begin developing techniques of "textual hermeneutics." "Seventy-Two Letters" (2000) poses the theory that "there [is] a lexical universe as well as a physical one, and bringing an object together with a compatible name [causes] the latent potentialities of both to be realized." The narrator of "The Truth of Fact, The Truth of Feeling" (2013) observes, "We don't normally think of it as such, but writing is a technology, which means that a literate person is someone whose thought processes are technologically mediated. We became cognitive cyborgs as soon as we became fluent readers, and the consequences of that were profound." Motivating these thought experiments is a fantasy about the "melancholy transcendence" of technical writing itself, which, as I have suggested, is a particular distillation of modernization theory's utopian fantasies about the end of history.

As Louise builds fluency in Heptapod B she discovers that it is transforming her own consciousness. Her thoughts become "graphically coded," and she begins experiencing "trance-like moments" in which she perceives "past and future all at once." Via the Sapir-Whorf hypothesis, she undergoes a racial transformation from human to human-heptapod hybrid that proceeds by language learning, not biology: a kind of postracial racialization. We now understand that what we have thus far been reading as Louise's prosopopoeic address to her daughter has in fact been taking place in the tenseless, simultaneous temporality of Heptapod B. The story's contrapuntal narration becomes, from the standpoint of this realization, a representation of Heptapod B as well as Louise's racial difference. This mode of narration reveals its postrace aesthetics in its movement away from a mimetic economy of racial representation to a narrative one, recapitulating modernization theory's influential displacement of race to a putatively nonracist, sequential narrative about culture and stages of development. Tension between these two temporalities registers modernization theory's paradoxical temporal schema in which the sequential is coded as modern, and simultaneity is coded as traditional as well as posthistorical and utopian. While this tension itself is not an adequate reduction of modernization theory's basic assumptions, the fact that it buttresses a theme of disinterested observation aligns it with modernization's credo of scientific objectivity. One of the central mysteries of Chiang's story is why the heptapods have visited; when asked, their response is always "'to see,' or 'to observe.'" The detached quality of this response is, within the story's thematic matrix, designed to resonate with the mystery of agency in a simultaneous experience of time. The humans are frustrated by the fact that the heptapods don't seem to want anything, and when they gift knowledge to the humans, it is of science that is already known. This symmetry is captured in the metaphor of the looking glasses themselves, which turn out to be nothing more than mundane glass.

The only substantive change that takes place after the heptapods arrive occurs within those who have learned Heptapod A and B. As a metaphor for a racialization via modernization, this handful of heptapod proficients allegorizes the model minority and Pacific ruling class—or at least the comprador class position that they occupy. A key register in which this class was conceptualized by modernizers was the temporality of "catch-up" and "skipping stages." As Latham puts it, "Modernization, above all, had framed a compelling *narrative*, an integrated plotline of rapid, universal, linear advance promising nothing less than an *acceleration* of history."[81] The modernization theorist Karl Deutsch's narration of this process was typical: "The developing countries of Asia, Africa, and parts of Latin America may have to accomplish ... within a few decades a process of political change which in the history of Western Europe and North America took at least as many generations; and they may have to accomplish this accelerated change almost in the manner of a jump, omitting as impractical some of the historic stages of transition through a period of near laissez-faire that occurred in the West."[82] Even nonaligned nations like India felt the urgency of catching up: Jawaharlal Nehru would often say in the 1950s, "What Europe did in a hundred or a hundred and fifty years, we must do in ten or fifteen years."[83] By no means immune to this narrative were critics of modernization theory like C. P. Snow, who, reflecting on the first decade of Mao's industrialization, nonetheless admired China for rapidly building up its human capital: "in ten years [they] have transformed their universities and built so many new ones that they are now nearly independent of scientists and engineers from outside. Ten years."[84] Just like in the economic figure of the model minority itself, however, a social evolutionist teleology is buried in the temporality of "jumping" stages. Adas writes: "the modernizers drastically reduced the time frame in which the process of social advance was to occur. In contrast to the centuries envisioned by the improvers (or the millennia calculated by those inclined to racist explanations for human disparities), the transition to modernity was plotted in decades."[85] Because proficiency in Heptapod B results in a reorientation to simultaneous time—depicted in the story as racial/species hybridity—one might surmise that the heptapods' goals boil down to the promulgation of their unique mode of temporality; this could be taken as a capsule description of modernization theory's historical enactment.

Paradoxically, modernization theorists saw the acceleration of history less as a progress narrative than as a realization of universal principles governing human society: a performative act that, performed correctly, would conjure a utopian cul-de-sac of history. The ideological coordinates I have been tracking—technical writing, the model minority/Pacific ruling class, and modernization's utopian scientific universalism—might therefore be understood as expressions of a temporal trope in which a sequential temporality seeks to terminate in a simultaneity that collapses traditional and modern. Despite the protestations of modernization theorists, this vision was not dissimilar to communism's dream of a world without scarcity.[86] In fact, it has become conventional to point out the overlap between modernization theory and Marxism's deterministic positivism. In Nils Gilman's estimation, Rostow's stages in fact offer a "contrapuntal Marxism" that wants "to reclaim Marx from the Communism of the Soviet Union."[87] Indeed, Walt Rostow found his theory so closely resembling Marx's that he devoted the final chapter of *Stages* to parsing what he saw as the theoretical divergences between the two—a narcissism of small differences so deeply felt that his book's infamous subtitle, "A Non-Communist Manifesto," now reads as an attempt at smuggling in Marx without the communism. Rostow would insist that his theory's point of departure from Marx was his presumption of a range of human rationality exceeding "profit maximization": "In the stages-of-growth sequence man is viewed as a more complex unit. He seeks, not merely economic advantage, but also power, leisure, adventure, continuity of experience and securing, he is concerned with his family, the familiar values of his regional and national culture, and a bit of fun down at the local."[88]

In "Story of Your Life," the illustration of simultaneous time that most directly aligns with Rostow's and Marx's end of history is Fermat's principle of least time, which proposes that light travels along the fastest and not the physically shortest path when refracted through a medium like water. When Gary explains this, it "feels odd" to Louise because it lures one into thinking about physics "anthropomorphic-projectionally," suggesting that "the light has to examine the possible paths and compute how long each one would take" (125). The illusion of agency is produced by light's seeming to *choose* either a minimum, or even in some cases a maximum, of time to its destination, even though what the variational principle of these two limit cases demonstrates is less a physical fact about light than the existence of a universal law. Later, as Louise's proficiency in Heptapod B improves, she begins to understand that:

Every physical event was an utterance that could be parsed in two entirely different ways, one causal and the other teleological, both valid, neither one disqualifiable no matter how much context was available.

When the ancestors of humans and heptapods first acquired the spark of consciousness, they both perceived the same physical world, but they parsed their perceptions differently; the worldviews that ultimately arose were the end result of that divergence. Humans had developed a sequential mode of awareness, while heptapods had developed a simultaneous mode of awareness. We experienced events in an order, and perceived their relationship as cause and effect. They experienced all events at once, and perceived a purpose underlying them all. A minimizing, maximizing purpose. (134)

A purpose, we might say, analogous to a conception of traditional society as providing for only a minimum of human needs, while a maximum is provided by the "high-consumption" society that modernizationists saw as the most advanced stage of humanity. The enigma of the Marxism underlying modernization theory, as Rostow himself admits, was that "both would pose, in the end, the goal or the problem of true affluence—of the time when, in Marx's good phrase—labour 'has of itself become the prime necessity of life.'"[89] In contrast to Marx's minimum of human agency, Rostow saw modernization theory as proceeding from an assumption about its maximum. Both are potentially "valid" perceptions of a universal telos that, in Gilman's words, consists of a "total knowledge about a society free of both want and dissent, with boredom as its most threatening feature."[90] Marx's famous line from the *Critique of the Gotha Programme*, "From each according to his ability, to each according to his needs," proposes the same mirror symmetry of knowledge transfer and desire that so frustrates the humans about the heptapods and that accompanies a version of the end of history that comes about with knowledge of the totality of the universe's events and their relation to an overarching plan.

Chiang's writerly struggle for aesthetic freedom (and concomitant aversion to "history") certainly has a racial dimension, but it is quite a bit more complicated than a struggle against the claims of the ethnographic imperative upon the ethnic author. What is so resonant between Chiang's affective attachment to aesthetic freedom and modernization theory's hegemony is how both in fact foreclose the transcendent possibility of freedom and agency while at the same time embracing a melancholic ontology of performance in which meaning is created not through the ultimate agential act of revolution, but, in Gilman's phrase, only through "the *right* kind of revolution."[91] Simultaneous temporality's presumption that everything possible has always already happened mirrors modernization theory's belief in the immutable stages of economic growth. While U.S.-led economic growth was welcomed by developing Northeast Asian countries, it solved an existential political threat of national delegitimacy while at the same time foreclosing the possibility of an independent national identity separate from the U.S. security umbrella. Louise's meditation on the question of agency recapitulates the interventionist rationale of the modernization theorists themselves: "Within the context of simultaneous consciousness, freedom is not meaningful, but neither is coercion; it's simply a different context, no more or less valid than the other" (163).

THE EXPOSITORY IMPULSE

In an author's note appended to "The Man Who Ended History: A Documentary," Ken Liu acknowledges that he "got the idea for writing a story in the form of a documentary after reading Ted Chiang's 'Liking What You See: A Documentary.'" Liu goes on to list bibliographical sources for the story's historical material, and also includes a dedication to the Chinese American journalist Iris Chang (on whom the story's main character Evan Wei is based) as well as the victims of Japan's Unit 731. Similar notes are appended to many of Liu's stories. Chiang also frequently appends detailed author's notes to many of his stories and has included them in appendixes to his two short story collections. Similar amendments can be found in the work of other Asian American SF authors. Claire Light's collection *Slightly Behind and to the Left* (2009) includes an explanatory afterword that explicitly problematizes the author's "childish" desire for the reader to "just *get it*," as well as decodes some of its stories' less transparent elements.[92] The pages of Kawika Guillermo's *All Flowers Bloom* (2020) feature handwritten marginalia. R. F. Kuang includes an annotated bibliography at the end of some editions of her alternate history *The Poppy War* (2018). Charles Yu's *How to Live Safely in a Science Fictional Universe* (2010) contains graphical schematics depicting the novel's plot as well as character relationships (figures 2.2 and 2.3). The annotations, explanations, and illustrations offered

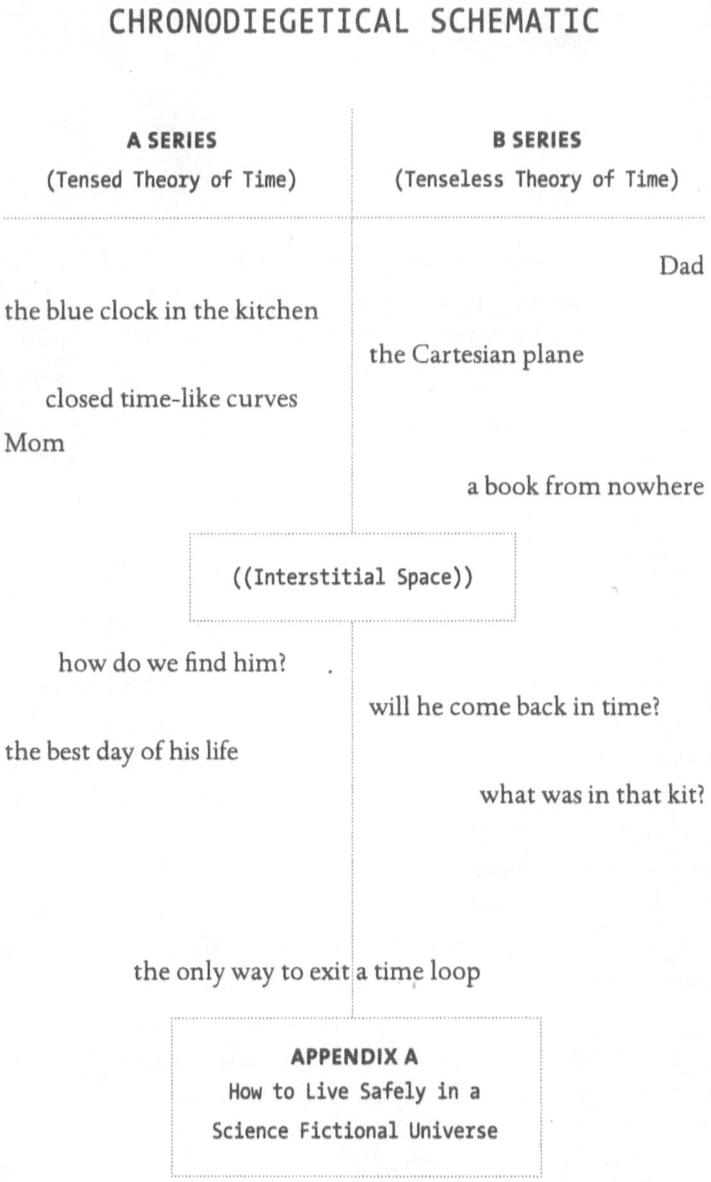

CHRONODIEGETICAL SCHEMATIC

| **A SERIES** | **B SERIES** |
| (Tensed Theory of Time) | (Tenseless Theory of Time) |

                                                    Dad

the blue clock in the kitchen

                              the Cartesian plane

closed time-like curves

Mom

                                    a book from nowhere

((Interstitial Space))

how do we find him?

                            will he come back in time?

the best day of his life

                                  what was in that kit?

the only way to exit a time loop

APPENDIX A
How to Live Safely in a
Science Fictional Universe

FIGURE 2.2. Schematics from Charles Yu's *How to Live Safely in a Science Fictional Universe* (2010).

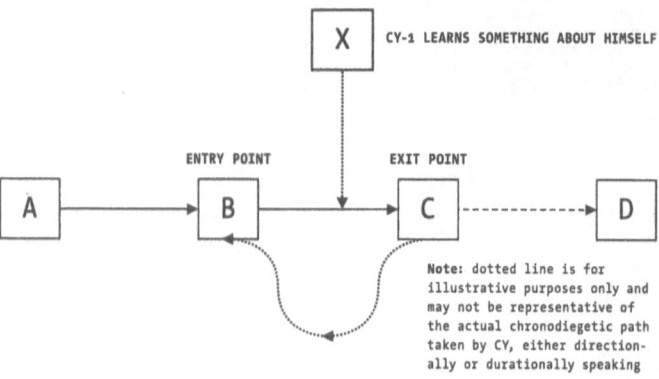

FIGURE 2.3. Schematics from Charles Yu's *How to Live Safely in a Science Fictional Universe* (2010).

by these authors attest to an *expository impulse* that is shared among post-65 Asian American authors. It is an impulse to concretize one's fiction via citation, explanation, and technical rigor—in a word, to never allow the imaginative flight of SF to lose sight of technical writing's groundedness. It is the same impulse that Yoon Sun Lee describes as the "utopian dimension" of Asian American realism that emerges with the everyday in the gaps of modernity's failures and that goads Asian American authors toward the "something more" that is the aspiration toward totality.

The expository impulse often manifests as a contrapuntal movement or dialogism.[93] In "Story of Your Life," this can be seen in the devices of interdependent narration, the tension between ekphrasis and the unrepresentable script of Heptapod B, and indeed the novum of simultaneous time itself. Even if Liu's "The Man Who Ended History: A Documentary" does not directly explicate Chiang's story, the impulse manifests in its own internal ekphrastic dynamic, as well as in its exposure and performative explanation of aspects of Chiang's story. Liu's story's concern with the racialized entanglements of Northeast Asia proposes a subtext to the thought experiment in Chiang's story, which explores the personal and collective consequences of unseeing "race" and other putatively phenotypical features. The genre of the author's note is a literalization of the expository impulse, which can also be internalized through modes of irony, such as the autopoetic tendency that we will examine more closely in chapter 4. In the next chapter, when we turn to Chang-rae Lee's style, we will see the expository impulse manifest as a surplus of style that fills the asymptotic gap in status between the PMC and the Pacific ruling class.

The excesses generated by the expository impulse can be contextualized through Jasper Bernes's account of the ethos of technical writing. Building on Andrew Hoberek's account of the rise of the postwar PMC in the United States, for whom "mental labor is the site of both transcendence and disempowerment," Bernes argues that "the former [indexes] a past life of petit-bourgeois entrepreneurialism and the latter a future life of thoroughly proletarianized drudge work."[94] The distance of class and developmental stage indexed by this "past life" is sublimated as modernist literary form: "If early modernist experiments, under the ethos of industrialization, could imagine the artist as maker, as fabricator and artisan of social forms—as the creator of a new language, sui generis—deskilling and, later, deindustrialization remove this contact with primary materials and reposition the artist as administrator of prefabricated forms, received from elsewhere, made by unknown characters."[95] For post-65 Asian American writers, this "past life" is differently constituted, and their distance from it is filled less by a nostalgia for what Bernes calls "contact" than the racial structures of transimperial modernization. The hypercathected force of hyper-selection and occupational concentration, which, as I have attempted to show, is shaped by modernization theory's fantasies and enactment through industrial policy, sublimates as the expository impulse. The impulse is in part a response to the "racial expectations" of assimilation and the ethnographic imperative. But it is also at least as much a response to the fraught choice by the Asian American author to veer away from occupational concentration, and perhaps even more a response to the affective disorientation experienced by Northeast Asian students and professionals arriving in the United States in the 1960s and 1970s, who were forced to grapple with the resonant distance between industrializing Asia, where they were national heroes, and the deindustrializing United States, where they are proletarianized. There is a homology between the Asian American SF writer as the agent who valorizes modernization's positivist utopia as aesthetic value via the medium of literary form, and the engineer—or, better, Okada's BA/BS Eng(lish/ineer)—who valorizes scientific knowledge as economic value via the "spurious coin" (to use Bernadette Longo's phrase) of technical writing. Like technical writing, SF mediates these contradictions and offers the possibility of valorization—as aesthetic capital at the very least, if not social and economic capital.

The next chapter tackles head-on the mounting issue of the Asian American *author*'s mediation of U.S.-Asia Cold War political economy and the post-65 racialization of economic identity. As the prose poet of the post-65 Asian American PMC, Chang-rae Lee and his oeuvre offer a preeminent case study in how literary style attempts to resolve contradictions produced by a mismatch in modes of production: Asia's industrialization and upward mobility on one hand and America's deindustrialization and downward mobility on the other. In preview, we might say that Lee's most autobiographical character, Henry Park, a self-described "sentient machine of transcription," is nothing if not the most stylish technical writer in all of Asian American literature.

Chapter Three

SHAKESPEARE WORDS
Professional Identity and Literary Style

> Any concrete description of a literary or philosophical phenomenon—if it is to be really complete—has an ultimate obligation to come to terms with the shape of the individual sentences themselves, to give an account of their origin and formation.
>
> —FREDRIC JAMESON, *MARXISM AND FORM*

There is a moment in Chang-rae Lee's 1995 novel *Native Speaker* that I would like to read as the kernel of his literary style. It presents a puzzle to which he repeatedly returns in his five subsequent novels. It is a paradigmatically post-65 scene.

Our protagonist, Henry Park, recalls his adolescent years working in his father's Upper East Side bodega in the 1970s. Their customers in the tony neighborhood are "the blue-haired matrons, and the fancy dogs, and the sensible young mothers pushing antique velvet-draped prams, and their most quiet of infants, and the banker fathers brooding about annoyed and aloof and humorless." Along with his other employees—recent immigrants from South Korea who "had college degrees and knew no one in the country and spoke little English"—Henry's father (who has given himself the name George Washington Park) requires his son to wear "a white apron over [his] slacks and dress shirt and tie." The motivation for these style guidelines is never given, but one hint resonates with the novel's titular expression of assimilation anxiety: perhaps the uniforms are a tactic to forestall or buffer the racial difference that customers like one "rich old woman whose tight strand of pearls pinched in the sags of her neck" sometimes respond to with epithets like "Oriental Jews." Another hint resonates with an economic dimension of the novel that operates not so much on the surface of the text as in the background, constantly structuring the relations between characters, intruding on their narrative trajectories, even shaping the sentences that breathe life into them. Flattering his wealthy white clientele, Henry's father suspects, "might be good for business." So he asks Henry to do one more thing: "to show [the customers] how well I spoke English, to make a display of it, to casually recite 'some Shakespeare words'" (49).

It is not at all clear how such a performance would improve the bottom line, and Henry's father doesn't elaborate. What is clear, however, is just how awkward such a performance would be. It is at least this that Henry (now referring to himself not just as "princely Hal" but more stylishly as "I, his princely Hal") seeks to avoid when "instead, and only in part to spite him, I grunted my best Korean to the other men." Falstaff his father certainly is not, but it's funny to think that if those Shakespeare words were performed stylishly enough, awkwardness might be avoided. Henry might even bring some customers back for more. To be sure, no matter how anodyne or playful Henry's father's request might seem on the surface, there is something lurid about trotting one's child out to perform for money. We can certainly forgive Henry's irritation, but long before we get there more needs to be said about the exquisite awkwardness of the request itself.

Why would "Shakespeare words" and "business" come to be associated in the first place? The awkwardness of Henry's father's request oozes out of a tension that suffuses all of Lee's novels, between aesthetic particularity and economic subjectivity. In Lee's novels we constantly witness a staging of this confrontation as well as attempts at making space for compromise formations. However, because of the predominance of occupational concentration in post-65 Asian American life, and thus the centrality of economic subjectivity, this compromise is jammed through professional identity: an ideal subject form of science fictionality that provides a container for a whole range of meanings and strategies, from national identity and racial identity to assimilation and citizenship to the arts and sciences. Lee's novels make clear how professional identity takes a specific shape in the case of the post-65 Asian American author that compels us to rethink how Asian American literature fits into accounts of postwar U.S. literary history that center the relationship between professional identity and what Sean McCann describes as the "rapid expansion of the long-term trend toward the development of large-scale systems of interlocking social and economic organization" that characterized the postwar years.[1] The old modernist anxiety over the commodification of the aesthetic is thus heightened—and vexed, because, for minority writers, it is difficult for style to escape the ethnographic imperative's grip on self-expression. Either way, what these factors create is a slippery surface for post-65 Asian American authors to perform upon.

Perhaps anxiety isn't the right word here because it is too psychologizing and individuating when the issue at hand is a social relation. That said, fictional characters provide a relatively stable set of forms and terms with which to construct psychological models that can offer useful clues for describing and analyzing the social relation. At best such models can help us to understand in sharper detail the *typicality* joining fictional characters to these social relations. Yoon Sun Lee, evoking Lukács, clarifies that typicality and stereotype are fundamentally different: "type embodies the contradictions of a historical moment rather than a reified social or demographic category."[2] For Henry and his parents, typicality is a source of pride while stereotype is a source of shame. Henry's father's request for Shakespeare words in the bodega scene arises from a complementary humiliation over stereotypically never having mastered English and over working in a bodega in the first place when he was trained for an altogether different life as an industrial engineer (51). But as Henry's late mother would remind him, his father's "true courage and sacrifice" after emigrating to the United States from South Korea in the late 1960s was to exchange a national typicality for a vulnerability to stereotype: "how he was able to discard his excellent Korean education and training, which were once his greatest pride, the very markings by which he had known himself, before he was able to set straight his mind and spirit and make a life for his family" (309).

The register of typicality preserves their connection to Korea. The abandonment of one life for another is one origin of the twoness that pursues Henry throughout the novel: a dehiscence at the very core of his being, emblematized by the titular trope of the native speaker. A twoness, moreover, that by turns resembles other psychic and formal structures like W. E. B. Du Bois's "double consciousness" but is particular to post-65 Asian America insofar as it indexes mismatched categories of economic subjectivity rather than racial standpoints. The job of style here is to smooth over the places where this twoness juts out, to affect a "poietic configuration," as Daniel Hartley argues in his account of the politics of style, that "forces the multiple voices of a text to cohere."[3] If we sense something distinctly

Asian American about Lee's project, something distinctly post-65, it is because what is playing out is a dynamic in which racially entangled formations of economic subjectivity, inhering preeminently in the position of the Asian American author, enter an agon with the aesthetic. Along these lines, Lee's style is that which attempts to establish a continuity between the dilemmas allegorized by the uniforms worn by Henry and the other employees, which function to neutralize racial interruptions to the smooth transaction of commerce, and the dream of the "Shakespeare words" themselves: a linguistic excess that yields not only aesthetic but also economic happiness.

A preoccupation with the economic, especially as it pertains to subject formation, is a core feature of post-65 Asian American literature. If this preoccupation is amplified in Lee's work, it is perhaps not so surprising when we consider that his first job out of college was a position as an equities analyst at the Wall Street investment bank Donaldson, Lufkin & Jenrette (DLJ). The job might have been an unlikely outcome for an English major, but perhaps not so much for a Yale graduate with an interest in wine. Lee joined DLJ in the fated year of 1987, the apex of the "greed is good" era that Oliver Stone's infamous character Gordon Gekko would emblematize when *Wall Street* was released in theaters that December. DLJ's success in the junk bond market brought it renown as "the new Drexel," referring to the firm of "junk bond King" Michael Milken, who, along with his insider trading henchman Ivan Boesky, was the inspiration for Gekko. As recounted by one of Lee's close friends at the time, who was also then an investment banker, that year "was a very heady period. It seemed very easy to make money." The apartment on East 23rd Street that Lee shared with the budding novelist Brooks Hansen became "the informal headquarters for what amounted to a postgraduate fraternity of young Korean-American professionals working in New York, all of whom still remember the epic parties there."[4] A small scene of the Reagan-era culture of financial deregulation that Doug Henwood describes in his history of Wall Street: a "wildness" that "included showering money on superfluous shopping centers in the middle of nowhere, windmill farms, prostitutes, speculative housing, speculative office buildings, cocaine, junk bonds, art for the CEO's house, the Nicaraguan contras, and yacht parties on the Potomac."[5]

By the time Lee left DLJ—he would be there for only a year—the junk bond market had bottomed out and the stock market had crashed. One wonders if this downward slump factored into the mood in which Lee slouched toward his typewriter every day to write his first novel, *Agnew Belittlehead*. According to Charles McGrath, to whom Lee recounted details about the manuscript, it was not only never published but "unpublishable." Although Lee has been reluctant to talk about the novel, McGrath relays that it was "about 500 pages long and heavily influenced by Thomas Pynchon" and that it contained "both Byronic verse and fantastical or science-fiction elements."[6] Much of the novel was written while Lee was commuting between New York City and Syracuse, where he was caring for his dying mother. Publishable or not, the manuscript was strong enough to secure Lee an agent as well as admission to the University of Oregon's MFA program, headed at the time by Garrett Hongo.[7] Lee's bet has certainly paid off.

My aim in this chapter is to locate in Lee's novels a sustained account of post-65 Asian American racial form that is especially sensitive to shifts in global political economy. Something of this perhaps comes from his time at DLJ, but more substantially it is traceable to the factors behind his family's arrival in the United States in the first place and Lee's sense of the typicality of their story. It thus helps us to perceive how for the Asian American author the category of Asian America has far exceeded its initial brief of ethnographic self-expression to become, among many other things, an optic for perceiving the subject-level consequences of material forces that have increasingly been interpreted as global and economic. Using Lee and his oeuvre as a case study, this chapter addresses directly what has been in the previous chapters a forestalled question about the mediating function of the post-65 Asian American author. In the following I lean particularly hard on *style* as an analytic for discussing this mediating function, though my purpose with it is to illuminate the *typicality* of the post-65 Asian American author rather than a formal accounting of, say, the distinctiveness of Lee's style. What I would like to show is how the apparently personal factors that bring the post-65 Asian American into the profession of authorship in the first place are strongly determined by the professional forms and class anxieties that modernization charted for Northeast Asian countries. This tension between personal agency and determinism opens an aperture of autopoetic self-reflection through which science fictional totality seeps into the literary text.

"Shakespeare words." The awkward appellation for an enigma of style, and the ultimate sign of post-65 Asian American literature; an emblem of the economic trope at the heart of its racial form and the reverse-image of Asian American technoscientific professional character. Henry never actually recites the words, however. In a way, it is Lee himself who eventually gets around to them in the title of his 2014 novel *On Such a Full Sea*, which is taken from act IV, scene III of *Julius Caesar*.[8] Not incidentally, it is also in *On Such a Full Sea* that the science fictional orientation that had been submerged in Lee's previous novels finally breaches the surface as dystopian SF. To be sure, Lee and his protagonists are not the same people, and in what follows I will take care to distinguish between each and how each relates to style. I will not ultimately be precious about this distinction, however, because *Native Speaker*'s commitment to metafictional reflexivity is just one aspect of the autopoetic tendency that can be found across Lee's work, and indeed of the expository impulse underlying post-65 Asian American fiction that I tracked in the previous chapter. It is more useful to think of Park and Lee together as co-stylists and of Lee's novels as their joint literary production. Style, to quote Hartley again, offers us "that elusive point at which the 'inner' necessity of the work coincides with the 'external' necessity of the historical situation."[9] It is through an analysis of Park and Lee's co-styling that the "inner" and "external" necessities of post-65 Asian American fiction become clear.

STYLE AND ECONOMIC SUBJECTIVITY

First in *Marxism and Form*, and then repeated throughout his later work, Fredric Jameson has argued that style is "a relatively recent phenomenon and comes into being along with the middle-class world itself." As the educational system that privileged Greek and Latin loses its hold so does the field of rhetoric, and it is an ideology of style, "the very element of individuality itself," that replaces it.[10] For Raymond Williams, "good prose and style are not things but relationships," and a critical analysis of style must attempt to recover "the relation between writer and reader which the ordinary version of style is designed to suppress."[11] Hartley unpacks this relation thus: "Each formal element of a literary work has its origins in a specific social formation (in this case, narrative and (modern) style); consequently, as that social formation undergoes major shifts in its mode of production (or the mode of production's stage of development), ruling ideology, or political configuration, each element is (potentially) transformed."[12]

Echoing Williams, Hartley emphasizes that, "Styles are at once expressions and embodiments of transindividual subjectivity, and are especially important as indices of newly emergent social subjectivity."[13] Even as an analysis of style must focus on the internal formal features of a literary text, such as diction, syntax, mood, genre, theme, etc., it must also pursue the difficult historical question that Williams places at the beginning of any such analysis: Why?[14] In fact, there are two questions here. To pursue the question of *why an author writes* as part of the question of *why an author writes in the way that they do* is to foreground not only the social relations that are reproduced through style but also those relations' conditions of emergence. Williams makes a key distinction between the "precise relationships" it contains—the author's private psychological motivations, for instance—and the "real relationships" that structure it.[15] Hartley glosses the latter category as "the level of unconscious actuality, in which the underlying 'pressures and limits' of precise historical situations are played out through the writer without her awareness."[16]

A sense of a shift in modes of production is a key thematic in all of Lee's novels. In *Native Speaker* we are offered glimpses into the dangerous new world of high finance through mentions, for instance, of the husband of a key staffer to the city councilman John Kwang, who is a "garden-variety investment banker . . . working on bridge financing for an industrial complex in Bangladesh" (286). Kwang himself holds his political coalition together via a scaled-up version of a Korean money club (*ggeh*), which is a financial instrument dating back hundreds of years that South Korea promoted domestically in the 1950s through 1970s as a way to integrate small businesses and rural regions into the national and international economy.[17] His constituents are predominantly documented and undocumented immigrants whose expansive informal economy makes possible the operation of the formal economy, and whose power Kwang has learned to tap into via the *ggeh*. An important point of contention in *A Gesture Life* (1999) is that the protagonist, Doc Hata, benefited financially and socially from an extended period of postwar American economic growth (in stark contrast to his suppressed past life as a medical officer in the Japanese army) before selling his medical equipment store to a struggling young couple knowing full well that their business prospects were dim and that their mortgage would soon be underwater. In *Aloft* (2004) the tense relationship between the protagonist Jerry Battle and his son Jack is complicated even further by the fact that Jack has been leveraging the assets of the family landscaping business to finance its expansion and public offering, as well as a lavish lifestyle for himself and his family. While the political unconscious of *On Such a Full Sea* (2014) is China's rise and U.S. decline, *My Year Abroad* (2021) explicitly engages China's rise through a narrative of apprenticeship and venture financing involving a charismatic, Kwang-like Chinese American flexible citizen, Pong Lou, mentor to protagonist Tiller Bardmon. Through Tiller, Lee revisits one of his central themes, the fragility of middle-class economic status. Tagging along with Pong on the latter's high-rolling travels in and out of Pacific Rim financial centers, Tiller is never certain whether he is working or not, an employee or not. This uncertainty is captured in his curious name, which evokes, variously, a liminal temporality, farming, and money transactions. Until the novel's gothic conclusion, he merely observes and enjoys. In Lee's fiction the figure thrust against the backdrop of these epochal transitions—the ur-trope for which is Korea's transition from Japanese colonialism to U.S. imperialism—is a solitary figure capable of weathering the storms of transition by clinging to a professional identity.

The answers to why Lee writes are multiple and complex, but his own accounts of the act of writing—which he will refer to as "the work of voice"—offer clues pertaining to the "pressures and limits" that have shaped his style. In two early essays about his deceased mother, "The Faintest Echo of Our Language" (1993) and "Coming Home Again" (1995), Lee traces his investment in language to his mother's childhood in Korea, where the Japanese colonial government suppressed the Korean language and imposed Japanese language instruction. In "The Faintest Echo" Lee tells us that his mother's name, Inja, is "Japanese in style and origin." He recalls her stories about how she "could only whisper to her sisters in the midnight safety of their house the Korean words folding inside her all day like mortal secrets" and how these stories imparted to him "the same burning, troubling lode of utter pride and utter shame still jabbing at the sweet belly of her life, that awful gem, about who she was and where her mother tongue and her land had gone" (87). We will flag for later the pregnant, Oedipal images of "jabbing," "words folding inside," and "belly of her life."

The trauma of colonial violence and cultural genocide that Lee inherits from his mother surfaces in unexpected ways after their emigration to the United States. In his teenage years, Lee's mother worries that he is losing his Korean—a worry that turns out to be less about nostalgia than a belated expression of anticolonial resistance. The truth is, Lee explains, "it had been whole years since I had lost the language," tracing the loss back to a reading contest in the first grade. With his mother's encouragement he won the contest after reading fifty books: "She had helped me then, pushed me to read and then read more to exhaustion until I fell asleep, because she warned me that if I didn't learn English I wouldn't be anybody and couldn't really live here like a true American." Lee had quite a deficit to overcome: just a year earlier he could "barely speak a word of English." For evidence of the urgency of learning English, his mother offers herself: "*Look at me . . . look how hard it is for me to shop for food or speak to your teachers, look how shameful I am, how embarrassing*" (87, original emphasis).

Lee's account of the urgency and shame surrounding English-language acquisition reproduces the devil's bargain of assimilation at the cost of one's home culture that stares down all immigrants, and especially the children of immigrants. This is especially evident in his recollection of his most awkward language-related memories as having to do with interactions with service workers. Not just grocery store employees and teachers:

> I would have to speak to a mechanic for her, I had to call the school myself when I was sick, I would write out notes to neighbors, the postman, the paper carrier. *Do the work of voice.* . . . I remember often fuming because of it, this one of the recurring pangs of my adolescence, feeling frustrated with her inabilities, her *misplacement*, and when she asked me one morning to call up the bank for her I told her I wouldn't do it and suggested that she needed "to practice" the language anyway.
>
> Gracious god, I wished right then for her to slap me. (88–89, my emphasis)

The "misplacement" that drives Lee's frustration appears to have something to do, if only in a small way, with how his mother's "inabilities" situate her social status in relation to service workers. It is in part this misplacement that Lee attempts to rectify later in the essay when he brings up the fact that his mother was a basketball star in high school, thus exonerating her misplaced low social status via a memory of her once high status. Published in 1993, two years before *Native Speaker*, "The Faintest Echo" clearly foreshadows core themes in the novel. Lee's mother's "misplacement" finds an especially striking echo in the character of Ahjuhma. After Henry's mother passes away (also from cancer), his father brings a middle-aged Korean woman over from South Korea to live with them as a cook and a maid. Lacking English and effectively confined to the tight "sphere" of the kitchen and her rooms behind it, she is a complete cipher to adolescent Henry and his friends: "Sometimes I thought she was some kind of zombie." "She's a total alien." "She's completely bizarre" (60, 72). What appears to evade their understanding is the same confusion that frustrates the young Lee when he is translating for his mother. It is not clear to them whether Ahjuhma is a worker or a family member—a point underscored by the term *"ahjuhma,"* which refers to a woman with no familial connection—just as it is momentarily unclear to the young Lee whether he is his mother's child or a kind of employee.[18]

Henry's belated regret over his and his father's treatment of Ahjuhma registers an awareness of the gendered blurring of familial and employment status that has historically been a key strategy for exploiting domestic workers' low-skill and unwaged labor.[19] Henry's regret does not rise to the level of critique, however; Ahjuhma is an instance of a prevalent trope in Lee's novels of the fracturing of domestic space by economic forces. Henry recalls, for instance, that his mother treated her role as a mother "like a job" (205). Doc Hata's house in *A Gesture Life* is constantly a target for real estate speculation and thus the awkward basis for one of his closest friendships, with the real estate agent Liv Crawford. In *Aloft* there is no distinction between domestic space and the family business, which is landscaping and home renovation. As soon as we are introduced to the grown-up June in *The Surrendered* (2010) and invited into her Manhattan apartment we learn that she has sold it and is in the process of selling off anything that isn't nailed down. In *On Such a Full Sea*, home is also either a factory or space for neoliberal self-valorization. In *My Year Abroad*, not only does Tiller Bardmon live precariously with his girlfriend and her son, who are in the Witness Protection Program, but they also tempt fate by transforming their house into a pop-up restaurant that becomes extremely popular.

In Lee's novels the fractured domestic space provides an objective correlative for an economic subjectivity that at all times threatens to engulf all other subject positions. For Lee himself, the motivation behind literary expression emanates from insight into the contradictions of his mother's unwaged reproductive labor: an insight that Ahjuhma amplifies. In the previous scene the power relationship between parent and child is disrupted when the "work of voice" momentarily unveils the economic relation between Lee and his mother. Lee takes advantage of the awkwardness and impropriety of this disruption by telling his mother "to practice" speaking English. This is a phrase that he remembers distinctly enough to quote verbatim, and this scene is in fact so deeply inscribed in Lee's memory that he brings it up again in his 1995 essay "Coming Home Again." This time he offers a fuller account of what happened and what was said.[20]

> One day, we got into a terrible argument when she asked me to call the bank, to question a discrepancy she had discovered in the monthly statement. I asked her why she couldn't call herself. I was stupid and brutal, and I knew exactly how to wound her.
>   "Whom do I talk to?" she said. She would mostly speak to me in Korean, and I would answer in English.
>   "The bank manager, who else?"
>   "What do I say?"
>   "Whatever you want to say."
>   "Don't speak to me like that!" she cried.
>   "It's just that you should be able to do it yourself," I said.
>   "You know how I feel about this!"
>   "Well, maybe then you should consider it practice," I answered lightly, using the Korean word to make sure she understood.
>   Her face blanched, and her neck suddenly became rigid, as if I were throttling her. She nearly struck me right then, but instead she bit her lip and ran upstairs. I followed her, pleading for forgiveness at her door. But it was the one time in our life that I couldn't convince her, melt her resolve with the blandishments of a spoiled son.[21]

His mother never slaps him, but not for want of Lee's trying.[22] In the earlier essay there was no admission of "brutal" behavior, which Lee quickly cleans up with softening language ("It's just that," "maybe," "I answered lightly"). To use King-kok Cheung's phrase, Lee's mother's "articulate silence" in this moment, her biting of her lip, speaks volumes about her childhood under Japanese rule, as well as the emotional stress of secondariness. As Lee has explained, the anger that consumes them—unresolvable because it is a symptom of large forces operating impersonally through them, because it is simultaneously the most impersonal and most personal of symptoms—has been "recurring" throughout their relationship. What seems to make this particular fight so unresolvable, so traumatically unforgettable and unclaimable, is that it lays bare how the forces involved aren't just colonialism and gender hierarchies. Something else besides muddles the mother-son relation into a flat social relation, extinguishing intimacy while at the same time amplifying its contradictions. That something else is the economic. The issue at hand, an erroneous bank statement, is not incidental. The root of Lee's genuine "fear" for his mother, as he describes it, and her resentment over her secondariness is that her lack of English means—for Lee—that she is outside of the economy in an important way. That she is out of circulation. Christine So might argue that this economic/interpersonal conflict's appearance within a narrative about Lee's dying mother, and the mediation of their relationship via the racialized symbolism of language, is guided by a distinctly Asiatic racial form in which economic subjectivity is inextricable from modes of racial "disembodiment or hyperembodiment."[23] That is, in representations of Asian Americans, the trope of capital's circulation (and noncirculation) is often associated with a bodily idiom of hyperracialization. In "The Faintest Echo," Lee stretches this idiom into an allegory about the origins of his writing career and style. This allegory operates through a reversal of mother-son relations, a confusion of who is bearing whom into subjectivity that resonates with the confusion over Lee's status as child or employee.

After leaving DLJ, Lee moves back home to care for his mother, who is dying from stomach cancer. It is during this time that he completes "the final push of work on what would prove a dismal failure of a novel."[24] In a striking scene, he administers morphine with a syringe that he has prepared:

> Even the sight of her pubic hair, darkly coursing out from under her, is now, if anything, of a certain more universal reminiscence, a kind of metonymic reminder that not long before she was truly in the world, one of its own, a woman, fully alive, historical, a mother, a bearer of life.
>
> I feel around for unseeable bruises until I find a spot we can both agree on.
>
> "Are you ready?" I say. "I'm going to poke."
>
> "*Gu-rhaeh*," she answers, which, in this context, means some cross between "That's right" and "Go ahead, damn it."

I jab and she sucks in air between her teeth, wincing.

"*Ay, ah-po.*" *It hurts. . . .*

Now I dab the pinpoint of blood. I'm trying to be careful.

"*Gaen-cha-na*," she says. *It is fine.*

"Do you need anything?"

"*Ggah*," she says flitting her head, "*kul suh.*" *Go, go and write.*[25]

We recall the Oedipal imagery that we flagged earlier. Lee's mother's childhood acts of transgression, whispering Korean to her sisters at night, filled her with shame and pride: a "lode" "still jabbing at the sweet belly of her life." In this scene it is Lee doing the jabbing, inseminating his mother, whose "lode" of linguistic ressentiment is delivered via a command to "*go and write*" the manuscript that would become *Agnew Belittlehead*, secure him a literary agent, and kickstart his career.

To drive home this allegory about the affective and economic transactions that constitute the mother-son relationship, in the midst of the passage just quoted—where I have placed the ellipses—Lee interpolates a section about his literary adolescence, which touches on the forebears of his style.[26] In all of Lee's published work this is the clearest account he offers of the Asian American–ness of his writing.

> I remember writing short stories in high school with narrators or chief characters of unidentified race and ethnicity. Of course this meant they were white, everything in my stories was some kind of white, though I always avoided physical descriptions of them or passages on their lineage and they always had cryptic first names like Garlo or Kram.
>
> Mostly, though, they were figures who (I thought) could appear in an *authentic* short story, *belong* to one, that no reader would notice anything amiss in them, as if they'd inhabited forever those visionary landscapes of tales and telling, where a snow still falls faintly and faintly falls over all of Joyce's Ireland, that great muting descent, all over Hemingway's Spain, and Cheever's Suburbia, and Bellow's City of Big Shoulders.
>
> I was to breach that various land, become its finest citizen and furiously speak its dialects. And it was only with one story that I wrote back then, in which the character is still unidentified but his *mother* is Asian (maybe even Korean), that a cleaving happened. That the land broke open at my feet. At the end of the story, the protagonist returns to his parents' home after a long

journey; he is ill, feverish, and his mother tends to him, offers him cool drink, compresses, and she doesn't care where he's been in the strange wide country. They do not speak; she simply knows that he is home.[27]

Not lost on us is the resonance of the language of "cleaving" and reunification with the colonization and partition of the Korean Peninsula. But as I have been arguing, these wounded attachments should not distract us from their coexistence with an economic metaphor. In this passage, speaking—that is, language and style—is unnecessary after reunification, which is also a condition of noncirculation. By the logic of this narrative, the space of the economic and the colonial is "the strange wide country" of mythical literary whiteness: another kind of "blank space" on the map that appears to invert the scene of a young Marlow fantasizing about the "blank spaces" of Africa in Joseph Conrad's *Heart of Darkness*. Lee's gestural description of his youthful style—its aspiration, at least—as "authentic[ally]" at home with these writers in a kind of space out of time, where the snow glows white forever (not a footprint to be seen), puts forth a racial and indeed heteronormative vision of literary aesthetics that comes about through his rediscovery of a gendered racial form. This compels us to reevaluate the silence between Henry and Ahjuhma as, in fact, a compromise formation that sustains the mismatch between her kinship and economic roles: a mismatch that is conspicuous when Ahjuhma circulates outside of the domestic space. Henry and his friends only come up with nicknames for her ("total alien," "Aunt Scallion") when they see her shopping in town on her off day. Linguistic style—"the work of voice"—becomes a resource for resuturing the contradiction and restoring the heteronormative sense of belonging to "that various land."

THE TROPE OF MISMATCH

This account of the "pressures and limits" shaping Lee's style—why he writes at all—brings into relief a dynamic in which cultural/racial assimilation and linguistic mastery are indistinguishable from a reconciled bank statement; the standard for "authentic" style and literary prestige is rooted in the eternal, autonomous circulation of white, Anglo-European writers; and the maternal injunction to write stuffs Lee into a subjectivity in which he is, confusingly, both child and worker. Or, put differently, the injunction lays bare the dialectic of productive and reproductive labor: of intimate relations and the real abstractions of economic relations. Turning now to the question of why Lee writes in the way he does, I need to distinguish my approach from the predominant approach in criticism on Lee's work, which establishes a relation between style and race that undergirds what Christopher Lee calls the "idealized critical subject": a figure that presumes a politics of resistance, and that, when deployed in literary criticism, presumes a relation, however complex, between the politics of the author and the politics of their fictional characters.[28]

The hypercanonical status that *Native Speaker* now enjoys in the field is due to its powerful allegorization of race as style. As Sunny Xiang observes, the novel "has been a shoo-in for Asian American studies syllabi because the tension between [Henry] Park's spy reports and his 'lyrical modes' animates the tension between the politically compromised voice of the model ethnic assimilator and that of the 'idealized critical subject.'"[29] The year 2002 seemed to be a turning point. In separate articles that year, Tina Chen, James Kyung-Jin Lee, and Crystal Parikh offered influential readings of *Native Speaker*'s allegorization of the spy and spy genre with Asian American racialization.[30] Each independently takes as their point of departure that, in Chen's words, "Lee deliberately reworks the genre of the spy story, altering it to accommodate the exigencies of a spy whose racially determined invisibility signals not license but a debilitating erasure of self and power."[31] Subsequent critics have developed sophisticated accounts of the historicity of the race-style allegory. For Xiang the trope of unreliable narration is the key to the style that Lee develops in the *Native Speaker*, and moreover constitutes Lee's "critical response" to "America's projection of Cold War Korea's forceful, passionate, and far-reaching anticommunist voice."[32] Jodi Kim, whose work Xiang's argument builds upon, offers one of the few readings that directly engages with the economic, arguing that the novel "gives narrative form to the Korean War and its Cold War aftereffects."[33] Kim zeroes in on Kwang's *ggeh*, which she describes as a form of "racialized undocumented capital" owing to its status as an unregistered and untaxed banking structure as well as its nonwhite, mostly immigrant members who operate primarily in the informal economy. From one angle this form of capital accords with model minority stereotypes in that it leverages the socially marginal, unbanked status of its members to facilitate capital accumulation and exchange. But when that capital becomes the basis for a new political machine, it becomes threatening and thus the target of Glimmer & Co.'s client, the Immigration and Naturalization Service. "Racialized undocumented capital, then . . . exposes the limits of liberal democracy," whose residual Cold War rhetoric trumpets "free-flowing global capitalism" while at the same time surveilling and criminalizing nonwhite migrant populations that are too free-flowing, too global, too capitalistic."[34] While Jodi Kim stops short of connecting this to an analysis of style, for Daniel Kim, it is literary style itself that materializes the inchoate collectivity manifested through Kwang's *ggeh*: as Lee writes, his is "the party of livery drivers and nannies and wok cooks and seamstresses and delivery boys, and his wealthiest patrons were the armies of small-business owners through whose coffers passed all of Queens, by the nickel and dime" (133). For Henry, Kwang's political achievement is his achievement of linguistic style: Kwang, he notes admiringly, is "unafraid to speak the language like a Puritan and like a Chinaman and like every boat person in between" (283).

Although *Native Speaker* is clearly interested in exploring the affordances of liberal multiculturalism it is more interested in accounting for that discourse's limitations. As Daniel Kim points out, Kwang's fearless creole is ultimately a melancholic structure because it substitutes literary representation for political representation. Kwang's political rise from city councilman to insurgent favorite for the mayorship is just as impressive as his ignominious downfall, through which, Kim explains, "*Native Speaker* makes quite plain . . . that no novel can serve to satisfy desires that are, at bottom, political."[35] This frustrated, unrealizable connection between aesthetics and politics, Kim goes on to argue, is particular to "a certain Asian American political fantasy which was particularly urgent in the late '80s and early '90s, a time when black-Asian racial tensions were exceptionally palpable."[36] At one point Kwang forges a truce between Korean small business owners and the African American community after a season of tensions.[37] As Parikh points out, Kwang's coalition is transparently inspired by Jesse Jackson's Rainbow Coalition.[38]

What joins these accounts of Lee's style is an insistence on style's politically resistant capacity as an "unsettling hermeneutic," to use Jodi Kim's phrase, that might reveal the contradictions of Cold War ideology, liberal multiculturalism, and U.S. racial capitalism. Lee's orientation to resistance seems to me overstated in these accounts, especially to the extent that they presume that the creative imagination might replace politics (a presumption that, again, *Native Speaker* is at pains to reject). Moreover, the race-style allegory clings to the reified racial tropes of liberal multiculturalism while neglecting to account for how *Native Speaker* not only ironizes that whole regime of racial meanings and rhetoric but also narrates its transition into what is in the 1990s an emergent regime in which economic subjectivity subsumes identitarian categories like race: what Jodi Melamed calls "neoliberal multiculturalism."[39]

Xiang offers a helpful starting point for tracking how Lee's style responds to this transition. In her reading of *Native Speaker*, Lee's style hinges on a juxtaposition of "spy theme" and "lyrical modality," the one set apart from the other, with the lyrical modes tending to appear "at the ends of chapters."[40] What Xiang is picking up on is a main feature of Lee's style more broadly: a kind of surplus of language in which concatenations, sentences, and chapters extend just slightly beyond a felt limit. This can be seen, for instance, in the interpolated adjectives in these passages: "Pete Ichibata was gloomy, ironical, pale. I liked him immensely, his sullenness, his corpselike color, except when he was lodged in a good mood, when he became overbearing and megalomaniacal. . . . My mother, in her hurt, invaded, Korean way, would have counseled me to distrust him, this clever Japanese" (14). The adjective "ironical" disrupts the resonance between "gloomy" and "pale." Almost as "sullenness" completes its job of conveying a mood, "corpselike" jumps out at us, devouring our attention, which is gutted by the time we are called upon to discern what it might mean to be "lodged" in a "good mood." In the second sentence, the standout modifier is "invaded," a word more admirable in this context for its efficient evocation of Japanese colonialism and American military occupation than for what it appears to be attempting, namely, the stuck landing of *le mot juste*. One gets the sense that Lee is cramming into his sentences, phrases, and modifiers more meaning and context than they can comfortably accommodate. That said, something larger is at work here than a private predilection for adjectival insistence—something like the expository impulse described in the previous chapter. To use Williams's distinction, we can say a lot more about the "real relationships" (material determinants) congealed in these sentences before we have to resort to guesses about the "precise relationships" (psychological motivations) embedded in Lee's style.

We can begin with the basic observation that Lee's style involves elevating one level of meaning into another. This effort is especially pronounced in what Xiang calls the novel's "lyrical" passages. Exemplary of these is the one that ends *Native Speaker*'s first chapter:

> And yet you may know me. I am an amiable man. I can be most personable, if not charming, and whatever I possess in this life is more or less the result of a talent I have for making you feel good about yourself when you are with me. In this sense I am not a seducer. I am hardly seen. I won't speak untruths to you, I won't pass easy compliments or odious offerings of flattery. I make do with on-hand materials, what I can chip out of you, your natural ore. Then I fuel the fire of your most secret vanity. (6)

We get the sense of elevated meaning as Lee takes a description of the most boring person imaginable and then inverts those qualities so that, with a snap of his fingers, they are suddenly the powers of a supervillain. What Lee's style manages to lift is our impression of Henry's hidden social status. The irony is that Henry almost never actually engages in the kind of psychological manipulation mentioned here. (The psychiatrist Emile Luzan being the one exception.) If anything, it is Kwang who possesses the superpowers of manipulation and Henry is his easy mark.

What do we make of this mismatch? We could chalk it up to a mistake on Lee's part, an aesthetic lapse in which he has overdrawn a character who is actually rather constrained, passive, and indistinctive ("invisible," even). Alternatively, we could follow Xiang's lead and attribute Henry's high opinion of himself to unreliable narration. The reason I hesitate to take up either of these entirely reasonable options is that Henry's self-description is rhetorically identical to the ironic descriptions of Pete Ichibata and Henry's mother, and, more important, we find the same kinds of mismatches across Lee's novels. If it's a mistake, then why is it such a consistent one? If it's symptomatic of a Cold War structure of feeling, why does it appear in novels where that structure and context are absent? I suspect what Lee is attempting to navigate are the dilemmas and contradictions thrown off by a mismatch between professional identity and social status. Henry's self-aggrandizing elevation of his boringness is a compensation for something: an alibi, we might say, for a hopelessly typical and unremarkable—and in the end, racial—character that he fears is *deserving* of invisibility. To be sure, this dilemma is from one angle nothing more than a depiction of interiority, but the indication that Henry's dilemma is distinctly situated in a post-65 Asian American racial form is how that interiority is fundamentally mediated by professional identity.

For post-65 Asian American authors professional identity is both an epistemological and a literary crux. In an interview, Lee explains that *Native Speaker* was written as "a response to what was, I think, becoming expected of Asian-American writers—which was that we write these very circumscribed family stories, within-the-house kind of stories, where there's also a keen intergenerational conflict. As wonderful as those stories are, I wanted to *widen the stage* in which my character was going to act. *I wanted an occupation for him* in which he'd have to get out in the world and see others, particularly the politician John Kwang."[41] Professional identity, in other words, not only mediates between the private and the public, but it is also the hinge between an older, thematically narrow genre of Asian American fiction and the new Asian American social realism that Lee clearly intends *Native Speaker* to inaugurate.[42] We will see another version of this at work in the next chapter's examination of how the trope of professional identity has offered Chinese American women writers narrative alternatives to various modes of normative femininity, as well as a capacious opening for literary innovation via science fictional genre manipulations that facilitate correspondences between interiority and various registers of material reality (especially economic and geopolitical).

Professional identity's mediation of the wider stage of economic circulation and transcendent humanistic value is especially pronounced in *My Year Abroad*, in which Tiller returns over and over again to the mystery of what exactly it is about his mentor Pong Lou's style that has such a profound impact on him. Here he explains:

> If I had simply bumped into him [Pong] on a Dunbar street, I couldn't have imagined him being all the other ways he was. I would have assumed he was like any other latecomer Asian immigrant, focused and industrious and leaving nothing to chance. A worker-bee bench chemist at a mega-pharma, but only that. . . . I couldn't have seen him as the multitargeting entrepreneur with ventures as varied in scale and kind as a fro-yo shop and car washes and an Indian wedding hall, and personal interests like yoga and surfing. I couldn't have placed him at the center of so many orbiting bodies, how each of us was drawn and held by the force of his peerless competence, the diverse

skills and discerning aptitudes and effortless generosity that made him seem like he was the wealthiest person in the world.[43]

There is a substantial gap between this Pong of impressive charisma and the nondescript Pong we follow in the rest of the novel. Tiller's recounting in this passage of how he underestimated Pong literalizes this mismatch, and at the same time betrays his personal investment in an overestimation of Pong's character. Tiller's transformation of Pong from "industrious" "bench chemist" into "the wealthiest person in the world" offers a glimpse into how the irony in Lee's style is grounded in a trope of class anxiety. Thus we see how unreliability is not only a matter of inscrutability or imposture. At a more basic level, it comes from a discrepancy between description and actuality that is at least as much economic in origin as it is, say, cognitive and cultural. While Tiller might understandably be read here as doting on Pong's inscrutability, and thus rehearsing a longstanding Western stereotype of Asians, I would argue that his compulsive habit of describing and redescribing Pong is aimed at generating literary style—the excessive parataxis in the last sentence, for instance—in order to smooth over the mismatch between the registers of Pong's personal style and his economic meaning. While perhaps not exactly Shakespeare, Tiller's words serve the spirit of Henry's father's request to perform them.

These registers manifest in Lee's novels not only thematically as professional identity versus social status but also generically as novel versus epic, and thus they reflect how the problem of protagonicity in Lee's fiction is a version of the problem of the universal subject of history. These ironies achieve their most explicit and intense form in *On Such a Full Sea*. The novel's collective narrator, meant to evoke a commenting Greek chorus, recounts events in the life of the protagonist—a teenage diver named Fan whose job it is to clean fish tanks—in an attempt to bridge her naturalistic, quotidian narrative to a kind of epic temporality in which revolutionary change might be narratable.

> She once told us that she almost preferred being in the tanks than out in the air . . . that she liked the feeling of having to hold her breath and go against her nature . . . she would pull her knees to her chest and drift to the bottom and stay there in that crouch until her lungs screamed for forgiveness. She wasn't inviting oblivion or even testing herself but rather summoning a

different kind of force that would transform not her but the composition of the realm, make it so the water could not harm her. . . .

But let's suppose another way of considering her, which was that she had a special conviction of imagination. Few of us do, to be honest. We wish and wish and often with fury but never very deeply. For if we did, we'd see how the world can sometimes split open, in just the way we hope. That it and we are, in fact, unbounded. Free.[44]

The uncertain status of "us"—which could refer either to an actual character or characters speaking for or as a collectivity, or to a limited omniscient consciousness (perhaps the voice of the facility's surveillance apparatus)—is of a piece with the uncertain status of Fan's capacity for interiority and agency: in other words, her capacity for the liberal protagonicity of the bourgeois novel. The bridging between novel and epic that the collective narrator attempts in this passage, a task that they return to repeatedly, hinges on whether or not Fan possesses this capacity. Indeed, the aesthetic success of *On Such a Full Sea*—as novel, epic, whatever—hinges on this very capacity. If Fan is free then they are all free, and the novel can rise to the status of epic. Fan never achieves protagonicity, however, and the novel barely holds together as a novel (as opposed, say, to a loosely interconnected collection of short stories) much less ascends to epic. Critics have noted this by describing Fan's characterization as "flat" and lacking in the libidinal developmental dynamic that propels the bourgeois novel. Rather than frame this as an aesthetic shortcoming, we can place it alongside the other mismatches between description and character in Lee's novels. Pete Ichibata never acts "megalomaniacal." Doc Hata is both model citizen and war criminal. And Pong just isn't that magnetic.

What we will call the trope of mismatch has been registered by other critics, though in different terms. Tina Chen notes Lee's "excessive and theatrical" deployments of spy genre conventions.[45] Daniel Kim writes of *Native Speaker*: "The central irony of Lee's immaculate prose style . . . is that it seems so entirely evacuated of the immigrant sensibility it memorializes."[46] Christopher Lee is of the opinion that *A Gesture Life* "finds itself mired in formal conventions that fail to adequately resolve its narrative form."[47] Viet Thanh Nguyen is more direct when he writes of Lee, "as beautifully written as his novels are, there is something of the anxious student in them, the longing for belonging, the evident desire never to write a bad sentence, and indeed always to write the perfect sentence"—an evaluation he quickly follows with his own self-effacement: "But that is just my feeling about Lee's writing. The same things I say of Lee could be said of me as a novelist."[48] What each of these critics points out is a mismatch between stylistic excess ("mired," "immaculate," "too perfect") and imperatives of theme and narrative—the contours, in other words, of the expository impulse. The issue is not so much whether Lee has succeeded or failed aesthetically. Instead the more interesting question concerns the affective and material structures that, in a way, impede Lee's relation to his objects and that register as stylistic awkwardness.[49] Lee's stylistic interest is in circumventing them. As I have been arguing, the trope of mismatch maps onto the mismatch between professional identity and social status that is the affective and material core of the post-65 Asian American experience: a mismatch that it falls upon the Asian American author to exonerate through style.

Indeed, this is the core dilemma that *Native Speaker* metafictionally stages through Henry's style, which is his stock-in-trade. The style that Henry aims to inhabit, however, is less like James Bond's phallic bravado than George Smiley's self-deprecating meticulousness: "We systematically overassessed risk, made it a bad word. Guns spooked us.... We knew nothing of weaponry, torture, psychological warfare, extortion, electronics, supercomputers, explosives. Never anything like that" (15). The success of Henry's assignments depends on his ability to evade description. "I am hardly seen," he tells us; his goal is to be "at once convincing and unremarkable" (6). His boss, Hoagland, praises his performances as "Tony, Emmy, Academy-fucking-Award" worthy (38). The effort he puts into appearing effortless invites teasing when one of Kwang's staffers accuses him of harboring "a secret literary career" (83). Henry's stylized elimination of all traces of style applies equally to his writing, and it is in his own accounts of his writing that it becomes clear that his style is the result of a negotiation of a two-cultures conflict that binds together yet more conflicts of the Oedipal and racial variety. These conflicts certainly contain a private dimension, but they are also, as Lee explores, antinomies generated by economic and historical forces, and so never exclusively attributes of the individuals through which they manifest.

In preparation for each assignment, Henry pens an extensive "legend": a cover story for his persona that overlaps significantly with his actual biography (20). And when in the field collecting intelligence on a mark, he generates "registers": dispatches to the central office about his target's personality, movements, activities, and associations. Here is how Henry describes his compositions in one of the novel's most widely quoted passages:

> I am supposed to do it this way, precisely but fast, checking off the day hour by hour the way a bright-eyed kid might reel off what he just got for Christmas. If I pore over the events too long . . . I might get the proportions wrong, lend an act or word a note of too much significance and weight.
>
> I am to be a *clean writer*, of the most reasonable eye, and present the subject in question like some sentient machine of transcription. In the commentary, I won't employ anything that even smacks of theme or moral. I will know nothing of the crafts of argument or narrative or drama. Nothing of beauty or art. And I am to stay on my uncomplicated task of rendering a man's life and ambition and leave to the unseen experts the arcana of human interpretation. The palmistry, the scriptology, the rest of their esoterica. The deep science. . . .
>
> What I am paid to do is observe him [Kwang] in a rigorous present tense, as a subject dynamically inhabiting a scene, as a phenomenon of study. (189)

To disturb "proportions" would undermine a professional duty for "perspicuity"—the linguistic clarity valued by technical writers—and degrade the quality of information that he is "paid" to produce.[50] Henry's methodical rejection of the aesthetic is so complete that the humanity of his subjects is in effect freeze-dried, left to be rehydrated via the "deep science" administered by "experts." If we find here that "science" has been given an unexpectedly artful status, then we have detected an aspect of the novel's science fictionality. Indeed, we are struck by just how unscientific, "uncomplicated," and un-transcript-like Henry's style is here. An Oedipal tension suffuses the racial and stylistic distinctions that it brings forth, and that are reminiscent of Lee's account of his white male modernist forebears. Henry's fetishization of language isn't only an efficient metaphor for racial anxiety but also the substance of the professional's knowledge work: "symbolic analysis," in Robert Reich's memorable formulation.[51] As C. Wright Mills puts it in his account of the "white collar" class that begins to emerge at the turn of the twentieth century, "fewer individuals manipulate things, more handle people and symbols. . . . They are the people who keep track."[52]

Henry certainly knows how to keep track, as does John Kwang with his massive database of *ggeh* members. *Native Speaker* is very much a novel about how big data transforms ethnic and political identity into what Mills calls a "picture of society as a great salesroom, an enormous file, an incorporated brain, a new universe of management and manipulation."[53] As Xiang argues, Henry is relegated to an inhuman, machine-like status while it is the experts—like his boss Hoagland, who is white—who are the stewards of the Cold War category of the human.[54] To recall the previous two chapters, what is this but the neoimperial blowback of modernization theory?

The style of the preceding passage—like many such passages in the novel, it is a soliloquy—hovers anxiously between "machine" and "Shakespeare" in its list of commands and lyrical depiction of interiority. To use our terms from the previous chapter, somewhere closer to technical writing than SF in the spectrum of post-65 Asian American genre forms. Henry's style is therefore a sublimation of the science fictional conflict staged in the bodega scene: between his father's request to perform for money and his rejection of that request. The fact that we never see Henry's "registers" and instead only get stylistic descriptions of them is related to the trope of mismatch. Whatever equanimity the style of the "clean writer" achieves for Henry is entirely thrown off by Kwang, who provokes all kinds of excess and hyperbole:

> I realized that Kwang presented a profound problem for me. I couldn't write the usual about him, at least in that automatic, half-conscious way. I had trouble again. I could not picture him. It seemed I had no profile from which to work. I was prolific, however, I wrote other pieces, entire tracts on him, tones and notes of him, but nothing I could use. I transmitted what I had on hand, two or three pages of vague and aimless reporting.... As I flesh out the day's register, as I am tonight, I feel as if I am desperately prospecting for an alibi, one mine more than Kwang's. (190)

What Henry describes here is a version of the "work of voice" that Lee was tasked to undertake on behalf of his mother's translation needs. In the same way that this work forced Lee into the awkward position of both son and employee, it is precisely Henry's professional composure that Kwang disrupts by provoking Henry's intense identification. The "alibi" Henry mentions is therefore not only a kind of exonerating narrative but also a "work of voice" that worries over an excess of racial and personal meaning that Henry must translate to his white "expert" readers while simultaneously deleting himself from that translation. After all, Hoagland pays Henry for the registers, not the alibi.

The alibi is a supplement that is both integral to the register and surplus to it, a homologous form to what we referred to above as Lee's stylistic tendency to exceed a felt limit: yet another form related to the expository impulse. The alibi is what is contained in the "tracts" that Henry writes about Kwang and that he discards because they are of no "use." Henry's racial and professional identities, schematically indexed to literary excess and waged labor, are in direct conflict here. The alibi is a figure for a post-65 Asian American style yoked to the burden of constantly justifying its own existence without the resources of what Daniel Kim calls a "monumental Asian American tradition of political and literary representation upon which to look back."[55] Lacking this tradition, Henry feels compelled to generate it on the fly—that is what we would find in those discarded tracts. The post-65 Asian American situation is different though consistent with the ethnographic imperative that hectors all minority writers. For Henry, and Lee, to worry about style is to worry about how to exonerate the mismatch between professional identity and social status.

Part of what I want us to see in these passages is Lee's depiction of a structure that mediates between an economic unconscious and a form of secondary elaboration in which the two-cultures trope does the work of binding a great deal of free-floating libidinal energy. There is a diachronic dimension to this structure that manifests in Lee's novels through intergenerational conflict and difference and that often explicitly indexes modes of production. In *Aloft*, Jerry Battle and his father are uncomfortable with the fact that Jerry's son Jack wants to take the three-generation-old family business public. The facilities and charters in *On Such a Full Sea* are clearly distinguished by industrial and postindustrial modes of production, respectively. *My Year Abroad* associates China's reform and opening period with Pong (whose name perhaps references the "ping-pong diplomacy" that paved the way to reform and opening), while Tiller is a figure for a kind of post-2008 American vulnerability and residual exceptionalism. In *Native Speaker*, the thing about Kwang that throws Henry off his game is that he attracts a transference of Henry's Oedipal conflict with his father. This shines a light on not just Henry's relationship with his father but also the "wider stage" upon which their relationship plays out, in which the roles they play are defined as much by profession as by character.

> Before I knew of [Kwang], I had never even conceived of someone like him. A Korean man, of his age, as part of the vernacular. Not just a respectable grocer or dry cleaner or doctor, but a larger public figure who was willing to speak and act outside the tight sphere of his family. He displayed an ambition I didn't recognize, or more, one I hadn't yet envisioned as something a Korean man would find significant or worthy of energy and devotion; he didn't seem afraid like my mother and father, who were always wary of those who would try to shame us or mistreat us. (129)

Kwang is Henry's father's stylistic opposite: "part of the vernacular," "willing to speak and act," and unimaginably ambitious. Henry's reliance on professional categories to convey this difference is symptomatic of his—and Lee's—economic unconscious. The homology between libidinal and economic difference is deepened at several moments in the novel, often via the trope of intergenerational difference. Henry remarks, "My father would not have believed in the possibility of sub-rosa vocations," thus marking a difference between the practical consciousness of a paradigmatic post-Fordist knowledge worker and the kind of small business owner who preaches to his son "you are your own cheapest labor" (43). So when Henry tells us that his father "couldn't care for the importance of *career*," he is also telling us that there is a genre of narration that is appropriate to his father's generation and another—the career—that is appropriate to his. We see the "work of voice," also known as "prospecting for an alibi," in how this transference isn't merely about Oedipal conflict and how that Oedipal conflict isn't merely about Henry and his father. Rather, this transference is merely one wrinkle folded into a far vaster fabric.

As stylistically opposite as Kwang is from Henry's father, there are structural similarities to their biographies that emphasize their shared typicality. Namely, both are born poor in South Korea and after emigrating to the United States make their fortunes through small business ownership. Walking through the streets of Flushing with Henry, Kwang shows him where he once had a storefront business selling and leasing "dry-cleaning machines and commercial washers and dryers, only high-end equipment." Kwang's mastery of English allows him to expand his business beyond Queens "to deal with non-Korean suppliers and distributors in other cities and Europe." Still, his clients were "Other Koreans" who "depended on him to find good deals and transact them" (169). Eventually, Kwang invests in "car dealerships and a local chain of electronics stores."

For Henry, what is so improbable about Kwang is that he is cut from the same cloth as his parents and their generation of Korean immigrants, and yet he has managed to match his social status with his professional identity. He has also managed to range beyond the ethnic enclave, largely through the force of his own personal style, to consolidate an insurgent political coalition. Even more improbably, it is a multiracial coalition that contrasts diametrically with the multiracial constituents of Kwang's mayoral contest rival, the incumbent De Roos: "strong-arm cadres of unionized workers and tradespeople, white ethnic old New York" (133). Jodi Kim argues that Kwang's insurgent political success is made possible by his mastery of liberal discourse and expansion of his *ggeh* to include thousands of unbanked informal workers, Korean and non-Korean alike. However, we might look to even earlier in Kwang's career for the origins of his style: his mastery of English as an orphaned child, which facilitates his ethnically exogamous business relationships. A reflection of Lee's stylistic preoccupation with the economic basis of multicultural politics and ethnic identity can thus be observed in the previous passages' conflation of racial identity with profession. To refashion a formulation often attributed to Stuart Hall, professional identity in Lee's novels is a modality through which race is lived.

What Lee's oeuvre tracks is how the purpose behind exonerating a diminished social status for an elevated professional identity—alibi-making, as it were—has shifted over the post-65 period, away from an assimilationist desire to translate "authentic" ethnic experience for a predominantly white readership to a desire to reconcile social contradictions that are increasingly economic in nature and global in scope. The ethnographic imperative certainly hasn't disappeared, but its command over literary form has diminished in direct proportion with multiculturalism's diminishing capacity to express Asian American realities. This diminishment in *Native Speaker* is often mediated by globalization's language of space and time. The detective genre's concentric narrative structure, at the center of which is the discovery of a hidden truth, allegorizes liberal multiculturalism's fetishization of racial authenticity. But by the time we get to *My Year Abroad*'s fetishization of transnational Chinese American identity as a value form, rigorous narrative structure has given way to a picaresque mode that is more appropriate to Pong's improvisational—and increasingly desperate—pursuit of spatial fixes to stagnant capitalist accumulation.

WRITING LIKE THE CHILD OF AN ENGINEER

Lee's novels display a pronounced stylistic interest in depicting an unfolding set of actually existing historical relations. Though *On Such a Full Sea* would appear anomalous alongside the realism of Lee's other novels because of its status as SF, in fact it merely exaggerates formal solutions that Lee has developed to address a consistent set of themes pertaining to the material determinants of contemporary Asiatic racial form. In other words, the novel is an extreme focalization of science fictionality. In regard to the movement of history, as well as Lee's preoccupation with the economic, the origin of the novel's title in *Julius Caesar* offers a rather efficient indication of this consistency:

> We at the height are ready to decline.
> There is a tide in the affairs of men
> Which, taken at the flood, leads on to fortune;
> Omitted, all the voyage of their life
> Is bound in shallows and in miseries.
> On such a full sea are we now afloat,
> And we must take the current when it serves,
> Or lose our ventures. (IV.ii.269–76)

In this speech Brutus attempts to convince Cassius to march on Philippi at a decisive moment. His reliance on a metaphor of financial speculation echoes one of the main dilemmas at this moment in the play, which is how to raise funds for the war. These might not be the "Shakespeare words" that Henry's father had in mind, but the drama of fate and free will staged in this passage offers a metafictional reflection on the two-cultures dynamic that brought Henry's father to make his request in the first place. In *Native Speaker* Lee's attempt at locating his characters—especially Henry's father and Kwang—amid a "tide in the affairs of men" produces clues for why Henry speaks and writes in the way he does. Specifically, clues for why and how "Shakespeare words" are dialectically bound to the science fictionality of Park Chung-hee's South Korea. The trail leads us back to the circumstances of Henry's father's emigration and provides a kind of ur-narrative of the origins of post-65 Northeast Asian American style.

We learn that Henry's father earned a master's in industrial engineering from what Henry's mother calls South Korea's "best university," most likely in the mid- to late 1960s (51). "Best university" is a reference to Seoul National, which was established in 1948 with U.S. military funding and then rebuilt after the Korean War through a partnership with the University of Minnesota. Henry's father's professional training was directed in no small way by Korean and American geopolitical and national interests. His degree field, "industrial engineering," held a great deal of symbolic meaning, focalizing as it did a set of state-sponsored nationalist, economic, and professional narratives. It is during the 1960s that Park Chung-hee launched a series of five-year plans focused on rapid industrialization, beginning with the development of energy and agricultural infrastructure, from 1962–1966, followed by a series of heavy and chemical industry-focused plans. These plans entailed the production of new categories of technical worker and of propaganda campaigns promoting such professions. The identification of the engineer with national identity and dignity was a legacy of nineteenth-and twentieth-century modernization discourse and Japanese colonialism.[56]

Just prior to Japanese rule, Korea had been in the early stages of developing institutions and social structures promoting technical professions. Although Western education was seen during the Joseon era as morally objectionable and counter to Confucian ethics, extensive debates took place over whether and how to promote technical training, which the scholar-official class saw as obviously valuable.[57] Amid these heady discussions, Koreans increasingly saw vocational technical training as a means of social and economic mobility. Japanese colonialism interrupted this development, relegating Korean technical trainees to low-level professions. Technical schools became "havens for students who failed to get into academic high schools or were poor."[58] While Henry "never learned the exact reason [his father] chose to come to America," he believes it had something to do with what his father calls "the big network in Korean business" and "how someone from the rural regions of the country could only get so far in Seoul" (52). After the Korean War, despite efforts by Park and other modernizers at elevating their status, the engineering profession nonetheless retained a nineteenth-century association with manual labor and the peasantry, which is why it is relevant that Henry's father is the son of a "poor cabbage farmer" (245). This was due in part to the post–World War II restoration of the Japanese dual-track educational system, which distinguished between academic and vocational tracks. In this system industrial engineering straddled the two tracks, which, read back into the characterizations of Henry and his father, informs the ambiguities over race, class, and language that structure their dilemmas of identity. Henry's father's story of blocked social and economic upward mobility and the class ressentiment it provokes gestures at one of the primary push factors of South Korean emigration during this period, namely the elitist confines of the *chaebols*, the closed nature of the patronage networks extending from Park's inner circle, and the general instability of the Park regime. Also significant would have been the government's active encouragement of emigration as a way to control population growth, deal with its surplus of technical professionals, and reap the benefits of a remittance economy.[59]

While highly trained technical professionals like Henry's father tended to have better chances at transcending their poverty, it was also true that South Korea in the 1960s and 1970s fell into the same trap that other Northeast Asian countries fell into during this period, which was an overproduction of STEM professionals and an underproduction of industries and jobs to absorb them. As Michael J. Seth writes, despite the consistent promotion of scientific and technical education in five-year plans, "neither the content nor the structure of education was ever comprehensively coordinated with the needs perceived by state economic planners and industrial managers, although the quality and numbers of engineering students improved and some of the industrial training programs were useful."[60] The mismatch between Henry's father's professional identity and social status is thus a direct consequence of U.S. pressure on South Korean industrial policy, and it long predated his arrival in the United States. The structural factors behind Lee's own father's emigration to the United States in 1965 to take up a residency in psychiatry are identical to those of Henry's father. Whether or not this indicates Lee's autobiographical interest in *Native Speaker*, what interests us is how it forms a concrete basis for the novel's autopoetic style. The puzzle of the Shakespeare words is that their evocation of the aesthetic is motivated not by a relation to the aesthetic but to the economic. Indeed, a very specific form of the economic: a misplaced economic subjectivity that sees in the aesthetic a potential alibi for the shame of deprofessionalization. It is relevant that Henry's father evokes a *literary* mode of the aesthetic. What is at work here is a nonmetaphorical two-cultures conflict in which Henry's father's overdetermined specialization in the sciences results in linguistic deficits that Henry is called upon to reconcile.

CODA: TEAMWORK

The scene in *Native Speaker* where we most clearly see racial identity routed through professional identity comes about halfway into the novel, when Lelia and Henry are attempting to reconcile. Lelia has just returned from an extended trip to Italy, where she decamped to initiate a trial separation. Just before her departure she hands Henry a list "of who [he] was" (1).[61] While the list contains a few positive statements, it is mostly a racially inflected indictment of Henry's nonpresence, inscrutability, and moral character. "Illegal alien," it accuses; "emotional alien," "stranger," "follower," "traitor," "spy." The cruelest diss isn't even on the list. Henry finds it on a scrap of paper under their bed: *"False speaker of language"* (5, original emphasis). Cruelest because Lelia knows very well that the entire edifice of Henry's ego is structured and balanced by language's capacity to arbitrate forms of twoness.

Now reunited with Henry but uncertain about their future together, Lelia apologizes for writing the list. Then she drops a bomb: in Italy she had an affair. When she explains to Henry how the affair helped her to clarify some things about their marriage, she rehashes the list's main theme, which is Henry's inscrutability:

> I told him we were separated. He thought I meant divorce but I said that wasn't it. I told him how I still felt love, but that I didn't trust you anymore. That I didn't know how you really felt about anything, our marriage. Me. You. I realized one day that I didn't know the first thing about what was going on inside your head. Sometimes I think you're not even here, with the rest of us, you know, engaged, present. I don't know anymore why you do

things. What you really want from me. I don't know what you need in life. For example, do you need your job? (118)

"Do you need your job?"—quite the swerve! Rather than suggest the mutual exclusivity of profession and racial form, Lelia's question has the effect of emphasizing their mutual determination, as well as their connection to style (albeit, for Lelia, a maddeningly inscrutable one). Henry's response is as revealing as it is unhelpful: "I'm not understanding what you mean by *need*."

The answer to Lelia's question, we can surmise, is yes and no. And what exactly "need" means makes all the difference in regard to the novel's ultimate puzzle, which is how the complexities of racial identification disrupt Henry's otherwise unimpeachable class position, alienating him from himself. Henry needs his job because of his wounded attachment to a debased racial identity in which his only access to authenticity is through an embrace of falseness. Espionage is the "perfect vocation for the person I was," Henry explains, which is "someone who could reside in his one place and take half-steps out whenever he wished" (118). As a spy, being a "false speaker of language" secures what Henry sees as his "truest place in the culture" (118). The spy genre is thus salient not only in how it allegorizes double consciousness but also in how the figure of the spy is the most exaggerated, crystalline version of the professional: someone who exchanges their identity for another, not as part of a contractual wage relationship but out of identification with an institution and an ideology. Despite his racial insecurity, Henry is economically quite secure. Henry's father left him "many millions," and long before his death he had driven home to Henry a very simple point: "You rich boy now" (149). However, Henry's father's bequest is a hoard, not capital: not the value in motion that Henry associates with whiteness. The counterpoint for Henry's uncertainty over the meaning of "need" is Lelia's father, Stew, the CEO of a "Boston-based holding company," whose whiteness and wealth know no uncertainty over petty concepts like "need": a point he emphasizes in the midst of a diatribe about a news segment on welfare recipients who say they "need" extravagances like "cable and long distance." "They probably do," Henry says. "Balls!" responds Stew (113). For Henry, Stew's whiteness inheres in his clarity about who needs what, his balance of economic and racial security. It is precisely this form of whiteness that he envies in Lelia: "what it was about Lelia that I desired and feared came partly through [Stew's] bloodline running through her" (111).

Moreover, the fact that Stew can tell exactly what Henry does for a living, despite Henry's not having told him and Lelia's refusing to say, emphasizes how Henry's need for his job is so strongly determined by his desire for whiteness. No matter his feelings of invisibility, he is perfectly legible in Stew's racial-professional schema.

When Henry and Lelia finally reconcile, it is not because Henry has undergone a psychological process in which he has somehow worked through his wounded attachment to racial identification. Instead, the whole problematic of racial identity is fundamentally transformed after he quits his job at Glimmer and takes up a new one as Lelia's assistant speech therapist. This is more than a straightforward career change: Henry symbolically traverses the liberal multiculturalism emblematized by Glimmer's Cold War configuration and arrives in a space of neoliberal multiculturalism. For Jodi Melamed, postwar liberal multiculturalism's domination of racial meanings constituted "a means of containing and managing [post–civil rights] social movements' deployment of culture by turning it into aesthetics, identity, recognition, and representation" (xix–xx). The culmination of neoliberal globalization in the 1990s displaces liberal multiculturalism with neoliberal multiculturalism's sorting of the world into two groups: "worthy multicultural citizens" and "losers" who are racialized as "unworthy and excludable on the basis of monoculturalism, deviance, inflexibility, criminality, and other historico-cultural deficiencies" (xxi).

The novel's final scene is keenly aware of this transition and the ironies it generates. We are brought into one of Lelia's ESL classes at a public elementary school on the Lower East Side. Henry dons a costume as a "Speech Monster" whose role is to act fierce and then cower when the children correctly pronounce a special phrase. At the end of the session, Henry takes off his "mask"/hood, and he and Lelia hug and kiss each child. Lelia distributes stickers and then "calls out each one as best she can, taking care of every last pitch and accent"; she speaks "a dozen lovely and native languages, calling all the difficult names of who we are." There are in American literature perhaps few more finely tuned deployments than this of the rhetoric of recognition. Despite the lesson plan consisting of "three active hours of video and mouth models and recorded sounds," the real point of it all is to "offer up a pale white woman horsing with the language to show them it's fine to mess it all up," and to have that same pale white woman speak each child's name with tonal authenticity (324).

However, this tender realization of liberal multiculturalism's pluralist dream is repeatedly ironized. For one thing, there are material limits to the dream of recognition portrayed here. Henry draws attention to the fact that "many freelancers rotate in these weekly assignments, and we probably won't see [the children] again this summer." Moreover, there is something cloying and supererogatory about Henry and Lelia's affection for the kids. Henry explains: "I tell them I will miss them. They don't quite know how to respond" (324). What the kids appear to be keenly aware of is the awkward simultaneity of economic and libidinal subjectivity: that what Henry and Lelia *actually* are is contingent contract workers whom they might never see again, *and* that Henry and Lelia are more than just coworkers (though, in my reading, not much more).

As we are informed a number of times, the stresses of defunded public schools are the conditions of Lelia's employment in the first place: "The city hires people like her to work with summer students whose schools don't have speech facilities, or not enough of them."[62] In the novel's opening pages, Lelia is burned out because "there are too many students in a class for her to make much difference"; and it is in part because of this burnout that she leaves to Italy (323). Henry and Lelia's reconciliation doesn't so much turn on the mending of their romantic relationship as their mutual realization that the work is easier when Lelia has help and that they work better together as what Alan Liu calls a "team." As Liu writes, the "team" in late capitalism is "a unit of ephemeral identity that most flexibly fuses technologies and techniques into skill sets (called 'innovation,' 'creativity,' or 'resourcefulness') adapted to the changefulness of the global economy."[63] It is, Liu goes on to argue, a "style of unreal identity . . . designed to 'simulate away' identity groups and class by incorporating them."[64] The team is a quintessentially neoliberal multiculturalist unit of social reproduction, and, accordingly, what Henry and Lelia offer up is a bravura performance of their status as "worthy multicultural citizens." Far from a rosy depiction of racial identity politics, neither is this a depiction of a straightforward class politics.

What saves Henry and Lelia's marriage, in other words, is Henry's (literal) embrace of his status as a member of the professional-managerial class (PMC). One of the most peculiar aspects of the PMC's structural position is the mismatch between its class status—that is, they are decidedly *not* owners of the means of production—and its relative power over the wage workers and surplus populations whose management they have been tasked to effectuate. Structurally aligned with the proletariat while at the same time ideologically and culturally identified with the bourgeoisie, the PMC's divided loyalties bear a strong resemblance to the classic trope of Asiatic racial form, inscrutability: a trope that itself derives from the antinomy of the model minority and perpetual foreigner. These resemblances precede and indeed prefigure the professional resemblances between post-65 Asian Americans and the PMC. Henry matches his PMC status to his post-65 Asian American identity.

By abandoning the liberal multiculturalist style that Kwang represents and embracing the PMC's multicultural politics, Henry's relation to race and class is mystified. In the same way that the Clinton administration signaled not the demise of the Reagan-Thatcher revolution but its apotheosis, Henry has by no means arrived on safer political shores. This mystification has nothing to do with any personal failing on his part, nothing that might have been named on the list, but instead with his material reorientation, via employment, to contemporaneous conditions of racial and economic subjectivity that are, in the early 1990s, undergoing radical change. *Native Speaker* is in many ways a novel *about* these changes.[65] Kwang's fortunes rise on the swelling waves of immigrants flooding into Queens and especially on the collective power of their informal economic relations. The children that Henry and Lelia tutor are members of these waves; they find themselves entering a world in which a pale white woman feels obliged to pronounce their names correctly: "lovely" and "difficult" words that, while not from Shakespeare, fulfill the same function of economic integration via the aesthetic mediation of racial identity.

These are features of the emerging mode of production whose contours *Native Speaker* is tracing (and whose themes Lee will not engage fully again until *On Such a Full Sea* in 2014). In a final, proleptic gesture, the novel turns its attention to one more feature of this regime pertaining to the consequences of a new phase of U.S. immigration law. Culminating in the 1990 Immigration Act, this phase is not a break from the 1965 act's reorientation to economic principles of selection but an intensification of those priorities. The 1990 act raised the annual ceiling on immigration by 35 percent, leading to a sharp rise in applications. It dramatically expanded existing temporary worker visa programs for highly skilled immigrants like the H-1B and created new "golden visa" programs like the EB-5 that offer foreign investors a pathway to citizenship. At the same time it dramatically decreased the number of slots offered to unskilled immigrants. As Mae Ngai explains, by further stratifying class distinctions between immigrant groups, "the legislation of the 1990s reconfigured the line between legal and illegal alienage, enlarging the grounds that turn legal immigrants into illegal aliens and making it nearly impossible for illegal aliens to legalize their status."[66] This is one of the reasons that "twenty-five years later, the unauthorized population in the United States has grown almost threefold, to an estimated 11.02 million."[67] A key legacy of the neoliberalization of this period has been the militarization of the southern border with Mexico and the intensification of enforcement and criminalization of illegal immigration: a development to which Henry, as it turns out, directly contributes. The anonymous client contracting his services is the Immigration and Naturalization Service, an agency of the Department of Justice from 1940 to 2003, and predecessor to the Immigration and Customs Enforcement and Customs and Border Protection agencies that were established under the aegis of the Department of Homeland Security.

Native Speaker registers but is unable to fully process or represent how this new immigration introduces complications to the dynamics between race and class, especially for Asian Americans and the Pacific ruling class. A striking example comes at the novel's end, when Henry is watching a segment on the evening news in which a reporter is interviewing some of the Chinese passengers from a smuggling ship that had run aground near Far Rockaway, Queens: "I listen closely to what they say. Or at least, how they are translated by a woman who sounds Chinese American, her tones over-round and bulky like Sherrie's. She imparts a formality and respect to their statements, and they seem to be interviewing for a position rather than telling their story, unceasingly nodding and bowing and grinning exuberantly with the joy of their good fortune. They keep repeating the words *America* and *new life*" (304). What might otherwise be a straightforward racialization of these undocumented immigrants is complicated by the mediation not just of a Chinese American voice but of one that has a specific tone of "formality and respect" and that suggests a specific social relation of waged employment: "they seem to be interviewing for a position" (304). Lurking behind this reconfiguration of racial and economic meanings is a neoliberal regime that also undermines the ideological synthesis of "America" and "new life." Lee draws this episode from a real event on June 3, 1993, in which a cargo ship called the Golden Venture ran aground near the Rockaway Peninsula. It carried nearly three hundred smuggled Chinese migrants, many of whom escaped the ship and tried to swim to shore; ten of them drowned.[68] By evoking the Golden Venture, Lee gestures at an analogy between Chinese and American capitalisms that he will later explore through the full-throated SF of *On Such a Full Sea* and the retro, postmodern picaresque of *My Year Abroad*—and that we will explore together in the next chapter through literary works by that analogy's preeminent interpreters: Chinese American women writers.

Chapter Four

GENRES OF DEPROFESSIONALIZATION

Economic Subjectivity and
Chinese American Women Writers

My job is my own only land.

—MAXINE HONG KINGSTON, *WOMAN WARRIOR*

The gloves are off. In "A Song for a Barbarian Reed Pipe," the last chapter of Maxine Hong Kingston's *The Woman Warrior: Memoirs of a Girlhood Among Ghosts* (1976), the narrator, Maxine, and her mother, Brave Orchid, finally go at it. Although their argument is instigated by what Maxine sees as her mother's plan to marry her off to an undesirable man, its focus quickly shifts to Maxine's future professional prospects. But it's kind of all the same thing: "Do you know what the Teacher Ghosts say about me?" Maxine says. "They tell me I'm smart, and I can win scholarships. I can get into colleges. I've already applied. I'm smart. I can do all kinds of things. I know how to get A's, and they say I could be a scientist or a mathematician if I want. I can make a living and take care of myself . . . I am not going to be a slave or a wife. . . . I'm never getting married, never!" (201–2). What is so striking here is that, for Maxine, imagining a professional future—and not just any future, but one in science or mathematics—is part and parcel of her struggle against prescribed forms of femininity, a struggle for which *Woman Warrior* is perhaps best known. "Chinese-feminine," as Maxine calls it at one point, is rejected here along with being a "slave or a wife," and "American-feminine" is rejected by cathecting lucrative, masculine professions in science or mathematics (11). As Christine So points out in her reading of the spate of Chinese American women's memoirs that were published in the wake of *Woman Warrior,* "acceptable forms of economic success can also be a marker of women's resistance to traditional gender roles."[1]

Yet the forces bringing professional identity to bear on femininity, and vice versa, far exceed any beef between mother and daughter or any designs that the "teacher ghosts" might have on their star pupil. In the late 1950s, when this fight takes place, Maxine could be only dimly aware of the emerging factors that would eventually coalesce in the process of occupational concentration and that would lead her to enroll at UC Berkeley with no fewer than eleven scholarships to support her intended major of engineering.[2] The confluence of these factors matters hugely to the fight between Maxine and her mother. When Maxine says that she could be a "scientist or a mathematician," the subtext she is activating is the history of her mother's erstwhile pursuit of the same professional path and her eventual failure to escape wifehood. Essentially, Maxine is saying that she will succeed where her mother failed and that times have changed since her mother's days in medical school in the late 1930s. If their fight were to have taken place today, however, Maxine's embrace of STEM fields might betray that she has yet to kick "the nerd syndrome," which is the revealing formulation that Sau-ling Wong once borrowed to refer to the temptations of whiteness, social status, and political quietude associated with the model minority stereotype. If, in Wong's words, rejecting the model minority means "abandoning traditionally 'safe' fields like science, engineering, or medicine," then it wasn't until Kingston's sophomore year at Berkeley, when she changed her major to English, that she finally kicked the nerd syndrome.[3] In the decades since *Woman Warrior*'s publication, occupational concentration has facilitated the injection of the nerd syndrome into the very DNA of Asian American identity—especially that of the Asian American author.

In a fundamental way, *Woman Warrior* is concerned not only with gender and race, which are the two dominant frameworks through which the memoir-cum-novel has been read, but also with how those categories have been shaped and directed by economic subjectivity. We might thus establish a continuity extending from *Woman Warrior* to a recent group of 1.5- and second-generation Chinese American women writers who debuted within recent years and whose debut works feature a very similar structure of concerns. One might include in this cohort Meng Jin, Ling Ma, Chanel Miller, Celeste Ng, Lucy Tan, Weike Wang, Xuan Juliana Wang, and Jenny Zhang. The parents of each of these writers (generally their fathers) were or are professionals (generally STEM professionals) who emigrated to the United States after 1965 for employment or education. Jin's parents are both scientists, and she herself intended to study physics in college. Ma's father is an economics professor, and her mother is an accountant. Ng's father was a physicist at NASA and her mother was a chemistry professor. Tan's parents both came to the United States from China for graduate study. Weike Wang's father is an engineer, and she herself has a BS in chemistry and a PhD in public health. Xuan Juliana Wang's father is an IT professional and computer repair technician. Zhang's father started but didn't complete a PhD in linguistics at NYU before becoming an IT professional. I include Chanel Miller, whose mother, a writer, emigrated from China and studied literature, as a limit case for understanding how these forms of economic and racial subjectivity exert a force beyond their empirical boundaries. As Miller explains in her memoir *Know My Name* (2019), attending Gunn High School in Palo Alto, California—a school whose student body is more than 45 percent Asian American, and where "winners of national math competitions were posted on windows" while "no one aspired to become a painter or sailor or literary recluse"—immersed her in the racialized culture of occupational concentration and the two cultures conflict.[4] With all of the writers in this cohort, my interest is how their particularity reveals their typicality as post-65 Northeast Asian American authors—their *social experience*, in other words, rather than their *personal experience*.[5] Taking this cohort's fiction as a whole, patriarchal dilemmas over professional identity, womanhood, and liberation feature prominently: sometimes as a two cultures conflict between the arts and sciences, sometimes as intergenerational conflict, and sometimes as the ressentiment that Susan Koshy calls "secondariness," a condition in which women immigrants are deprofessionalized or otherwise made dependent upon men for financial reasons and for citizenship.[6]

Key to this chapter's argument is that these authors' works often reflect aspects of their parents' biographies, especially those pertaining to professional identity. Jin's *Little Gods* (2020) centers on a brilliant Chinese physicist whose career fails to offer an escape from the limitations of motherhood. In Ma's *Severance* (2018), a novel informed by the Obama-era's strained U.S.-China relationship and set in a zombie pandemic, the protagonist's father is an economist and her mother a once-successful accountant. Miller's memoir is both an account of her sexual assault and struggle for justice as well as a *Künstlerbiografie* charting her path through tangles of cultural and professional expectations into subjectivity as a visual and literary artist: a path into art that resonates strongly with her mother's. The parents in Ng's debut novel *Everything I Never Told You* (2014) are, by profession, a history professor and a would-be doctor. Their daughter, Lydia, is pushed to the brink by her mother's tiger parenting. Tan's *What We Were Promised* (2018) is about a family of elite Chinese professionals who move back to Shanghai after years in the United States only to find themselves struggling with cultural difference and the isolation of career and wealth. Weike Wang's *Chemistry* (2017) features an unnamed Chinese American PhD student in chemistry and undercover creative writer who drops out of her PhD program. The stories in Xuan Juliana Wang's *Home Remedies* (2019) range formally from realism to allegory to SF and take as their subjects young Chinese and Chinese Americans navigating upward mobility and economic precarity in the midst of China's global rise, as well as characters like one story's computer scientist father whose rigid attachment to putatively logical thinking estranges him from his daughter. Finally, Zhang's short story collection *Sour Heart* (2017) focuses on the lives of impoverished Chinese artists who emigrated to the United States after the 1989 Tiananmen Square massacre, rejecting China's politics as well as its industrializing ethos, and struggle to live, make art, and raise children in New York City.

What these texts tellingly share is a thematic continuity with *Woman Warrior*'s interest in the inheritances of professional and feminine identity.[7] To be sure, such a thread could describe any number of novels, Asian American and non–Asian American alike. Making these works paradigmatic of post-65 Asian American literature as a whole is how these thematic continuities are sustained by the material processes underlying each of these authors' emergence *as* authors. These processes enter this cohort's texts, as well as *Woman Warrior*, through a fantasy of endless, science-led economic expansion in which scientific and technical professionals play heroic roles, and for which post-65 Asian America has become emblematic: the fantasy of social assimilation via economic mobility. This fantasy transforms what are largely political economic forces into the most deeply personal forms of conflict: like the fight between Brave Orchid and Maxine, in which rifts between mother and daughter and within Maxine's own sense of futurity and identity formation are so apparently private. As our previous chapters have attempted to show, this fantasy can be traced at least as far back as Northeast Asia's postwar struggle with "modernization." For us as readers and critics, the easy conceptual slippage between science fictionality and SF is due to a very particular kind of mediating fantasy called *genre*. The longing for form that genre names only ever gets us so far, however, and never ultimately closes the distance to its object either conceptually or aesthetically because, as with all longings, it can be satisfied only by the impossible: the gold of an ideal form extracted from the lead of concrete particularity. The brief descriptions here of the cohort's texts and their continuities with *Woman Warrior* certainly *appear* to be moving toward an account of a post-65 genre. But my point is that what is needed to understand the continuities among them is not a checklist of formal features but an engagement with the very autopoetic tendencies that transform a parent's life into their child's art, and how those tendencies are structurally determined. While psychological accounts of autopoetic irony in Asian American literature certainly provide forceful explanations for formal tendencies found in the work of specific authors, this chapter aims to account for how various material processes have come to constrain the formal tendencies in this cohort's Chinese American fiction.[8]

What I am after isn't a description of how a set of formal conventions reproduces itself, but instead how literary form mediates a racialized class of economic subjects and their conditions of emergence. As I argued in the introduction, the profile of familial and professional orientation sketched out above is strikingly consistent across post-65 Asian American authors, and even more so among Northeast Asian American and Chinese American writers. Importantly, while all of the above authors hold MFAs (with the exception of Kingston), this should not strike us as a contradiction of occupational concentration's STEM focus. If we approach occupational concentration not only as a demographic term but also as a dominant expression of the fantasy of economic mobility described earlier, it should instead strike us as affirmation of the libidinal identity of the arts and sciences within the fantasy of economic mobility. In many ways it is the advanced degree credential itself that satisfies this fantasy.[9]

If I am at pains to distance my approach in this chapter from a genre account, it is because genre offers one of two highly tempting frameworks for understanding how Chinese American fiction can be understood internally rather than through analogies with proximal but overly general categories like Asian American fiction and postwar American fiction (about which I will have more to say in a moment). The other framework is an essentialist one that centers race, culture, or both. What is Chinese American about post-65 Chinese American literature, my premise goes, is not an essence residing in the body of a specific author—a Chinese Americanness that we smuggle into our discourse when we say that a text is *by* a Chinese American writer. What makes it Chinese American is the complicated set of facts and contradictions that is conjured when we say that an author is *from* China and writing from the standpoint of a Chinese American. In the case of the preceding cohort of writers, their Chinese Americanness inheres in the narrative vehicle of occupational concentration, their characterization of feminist resistance to patriarchy, and the rich, dichotomous tension between the arts and sciences that reveals them as two sides of the same coin. The traces of these material relations, moreover, enable us to track science fictionality outside of the institutional and genre loci of SF. With the exception of *Severance* (even there, only after qualifications), these works are not readily described as SF, yet, as I explained in the introduction, they are under the sway of science fictionality's gravitational pull.

A significant challenge in telling this story, which is ultimately about the distinctiveness of Chinese American fiction, is that the itinerary of the post-65 Asian American author tracks quite closely with the rise of what Mark McGurl calls the "program era" of U.S. fiction, such that the science fictionality of post-65 Asian American fiction, the dialectic of its material conditions and formal articulations, brings it into resemblance with "program era" fiction, which also emerges under the sign of STEM. As McGurl argues, the postwar research university became "the realm not only of institutions but also of technologies, the hard and soft machines in and by which literature comes into being."[10] Although it is merely a coincidence that between 1965 and 2005 the number of creative writing programs in the United States rose from about a dozen to more than three hundred—that is, roughly by the same multiple, twenty-five, that the Asian American population increased over the same period—these are two histories of professionalization that, when viewed from the standpoint of literary history, might look startlingly the same.[11] Moreover, many of the signature features of program-era fiction, namely autopoesis and genre play, are also the sites in which the science fictionality of post-65 Asian American fiction is most pronounced. A similar and perhaps more potentially muddling set of features corresponds with the "genre turn," which critics like Andrew Hoberek and Jeremy Rosen have described as a trend, beginning in the late 1980s, in which writers of so-called "literary fiction" have adopted elements of "genre" fiction. Michael Chabon, Kazuo Ishiguro, Emily St. John Mandel, Cormac McCarthy, Ruth Ozeki, Colson Whitehead, and, indeed, Ling Ma are often cited as exemplars. A common feature of these accounts of program era, postwar, and genre-turn fiction is that they all default to an account of a general phenomenon in anglophone, and especially U.S. fiction. The larger issue I am grappling with here is that such accounts risk exchanging minority literary and social histories for the synthetic force of periodization and other modes of generalization. Daniel Hartley dubs this an "epic" critical scope that he finds emblematized by the work of Fredric Jameson: "A mind attuned to the shifts between modes of production or the transitions between stages within a single mode of production . . . is sketched out on so vast a scale as to lose all sight of the more immediate formal and political configurations in which literary works arise."[12] It is an approach, moreover, that Lisa Lowe warns about when she argues that that the "formal deviations" of Asian American literature "are misread if simply assimilated as modernist or post-modernist aesthetic modes."[13] Hartley is quick to offer this qualification, however: "In the context of a Marxist poetics . . . the epic mode of criticism is a necessary failure; its success relies on its being coupled with less sweeping modes of analysis."[14] The way I see it, an account of post-65 Asian American fiction as science fictional compels us to pause and reconsider our literary historical claims precisely at moments when the epic mode is at its most seductive.

In my attempt at describing an alternate genealogy of Chinese American fiction that *is not reducible* to the program-era, genre-turn, or even Asian American fiction, I will not stubbornly deny the gravitational pull of any of these. Instead I will try to find moments in which the interactions between all three are especially pronounced. Put slightly differently, an important part of this story is, as we saw in chapter 2, how occupational concentration has extended its domain over the profession of fiction writing such that the distance between, say, a computer program (writing like an engineer) and program fiction (writing like a professional author) has narrowed. Had *Woman Warrior*—part memoir, part fabulation, part novel—been published in 2016 rather than 1976, for instance, it might very well have been placed under the rubric of the genre turn. But as I will show, its approach to genre responds quite directly to occupational concentration. Among the tropes I take up in this chapter, occupational concentration—especially its narrative form, the drama of professional identity formation exemplified in Maxine and Brave Orchid's fight scene—is the red thread that allows us to track what is distinctly Asian American in broader processes of embourgeoisement and professionalization so strongly shaping the persona of postwar U.S. authors and the literature they produce. Professional identity formation isn't the whole story, but it is an aperture through which we can glimpse the interaction between occupational concentration as an economic process and its subject-level consequences. Where critics like McGurl and Sean McCann see in postmodern U.S. literature a fundamental resistance to the research university by an expanding PMC as emblematic of resistance to what McCann calls "bureaucratic confinement," post-65 Chinese American writers like Kingston are more likely to view the technoscientific research university as a space of freedom in which dilemmas pertaining to identity might be productively resolved.[15] Relatedly, a character like *Severance*'s protagonist Candace Chen sees office work and consumerism as adequate compensation for the lost plenitude of collegiate life. For Maxine and Candace, professional identity is one way to embrace a capitalist subjectivity that is a rosier alternative to secondariness and the incarceration of normative femininity. If the Asian American campus novel is a relatively new and small genre, then it is perhaps because the postwar technoscientific research university is such a fundamental precondition for post-65 Asian American literary expression that it goes without saying.[16] Therefore, to suggest that post-65 Asian American literature is always already campus fiction is another way of saying that it is all science fictional.

In this chapter, after accounting for the science fictionality of *Woman Warrior*, I leap ahead some forty years to examine the cohort of Chinese American writers mentioned earlier. My goal is not to provide an exhaustive account of these decades but to model a methodology for such an account by focusing on a hypercanonical text that has had an enormous downstream influence, and that is especially sensitive to science fictionality's subjective dimension via the register of fantasy. Across the post-65 period, literary articulations of science fictionality modulate between subjective and objective foci, and in this cohort's texts, I will be very interested in how China's geopolitical rise becomes one of the predominant drivers of this process and turn to a cohort case study to examine how science fictionality has become a predominantly *objective* condition. In this regard, *Severance* is emblematic of the new cohort's debut works. Its science fictional qualities are best understood when placed in relation to what we might call the *trope of China's rise*, which is a central locus in this cohort's texts. It appears mainly vis-à-vis narratives of professional identity formation that bring into relief the political and social contradictions particular to the Chinese American experience of China's rise.

DEPROFESSIONALIZATION IN *WOMAN WARRIOR*

Perhaps the most written-about text in Asian American literary studies, *Woman Warrior* has also enjoyed a wide readership outside of Asian American studies, especially in the fields of feminist criticism and autobiography studies. According to several anecdotal accounts, *Woman Warrior* was, at least at one moment in the late 1990s, the most widely read and taught literary text in U.S. colleges and universities by a living American author.[17] Of its five unnumbered chapters, the first, second, and fifth—"No Name Woman," "White Tigers," and "A Song for a Barbarian Reed Pipe"— have received the most attention and have been foundational to the development of Asian American critique. "No Name Woman," with its nod to Betty Friedan's "The Problem That Has No Name," is one of the most powerful depictions that we have of how the violence of patriarchy is sustained in mother-daughter relations, as erin Khuê Ninh has shown in her account of the "debt-bound daughter." Sau-ling Wong has shown how the feminist reimagining of the Fa Mulan folktale in "White Tigers" activates a tension between "necessity" and "extravagance" that allegorizes the internal conflicts of Asian Americanist critique. And the bullying scene at the center of "A Song for a Barbarian Reed Pipe" has become the paradigmatic illustration of what Anne Cheng calls "racial melancholia" and that King-Kok Cheung calls "articulate silence."[18]

If its third and fourth chapters, "Shaman" and "At the Western Palace," have been proportionally underexamined, it is perhaps because their focus on class instability does not obviously accord with the feminist, antiracist, and anti-orientalist politics of Asian American critique. While the argument I will be making is that these two chapters reveal how Kingston's feminism and formal choices are tied to a post-65 context, my intention is not to bring these chapters into line with the normative practices of Asian American critique. Instead, it is to demonstrate in this highly influential text how post-65 economic realities have generated strong social and aesthetic guidelines for Asian American subject formation and literary expression.

"At the Western Palace" opens with an extended scene of misrecognition at the San Francisco International Airport (SFO). The international terminal is filled with travelers milling about, and it is into this hubbub that Maxine's mother, Brave Orchid, has brought her children and her niece to pick up her younger sister, Moon Orchid, whose flight from Hong Kong has arrived early. As the passengers exit immigration and the customs checkpoint, Brave Orchid keeps mistaking various women for her sister. "There she is," she shouts, pointing to a woman so unlike her sister that "it shocked [her niece] to discover the woman her aunt was pointing out. This was a young woman, younger than herself" (116). Almost as soon as Brave Orchid realizes her error, she errs again when "another Moon Orchid" appears. Her niece finally makes a positive identification, spotting her mother on the other side of the glass partitions, making her way through customs. She yells, "Mama! Mama!" which strikes Brave Orchid as odd: "What a strange word in an adult voice. . . . like a child" (117). When Brave Orchid lays eyes on her sister, she is shocked: "*That* old lady? Yes, that old lady facing the ghost who stamped her papers *without questioning* her was her sister" (117, my emphasis). And when they are finally reunited—after thirty years of separation—the sisters, only one year apart in age, strike Maxine as "two old women with faces like mirrors." For a moment, they are each transfixed by the other's visage: "Their hands reached out as if to touch the other's face, then returned to their own, the fingers checking the grooves in the forehead and along the sides of the mouth" (118). On their way to the car, Moon Orchid accuses her older sister of "wearing an old mask to tease me" (119). Indeed, nothing quite lines up in this scene, epistemologically speaking. Visual information is unreliable and undermines assumptions about the normal flow of time. This irreconcilability intensifies and proliferates through the chapter, providing an objective correlative for Moon Orchid's unraveling sense of reality.

For Brave Orchid the scene at SFO dredges up memories of her own entry into the United States decades earlier: "These new immigrants had it easy [Brave Orchid thinks to herself]. On [Angel] Island the people were thin after forty days at sea and had no fancy luggage . . . [Angel] Island had been made out of wood and iron. Here everything was new plastic, a ghost trick to lure immigrants into feeling safe and spilling their secrets" (115). By the time Moon Orchid has arrived at the airport, the "wood and iron" world of Angel Island has transformed radically, into a "new plastic" world of deceptions and secrets—not least in terms of the labor skills and modes of production (industrialization, deindustrialization) indexed by each material.[19] Brave Orchid would have undergone a very different set of immigration screening protocols. After surviving "forty days at sea," she and other Chinese immigrants would have been subjected to medical examination, possible quarantine, and an entry interview whose goal was to extract points of fact that would be cross-checked against interviews with family members and fellow villagers. These interrogations were developed to ferret out "paper sons" who took advantage of the destruction of public records in the 1906 San Francisco fire by fraudulently claiming to be the children of American citizens. Paper sons and daughters would have to memorize almost comically minute details about the personas they claimed—the number of paces from the front door to a barn, for instance.

This is the kind of face-to-face and oddly intimate engagement with immigration authorities that Brave Orchid associates with "wood and iron" and that she contrasts from the impersonal yet somehow more threatening "plasticity" of her sister's experience. As Catherine Malabou argues, "plasticity" denotes both a capacity to "take form (as in the plasticity of clay) and to give form (as in the plastic arts and plastic surgery)."[20] What Brave Orchid registers here, in the taking and giving of form staged by her reunion with her sister, is the plasticity of the pre- and post-65 immigration regimes—a disorientation that quickly metabolizes into an anxiety over likeness. In *Woman Warrior* the logics driving resemblance and simile arise from anxieties pertaining to whether pre-65 Chinese America is *like* post-65 Chinese America. One way this distinction is made is through the apparent generic differences between the novel's chronologically pre- and post-65 chapters. "At the Western Palace" is the novel's pivotal chapter because it transitions readers from the magical realism and fabulation of the China chapters ("No Name Woman," "White Tigers," and "Shaman," which bring us up to the early 1940s) into the realism of the U.S. chapters ("At the Western Palace" and "A Song for a Barbarian Reed Pipe," which take place in the early 1970s). "At the Western Palace" facilitates this transition by mixing the fictionality of the China content with the realism of the U.S. content.

"At the Western Palace" reads like a straightforward realist narrative, but we later learn that it is an almost entirely imagined reconstruction of events based on thirdhand information: "In fact, it wasn't me my brother told [this story to]," Maxine explains; "one of my sisters told me what he'd told her" (163). To account for this genre reversal, critics have read *Woman Warrior* in terms of postmodern epistemology and formal experimentation. Indeed, McGurl holds it up as "perhaps *the* classic" of postmodern autopoetics.[21] In addition to these accounts, I propose that a salient feature of "At the Western Palace" is that it is a highly wrought product of what Yoon Sun Lee has described as Maxine's "laborious narrative work of mediation."[22] The question that then arises is *why* she chooses to undertake this not inconsiderable task. Why, moreover, would these events be so important to her that she displaces her pride of place in her own memoir even more than she had in the previous two chapters? The answer has to do with the stakes of professional identity as a solution to limitations of traditional femininity and how her mother's professional narrative models this strategy.

"At the Western Palace" and its predecessor, "Shaman," together form a narrative arc about Brave Orchid's deprofessionalization, and in so doing reveal *Woman Warrior*'s orientation to science fictionality. "Shaman" is an account of Brave Orchid's medical training in the mid-1930s and her subsequent years practicing as a field medic in the rural areas of Guangdong Province during the Japanese invasion of 1938. In its opening scene we find Maxine marveling over her mother's diploma, which cites her as possessing "Proficiency in Midwifery, Pediatrics, Gynecology, 'Medicine,' 'Surgary,' Therapeutics, Opthalmology, Bacteriology, Dermatology, Nursing, and Bandage [sic]" (57). As outlandish as this spread of specializations might appear, it is very much in line with the modernizing ethos of the Republican era in China and its emphasis on importing Western science. Indeed, at the beginning of her training, Brave Orchid and her fellow students are told, while gathered in an auditorium under a portrait of Dr. Sun Yat-Sen, "You will bring science to the villages" (63). Yet a different, if related, form of liberation was on Brave Orchid's mind when she decided to enroll in medical school. As she recounts to Maxine, she left her husband's family's household, where she was living at the time, in order to be "free from families" and to "live for two years without servitude" (62). Kingston has a second-wave feminist ethos very much in mind when she emphasizes how Brave Orchid's name is actually emblematic of the liberatory potential of the career: "Professional women have the right to use their maiden names if they like. Even when she emigrated, my mother kept Brave Orchid, adding no American name nor holding one in reserve for American emergencies" (77).

By the time we arrive at "At the Western Palace," decades have passed since Brave Orchid received her degree, and much has changed. "You have no idea how much I have fallen coming to America," Brave Orchid tells Maxine (77). This is a key point not just for our reading of *Woman Warrior* but for making sense of post-65 Asian American fiction. Differences in training and her lack of English meant that Brave Orchid could no longer practice medicine in the United States (149). Instead she spends long hours working in her husband's laundry. Thus, while her professional and class statuses in the United States carry with them an abject racial charge, they in fact conceal the complicated itineraries of how those statuses transform across the space-times of immigration. What is important is not that Brave Orchid works in a laundry, but that she doesn't see herself as the kind of person who works in a laundry and that, had fate intervened differently, she should by rights be enjoying a far loftier class position. In many ways these two chapters in *Woman Warrior* are entirely about rectifying these status contradictions by any means necessary—including bullying and the total embrace of fantasy.

It is for these reasons that even though Moon Orchid is ostensibly the protagonist of "At the Western Palace," the chapter's plot actually centers on Brave Orchid and the caper she hatches to reunite Moon Orchid with her long-estranged husband, from whom she has been separated for some thirty years. In those decades of separation Moon Orchid's husband started two things: a successful medical practice as a brain surgeon and a second family with a young Chinese American wife. For Brave Orchid this situation is totally unacceptable, but for Moon Orchid, who was living a comfortable life in Hong Kong funded by her husband's generous remittances, the situation had been, well, pretty darn great (125). Nonetheless, Brave Orchid convinces Moon Orchid to go along with her plan to drive the three hundred miles from Stockton to her husband's office in "a skyscraper in downtown Los Angeles" and force him to take her back (146). When they arrive, Brave Orchid tells Moon Orchid to wait in the car as she goes up to

GENRES OF DEPROFESSIONALIZATION

the office to scope out the scene. After weeks of living with her sister cheek-by-jowl, Brave Orchid finally has a few moments to herself. Entering the building, she finds the "lobby was chrome and glass, with ashtray stands and plastic couches arranged in semicircles" (147). Once she exits the elevator into the medical office's waiting room, we get a hint of the true reason why Brave Orchid hatched this plan in the first place: "A roomful of men and women looked up from their magazines. She could tell by their eagerness for change that this was a waiting room. Behind a sliding glass partition sat a young woman in a modern nurse's uniform. . . . It was an expensive waiting room. Brave Orchid approved. The patients looked well dressed, not sickly and poor" (147–48). What a weird reaction! "Brave Orchid approved." This description of the lobby echoes that of the waiting area at SFO, with its glass partitions and "new plastic," even as it parallels Brave Orchid's envy and resentment for how easy the "new immigrants" have it (115). But why is her reaction to the waiting room one of *approval*? One answer may be found in the play of similes that opens the chapter—the trope of likeness that mediates the difference between pre- and post-65 immigration regimes. In her efforts to recruit Moon Orchid into her scheme, Brave Orchid tells her at one point, "He's a doctor *like* me" (149, my emphasis). Condensed into Brave Orchid's approval is an identification with Moon Orchid's husband's profession as a doctor, and perhaps also a vertiginous realization that if she had immigrated *after* 1965 that medical office, or one like it, could well have been her own. She never utters the words *social assimilation via economic mobility*, but that fantasy engulfs the room.

Even as Maxine inherits her mother's investment in the connection between science and liberation from patriarchy, the science fictionality of *Woman Warrior* isn't limited to that inheritance. Where that inheritance opens onto the broader context of post-65 science fictionality is when the memoir turns to the problem of Maxine's academic and professional future, which, as we saw earlier, is consistently oriented to scientific and technical fields. It is Maxine's antipatriarchal investment in science fictionality that helps us to unlock the mystery of the last two sentences of "At the Western Palace": "Brave Orchid's daughters decided fiercely that they would never let men be unfaithful to them. All her children made up their minds to major in science or mathematics" (160). Laura Hyun Yi Kang has called these sentences "cryptic"; Sau-ling Wong has called them a "non-sequitur."[23] I read them as conclusions overdetermined by the pressures of occupational concentration, which at this point, in the early 1970s, are still emergent and only perceptible as structures of feeling. "Science or mathematics" refers not only to academic and professional fields but also to an emerging post-65 Asian American social formation in which professional values promise to supersede the cultural values of pre-65 Chinese immigrants. Brave Orchid might have arrived too early to catch the wave of occupational concentration, but her daughters are right on time.

SHENZHEN DRIFT

Imagine, for a moment, Brave Orchid sitting down to share a meal with Ruifang Yang, the mother of the protagonist of Ling Ma's 2018 novel *Severance*. They might chat about the differences between their immigration experiences: Brave Orchid's arrival by ship at Angel Island in the 1930s and Ruifang's arrival by airplane in Salt Lake City in 1988 to join her husband, a would-be literature professor whose exam scores unhappily funnel him into a PhD in economics at the University of Utah (170). They might commiserate over their shared sense of isolation in the United States and their negative feelings about assimilation. But where they would truly bond would be over the topic of deprofessionalization. Brave Orchid would recount to Ruifang the story of how far she has fallen since emigrating to the United States, and Ruifang would tell Brave Orchid the story of "how far she had come" in her hometown of Fuzhou, where "she had been a certified accountant, and she counted among her clients various city and regional government officials" (172, 176). She would explain that she had to give all of that up in order to join her husband and that the only work she could find in the United States was piecework for a wig manufacturer (173). The two women would recognize in each other a ressentiment roiling around their shared secondariness. At this point in their conversation they might opt to change the subject to their hopes for and worries over their daughters. Ruifang might convey to Brave Orchid, as she did to her daughter Candace, what she and her husband wanted most dearly for Candace when they chose to emigrate to the United States: "I just want for you what your father wanted: to make use of yourself.... No matter what, we just want you to be of use" (190).[24]

My point here is that these very different characters and very different books share deep similarities, perceptible here in characterization and theme. And while genre might count as another one of these differences, it is a bit of a red herring. Where *Woman Warrior*'s orientation to science fictionality is interior and psychologically mediated, and resolved aesthetically as magical realism ("talk-story" as Kingston calls it), *Severance*'s is right there on the surface as SF. That said, each novel's approach to genre—the work that each tasks genre with doing—is similar insofar as each responds to science fictionality. The conspicuously fantastical elements of *Woman Warrior* (i.e., the mundane existence of ghosts) are a mediation of traditional culture and the science fictionality of China's modernization throughout the 1930s. This is most clearly illustrated in the chapter "Shaman," in which Brave Orchid and her medical school classmates engage in intense debates over their empirical observations about ghost behavior in their dormitory. *Severance* tasks its SF conceits with the same mediating function. Set in New York City in the year 2011, *Severance*'s conceit is a mysterious pandemic that has stricken much of the world, dooming its victims to a zombie-like state in which they are locked to a location, performing gestures in an endless time loop until their bodies waste away.[25] The disease, called "Shen Fever," is believed to be a fungal infection and is named after Shenzhen, the iconic industrial hub in southeast China, providing a rather on-the-nose allegory for Chinese capital that lowers the barriers of national difference, allowing for easier traffic of comparison. Shen Fever provincializes the United States and China alike (as well as Chinese American and Chinese identity, as we will see in a moment) even as it secretes an orientalist residue.

The novel's settings in deserted, postapocalyptic cities and malls are familiar conventions of the zombie genre as shaped by George Romero's *Night of the Living Dead* (1968) and Boris Sagal's *The Omega Man* (1971). However, much like Colson Whitehead's *Zone One* (2011), which many reviewers have cited as similar in style and approach to genre, *Severance* evades genre classification. For instance, its zombies aren't really zombies, but instead "the fevered." They're harmless and don't horde together or offer up on-the-nose allegories for race or class in the way that, say, Romero's living dead do for black-white racial conflict, and Whitehead's locating of the titular Zone One's base of operations in a Chinatown bank, Fort Wonton, draws the novel's zombies into an allegory of Chinese capital.[26] Moreover, the ambient threat so common to the zombie genre is, in *Severance*, converted into relentless banality, outdoing even *Zone One*. The "drift" of zombie conventions brings our attention to what is contemporary about the novel. As Theodore Martin puts it: "By holding certain features steady... genres first draw our attention to what changes; then they compel us to ask why."[27] Like *Zone One*, *Severance* seems like an obvious instance of the "genre turn" in anglophone fiction, which, as I have been arguing, has generally been understood as a recent phenomenon—after 1989-ish—in which the conventions of putatively low genre forms like SF, horror, and fantasy are accepted into the auspices of something called "literary fiction." But if we think of genre as an expression of what Martin calls "historical tendencies" rather than sets of formal features and hierarchies that distinguish (however provisionally, psychoanalytically, or market-oriented) between high and low, then, as it turns out, *Severance* has more in common with *Woman Warrior* than *Zone One*. *Severance* and *Zone One* might share the niche genre of the zombie office novel, but we shouldn't allow their formal resemblances to obscure either the differences in how they got there, or the deeper resemblances between them (i.e., Brave Orchid and Ruifang's shared deprofessionalization).

Together with our cohort's texts, *Severance* demonstrates how the "epic" literary histories that we have assembled—about postwar fiction, the genre turn, Asian American fiction—might benefit from disambiguation, not so much to salvage any of these concepts or periodizations but to understand how genre forms and social forms interoperate, especially in minority literatures. For instance, disambiguation might reveal evidence of a suggestion that Andrew Hoberek and Min Hyoung Song have each made, which is that Asian American literature anticipated the genre turn.[28] What more genre-turn-y text than *Woman Warrior*? In 1976 it was a clear outlier in what was then still a very small and stylistically uniform archive of Chinese and Asian American writing.[29] Elaine Kim, Robert G. Lee, and other critics have referred to this era as the "goodwill" or "ambassadorial" period in which U.S. writers of Asian descent like Pardee Lowe, Jade Snow Wong, and Younghill Kang sought through their writing and self-fashioning to "demonstrate how acceptable" they were to "American society."[30] As previous chapters have shown, the explosion of Asian American SF following this period tracks occupational concentration and its articulation with industrializing Asian economies that are producing more STEM professionals than their economies can absorb. Even when post-65 Asian American literature unambiguously takes the form of SF, we need to understand that genre status as an extreme focalization of science fictionality. And just as SF is an extreme focalization of science fictionality, the focalization of Asian Americans into STEM fields is an extreme form of the more general process of occupational concentration. It matters how Asian American authors got with the program (era).

What historical tendency is revealed in the science fictionality of post-65 Chinese American literature? It would help to sharpen this question with another: What is the literary function of China, Chineseness, and the trope of China's rise? Science fictionality conjures new forms when its imagined locus of industrialization shifts from the United States to China and its imagined ideal subjects begin to resonate with the prestige of global capital over against the racial form of nationally specific identities, a process that results in what Jane Hu calls "generic Asian-ness."[31] The debuts by these several Chinese American women writers offer us a useful sample for exploring these questions. In each of them we detect resonances with Kingston's negotiation of feminine and professional identity in *Woman Warrior*, and especially with how the figure of "China" intervenes in processes of Asian American and Chinese American identity formation that are already strongly influenced by occupational concentration's narrowing of life choices. This scenario aptly summarizes the central conflict in Lucy Tan's *What We Were Promised*, where one of the main characters grapples with deprofessionalization upward (the reverse, one might say, of Moon Orchid's itinerary): away from a life of career ambition in the United States and into a life in glitzy, twenty-first-century Shanghai as a "taitai," slang for "ladies of luxury who could not be called housewives because . . . they did no housework at all."[32] The mother of *Chemistry*'s unnamed protagonist might identify strongly with Ruifang's homesickness (but for Shanghai, not Fuzhou) and with her investments in beauty and STEM careers as stabilizers of the untenable agon of Chinese American–ness.

Puzzles of aesthetic, economic, and transnational identity also motivate the stories in Xuan Juliana Wang's *Home Remedies* and are most pronounced in the story "*Fuerdai* to the Max."[33] Like a *Better Luck Tomorrow* (2003) for the Orange County parachute-children set, the characters in this story, the *fuerdai*, are the bling-blingy scions of Chinese nouveau riche, sent alone to the United States as teenagers for an American education. Ignored by and indistinguishable to Asian Americans and non–Asian Americans alike, hovering indeterminately between Chinese and American, they are left with nothing but the shibboleths of global capital to anchor their identities. Their uncertain social status is further complicated by the hazy origins of their money: Does it come from political connections, the black market, or legitimate business? These are the factors that set the stage for the story's central conflict, in which Lily's reputation is besmirched by another girl, Wey, who is jealous of Lily's enormous wealth and accuses her of being an escort. Here, collapsed into the trope of twenty-first-century Chineseness, is the crystallized telos of narratives of occupational concentration: the absolute reduction of identity to economic subjectivity, and the ejection of professional identity as a meaningless waypoint in that itinerary.

The transformation of China's rise into a trope for the objective dimension of Chinese American economic identity also appears in Jenny Zhang's *Sour Heart*. There the logics driving resemblance and similarity arise from a historical comparison between China's pre-1989 ideological threat and China's post-1989 economic threat. The story "Our Mothers Before Them" exposes this structure by toggling sections of the narrative between the Cultural Revolution in 1966 and Washington Heights in 1996. In addition to an anxiety over historical analogy, another resonance with *Woman Warrior* is the theme of deprofessionalization. One of the titular mothers, Li Huiling, is tormented by her diminished status in the United States. In contrast to Brave Orchid, Huiling experiences this diminishment as a deaestheticization. A talented singer and aspiring film starlet in her Shanghai youth, she abandons her ambitions after Tiananmen to follow her artist husband to the United States. In what we might read as a modification of the two sentences at the end of "At the Western Palace," in which Maxine and her sisters resolve to major in "science and mathematics," Zhang depicts Huiling's children trying to assuage their mother's regrets: "I'll never attempt art when I get older. Only a sadist—a self-centered sadist—would put his family through that."[34] Occupational concentration—depicted here as rejecting the arts—resonates not only with a post-65 process originating in U.S. immigration policy. It also gives figure to a U.S.-China political unconscious in which science fictionality is mediated by the China trope's relentless economism: its flattening of Chineseness and Chinese American-ness into modes of subjectivity whose rejection of the arts and implicit privileging of the sciences is a no-brainer for a fundamentally economic ethos.

GENRES OF DEPROFESSIONALIZATION

A key indication that genre has drifted between *Woman Warrior* and this cohort's recent texts and yet retained its orientation is that the latter registers China as a material reality rather than an abstraction (for example, the private site of verification that Maxine has in mind when she declares, "I want to go to China and find out who's lying").[35] This dimension is often mediated by displacements of the two-cultures antinomy. Such displacements are registered, perhaps unexpectedly, in Chanel Miller's memoir *Know My Name*. Miller's mother, May May, is a well-known Chinese feminist writer who, Miller tells us, was famously featured in Wu Wenguang's celebrated 1990 documentary film *Bumming in Beijing: The Last Dreamers*, which tracks five bohemian artists before and after the events in Tiananmen—the same kind of post-Tiananmen exiles in the United States who are the subjects of *Sour Heart*.[36] Writing under her Chinese name, Zhang Ci, she is best known for a highly influential 1988 essay, "Life Alone," in which she claims an artistic identity as a writer by way of rejecting what Maxine would call "Chinese-feminine" as well as the (generally STEM-oriented) professional trajectories entailed by China's reform-era alignment of human capital development with its rapid industrialization. Thus, when Miller writes to her mother in the acknowledgments to *Know My Name*, "I grow in the direction of you," she captures with moving efficiency a two cultures dynamic that elevates artistic identity as an ideal of self-expression, but that also significantly mediates what Rey Chow calls a post-Tiananmen "transaction of ethnicity" in which Chinese artistic identity is inseparable from Chinese dissident political identity.[37] Crucially, this convergence of identities—mother's and daughter's, Chinese American and Chinese—is motivated by Miller's resistance to occupational concentration, which she pathologizes when she recounts a streak of student suicides at her high school in 2009, many by Asian Americans.[38]

The comorbidity of occupational concentration, expressed as toxic, STEM-oriented academic standards, helps to clarify the rather complicated historical orientations of Celeste Ng's *Everything I Never Told You*. The formal device organizing the novel's plot is a two-cultures trope subjected to a series of gendered and racial inversions: STEM is aligned with the white American Marilyn Lee, rather than her Chinese American husband, James Lee, a history professor. The narrative that follows explores the consequences of these inversions, which can only really be cathected with reference to the racial form of occupational concentration. Marilyn's aspirations to become a doctor are scuttled by her mother, who enforces the traditional gender roles that Maxine would label "American-feminine," and who Marilyn resolves, very much like Maxine, never to become. Marilyn transfers her aspirations to her daughter, Lydia, who struggles to meet her mother's high—and field-specific—academic expectations. Meanwhile, James's affair with a Chinese American graduate student is an explicit attempt at resolving feelings of being out of place academically, culturally, and racially that the novel meticulously traces back to his childhood as a poor, second-generation Chinese American isolated in 1940s Iowa. These conflicts hinge entirely upon the novel's setting in 1977. Situated just prior to Deng Xiaoping's inauguration of China's "Reform and Opening" era in 1978 and to the full normalization of U.S.-China relations in 1979, the 1977 U.S.-China relationship was one still largely defined by symbolic diplomatic gestures rather than the deep economic relations that have since joined both countries at the hip. Although this earlier phase of U.S.-China relations is barely depicted in the novel, it is nonetheless the sine qua non that enables Ng to bypass the unignorable, too-big-to-fail U.S.-China relationship of 2014, when the novel is published, and confine China and Chineseness entirely to the registers of the libidinal and affective. The concrete reality of China's economic rise is therefore registered precisely in its diegetic absence: a key part of the "everything" we are never told.

The post-65 features of these narratives—occupational concentration, the two cultures, gendered professional identity formation—certainly resonate with Amy Ling's foundational account of pre-1990 Chinese American women writers as negotiating a "between-worlds condition . . . that is characteristic of all people in a minority position" and a patriarchy for which being a woman writer "is not only an act of self-assertion but an act of defiance" (177, 1). They also offer us opportunities to situate these works and their authors in a specific historical context, and to unpack political complexities that do not solely follow the path of "defiance." In particular, they confirm Christine So's insight that "Chinese women's history [has become] a means of negotiating a global capitalist present."[39] China and Chineseness offer these writers means for evading occupational concentration and its Scylla and Charybdis of "Chinese-feminine" and "American-feminine." If *Woman Warrior*'s heroic professional fantasies were sustained by the momentum of China's agon with modernization in the 1930s, leading into the science fictionality of the early post-65 years, then four decades of those fantasies' displacements and deflations shape the science fictionality in *Severance*. The future itself—empty but for the frisson of Chinese capital—joins the casualties in *Severance*'s postapocalyptic setting, revealing itself as akin to the nationalism parodied in *Zone One*'s ironically named "American Phoenix," whose numbers-driven, corporate sponsored management of American civilization's rebound smacks of more of the same rather than its moniker's suggested rebirth. In *Severance*, if there ever was a future to speak of, it was in Shenzhen, not New York City.

Severance is a novel less about the heroic potential of science than it is about terminal economic stagnation that can only be imagined in national terms: the final severance of science fictionality's fantasies of expansion from the conditions that sustained them. Whereas in *Woman Warrior* science fictionality is detected in the attachment of science to women characters, in *Severance* science fictionality is detected in both the detachment of science from character and the relegation of science to the aesthetic—specifically, to the register of genre SF. While a genre-turn analysis of *Severance* might stop here, we may forge ahead to see that what distinguishes it from *Zone One*'s similar depiction of stagnation (most strikingly in the resemblance between its "stragglers" and *Severance*'s "fevered") is a dialectical working through of dilemmas in Chinese American identity. The exaggeration of the collapse of social and temporal relations as a result of prolonged economic stagnation in this allegory of the apocalypse merely intensifies what is a very real consequence of China's rise for the coherence of Chinese American identity, especially for paradigmatic post-65 professionals like Candace.

From our historical vantage point, if Maxine's commitment to science and mathematics is less than liberatory and instead charts a path out of the frying pan of normative femininity into the fryer of the PMC, then *Severance* makes this fraught pathway literal. For Candace Chen, a white-collar office job at the book manufacturing firm Spectra is initially an escape from the unfreedom of post-college unemployment and precarity, yet it's ultimately a prison sentence that she oddly embraces. Rather than revolt against the imprisonment of career and wage labor, as her white boyfriend Jonathan does, Candace finds comfort in it. In response to his question, "Why do you want to work a job you don't really even believe in?" Candace wants to answer but doesn't say out loud, "The way you choose to live is a luxury.... You think it's possible to opt out of the system.... In this world, money is freedom. Opting out is not a real choice."[40] Again, she *thinks* these responses but doesn't voice them.

Here the contradiction between racial identity and economic subjectivity running throughout the novel determines her "articulate silence" (to refer to King-kok Cheung's term for this prevalent trope in Asian American women's writing). That silence reflects Ma's habit of stopping just short of explicit racial markers, even when they are threatening to erupt through the surface. What Candace is clearly critiquing is Jonathan's cisgender, heterosexual white privilege. In other words, her silence is more than just a dilemma of deracinated economic subjectivity—the fate, as it were, of the "neoliberal subject" or the "post-Fordist" worker. What we might call Candace's and Ma's postracial affect is symptomatic of the perennially unresolved status of Chinese American racial form as it articulates to a specific moment in U.S.-China economic relations.[41] An anthropomorphic racial form that has been governed by the inhuman trope of economic subjectivity since the nineteenth century, it poses challenges for calibrating a vocabulary of race and racism. The racial form that hovers about Candace has everything to do with her convergence with the capitalist system, which she describes here as a kind of opting in and which amounts to a dissipation of racial form rather than a deracination. As I argued in chapter 2, such dissipation moves Asian racial form away from mimetic markers like Frantz Fanon's "epidermal racial schema" into other registers that are nonvisible, narrative, and relational.[42]

The complex process of economic subjectivity's absorption of racial subjectivity reaches its climax when Candace is touring a factory in Shenzhen. Candace's job at Spectra is to work with U.S.-based "publishers who paid [Spectra] to coordinate book production that we outsourced to printers in Southeast Asia, mostly China" (10–11). As a middle-level manager, Candace produces nothing but instead facilitates the smooth operation of a global supply chain. While touring one of her vendor's factories in Shenzhen, she realizes that her Chinese identity and her Chinese American identity are incoherent to the factory workers showing her around. After some awkward attempts at making conversation with her rudimentary Chinese, Candace realizes that the workers see her as neither Chinese nor Chinese American, and perhaps not even as American. Instead they see her, if they see her at all, as an economic entity: "The workers looked up at me with benign expressions as we walked past. My first impulse was to smile, but it seemed condescending. I didn't know them. I didn't know what their jobs were or what their lives were like. I was just passing through. I was just doing my job."[43] Bereft of Chineseness, or even Chinese Americanness, the only way Candace can connect with the workers is a smile, which they would find condescending because she is a buyer first and foremost. In her embrace of "passing through" and "just doing my job," we see Candace opting into the global supply chain. By thus converging with economic subjectivity, Candace brings into relief the post-65, Chinese American racial form that her mother once adumbrated: a usefulness with no use. Abject as it might seem, this is a compromise formation forged through the material processes underlying deprofessionalization, the shifting meanings of femininity, and occupational concentration. We misunderstand the historical variability of Asiatic racial form if we merely see in Candace a person who has yet to "kick the nerd syndrome": a model minority in the purely economic sense who cynically ignores opportunities for solidarity and critique, and whose horizon of ethical development is limited to the ever-narrowing racial liberalism of a fading U.S. empire.

Severance's indeterminate drift through the genres of the zombie novel, SF, literary fiction, the office novel, and any number of other genres tracks a drift of material relations from the United States to China. If, as Istvan Csicsery-Ronay Jr. argues, SF has historically served to manage "the abstract techno-political leap forward out of 'domestic' culture, from a nation among nations to a global culture," then the tendency to drift between genres— exhibited by *Severance*, *Woman Warrior*, and the debuts of the Chinese American writers discussed earlier—is connected to the ongoing, increasingly urgent recalibration of Asian American, and especially *Chinese* American, identity and racial forms in relation to China's rise.[44] Converging with economic subjectivity—embracing the nerd syndrome rather than "kicking" it—isn't a story just about model minoritization but a turn from the untenable genres of normative femininity to the perhaps less untenable genres of professional identity. Tracking the science fictionality of post-65 Asian American literature reveals how this turn is neither an entirely private process, nor one available to universalization. It is a process conditioned by the drifting meanings of "Chinese" and "American" and "Chinese American"—meanings that drift between Stockton and New York City, Mexico and India, Chicago and Shenzhen. In post-65 Asian American literature, Chinese American identity and "just doing my job" converge with one another.

As I hope this chapter has made clear, there is nothing smooth or seamless about this process of convergence or the global drift of meanings and political economic relations underlying its logic. In the next chapter we will examine more closely one dynamic of human capital circulation between the United States and Asia: fictionalized narratives of return. Going back is always complicated, but few have expressed those complications as efficiently as Candace's uncle in *Severance*, who, upon seeing his brother (her father, the prodigal "capitalist" son) for the first time in more than a decade, berates him thus: "You can't just come back. You can't just come back. You can't just come back."[45]

Chapter Five

ENOUGH?

Semiperipheral Structures of Feeling in the Taiwanese American Novel

> Taiwan exists in the between.
>
> —FUNIE HSU, BRIAN HIOE, AND WEN LIU, "COLLECTIVE STATEMENT ON TAIWAN INDEPENDENCE"

This chapter takes up the question of how Taiwanese American authors have grappled with forms of betweenness. These forms emerge from contradictions linking the racial and class status of Taiwanese Americans to the semiperipherality of Taiwan itself.[1] The bulk of Taiwanese American fiction has appeared in the last twenty-five years and is in many ways the paradigm of Min Hyoung Song's account of Asian American literature as a production of "the children of 1965."[2] This timing has marked Taiwanese American fiction in two ways. First, more so than other Northeast Asian American literatures, it has become strongly and self-consciously shaped by post-65 occupational concentration and the concerns of an upwardly mobile professional-managerial class (PMC). A class that Barbara and John Ehrenreich famously defined as a "derivative class" that is "concerned with the reproduction of capitalist culture and class relationships," the PMC is a class constituted by betweenness.[3] It is at once materially aligned with the working class and ideologically aligned with the interests of capital. Compounding these alignments has been the globalization of Taiwanese American PMC status in the post-65 period due to the "brain circulation" of human capital.[4] Moreover, the awkward noncorrespondence between economic success, geographical mobility, and racial abjection that has increasingly defined Asian American racial form, and is amplified in the case of Taiwanese Americans, has compelled Taiwanese

American authors to engage with race and racial hierarchy through autopoetic forms of irony.

Second, Taiwan's geopolitical positioning has generated its own forms of cognitive dissonance. A small country with a deep history of multiple colonizations, its postwar economic growth launched it into "semiperipheral" status in the 1970s. In Immanuel Wallerstein's well-known schema,

> The core-periphery distinction . . . differentiates those zones in which are concentrated high-profit, high-technology, high-wage diversified production (the core countries) from those in which are concentrated low-profit, low-technology, low-wage, less diversified production (the peripheral countries). But there has always been a series of countries which fall in between in a very concrete way, and play a different role. The productive activities of these semi-peripheral countries are more evenly divided. In part they act as a peripheral zone for core countries and in part they act as a core country for some peripheral areas.[5]

A central feature of semiperipherality is an alignment with the interests and needs of the core, which reflects at a macro scale the structure of interests that defines the PMC, making it, as Petrus Liu has argued, a kind of geopolitical model minority.[6] Consistent with this alignment, a "Taiwanese imperial desire," to use Chen Kuan-Hsing's phrase, was first announced in the 1994 "moving southward" (*nánxiàng*) policy that encouraged Taiwanese investment in Southeast Asia. All the while the country was at work capturing a crux in the global semiconductor supply chain that now serves as a "Silicon Shield" against Chinese invasion.[7] As I showed in chapter 1, Taiwan's semiperipherality, cultivated by the United States and Japan, entailed the reproduction of the core's STEM human capital priorities, and was a key factor contributing to the overproduction of STEM professionals on one side of the Pacific and the phenomena of hyper-selection and occupational concentration on the other.[8] Semiperipherality and the Taiwanese American PMC, in other words, are dialectically related facets of Taiwan's betweenness.

Looming over all of this is the geopolitical and discursive presence of the People's Republic of China. To be sure, China looms over twenty-first-century Asian American racial and literary forms more generally, but for Taiwanese Americans and Taiwanese American fiction it has had very specific effects. The tangle of historical, political, emotional, familial, and cultural issues that constitute the China-Taiwan conflict is captured with uncomfortable efficiency in the title of Melissa J. Brown's 2004 book *Is Taiwan Chinese?* But the more recent economic interdependency between the countries suggests that an inversion of the question is equally salient: Is China's economy Taiwanese? Within Taiwan these dilemmas and ambiguities have resulted in an array of positions on reunification and independence, with the vast majority of Taiwanese nonetheless rejecting reunification and preferring instead the continuation of the status quo's betweenness, in which Taiwan is effectively a sovereign nation.[9] Moreover, Taiwanese national identity and Taiwanese American identity have been vexed by a number of befuddling discourses. Preeminent among them is the nearly half-century-old U.S. policy of "strategic ambiguity" toward Taiwan, in which the United States refrains from clarifying whether it would intervene if China attempted to retake Taiwan. More prevalent in daily life are the times when Taiwan and China are conflated in sociological studies and legislation, or the indignities of Taiwanese athletes competing under the banner of "Chinese Taipei." The deteriorating U.S.-China relationship, furthermore, has increasingly compelled Taiwanese Americans to equivocate on their national origin. At the same time these same tensions have inspired some Taiwanese Americans to be more vocal about their Taiwanese identity; for instance, as I write, Charles Yu's Twitter bio simply reads: "Taiwanese American." While Taiwanese American authors have rarely expressed their personal stances on reunification versus independence, their fiction has become one of the premiere venues for working through what I am calling a *Taiwanese semiperipheral structure of feeling*. Two components of this structure are a revanchist desire for either independence or reunification with China and ressentiment over Taiwan's persistent coloniality.[10]

In this chapter I will examine a group of recent Taiwanese American novels that grapple with U.S.-Taiwan-Chinese relations from the self-conscious position of Taiwanese American subjects. Underlying this self-consciousness are material continuities that join class anxiety to semiperipherality. Wallerstein helps to clarify: "Under pressure from core states and putting pressure on peripheral states, their major concern is to keep themselves from slipping into the periphery and to do what they can to advance themselves toward the core."[11] The "concern" that Wallerstein describes is analogous to the "fear of falling" in class status that Barbara

Ehrenreich described as the "inner life" of the postwar American middle class, a fear that, in Asian American communities, is sublimated as the "success frame" of model minoritization.[12] Taiwanese American authors attempt to fashion narrative solutions for these semiperipheral anxieties. On one hand, there is the allure of the *Bildungs*, a legacy of modernization theory's single-vector narration. On the other hand, there is skepticism over linear development provoked by the facticity of uneven and combined economic development: the coexistence of multiple stages of development and their associated social forms. The semiperiphery is caught between a rock and a hard place, upending the teleology of "slipping" back and forth between stages that the modernization theorists wished into being. Torn between these contradictory narrative horizons, Taiwanese American writers often resort to deformations of temporality such as revisionist history and time travel.

Three interrelated tropes will aid in tracking these structures of feeling: return narratives, racial form, and ideological unreliability. Almost all Taiwanese American fiction falls under the heading of the transnational turn and features narratives or motifs of return.[13] In contrast to Chinese American return narratives, in which characters return to China, Taiwanese American return narratives rarely feature Taiwan as the setting of return. When they do, as in Tao Lin's *Taipei* (2013) and *Leave Society* (2021), they are usually emptied of particularity; or, as in Anna Yen's *Sophia of Silicon Valley* (2018) and Elysha Chang's *A Quitter's Paradise* (2023), returns to Taiwan are only mentioned in passing. Rather than Taiwan, the setting of return tends to be either China or elsewhere in Asia. This abstraction of return reflects the ambiguities of Taiwan's semiperipheral status even as it participates in a broader trend in Asian American fiction in which the psychological function of return is diminished in favor of depicting the material relations traversed in the process of return. These qualifications notwithstanding, return narratives provide a form for Taiwanese American authors to explore the lives of a transnational PMC that envisions themselves as members of what Jim Glassman calls the Pacific ruling class: "a transnationalized set of elite actors that include capitalists, but also state planners, military leaders, and others who help set in motion policies and projects connected to industrialisation."[14] Indeed, the narrative and symbolic priority given to return as a figure for the global circulation of capital makes these novels as much *about* the U.S.-China-Taiwan conjuncture as they are about their Taiwanese American characters. While race often plays a significant role in these narratives, it is often calibrated not to dilemmas of identity or cultural difference but instead to PMC status hierarchies that vary across geographies. Race is a modality through which semiperipherality is lived, in other words. Along these lines, the characters in these novels are often torn between a Taiwanese American racial identity that is losing its appeal and an ambiguous "Asian" racial identity that signifies capital and is more or less synonymous with China.[15] This dilemma, deeply rooted in Japan-U.S. transimperiality, gives rise to an ideological unreliability and comic tone that characterize much of Taiwanese American fiction.

In the next section I will flesh out Taiwan's colonial history and emergence as a semiperipheral country. These contexts will be crucial for understanding how deeply the colonial experience has shaped Taiwan's semiperipherality and how that experience connects to Taiwanese American racial form. As Arif Dirlik argues, "colonialism creates not merely oppositions but also new cultural affinities that in the long run become part of the cultural fabric of society."[16] I therefore follow this account with an analysis of the China trope that intervenes in the formulation of Taiwanese identity, warping the space-time of Taiwanese American fiction in ways that register through tropes of uneven and combined development. In my analysis of Kathy Wang's *Family Trust* (2018) and Charles Yu's *How to Live Safely in a Science Fictional Universe* (2010), as well as a handful of other novels, we will see revanchism and ressentiment emerge as responses to these dynamics.

FORMS OF BETWEENNESS

Before its recent semiperipheral emergence, the group of islands now known as Taiwan served as a periphery to empires.[17] For millennia prior to European contact in the sixteenth century, Taiwan was, and continues to be, home to an indigenous population that spread across the Pacific, seeding populations in Polynesia and Austronesia. In the early seventeenth century the Dutch East India Company established a base of operations, Fort Zeelandia, in the present-day southwestern city of Tainan. Spain established colonial outposts in the north for the Manila galleon trade but later surrendered its holdings to the Dutch. A few decades later it was time for the

Dutch to leave after being ousted by Ming loyalists, whom a newly regnant Qing dynasty would themselves oust shortly thereafter. Hundreds of years would pass before the Qing classified Taiwan as a province in 1885, more or less just in time for the island to be handed over to the Japanese in the Treaty of Shimonoseki that brought the first Sino-Japanese war to a close in 1895. For the next fifty years, until Taiwan's "retrocession" to the Republic of China (ROC) after Japan's defeat in 1945, the Japanese would manage Taiwan as a "model" colony.[18] As Leo Ching observes, "the Japanese colonial period remains a powerful subtext in which the questions of 'Taiwanese consciousness' and 'Chinese consciousness' are embedded and contested."[19] Indeed, for many Taiwanese the Japanese colonial period remains a focus of nostalgia, despite its expansive police state, ethnic repression, and violence against indigenous populations.[20]

When Chiang Kai-shek's Kuomintang party (KMT) was defeated on the mainland by the People's Liberation Army in 1949, they retreated to Taiwan, bringing two million soldiers and civilians with them. Chiang instituted marital law on the island later that year. The transition to KMT rule that had been underway since Japan's defeat was smooth in some ways and deadly in others. Imperial transition progressed largely without a hitch: "The potent colonial bureaucracy was preserved nearly intact; Japanese personnel in many cases stayed on well into 1946, training Taiwanese replacements, and native bureaucrats who had served in the colonial administration continued in office."[21] But on February 28, 1947, pent-up native anger at KMT corruption and the closing off of economic opportunities sparked an uprising when a woman caught selling loose cigarettes was beaten by Monopoly Bureau agents. The police and military response—known as the 228 Massacre—resulted in upward of 25,000 deaths. Although the KMT would remain hopelessly focused on revanchism for the better part of the next two decades, eventually its cooperation with U.S. aid and military projects, bolstered by regional synergy, created the conditions for economic takeoff in the 1960s. The cultivation of human capital was a crucial factor in this, as well as an instigator for ideological conflict around the issue of Taiwanese identity.

From the 1960s through the 1980s, Taiwanese foreign students in the United States, believing themselves beyond the reach of the repressive KMT police state, engaged in an independence movement that focalized widespread anti-KMT sentiment and occasionally erupted in violence.[22]

Consequences for this activism were severe. Many students were placed on blacklists prohibiting their return, and consequences could be meted out to relatives back home: "Speak a wrong word in New Haven and your cousin in Kaohsiung would lose his job," as one character puts it in Shawna Yang Ryan's 2016 novel *Green Island*.[23] One of the most significant events in this movement's history was a territorial dispute between Taiwan, China, and Japan in 1969 over the Diaoyu/Senkaku Islands, which provoked a worldwide movement opposed to Japan's U.S.-sponsored claim of sovereignty over them. What came to be known as the Baodiao movement connected these students to the "global revolutionary movements of the 1960s" and enabled them to give voice, often for the first time, to Taiwanese national identity and a desire for independence.[24] These possibilities were made all the more urgent by Nixon's visit to China in 1972 and America's move toward normalizing U.S.-China relations, a process that reached completion in 1979 with the United States severing ties with Taiwan and shifting diplomatic recognition to Beijing. According to Chih-ming Wang, the Baodiao movement would eventually fracture into "three irreconcilable positions" that track the major contours of Taiwan's semiperipheral geopolitical alignments and whose fault lines continue to organize Taiwanese politics around the issues of reunification and independence: a "pro-Republic of China reformist" position that wants to remain in Taiwan with a reformed KMT, a "pro-unification leftist" position desiring "socialist utopia," and finally an "independent Taiwan" position.[25]

When Chiang's son and successor, Chiang Ching-kuo, lifted martial law in 1987, he also authorized family visits to China for the first time. This quickly led to the establishment of business ties and investment in China. As economic historians like Shelley Rigger and Ho-fung Hung have shown, these entrepreneurs—the *táishāng*—brought supply chains, expertise, and capital into China and thus played a decisive role in China's leapfrogging and economic miracle. The present form of Taiwan's semiperipheral status came into focus during this period. As we discussed in previous chapters, for observers and participants with selective memories, including American modernization theorists, the World Bank, and Taiwan's own technocrats, Taiwan's success was proof positive of neoliberal principles of state nonintervention and free markets. Others have argued that Taiwan's performance was exemplary for the exact opposite reason: it was "a case of *etatisme* and a challenge to dependency theory," which theorized that peripheral states would remain peripheral.[26] In recent years, Taiwan has occasionally been able to treat the putative core—China and the United States—as peripheries, taking advantage of regions of underdevelopment within otherwise highly developed economic systems. Much has changed since Shu-mei Shih theorized Taiwan's geopolitical "(in)significance" in 2003.[27] Taiwanese firms like Foxconn and Taiwan Semiconductor Manufacturing Corporation have struck deals with U.S. locales that smack of a core-periphery relation, with the Taiwanese firms acting as the core to the low-value-added manufacturing contracts promised to peripheral U.S. locales near locations like Mount Pleasant, Wisconsin, and Phoenix, Arizona. Core behaviors like this have made it difficult for potential allies of Taiwan's sovereignty to voice their support. The U.S. left, for example, is generally unsure about how to navigate a critique of Chinese aggression and is uncomfortable with the complexities of nationalism and antinationalism within the Taiwanese independence movement, not to mention calls for civil defense training in the wake of Russia's 2022 invasion of Ukraine.[28] Even more difficult to process is the Sinitic, quasi-racial basis of left reunificationism. This political awkwardness is further complicated by the fact that Taiwan's staunchest allies in the United States have traditionally been anticommunist Republicans.[29] These forms of betweenness have been frozen in place by those "three irreconcilable positions" on one side, and the longstanding U.S. policy of "strategic ambiguity" on the other: a policy that for all its faults has so far succeeded in not only deterring China, but also in providing a check on Taiwan's "imperial desire."[30]

It will not be lost on students of Asian American history that "betweenness" also describes how Asians in the United States have been racialized since they began arriving in large numbers in the mid-nineteenth century. Core concepts in Asian American critique have been designed to capture this status. The "model minority," at once a model citizen and unassimilable, is the flip side of the "yellow peril," which is an anxiety over orientalization that is itself the flip side of a fantasy about Asia's infinite markets. The "model minority *myth*" critiques the rhetoric in which Asian Americans are used as a cudgel against Black Americans who rely on the excuse of racism for their difficulties assimilating to white norms. There is no betweenness without racialization, and if racialization is the name we give to a dynamic of socially mediated material relations, then Taiwanese American identity fits awkwardly within Asian American identity for the same reasons that Asian American identity fits awkwardly within American racial hierarchies: the cognitive dissonance that economic success introduces into narratives of racial abjection and minoritization.[31]

The material relations that make Asian Americans racialized figures of betweenness are intensified for post-65 Taiwanese Americans. While Asian Americans as an aggregated demographic group have the highest educational attainment and household incomes of any racial group in the United States, many scholars have pointed out that this average obscures a wide spread of inequality in which some groups—in particular Southeast Asians—struggle academically and are ensconced in endemic poverty, and others—in particular Northeast Asians, South Asians, and Filipinxs—have high educational attainment rates and household incomes. Critics like erin Khûe Ninh and Viet Thanh Nguyen have argued compellingly that Asian American cultural politics have been historically dominated by more privileged subgroups who use the material abjection of less privileged subgroups as rhetorical leverage. In Ninh's trenchant account, Asian American cultural politics "has taken to reflexively trotting out [Asian America's] subpar Southeast Asians, whose material deprivation is [the] only too-scant argument for the falseness of the model minority myth, and on whose continued failure must rest the hopes of entire academic and political platforms."[32] Model minorities—defined as highly educated, highly disciplined, and high-income subjects—are very real indeed. Demographically, few groups are more exemplary of the model minority than Taiwanese Americans. Taiwanese immigrants to the United States are among the most hyper-selected and occupationally concentrated of any immigrant group: 70 percent hold bachelor's degrees or higher, second only to Indian immigrants.[33] Prior to 1965, Taiwanese immigrants almost exclusively consisted of STEM students. Taiwanese Americans also have among the highest household incomes of any ethnic or racial group, again second only to Indian Americans.

If the capitalist form-determination of racial hierarchy has been more often noted than demonstrated in Asian American studies, then it is in part because of the continued predominance of racial formation frameworks for analyzing racial representation, which tend to diminish, if not entirely reject, class and political economy.[34] We are better served by attending to the dialectic interaction between Asian American racialization and what Bruce Cumings calls a "class-based archipelago" extending across sites in the United States and Asia that includes "at the top, a transnational power elite, intertwined in various networks and educated at top-rated American or British universities; then an echelon of urban middle and working classes; and, finally, a vast mass at the bottom."[35] As we will see in *Family Trust* and elsewhere, Taiwanese American fiction often draws focus on the interaction between racial forms and the inequalities of geopolitical dynamics through a trope of *shifting racial hierarchy* that registers the shifting meanings of class difference and unequal modernity at an international scale.

To illustrate the link between semiperipherality and racial form, we can turn to Charles Yu's 2010 novel *How to Live Safely in a Science Fictional Universe*, which offers the following dreamlike description of the protagonist's father's country of origin:

> My father had originally come from a faraway country, a part of reality, a tiny island in the ocean, a different part of the planet, really, a different time, where people still farmed with water buffalo and believed that stories, like life, were all straight lines of chronology, where there was *enough* magic left in the real, in the humidity of August and the mosquito and the sun and birth, *enough* magic and terror in the strangeness of family itself, that time travel devices were not only unnecessary, but would have diminished the world, would have changed its mechanic, its web of invisible dynamics. The technology of the day was *enough*, the technology of the sunrise and sunset, the week of work and rest in cycles, in rhythm, sixteen hours of hard rice-farming labor, the remainder of time in a day left for eating and sleeping, the seasons, the years passing by, each one a perfect machine. (70, my italics)

This passage constructs the "tiny island" out of feelings of "enough"-ness rather than concrete images. Its several concatenated clauses, betraying an expository impulse, generate a descriptive indistinctness. The geometry of time proceeds in "straight lines" and yet refuses, via an insistence on enoughness, any sense of development and teleology. Multiple spatial distancings, along with mentions of "strangeness" and "invisible dynamics," conflict with the passage's monadic insistence on self-containment. And there, hiding in the open and never explicitly named here or elsewhere in the novel, is the identity of the island, Taiwan. This authorial act of withholding becomes conspicuous when, at another moment, the protagonist mentions that his parents spoke "a home language, a private, family language, as well as the mainland language taught in schools by the nationalists," referring to the suppression of Taiwanese, Hakka, and indigenous languages by the Japanese and the KMT (82). The reference to linguistic and ethnic repression resonates with a dimension of the novel that the reader has already become aware of, if only at the peripheries of perception: the absence of explicit racial markers. This absence also becomes conspicuous amid the novel's richly developed racial forms (e.g., whiteness registered as "noblesse oblige" (174), Asian Americanness registered as "physically shrink[ing] with each professional defeat" (35)). Together, these absences suggest an association between nation and race in which the (non)enunciation of one necessarily implies the other. To be Taiwanese is to be racialized, and Taiwan itself is a racial object. In the preceding chapters I have explored the connection between occupational concentration and racial form and how an author's "postracial" stylistic choice to obscure or elide racial markers is guided by the legacies of transimperial modernization's racial contradictions. Yu's novel shows us how that choice can also be symptomatic of an unresolved ambiguity about Taiwan's modernity.

Associated with this ambiguity is an aspect of semiperipherality that modernization theory cannot abide—uneven and combined development—which the passage registers as the island's "different time," status as the "perfect machine," and juxtaposition of atavism and "technology." Leon Trotsky first elaborated uneven and combined development in an attempt to understand why the Bolshevik Revolution of 1917 occurred before classical conditions of socialist revolution were in place. His solution, to quote the political economists Justin Rosenberg and Chris Boyle, was "to uncover a specifically international layer of causality at work in the ongoing history of the global political economy," in which the relations between national entities comprise different modes of production, scales, and speeds, thus bringing into analysis "a dialectical, non-unilinear quality to historical change overall."[36] In the Warwick Research Collective's recent account of world literature as an archive of uneven and combined development, they note that these dynamics are often registered as deformations of temporality: "We might then see . . . uneven and combined development as a form of time travel . . . a spatial bridging of unlike times . . . that leads from the classic forms of nineteenth-century realism to the speculative methodologies of today's global science fiction."[37] As Trotsky found, the "dialectical, non-unilinear" temporality of uneven and combined development is not spatially distinct, but instead combines multiple temporalities within the same space. Uneven and combined development, in other words, is a key material condition of science fictionality.

The adjectival insistence on enoughness in the preceding passage is provoked by a semiperipheral anxiety that wishes on one hand to embrace the difference of unevenness and on the other to refuse the capitalist futurity of combination. It describes a "tiny island" that is a part of "reality" (a term for the capitalist everyday in the novel's parlance), yet also "faraway" from spaces where rice farming is not enough. The semiperipheral anxiety that these contradictions are designed to assuage becomes more apparent when we consider the function that this passage is playing at this moment in the novel. The protagonist, also named Charles Yu (Charles from here on), is in the car with his father, who is about to pull over to reveal his "secret plan, [his] *invention*," which turns out to be a theory of time travel. However, even more shocking to Charles than his father's theory is the fact that his father doesn't have just "dreams or ideas" but something much more volatile: "ambition." His sudden outburst of energy and personal disclosure is so shocking that Charles actually registers it as a threat ("I can't tell if he's mad") and even considers jumping out of the car (69). We already know at this point that Charles's father's theory will give rise to entire industries of time travel and artificial universes and that another inventor beats him to market, leaving him with nothing to show for his efforts. Perceiving in his father's "ambition" a hidden feeling of *not*-enoughness—perhaps the germ of a "Taiwanese imperial desire"—Charles softens the threat by recalling his father's origins and experiences with the total adequacy of enoughness. We detect in Charles's father's ambition a supremely inventive yet deeply buried ressentiment constituted by racial and national forms, bringing to our attention that it is not only Taiwan that is conspicuously unnamed in the novel but also the entire historical structure of Japan-U.S.-China transimperiality.[38]

A question then arises about *why* Charles feels compelled at this moment to respond to his father's ambition with a moving depiction of enoughness that implicitly critiques it. As I will explain at the end of this chapter when I return to *How to Live Safely*, for Yu, semiperipheral anxiety complicates what ultimately appears to be a deep political desire for expressing a Taiwanese identity beyond national and ethnic categories, one that refuses to assert Taiwan's significance via its integration into the global economy. It is for this reason that the preceding passage's depiction of the "tiny island" isn't exactly nostalgic. While the passage is certainly meant to depict an idyllic Taiwan, it is a Taiwan that has never existed and whose possible existence is vexed by powers that dwarf its tiny stature.

THE CHINA TROPE

Over the last decade or so return narratives have become a prevalent feature in mainstream Asian American fiction.[39] In regard to Chinese and Taiwanese American fiction, which will be my focus in this section, these include, in addition to *Family Trust* and *How to Live Safely*, Chieh Chieng's *A Long Stay in a Distant Land* (2005), Francie Lin's *The Foreigner* (2008), Tao Lin's *Taipei* (2013) and *Leave Society* (2021), Kevin Kwan's *Crazy Rich Asians* (2013), Ed Lin's *Ghost Month* (2014), Shawna Yang Ryan's *Green Island* (2016), Ling Ma's *Severance* (2018), Emily X. R. Pan's *The Astonishing Color of After* (2018), Lucy Tan's *What We Were Promised* (2018), Anna Yen's *Sophia of Silicon Valley* (2018), Chia-Chia Lin's *The Unpassing* (2019), Esme Weijun Wang's *The Border of Paradise* (2016), Xuan Juliana Wang's *Home Remedies* (2019), K-Ming Chang's *Bestiary* (2020), Meng Jin's *Little Gods* (2020), Ha Jin's *A Song Everlasting* (2021), and Lyn Liao Butler's *The Tiger Mom's Tale* (2021), as well as films like Lulu Wang's *The Farewell* (2019), Alan Yang's *Tigertail* (2020), Destin Daniel Cretton's *Shang-Chi and the Legend of the Ten Rings* (2021), Daniel Kwan and Daniel Scheinert's *Everything Everywhere All at Once* (2022), and Adele Lim's *Joyride* (2023). In these works major and minor characters physically return to or state their intention to return to locations figured as origins: sometimes to the country where they were born, sometimes to a location where that home country used to be, sometimes to an ancestral or parental point of origin, and sometimes to a location that signals a more symbolic than literal return. Before the 1990s depictions of return in Asian American fiction were few and far between, mostly appearing as short stories published in small circulation periodicals or community publications.[40] Themes of return in those texts tended to focalize psychological dilemmas of cultural identity and political loyalty, though they also raised questions about uneven and combined development.

While the depiction of return has long been a mainstay of Asian American autobiography and memoir, the recent availability of return narratives to *fictionalization* corresponds to the expansion of middle classes in Asia and to a socially and geographically mobile Asian American PMC for whom sites in Asia are accessible via travel and consumption. The backdrop to this convergence is the dusk of the American Century, which is associated with a sense that U.S. institutions and social mores are incapable of managing racial conflict. The bulk of the literary examples above appeared after the 2008 financial crisis, and in fact many of them explicitly make reference to the crisis. Within these texts, the signifier "China" plays an outsized role, dragging into its gravity well discourses of Asia's rise and U.S. decline, as well as more general anxieties about futurity and class reproduction. "China's" symbolic capture poses unique challenges to Taiwanese American writers due to the two countries' current economic interdependence and their fraught history, not to mention their easy conflation among readers unfamiliar with these contexts. To understand how these challenges shape Taiwanese American fiction we will first need to describe how the China trope operates in the present conjuncture.

Here it would help to examine an intertextual dialogue between Ling Ma's *Severance* and "A Pair of Tickets," the final chapter in Amy Tan's 1989 novel *The Joy Luck Club*.[41] Upon Jing-mei's return to China in the late 1980s, her astonishment at the modernity of her hotel in Guangzhou is paradigmatic of how Asia began appearing to Asian American authors around this time—that is, via the uncanny shock of global capital.[42] Jing-mei's astonishment is specifically provoked by the array of multinational brands greeting her in her room's mini-bar: "Heineken beer, Coke Classic, and Seven-Up, mini-bottles of Johnnie Walker Red" (277). If we examine how this scene functions in the chapter, we find that it is just one moment in Jing-mei's struggle to grasp the *unevenness* of capitalism. Outside of the hotel she encounters decidedly unmodern aspects of Chinese life: from the train she sees an "ox-driven cart" in the fields, her aunties unexpectedly greet her at the train station because their village has no telephone, and as she observes the urban environment she tsks, "Oh, would OSHA have a field day here" (268, 276). These discrete and paratactically linked signs of the simultaneity of ancient and advanced modes of production serve as objective correlatives to the chapter's central drama of unevenness: the story of Jing-mei's half-sisters, twins, whom their mother abandoned as infants decades ago as she was fleeing the Japanese. The twins were found and raised by a poor couple, and thus followed a very different developmental trajectory than Jing-mei's life of relative material comfort in the United States. However, the 1980s were too early for Tan to register the allegory of family reunification with emerging combinations like "capitalism with Chinese characteristics."[43] Rather, Tan processes that triumph's structure of feeling through Jing-mei's narrative of identity formation. "A Pair of Tickets" opens with Jing-mei's unhappy realization upon arriving in China that she is Chinese after all and ends with her happy acceptance of that identity, which she attributes to reuniting with her family.

Where Jing-mei is not quite able to grasp how her uncanny encounters with multinational brands and signs of uneven economic development are also key aspects of her Chineseness, *Severance*'s Candace explicitly locates these aspects at the core of her Chinese identity in a passage that appears to pay homage to Jing-mei's experience in Guangzhou. Over the course of Ma's novel, Candace returns to China multiple times: once in her teenage years to Fuzhou, her city of birth and where she spent her early childhood, and several more times as an adult to Hong Kong and Shenzhen for work. The trip to Fuzhou becomes a primal scene of sensual abundance and emotional confusion that she later dubs "Fuzhou Nighttime Feeling"; its memory content consists of "teenagers in fake American Eagle ... pajama pants printed with SpongeBob or fake Chanel logos. There is a Mickey D's and a KFC, street dumpling stands, bootleg shops, karaoke bars. ... If Fuzhou Nighttime Feeling ... were a flavor, it would be the ice-cold Pepsi we drink as we turn down tiny alleyways where little kids defecate wildly" (97–98). Just as key to this structure of feeling's historical origin in the 1990s—following Deng Xiaoping's 1992 "Southern Tour," which recommitted China to global capital after Tiananmen—are the stigmata of economic unevenness: "fake" brands and kids pooping in the street. When Candace returns to China as an adult, her perspective has widened. Not only is she able to locate these temporal asymmetries in a global supply chain, but she is also able to overcome the paratactical gaps between them, coming into consciousness of how uneven economic and social structures combine within the world-system. On a trip to Shenzhen, sometime in 2010 or 2011, to oversee the factory production of one of her products, Candace doesn't exclaim, "This is Communist China?" as Jing-mei does. But she has an equally sudden and transformative revelation that erupts in the middle of Ma's narration of the factory tour:

> What I knew about overseas labor came from a college Economics class. First, the U.S. manufacturing jobs went to Mexico, to the maquiladoras that

staffed laborers willing to work for cheaper rates than Americans. Duty-free, tariff-free. This was the 1980s and 1990s. Later, a portion of those jobs went to suppliers in China, which offered cheaper labor rates, even cheap enough to offset the shipping costs that coincided with a rise in oil prices. And after this, in another few years, the jobs will go elsewhere, to India or some other country willing to offer even cheaper rates, to produce iPods, Happy Meal toys, skateboards, American flags, sneakers, air conditioners. The American businessmen will come to visit these countries and tour their factories, inspect their manufacturing processes, sample their cuisines, while staying at their nicest hotels built to cater to them.

I was a part of this. (85)

The "this" of which Candace is a part, to quote Rosenberg and Boyle again, is China's "integration into global value chains created by foreign multinationals who were transnationalizing their production processes."[44] Where Jing-mei is able to register only the novelty of multinational brands seemingly out of place in a Chinese hotel, Candace is able to understand why the hotel was built in the first place and how the national identity categories that she and Jing-mei struggle with are drained of meaning under the flattening pressure of "this." Rather than alienation, this deformation of the terms of identity is somewhat recuperated by the double meaning of Candace's realization: being "a part of this" also produces a sense of belonging, and a consciousness of one's reproductive function within the system. This might explain why the proximal cause of Candace's revelation is a conversation about children (the American values that *The Very Hungry Caterpillar*—i.e., greed, individualism—imparts on them), as well as the novel's cryptic final image of a pregnant Candace going through the motions of commuting into a downtown Chicago made vacant by a zombie apocalypse.

If in 1989 Jing-mei's focus is drawn to the *unevenness* of China's economic development, then in 2011 Candace is attuned to China's *combined* development with the United States: the "real-time interaction of the advanced capitalist economies with the primitive accumulation stage of capitalist development in China" in which its vast rural labor force was brought online.[45] Candace's perspicuity about the lineaments of twenty-first-century global capitalism is due to libidinal and structural factors: Fuzhou Nighttime Feeling and the shittiness of her job, which she realizes has a stronger resemblance to the "cheaper labor" workers who are leading her factory tour than to the fashionable and effortless "Art Girls" back in the Manhattan office who emblematize Candace's PMC fantasies. That she is in Shenzhen when she has this realization is entirely apt. A city that has been both mythologized and demonized in the United States for its astonishing growth from a fishing village with a population of only thirty thousand in the late 1970s to one of the most high-tech, rapidly expanding cities in the world with a current population of over ten million. Impossibly futuristic, gothic, and seemingly unstoppable in its growth, Shenzhen has become a symbol of China's economic and geopolitical rise, as well as evocative of the anxieties pertaining to the end of the American Century and the inevitability of China's hegemony.

The dominance that "China" enjoys over categories like unevenness, global capitalism, and futurity is also reflected in racial form. In 2002, looking back on the first decade or so of the "sudden appearance of wealthy Asians" in the West,[46] Viet Thanh Nguyen observed that Asian flexible citizens displace the "assumption that traditional whiteness is associated with wealth and that both whiteness and wealth are to be earned over the passage of time. By putting traditional whiteness into crisis, the new Asian capital also puts Asian America as a whole—not just the model minority—into crisis in its efforts to claim a domestic authenticity that does not threaten whites."[47] Hindsight reveals to us that what Nguyen correctly foresaw is how unevenness, registered in the language of unearned economic and technological progress and rapid (i.e., *too* fast) growth, which provokes moral panics over technology transfer, protectionism, and knockoffs would become a central aspect of twenty-first-century Asian racial form, even if he is perhaps being too politic by not explicitly naming China as its primary determinant.[48] The most visible recent examples of refurbished "domestic authenticity" to placate white fragility include not only the obvious cases of Asian American conservative politicians but also defenders of American exceptionalism like Taiwanese American former presidential candidate Andrew Yang.[49] In contrast with Chinese American fiction, which, as we have seen in Ma's and Tan's novels, tends to use "China" as a figure for global capital and therefore largely bypasses the rhetoric of the China threat, Taiwanese American fiction tends to veer into a form of ressentiment in which stereotypes of Asia as capitalist threat are avowed, and in many cases explicitly embraced. This ressentiment is couched in the too-easy slippage between generic Asian-ness and Chinese-ness and is often registered in the language of race and revanchist return narratives.

One of the clearest depictions of the link between revanchism and ressentiment can be found in the Taiwanese American author Jade Chang's novel *The Wangs vs. The World* (2016). When the novel opens, the patriarch of the Wang family, Charles, is newly bankrupt. He sets off on a cross-country journey to gather up his children as he scrambles to pick up the pieces of his life after his cosmetics empire collapses. Traveling eastward from his repossessed mansion in Bel Air, his ultimate goal isn't a reevaluation of his place in America, as might be suggested by the road trip narrative. Instead, it is to conscript his children into the arc of an epic return narrative, which began in Taiwan, where he was born, and routed through the United States, but whose final destination is not Taiwan but China, where Charles sees himself "living out his unseen birthright on his family's ancestral acres, a pampered prince in silk robes" (1). His bankruptcy, which he blames on a "fickle," post-2008 United States, brings the contours of his ressentiment into stark relief: "The life that should have been his. China, where the Wangs truly belonged. Not America. Never Taiwan" (78). What is obvious to all around him is that these interconnected identifications and disidentifications, in addition to being annoying and disruptive, are prompted by his acute fear of falling.

Meanwhile, Charles's children have been pursuing career trajectories that leverage a generic Asian-ness rather than their Taiwanese American identities. For Saina, a successful installation artist, the slippages between generic Asian-ness, Taiwanese-ness, and Chinese-ness authorize her to aestheticize the China threat in her blockbuster shows, which have titles like "Made in China" and "Power Drum Song" (a reference to the classic of Chinese American fiction, Chin Yang Lee's 1957 novel *Flower Drum Song*, which is about a miserly patriarch). For Andrew, an aspiring comedian, the elision of his Taiwanese identity is overdetermined by his overabundance of privilege. As he explains to one audience, he lacks the "miserable" life experiences that "legit" comedians usually draw on for their jokes. On the contrary, he is athletic and good-looking, his father hugs him, and "worst of all," his family is rich. Robbed of misfortune, he explains that there is only one thing he can develop his act around: "Yep, I'm Asian" (188). In other words, part of Andrew's distinction as a Taiwanese American character is that he has only the narrowest purchase on ressentiment, and even then he cannot articulate it as a Taiwanese identity but must resort to the generic "Asian." In the novel's final pages, Charles is on his deathbed in a Chinese hospital, his children gathered round him, when he has a revelation: "The Indians were just a tribe of early Chinese people who took a long walk across the Bering Land Bridge and ended up in a New World. The true Americans were Chinese! It was too bad it had taken him so long to remember that" (350). He revises the arc of his return with his dying words: "Daddy discovered America!" (351). Charles's totalizing yet ineffectual claims upon China and the United States bear a notable resemblance to the "ambition" of *How to Live Safely*'s father character, whose invention of time travel technology and inability to reap its profits expresses, in the idiom of SF, Taiwan's semiperipheral relation to China. That is, both characters see themselves as the secret instigators of world-historical (even multiuniverse-historical) events, the corollary to which is the outsized role that Taiwanese *táishāng* played in China's explosive growth: the "tiger" leading the "dragon," to use Shelley Rigger's formation.[50] Where novels like *The Wangs vs. the World* (and *Family Trust*, as we will see in a moment) celebrate this asymmetry, novels like *How to Live Safely* explore its comic and melancholic dimensions.[51]

REVANCHISM AND IDEOLOGICAL UNRELIABILITY IN *FAMILY TRUST*

Kathy Wang's novel *Family Trust* (2018) turns on the intimate vicissitudes of semiperipherality and is especially concerned with how unevenness fractures the post-65 Taiwanese American family. A comic novel primarily interested in satirizing its characters' obsessions with social and financial status, *Family Trust* has no overt aspiration to a critical realism of twenty-first-century capitalism. However, it is precisely in the novel's pursuit of the racial contradictions of social and financial status that that totality comes into view via an ideological rather than epistemological unreliability.[52]

At the center of the novel is the Huang family. Specifically, the would-be patriarch Stanley Huang, a retired engineer and dropout from a Stanford PhD program who is dying of pancreatic cancer—would-be not only because Stanley is prone to physically and verbally abusive outbursts of anger when his patriarchal authority is challenged but also because we learn that his ex-wife, Linda Liang, a gold-watch IBM employee, was in fact the mastermind behind his supposed fortune of $7 million. That figure isn't revealed to the reader until three-quarters into the novel, however, and much of the drama up to that point concerns friends' and family members' speculations about the precise magnitude of Stanley's fortune and whether the fortune still exists. Stanley's children, Fred and Kate, are sweetly given to supporting rather than competing with each other, but Linda wants to make sure Stanley doesn't give an equal share to Mary, his wife of a decade ("only" a decade to those who would contest her inheritance). The Huangs are in many ways an exemplary post-65 Taiwanese American PMC family: model minorities in terms of their academic, professional, and economic success, as well as occupationally concentrated in STEM fields. Stanley and Linda, moreover, both attended Taiwan's most prestigious university, National Taiwan University, and Linda attended Beiyinu, the highly selective all-girls high school in Taipei.[53] Set in post-2008 Silicon Valley, the novel, as its punning title suggests, is interested in how finance structures intimate family relationships. Wang's studious refusal to render any of her characters *likeable* reveals in part her systematic rejection of the moral aspect of the model minority stereotype that depicts Asian Americans as passive and docile, even as her characters unabashedly embrace the stereotype's economic aspect. A significant, shared theme in these Taiwanese American novels is a rejection of model minority passivity via the counterproposition of the Asian American *asshole* and the hyperbole of the Asian American *loser*.[54] The Huangs certainly can't be faulted for shying away from action or expressing their opinions. It is the odiousness of their opinions through which the strangeness of the narrative voice emerges. Taiwanese American return fiction's depiction of flexible Asian American subjects often turns upon racial meanings that mediate the demographic emergences of Taiwan's semiperipheral status.

Family Trust features two return subplots. In one, Fred travels to Bali by way of Hong Kong to attend a prestigious business networking event called the "Founder's Retreat," an invitation-only annual gathering that brings together luminaries of Asian and Western capital. In the other, Stanley travels to Hong Kong with Mary, who consults experts in Chinese Traditional Medicine about Stanley's condition and tracks down herbal remedies. Stanley's arrival in Hong Kong carries with it none of the historical significance that might be associated with a return to China by a Taiwanese American of his generation. He is there for medical tourism and to close out some bank accounts. Mary's return is the most straightforward because she was born and raised in China, but Hong Kong's relevance to her has nothing to do with home, only with the cure for Stanley that might be found there. Fred was born in the United States and has no personal connection to Indonesia itself, so, in a way, his "return" is at best symbolic: he is a second-generation Asian American "returning" to "Asia." In fact, it is precisely his generic Asian-ness that becomes, in the context of the Founder's Retreat, a marker of ascendant social and, more important, *financial* capital.

Fred spends a great deal of time complaining about his invisibility in Silicon Valley, where he is a "banal paragon of the model minority, banished to an existence of mediocre achievement" (196). He is desperate to attend the Founder's Retreat because only there might he finalize a lucrative business deal with two classmates from Harvard Business School, both scions of wealthy Asia-based families: Reagan Kwon and Jack Hu. As he sees it, this is his best shot to rise above his $325,000 salary, "a pittance" in Silicon Valley (21), as a mid-rank venture capitalist at a mid-rank Taiwanese American firm and become "a man of significance!" (196). While Fred is perhaps in this regard a kindred spirit with *The Wangs vs. The World*'s Charles Wang, a key difference is the absence of national form in Fred's manifest expressions of his aspirations. Fred's return narrative, understood through a libidinal dynamic, has no distinctly Asian content. Understood as a narrative of capital circulation, however, Asia and Asian-ness are maximally significant for Fred's self-valorization. Reagan's familial connections to the Thai government have yielded him carte blanche decision-making power over a sovereign wealth fund, worth "multiple billions," that he calls "Opus" (189). Along with Jack's family's Hong Kong-based real estate business, Fred is to become the third leg in the scheme, directing the fund's U.S. investments in Silicon Valley. While the Taiwanese origins of Fred's employer, Lion Capital, are relevant, Fred's specific role is not so much to carry himself as a Taiwanese American or an employee of a Taiwanese firm but instead to leverage his expertise as an "Asia guy"—or, as he puts it, to perform "an excellent imitation of a moneyed mainland [Chinese] businessman on an acquisition spree, armed to spend recklessly abroad" (259). Key to the scheme, in other words, is the ability of its principals to project the dizzying magnitude of "Asian" capital.

One of the two primary ways that uneven and combined development is registered in *Family Trust* is in the novel's thematic association of *deregulation* with newly industrializing Asian countries like Thailand, and *regulation* with developed sites like Hong Kong and the United States. As Reagan and Jack explain, one of the main reasons why they are recruiting Fred is because Jack's family's Hong Kong-based firm, "Hu Land and Investment," is "pretty constrained in terms of risk" (188). Descriptions of Thailand as a place where corruption and nepotism proceed with impunity project a Pacific ruling class that Fred dearly wants to join so that he, like the aptly named Reagan, might be the one to decide where and how to regulate and where to deregulate. Reagan's captainship of Opus is the nepotistic outcome of his family's relationship with the Thai government, in which his sister Regina serves as the minister of education. More fundamentally, the drama at the center of the novel—how to ensure that Stanley not only distributes his wealth equitably but also reports on it transparently—is itself, as the novel's title suggests, a conflict over regulation.

We can read the puzzle of the novel's annoyance over racial stereotypes on one hand and its total lack of concern about racial group identity on the other as a further refraction of regulation's function in enforcing the difference between legitimate and fraudulent, real and fake. The expedited strategy of granting Reagan carte blanche betrays the Thai government's anxiety over its lagging modernization and development. Opus's mission is "to make Bangkok the technology hub of Asia. 'Silicon Valley of the East!' or whatever. The rest of Asia is booming, everyone's getting rich, and they don't want to be left behind" (189). As Sunny Xiang has shown, the political imperative of rapid economic development in Asia has dovetailed with a pervasive, persistent, and transnational racial stereotype of Asians—especially Chinese—as peddling knockoffs and as human counterfeits themselves. The travel of this stereotype also manifests as "economically successful yet morally suspect diasporan" subjects like Fred, who are in a constant state of racial and gendered self-alienation (and thus strongly resemble characters in Charles Yu's fiction).[55] The political economic origins of this stereotype are efficiently portrayed in Opus's strategy of investing in Silicon Valley companies whose technology they "rip off and copy for themselves" in order to foster protectionist import-substitution at home (192). As a kind of regulatory middle ground between Hong Kong and Thailand, Silicon Valley is for that precise reason a site of amplified unevenness and distortions of formal equality, where corruption and nepotism are thinly concealed beneath a veneer of liberal multiculturalist palaver.

ENOUGH?

"Some of us are more equal than others," quips an Indian American Lion employee who accuses the HR chief of "deliberately limiting Asian and Indian hires in order to meet certain diversity standards" (98). This contradiction emblematizes how uneven and combined development shapes racial meanings in a specific social context, here a neoliberal multiculturalism whose reproduction of white domination via the performance of diversity succeeds by suppressing expressions of class conflict.[56] Quip launched, the HR chief "pales," and the room falls silent. This discomfort affectively registers the ideological unreliability of the novel's narrative voice, which delights in puncturing neoliberal multiculturalism's mannered euphemisms. In another exemplary scene, Kate's boss tells her that he has "been under some pressure, to do promotions," and that he is considering her for one: "Was he bullshitting her? But then Sonny wasn't really a liar, Kate thought. He didn't know how. 'Really,' she said carefully. 'Because you're a woman [he continued] . . . Apparently, we don't have enough! So I'm supposed to promote females . . . The good news is, at the Labs we at least have enough Latinos and blacks . . . It would be best if you weren't Asian, but I can't be too picky'" (404). Ideological unreliability emerges in the unsettling effect that passages like these have on readers who are positively predisposed to a politics of representation. Notwithstanding the question of correspondence between narrative voice and readerly expectation, this passage participates in the novel's more pervasive effort to render undecidable where the narrative voice, and ultimately Wang herself, might stand in regard to racial politics.

The roots of the novel's ideological unreliability run deeper than what might be easily relegated to bad or incoherent politics on the part of the author or narrative voice and are in fact reflective of the regulation and deregulation to which semiperipheral countries are especially beholden. For Gerald Prince, unreliable narration includes ideological uncertainty; he defines the unreliable narrator as "a narrator whose norms and behavior are not in accordance with the implied author's norms; a narrator whose values (tastes, judgments, moral sense) diverge from those of the implied author's; a narrator the reliability of whose account is undermined by various features of that account."[57] But for Dorrit Cohn, ideological unreliability—what she calls "discordant narration"—is a unique mode in which, from a "reader's sense," the narrator is "normatively inappropriate for the story he or she tells" and there is a split between the author's intention and the narrator's understanding of the narrative.[58] For Cohn, the origin of this discordance—in the "reader's sense" or the author's intention—is undecidable. But the examples she draws from—Joseph Conrad's *Heart of Darkness*, Thomas Mann's *Death in Venice*, Emily Brontë's *Wuthering Heights*, and Kazuo Ishiguro's *Remains of the Day*—suggest to us that ideological unreliability might be a tendency of texts authored by marginalized subjects. In the case of the Taiwanese American novelists I am examining, it appears that ideological unreliability is reflective of an internal self-division that is structured and amplified by a post-65 mismatch between PMC class status and "Asian" racial identity. Taiwan's semiperipherality is the material basis for the undecidability between core and peripheral behavior, as well as national identity and generic Asian-ness.[59]

Monika Fludernik writes, "for unreliability to be present in the text, there needs to exist a secret."[60] On a superficial level, ideological unreliability in these novels proceeds in the register of anti–political correctness that, for example, is announced by Kate's white friend Camilla, who at one moment wags a finger at her and says, "Don't pretend I don't just say out loud what you secretly think" (358). The horizontal racial analogy implied here—that Kate's true thoughts are best expressed by a wealthy white woman—is given far lower priority in the novel than the shifting vertical hierarchies between various racialized characters and groups jockeying for status. Camilla, for example, unabashedly pursues Kate for friendship and apology after Kate forcefully confronts her for having an affair with her husband. An extreme frankness is broached between them, which becomes the basis for the rather unidirectional dynamic in their relationship, in which Camilla is the giver and Kate the receiver. This unevenness, homologous with their respective priorities in the novel's character system (minor, major), corresponds to a recurring agon between "white" and "Asian" capitalism, here voiced by Linda:

> Why did white people like to pick and choose from cultures with such zealous judgment? Of course they just *loved* Szechuan cuisine served by a young waitress in a cheap cheongsam, but as soon as you proved yourself just as adept at the form of capitalism *they* had invented? Then you were obsessed. Money crazed. Unworthy of sympathy. And God forbid your children end up at superior schools; then it became all about how much they must have been beaten, the investigative conjecturing over what creative instincts had been snuffed out in order to achieve such excellent test scores. (213)

These figurations of racialized (rather than racial) capitalism are central to other Taiwanese American novels as well. They also suggest, sometimes explicitly, that "white" capitalism's time is up. In this passage Linda's intense resentment betrays the true sentiment behind her feigned sportsmanship of "just as adept." There is no question that the Huangs consider themselves superior at capitalism; their warrant is proffered by characters like Reagan Kwon and Jack Hu (and for Linda specifically, her ostentatious friend Shirley Chang), who are unambiguously portrayed as money crazed and unworthy of sympathy.

Common in Taiwanese American fiction is a trope, a kind of pincer move, in which stereotypes are simultaneously affirmed and rejected (e.g., "Linda had herself avoided driving a luxury automobile for this very reason, the desire not to be seen as a stereotype" [55]).[61] For instance, Anna Yen's *Sophia of Silicon Valley* (2018), a novel that Cheryl Naruse would call a "coming-of-career" narrative that tracks the title character's exemplary performance as an employee whose loyalty, sharp tongue, and aggressiveness facilitate her rapid rise through the ranks of various Silicon Valley firms ("Wow," one character says to her, "You certainly do go against the stereotype of meek Asian girls, don't you?" [80]).[62] Notably unironic about the multiculturalist contradictions that provide fodder for Wang's and Chang's novels,[63] *Sophia* ends with a burst of patriotism that transports the model minority to the forefront of U.S.-led global capitalism. Surveying a lobby full of flowers and condolences sent to Ion (a thinly veiled Tesla Motors) after a group of employees dies in a plane crash, Sophia is overwhelmed: "A sudden rush of patriotism caught me off guard as I realized Ion wasn't just about profits and losses, stock options and employment agreements. It was about solidifying America's position as a leader in the automotive industry by bringing the world's first electric car to market."[64] Sophia's loudmouthed refutation of the model minority myth facilitates the wish-fulfillment of her economic nationalism.

In Taiwanese American fiction the ironization of race's materiality via ideological unreliability is symptomatic of a more fundamental political economic unevenness in U.S.-Asia relations. Post-65 Taiwanese American PMC characters, like the authors who invent them, find themselves at the point of articulation of these political economic shifts and regimes of racial meaning and so experience the most extreme gravitational effects of those forces. For *Wangs vs. the World*'s Charles Wang, racial meanings and hierarchies are fleeting and contingent—not so much because race itself is immaterial, but because its form-determination by material conditions is shifting so quickly:

> If the billion people of China ever chose to march *en masse*, they would be overwhelming in their similarity and horrific in their differences. There would be so many variations on the theme of human that all typologies would be completely bulldozed. This was why he had never worried himself about how America viewed his children, never bothered himself over unflattering stereotypes and prejudices. What did it matter how a country full of white people saw them when the whole world was theirs? (294)

Among the most privileged subjects riding the crest of the wave of transition from the United States to the China-led systemic cycle of accumulation, Taiwanese American PMCs like Charles are in some ways structurally positioned to glimpse what Christopher Chen calls "the limit point of capitalist equality": a speculative future—not necessarily a happy one—in which racial meanings are reconfigured if not beyond recognition, then at least into a transitional, uncanny otherness.[65] My goal here is not to make ethical claims about the politics of race and representation in any of these texts but instead to demonstrate how such reconfigurations might be more apparent to those occupying a specific structural position. That specificity can be further accounted for through the fact that Charles's theory of difference in this passage metastasizes a KMT revanchist politics that we might call, amending Wang's schema from earlier, "ultra-right reunificationism."

SPACE-TIMES OF RESSENTIMENT IN *HOW TO LIVE SAFELY IN A SCIENCE FICTIONAL UNIVERSE*

Mediated through memory, return narratives produce multiplicities of space-time. Sometimes these multiplicities bunch together; sometimes their tormented weight is so dense that they puncture the fabric of space-time to create new universes, new pockets of what the characters in *How to Live Safely* call "chronodiegetic" space. Yu's novel translates these vicissitudes into a SF idiom to tell a story about a post-65 Taiwanese immigrant family and the unhappiness of their lives in a locale that is never named but is highly reminiscent of Silicon Valley. While in many ways *How to Live Safely* is suffused with return narratives, they are quite different from the realist portrayals of return in the previously discussed novels. Charles is a time machine repair technician who almost always finds his time-traveling clients returning to the unhappiest moment in their lives. Unlike his clients, Charles lacks the courage to return to that moment and instead opts to spend decades of his life alone in his capsule-sized time machine living "at zero . . . the exact point between comfort and discomfort" (54). In the novel's main plot, Charles's father, having experienced too much disappointment, too much not-enoughness, escapes to a point in space-time without notifying his family of his whereabouts. After many years of absence, Charles finally sets out to find him. The time travel trope crystallizes the desires underlying return while at the same time transforming the otherwise straightforward spatial narrative of return. In contrast to revanchist novels like *Family Trust* and *The Wangs vs. the World*, which use return narratives as a vehicle for satirizing PMC aspirations to Pacific ruling class status, *How to Live Safely* depicts the underlying class ressentiment that sometimes motivates returns. And where revanchism compels authors to situate their narratives explicitly in relation to China, ressentiment and its constituent affects—anger and melancholia—tend to draw focus onto the contours of uneven and combined development, which are registered in what Yoon Sun Lee would call tropes of "side-by-sideness" like parataxis and juxtaposition and combined through forms of generic undecidability and spatialized abstractions.[66] Charles comes to learn that his father's disappearance was in fact a return—but not to the past, and not back to the idyll of his childhood on the "tiny island" in the sea. When Charles finally finds his father, the scene unfolds in an appendix to the novel's main text. They find each other in a place that has only ever existed in space, never in time, and that captures a structure of feeling underlying an impossible Taiwanese identity.

One of the most pronounced stylistic features of Yu's fiction is how it disorients readers in regard to genre. For instance, when Charles describes his father's habit of "regularly drifting five minutes into the past," it is unclear whether this description is of literal time travel, or, say, a metaphor for emotional distance.[67] Both are plausible. And when the novel turns to the stock convention of time travel SF, the infodump explaining the laws of time travel, here is how the question of whether one can change the past is handled:

> No matter how hard you try, you can't change the past.
>
> The universe just doesn't put up with that. We aren't important enough. No one is. Even in our own lives. We're not strong enough, willful enough, skilled enough in chronodiegetic manipulation to be able to just accidentally change the entire course of anything, even ourselves. . . . Time is an ocean of inertia, drowning out the small vibrations, absorbing the slosh and churn . . . and we're up here, flapping and slapping and just generally spazzing out . . . but that doesn't even register in the depths, in the powerful undercurrents miles below us, taking us wherever they are taking us. (14)

Invisible forces are as pervasive in this passage as they are cognitively indistinct. It is unclear if the reason we cannot change the past is because of physical or psychological limitations. Further agitated by the novel's metafictional conceit, it is always an open possibility that the novel is in fact an autofictional account of author Yu's own project of working through a psychological impasse, which makes the text's capacity for making diegetic truth claims unreliable. Generic undecidability can be read as an index of developmental distance from a more coherent core or periphery position. In contrast to the enoughness of the "tiny island" where Charles's father came from, the "not enough"-ness in this passage is a power relation that situates "us" between "the depths" and "small vibrations." Though perhaps not an exact schematization of semiperipherality, this passage nonetheless captures a distinct semiperipheral feeling of betweenness and scale that renders genre undecidable and undermines the teleology of core and periphery.[68]

At other moments in the novel ressentiment mediates uneven and combined economic development. In the description of "Minor Universe 31" (MU-31), which draws from naturalism's interest in scale and class conflict, we learn that it is composed of three regions: unincorporated areas that have "no particular look and feel, no genre," affluent areas of SF in which residents cultivate "reality gardens" that emulate the unincorporated areas, and finally an additional SF region, the largest, consisting of a stable middle class. "A few decades ago," the novel's titular handbook explains,

> It became permissible for families to emigrate from the unincorporated areas of "reality" into the science fictional zones.

Permissibility, however, has not necessarily translated into economic permeability.

Despite improvement in recent years, successful transition into the SF zone remains difficult to achieve for many immigrant families, and even after decades of an earnest and often desperate striving for acceptance and assimilation, many remain in the lower-middle reaches of the zone, along the border between SF and "reality."

Although technically SF, the look and feel of the world in these borderline neighborhoods is less thoroughly executed than elsewhere in the region, and outcomes of story lines can be more randomized, due to a comparatively weaker buffer from the effects of 31's incomplete physics. As a result, the overall quality of experience for the residents of these striving areas is thinner, poorer, and less substantial than of those in the middle and upper regions, while at the same time, due to its mixed and random and unthemed nature, less satisfying than that of reality, which, although gritty, is, at least, internally consistent. (77–78)

The origins of ressentiment are named in the "desperate striving," "randomized" outcomes, "unthemed nature," and the overall "thinner, poorer, less substantial . . . less satisfying" experiences available in these zones. Even though this passage's focus is on immigration, the tropes of simultaneity, compression, and juxtaposition are symptoms of uneven and combined development that in Yu's hands function as national allegories for semiperipheral Taiwan.[69]

An on-the-nose example of these national allegories is the capital city of MU-31, "NEW ANGELES/LOST TOKYO-2" (NA/LT2) whose name brings into the novel's symbolic economy two of the colonial powers that have shaped Taiwanese history. In an excerpt from the novel's titular manual, we are told that NA/LT2 formed in two steps, the first when "New York and Los Angeles, 2,462 miles apart, much to the surprise and consternation of residents and property owners and municipal officials and parking lot owners and westsiders from the eastern half and eastsiders from the western half, slowly and invisibly and irreversibly merged into each other." In the second phase, "Greater Tokyo spontaneously bifurcated along a spatiotemporal fault line. Half of this bifurcated Tokyo moved across the world and wrapped itself around the perimeter of the recently formed New York/Los Angeles chimera. This half is referred to as Lost Tokyo-2."[70] Meanwhile,

Lost Tokyo-1 "has not been located yet ... leaving two halves, bewildered ... unable to understand what has happened, or if things will ever go back to the way they were, hoping its other half might someday find its way back" (60). An allegory for transimperial history as well as Taiwan-China partition and conflict, Lost Tokyo-1 amplifies the melancholia that we have already encountered in Charles's father's revanchist "ambition" to bring time travel to market.

The novel's hints at the injuries of racism clarify how revanchism and ressentiment operate as semiperipheral structures of feeling and bring into focus the interactions between semiperipherality and racial form that I have been describing in this chapter. We have already discussed the way in which *How to Live Safely*'s conspicuous lack of racial and national markers fits into a literary trend toward "postracial" representation, as well as how it reflects ambiguity over Taiwan's modernity. This lack also literalizes the erasure of Taiwan and Taiwanese Americans from mainstream mythologies of Silicon Valley that locate its origins in the parental garages of white, cisgendered male founder-geniuses. As AnnaLee Saxenian has shown, Silicon Valley owes much of its success to Taiwanese American return narratives. Post-65 "New Argonauts," as she dubs them (borrowing from the Greek myth of Jason's crew, which leaves from Iolcus and ultimately returns with the Golden Fleece), charted a path of "brain circulation" that has facilitated the technology transfers and established the supply chains that have provided the inputs and infrastructure upon which Silicon Valley and much of the world's technology sectors depend (e.g., semiconductors). These diasporic returns, Saxenian observes, have been multiply motivated: sometimes by a nationalistic commitment to industrialization and economic development, sometimes by a simple entrepreneurial pursuit of profit, sometimes by a combination of these factors.[71] And sometimes by racial barriers like the "bamboo ceiling," which is only glancingly referred to in the novel:

> I noticed, on most nights, his jaw clenched at dinner, the way he closed his eyes slowly when my mother asked him about work ... seeming to physically shrink with each professional defeat ... with each year finding new and deep places to hide it all within himself, observed his absorption of tiny, daily frustrations that, over time (that one true damage-causing substance), accumulated into a reservoir of subterranean failure, like oil shale, like a volatile substance trapped in rock, a vast quantity of potential energy

locked in to an inert substrate, unmoving and silent at the present moment but in actuality building pressure and growing more combustive with each passing year.

"It's not fair," my mom would say. (35)

We have here something like Langston Hughes's sagging load, except the explosive creativity of ressentiment, for Charles's father, leads not to racial resistance or politics but to entrepreneurialism and a time machine prototype that fails to work during a crucial presentation to a venture capitalist. Another inventor succeeds in adapting Charles's father's theory, reaping the windfall of the ensuing world- and universe-creating industries. (In the 1970s and 1980s, Taiwanese technocrats like Lee Kuo-ting leveraged the disappointment of the bamboo ceiling to lure Taiwanese American STEM professionals back to Taiwan.) The science fictional universe of the novel's title is the product of Charles's father's half-failed revenge upon an America that had not given him enough, which is not dissimilar to the science fictional universe we putatively find ourselves in that is the result of Taiwan's half-failed revenge against the People's Republic of China. Charles's father's professional frustration is not only a personal tragedy. It is also a depiction of the human capital dimension of Taiwan's postwar industrialization as combined with what was in the 1960s and 1970s, when Charles's father arrived in the United States, a "global restructuring" that was well underway in which U.S. Cold War political economic priorities directed a Japan-led regional economic development.

For Charles's father, semiperipheral ressentiment is not only a response to the racial abjection that Charles perceives in the presence of the venture capitalist ("noblesse oblige" [174]). It is also a response to an imperative of accumulation, the fantasy of economic mobility that follows from a semiperipheral "fear of falling" that motivated the national priorities that led to his immigration in the first place and articulated a science fictional worldview that converts *enough* into *not enough*. The "jaw clenching thing" that Charles's father often does is a response to racism, but it is also a response to frustrated ambition borne out of an identification with capitalism and capitalist subjects like the venture capitalist and the Pacific ruling class that he emblematizes. On their way to present the time machine prototype to the venture capitalist, we get a description of what Charles's father is truly after:

> He had made a noise, and the world heard him, and the world was coming. And just as he had always imagined, it was coming with money. Or more accurately, the promise of money. More than money. Prestige.... He imagined the prospect of seeing his name in trade journals, rivals and admirers whispering about what he was working on, his method of working, how he got his ideas. He imagined how the people at work would react when he quit, when a month after he quit they realized what they had let slip away, how they could never afford him now, how they had ignored him all those years, put him in the cubicle, let him inch upward, never seeing the quality of his ideas. (168–69)

Insofar as racial meanings in the United States are only legible as signs of abjection, the wholehearted alignment with capital disclosed in this passage seems to disqualify Charles's father's warrant to self-identification as a racial subject. We might therefore read the novel's semiperipheral structure of feeling as a register of private and national experiences of racial downgrading and the desire to move up the global value chain. One thing that is behind the novel's evasions of racial markers is precisely that mote of PMC class identification with capital that undermines racial meaning in the United States.

THE MELANCHOLY AXIS

While there is no mystery why Charles's father is angry, it is never clear why Charles himself is so sad. What is the "secret," to recall Fludernik's term, behind that sadness, which also renders him, like other narrators of Taiwanese American fiction, so unreliable, so bad at being himself? What is the gravitational force that pulls him into a life lived "at zero?" Beneath all of this is a political desire about Taiwanese identity that defies expression for Yu and for many Taiwanese Americans of his generation. It was only in the late 1980s, as martial law was relaxing, that it first became possible in Taiwan to openly express political desires differing from the KMT, and even then not without consequences. The question of how to articulate those desires in relation to China—a culture, if not a state, with which pro-independence and pro-reunification partisans alike continue to identify and disidentify—further complicates the discourse around Taiwanese identity, which is complicated further still by the problem of Han settler colonialism and indigenous rights to the island, which are a matter of justice but also threaten to retrench capitalist regimes of property. What is often described as Taiwan's semicolonial dependency on the United States adds yet another layer of state-level mediation to Taiwanese identity, as well as a layer of diasporic meaning. As Chih-ming Wang argues, "Taiwan's future is... intimately linked to Taiwanese Americans, as their identity both depends on and contributes to Taiwan's de jure independence."[72] Taiwanese and Taiwanese Americans are linked by an axis that resists panethnicity and thus evades Asian Americanist frameworks. Through the framework of Northeast Asian America, that axis snaps into focus.

The novel's appendix, where Charles finally finds his father, opens with an image that materializes these tangles of mediation: "Look in the box. Inside it, there's another box. Look in that box and find another one. And then another one, until you get to the last one. The smallest one" (232). It is in that tiniest box that Charles finds a reproduction of the kitchen in his childhood home and a clock that gives him the final clue he needs to find his father. When they reunite, his father explains that "he got trapped in the past" and had never meant to disappear for so long (232). They then climb into Charles's time machine and return to "home, present day." This is what the appendix tells them to do once they arrive: "Step out into the world of time and risk and loss again. Move forward, into the empty plane. Find the book you wrote, and read it until the end, but don't turn the last page yet, keep stalling, see how long you can keep expanding the infinitely expandable moment. Enjoy the elastic present, which can accommodate as little or as much as you want to put in there. Stretch it out, live inside of it" (233). The contradictions in this passage (e.g., a never-ending book, an "infinitely expandable" present) evoke that other scene of Taiwanese identity formation, the "tiny island" and its location within capitalist "reality" that is somehow also "faraway" from capitalist temporality and its circuits of labor and exchange. The depiction of agency here, bolstered rather than undermined by the imperative verb forms in almost every sentence, suggests that at the core of the Taiwanese identity that the novel narrates in fits and starts is *self-determination*. It is to this theme that the novel's entire semiperipheral structure of feeling is oriented, as well as all of the formal strategies that Yu employs. The novel doesn't end there but goes on for one more page, where we find this text: "[this page intentionally left blank]" (234). This tiny island of text floating outside of the novel's spacetime names a political desire for a Taiwanese identity, a structure of feeling that for a diasporic Taiwanese American author in 2010 could only be conveyed formally—through the appendix's subjunctive mood, the novel's uncertain genre status, time travel plot, and science fictionality.[73]

We are given two indications of just how fundamental this desire is in the novel. In one of Charles's memories from his childhood, he witnesses his father crying: "I stood there in the hall, a few feet outside the threshold of my father's private study, watching him, looking at him framed by the door, while he looked at his own father, framed in the picture, *the three of us, son, father, and grandfather, forming a melancholy axis, forming a chain, a regress, a bridge into the past*" (194–96, my emphasis). The question of why his father is crying and what makes this axis "melancholy" is answered earlier in the novel, when Charles explains, "It was almost like [my father] was trying to get lost, like he knew what it would all lead to, this machine. He wanted to use it for sadness, to investigate the source of his own, his father's, and on and on, to the ultimate origin, some *dark radiating body*, trapped in its own severe curvature, cut off from the rest of the universe" (48, my emphasis). Like the inheritors of transimperial trauma that we met in chapter 1, the engineer legatees of modernization in chapter 2, the economic subjects in chapter 3, and the professionalized daughters of deprofessionalized mothers in chapter 4, Charles is pursued by his origins. The melancholy axis reaches out to him. If Charles and his father are both blocked from self-determination, then it is because Taiwan, throughout its many colonizations, has always been blocked from self-determination. If the novel's characters are alienated from themselves and each other, it is because Taiwan has been alienated from the international community and from its own capacity for expressing a national identity. If Charles is "not particularly good at being [himself]," it is because Taiwan has not been particularly good at being itself (10). This is the novel's deepest source of sadness—the "dark radiating body" that installs itself in Charles's grandfather, that Charles eventually inherits, and that, even more than the disappointments of professional failure, provokes Charles's father to use his STEM training to escape from reality.

There is a version of Taiwanese nationalism that wants to transcend the nation form itself, to escape the "reality" of global capitalism in which the nation form is an essential unit of political, economic, and social organization. For this kind of nationalism, self-determination and independence are necessary intermediary steps on the way to a building a world in which nations do not exist because they would not need to exist. This is ultimately a radical vision of a postcapitalist world that is, to borrow the journalist E. Tammy Kim's phrase, "anti-nationalist and internationalist": a nationalism that openly desires its own negation.[74] The venues and vocabulary for expressing Taiwanese identities such as these have been magnificently expanded by a younger generation of Taiwanese and Taiwanese Americans leftists. Associated with the 2014 Sunflower Movement, in which students and activists occupied the chambers of Taiwan's legislature for three weeks that spring to oppose a KMT-sponsored bill that would deepen China's economic ties with Taiwan, these writers, thinkers, and activists have reframed the geopolitical challenges of Taiwan's self-determination as an opportunity for "working in solidarity with other liberation movements [around the world] instead of pandering to the political-economic desires of the US Empire."[75] Rather than solely focus on Taiwan, they have forged an axis of solidarity with movements in Hong Kong, Southeast Asia, and beyond.[76] In many ways this identity returns us to a vision expressed in the 1960s and 1970s by some of the very same hyper-selected Taiwanese STEM students who comprised the first wave of post-65 immigrants: a democratic vision that the Taiwanese American scholar Wendy Cheng's late father Edward, who was trained as a nuclear engineer, once called a "contradictory, but fantastic thing."[77] If, as Cheng documents, this vision got trapped in the past, it is because it was suppressed—not only by the surveillance and machinations of the KMT but also by the semiperipheral desires of Taiwanese Americans for whom capitalist subjectivity was an adequate compensation for the hurt of political defeat. This vision's traversal of the space-times of Taiwan's postwar development and the careers of post-65 Taiwanese Americans compels us to ask whether independence will ever be enough. Whether it should be enough, and whether our goal is to live safely or by some other principle.

CONCLUSION
Asian Fetish

> The bourgeoisie, by the rapid improvement of all instruments of production, by the immensely facilitated means of communication, draws all, even the most barbarian, nations into civilisation. The cheap prices of its commodities are the heavy artillery with which it batters down all Chinese walls, with which it forces the barbarians' intensely obstinate hatred of foreigners to capitulate. It compels all nations, on pain of extinction, to adopt the bourgeois mode of production; it compels them to introduce what it calls civilisation into their midst, i.e., to become bourgeois themselves. In one word, it creates a world after its own image.
>
> —KARL MARX AND FREDERICK ENGELS, "MANIFESTO OF THE COMMUNIST PARTY"

This book has offered a deliberately partial account of post-65 Asian American literature. Its focus on Northeast Asian American literature and its authors arises from an inductive approach that proceeds from specific material histories, and its aim has been to show how works of post-65 Northeast Asian American literature share a set of racial and literary forms that extend from the class typicality of its authors. Against the backdrop of rising economic fortunes in Northeast Asia and existential doubts about American democracy and capitalism, these authors and their texts grapple with what it means to be *Asian* American: how the shifting emphasis of that identity broadens geographical and cultural horizons even as it raises questions about capitalist subjectivity and historical justice. What lessons does this account offer for scholars of Asian American literature as a whole? I would like to think that there are many, but I will focus on just one, which pertains to Asian racial form in the era of deindustrialization. As open as many of these texts are to identifications beyond the United States, they cannot escape U.S. racial forms. One lesson we might draw from them is that the racial forms that have traditionally organized Asian Americanist scholarship and critique—forms of bodily abjection associated with spatial and juridical exclusion—no longer appear to be the predominant forms that structure Asian American life and racial representation.

CONCLUSION

Among the clearest and most convincing theories of Asian racial form that we have is offered by Iyko Day in her 2016 book *Alien Capital: Asian Racialization and the Logic of Settler Colonial Capitalism*. Drawing from Colleen Lye's work on nineteenth- and early twentieth-century U.S. discourses of Asian exclusion and transpacific political economy and Moishe Postone's work on the racialization of capitalist domination, Day argues that Asiatic racial form in North America is primordially anchored to a false antinomy of "abstract" versus "concrete" labor. Adapting Postone, she traces this to a "settler colonial ideology of romantic anticapitalism," which creates three positions: "Indigenous, alien, and settler." To these positions, a variety of social meanings are assigned. Asians, as "free," imported labor, occupy the role of aliens who can be excluded and expelled. They are contradistinguished from Native Americans who can be eliminated but not expelled, Blacks who can be excluded but also not expelled, and the white settlers who have an interest in naturalizing the whole scheme. Following the narrative of romantic anticapitalism, "the Asian signals the overthrow of traditional, pure, concrete conceptions of labor for an era that reduces human individuality to an abstract form of repetition and equivalence."[1] Key to Day's account is how the materiality of the Asian body sustains romantic anticapitalism's false antinomy, concealing, in the manner of what Marx calls "fetishism," the commensurability of all forms of labor under capitalism, concrete or not, as well as capitalism's core operation of extracting profit by abstracting labor as a quantity of time.[2] In Yoon Sun Lee's helpful gloss, the Asian body serves a primarily *visual* function in Day's argument.[3] Indeed, Day opens her book with a brilliant analysis of a visual object. She recounts an incident in 2012 when the Bank of Canada replaced an image of a female Asian scientist on its newly designed hundred-dollar bill with an allegedly "neutral" "Caucasian-looking woman." In Day's reading, an image of a female Asian scientist on a banknote was too upsetting as an emblem of Canadian national identity for the focus groups that the Bank consulted because it crystallized a racial form in which Asians personify "capital itself."[4] The decision to "neutralize" the image thus demonstrates how "the contemporary economism of Asian racial form does not represent a break from the past" but rather a continuity with its nineteenth-century forms.[5]

As Day makes clear, her account of Asian racial form is tightly associated with *industrialization*: a period in which Asian waged labor—primarily

Chinese, Japanese, and Filipino—was recruited as reserve armies to serve America's rapidly expanding industrial needs. These populations were disciplined through segregation policies and exclusion laws that continued in various forms until the passage of the Immigration and Nationality Act in 1965, which, as I outlined in the introduction, made immigration a matter of fiscal policy and shifted its orientation from exclusion and restriction to inclusion and selection.[6] This connection between racial abjection and juridical exclusion—for Day, emblematized by the figure of the *coolie*—has formed the basis of Asian Americanist historiography and political expression.[7] Consequently, as Christopher Lee argues, it has also formed the basis of Asian Americanist hermeneutics, which have been committed to producing accounts of an "idealized critical subject" of resistance.[8] The political and institutional stakes involved in maintaining these orthodoxies are high. As Viet Thanh Nguyen has argued, "Without the compelling narrative of assimilation and political resistance against exclusion, the possibilities for uniting Asian America over its heterogeneous constitution rapidly begin to fracture."[9] Although the *visual* basis of Asian racial form's nineteenth-century logics is undeniably still with us, as Yoon Sun Lee goes on to point out, "visuality cannot account for everything."[10] Lee's point is that the visual, and the exclusion thesis through which it is expressed, can tell us only part of the story of Asian racialization. The racialization of Asians as the embodiment of all of capitalism's evils depends in no small way upon a prevalence of opportunities to set one's eyes on Asian bodies performing labor—to register, in Marx's words, their "sensuous" qualities as labor commodities.[11] We recall in Marx's account of fetishism, however, that commodities possess another dimension besides this. Commodities, he writes, are "sensuous things which are at the same time *supra-sensible or social*."[12] It is along these lines that Lee argues that "Asians can be most vividly and consequentially represented *when they are not explicitly represented or visualized at all*."[13] The nonvisual, "supra-sensible" dimension of racial form—Lee names "narrative ... the aesthetic ... [and] concepts, such as realism"—are where we might find, through analysis, an additional register of the "social."[14] What Day helps us to see is how in Asian American studies the visual is a preeminent vehicle of the "metaphorical duplicity at the heart of capitalist value"[15] and that the visual is not only an analytical crux but a whole historiographical apparatus anchored to North American industrialization.

CONCLUSION

Critiques of the exclusion thesis, like Nguyen's, have focused mostly on how it serves institutional reproduction and the accumulation of professional capital.[16] Day's distinction between a racial form that welds the visuality of the Asian body to processes of abstraction and a racial form that welds Asian visual representation to "capital itself" helps us to grasp Takeo Rivera's observation that "Asiatic racial form shifts according to the status of material labor conditions."[17] It also helps us to approach the exclusion thesis and Asian racial form from a different direction, as matters of periodization.[18] What happens to Asian racial form when U.S. industrial expansion gives way to an extended period of deindustrialization? In industrialization, Asians, especially Chinese and Japanese, were occupationally concentrated in labor-intensive productive occupations (e.g., farming, railroads, mining, factories, laundries) that brought them in physical proximity to processes of labor abstraction. Day's examples include Chinese railroad workers whose labor efficiency amplified the contradictions of how value is derived from socially necessary labor time, much to the ire of the white workers whom they outnumbered four to one. Then there were the Chinese enclaves in which reproductive, domestic spaces were conflated with productive spaces and there was no distinction in the working day between reproductive necessary labor time and productive surplus labor time.[19] This seemingly natural acceptance of dehumanization, Day writes, "fed into romantic anticapitalism's dehumanization of Chinese workers as abstract labor."[20]

Since the end of World War II, industrial activity, manufacturing, and the corporate rate of profit have declined steadily in the United States, a trend called *deindustrialization*.[21] As Jasper Bernes writes, deindustrialization marks a period in which "people, by and large, turn from work based on making things or objects to work oriented around the performance of administrative and technical processes or the provision of services to customers."[22] This turn away from the kind of work in which bodily labor is highly visible has been even more pronounced among post-65 Asian Americans who, as we have seen, are occupationally concentrated into STEM fields and "knowledge work" in much higher proportions compared to other racial groups. It's relevant that the female Asian scientist in Day's anecdote is a *scientist*. The history behind the scientist's heavily mediated representation, even its multicultural forms, is more a legacy of mid-twentieth-century modernization projects than nineteenth-century industrialization. Moreover, work visas like the H-1B have accelerated transformations in labor that are associated with deindustrialization like deskilling and casualization. By virtue of their short terms and sponsorship requirements, such work arrangements build exclusion and restriction into what appear to be policies of professional selection. And because the vast majority of these visas go to workers from China and India, they are strongly determinative of Asian racial form.

Romantic anticapitalism is an irrational, utopian story that projects a fantastical *beyond* from capitalism where we have an authentic, unalienated relation to our labor. In Asian American studies, its impact is felt in an analytical tendency to separate race from class and to associate concrete labor (activism, critique) with race and anticapitalist resistance and abstract labor (institutional reproduction) with class and model minority desire. If there has been a revival of the dialectical analysis of race and class in Asian American studies, of which Day's book is a powerful example,[23] I suspect that what has prompted it is due as much to developments outside of Asian American studies as with contradictions that have unfolded within the field. Here I have in mind how the fetishistic power of romantic anticapitalism has diminished. The question posed by capitalism today is overwhelmingly whether or not we can survive it as a species, not to mention as immiserated workers whose wages have been stagnant for the past half century; it is not whether we can rescue our concrete labor from the alienation of capitalist abstraction. Our collective sense that "there is no alternative" to free market capitalism, which Mark Fisher famously dubbed "capitalist realism," reigns supreme.[24] Just as industrial processes are still with us, though residually, the contours of romantic anticapitalism are still with us as well, but its narrative has morphed into an ideology that places the hyperawareness of capitalist realism's foreclosure on one side and the openness of liberation on the other. We might call this a science fictional ideology that sustains a dichotomy in which the technological extensions of capital are assigned to the monstrous processes of labor abstraction, and human production and reproduction to concrete labor. As Annie McClanahan puts it: "machinic autonomy *or* human labor . . . automated factories *or* a labor-driven service sector . . . automation and growth *or* technological and economic stagnation."[25]

The comedian Scott Seiss helps us to grasp this antinomy. In response to the boosterism around the latest version of the automation threat—"A.I.

CONCLUSION

is a wonder! It can do things you never thought possible"—Seiss quips: "Yeah, like make me admit I want to keep my job." The threat of total automation fails to sustain a romantic narrative about the concreteness of human labor. What's cathartic about Seiss's jokes is how his characters, who are fully aware of how labor is abstracted, immediately leap past romantic tropes of concrete labor. There's nothing particularly Asian American about Seiss's jokes, but Asian racial form has facilitated the deromanticization of romantic anticapitalism by articulating race to the threat of labor automation. While the industrial version of the automation threat centers on inhumanly efficient Asian bodies who work for inhumane wages and replace white jobs, the deindustrial version involves "techno-orientalist" fears of Asian subjects and states developing technologies that will not only do our jobs for us, but obsolesce those jobs altogether.[26] This was the well-nigh Oedipal irony suffusing Andrew Yang's short-lived presidential candidacy, in which he touted an automation threat narrative to advocate for universal basic income. Yang's father, Kei Hsiung, who holds a PhD in physics, spent much of his career generating patents for the TFT/LCD technologies used in the self-service kiosks that Yang blames for automating away retail jobs.[27] Meanwhile, Asian subjects and states—China especially—continue to be scapegoated for labor obsolescence in the United States and the West more broadly, rather than the "moving contradiction" of capital that disposes of the very source of its value creation, human labor.[28] Whether or not the job apocalypse that generative large language models and high-tech automation portend is a real possibility or if critics of that narrative are correct that underemployment and immiseration are the more likely outcomes, either way we are staring down a science fictional future in which human reproduction is an increasingly inefficient component of capitalist value extraction.[29] Under these conditions, in which people are increasingly aware of the systemic origins of crises that cannot be personified—indeed, to the point of capitalist realist pessimism—Asian racial form has shifted its orientation from the visual to the social.

So how does Asian racial form in the era of deindustrialization fix to the "supra-sensual" dimension of the commodity, and what does this tell us? Throughout this book we have encountered a number of characters who have helped us to formulate responses to these questions. Ruth Ozeki's Nao and her father Haruki #2, Ted Chiang's postracial heptapods and their impossible language, Chang-rae Lee's Henry Park and Pong Lou, Ling Ma's

Candace Chen, Kathy Wang's Fred Huang, and Charles Yu's father-son pair: all of these point us to a key feature of Asian racial form in the era of deindustrialization. What makes these characters Asian American is how their authors use them to remediate legacies of modernization through narratives of economic mobility, the aestheticization of the two-cultures conflict, and more often than not the literal movement of characters between Asia and the United States. Their racial form is associated not with their bodily capacity to produce commodities (which reminds us of capitalism's abstraction of labor), but with their capacity to reproduce capital (which reminds us of exchange, circulation, and mobility). *In the era of deindustrialization, it is the STEM professional rather than the coolie who is the preeminent figure for Asian racial form.* Whereas the locus of Asian racialization during industrialization was the sensuous dimension of production and labor, these characters and the forms through which they come into existence demonstrate to us that this locus has expanded to encompass the "supra-sensory" dimensions of "capital itself." This doesn't mean that surplus value is no longer generated through the abstraction of labor. It means that deindustrialization has different needs for Asian labor than industrialization did and that the social forms that we call race have shifted accordingly. These characters help us to track the "supra-sensual" dimension of the "social" and its entanglement with the "sensuous": a whole depth of history and material relations in which the economic, cultural, and ideological routes that transimperial modernization established are traced and retraced. They also bring into relief one of the main points that this book has tried to make, which is that Asian American identity—especially Northeast Asian American identity—is today as much a class identity as it is a racial identity.

For me this last point is a particularly important one because the disavowal of class in Asian American studies has facilitated the neglect of Taiwan and Taiwanese American histories. So I hope the reader will forgive me, at the very least in the spirit of disrupting the illusory sense of an ending that the genre of the conclusion is designed to generate, for leaping abruptly ahead to a set of questions that follow from all this. Coupled with the relatively small size of Taiwan and the Taiwanese American community and the easy elisions with China and Chinese Americans, the fact that Taiwanese Americans possess among the highest education and income attainments of any ethnic group in the United States gives the community a unique class character and racial status that makes it incompatible with the Asian American exclusion thesis—an awkward fit at best. Consequently, as Wendy Cheng quite correctly observes, "In most accounts of the Asian American Movement as well as collections concerning Asian American political activism more generally, Taiwanese are not mentioned at all."[30] There are two ways in which the effects of this aporia can be addressed: by recovering Taiwanese American histories and by reflecting upon the aporia's underlying conditions. This book has taken both of these approaches by attending to Taiwanese American authors and to Taiwan's transimperial entanglements with Japan, the United States, and China. In many ways this book's inductive approach is a response to Taiwan's elision in Asian American studies, an attempt at broadening our historical lens and deepening our dialectical commitments to show how Taiwan's specificity is foundational not only to Northeast Asian regional development but also to the coherence of all of those things we call Asian American.

There is much more at stake here than adding a space for Taiwanese Americans within Asian American studies: deeper questions about the field itself, the kind of knowledge it is capable of producing, and the kind of political force it is capable of projecting. What impact would war over Taiwan, or Taiwan's abandonment by the international community in order to avert war between the United States and China, have on Asian America? How might Asian American studies, as an intellectual and political formation, respond? In a field that traces its roots to the antiwar movement, what are the limits of a critique of race and U.S. empire in such a situation? What opportunities would such a critique present? This is a thought exercise to which I often return.

ACKNOWLEDGMENTS

I'm not capable of writing a book on my own. Thank goodness for other people.

I am grateful to my colleagues at UC Irvine for creating a nurturing intellectual, infrastructural, and institutional environment for this book: Annabel Adams, Jonathan Alexander, Elizabeth Allen, Colin Andrews, Jami Bartlett, Philip Broadbent, Kassandra Ceja, Jasmine Diaz, David Fedman, Lisa Florentes-Mullens, Audrey Fong, Richard Godden, Kyle Grady, Chad Horn, Hu Ying, Joe Jeon, Eleana Kim, Camille Laws, Jerry Lee, Jim Lee, Julia Lee, Mimi Long, Julia Lupton, Daren Mai, Ted Martin, Annie McClanahan, Liz Nguyen, Dee Dee Nunez, Beth Pace, Dwayne Pack, Brad Queen, Valentina Montero Roman, Jeremy Saine, Joo Hoon Sin, Jim Steintrager, Amanda Swain, Michael Szalay, and Monica Youn. Annie, Joe, Michael, Richard, and Ted made all the difference upon my arrival by bringing me into the intense embrace of their reading group. My graduate students Jacob Baumgartner, Jiyon Byun, Toni Hays, Chenglin Lee, Jung Soo Lee, and Alden Sajor Marte-Wood were sources of inspiration and motivation for this book—I count them among my most valued teachers. Thanks also to my research assistant Danielle Shi.

At UC Berkeley, where the ideas for this book were first stuttered into the world, I have many friends and mentors to thank: Janet Adelman, Aaron Bady, Alex Benson, Ashley Barnes, Jasper Bernes, Ben Cannon, Chris Chen,

ACKNOWLEDGMENTS

Jeehyun Choi, Dan Clinton, Jean Day, Lyn Hejinian, Jane Hu, Shannon Jackson, Azusa Kobayashi, David Landreth, James Jaehoon Lee, Seulghee Lee, Steven Lee, Andrew Leong, Lili Loofbourow, Trinh Luu, Swami Medhananda, Gabe Milner, PJ Nadal, Gina Patnaik, Luke Terlaak Poot, Gautam Premnath, Kent Puckett, Megan Pugh, Takeo Rivera, Becca Schonberg, Scott Saul, Matt Seidel, Jonathan Shelley, Katie Snyder, Ragini Tharoor Srinivasan, Amanda Su, Michelle Ty, Sunny Xiang, Wendy Xin, Irene Yoon, and Mia You. Every thought in this book was shaped by Colleen Lye and prototyped with PJ, Ragini, and Sunny.

Portions of this book received valuable feedback at the 2015 Penn State Asian Studies Institute. My thanks to Crystal Baik, Akash Belsare, Tina Chen, Chris Eng, Eric Hayot, Michelle Nancy Huang, Andrew Leong, Cheryl Naruse, Vinh Nguyen, Leland Tabares, Darwin Tsen, Grace Wu, and Hentyle Yapp. I also received valuable feedback from the participants in Grace Wang's Fulbright seminar in Hong Kong: Ackbar Abbas, King-kok Cheung, Jason Coe, Joe Jeon, Eleana Kim, Andrea Louie, Susette Min, Kim Park Nelson, erin Khuê Ninh, LeiLani Nishime, Christopher Patterson, Valerie Soe, and Thuy Linh Tu.

I thank Gordon Hutner for providing me with multiple opportunities to share my work in *American Literary History*, and to Philip Leventhal for reading one those articles and then guiding me so calmly and expertly through publication. This book has been improved by Philip's sharp editorial eye and perspicuity, as well as the care and attention of Monique Laban, Marisa Lastres, Gregory McNamee, and Chang Jae Lee. I would also like to thank Yu-wen Wu for her art, which grasps the essence of this book, and more specifically for her permission to use for the book's cover an image from her aptly titled installation *The Accumulation of Dreams*.

Over the years, I was given encouragement at key moments by Rachel Lee, Gautam Premnath, David Roh, Stephen Hong Sohn, and Sherryl Vint. They might not even realize how pivotal they've been for me, but I will never forget. On more than one occasion, especially during my many years on the job market, Aimee Bahng lifted me out of despair.

Several people came together to help me over the finish line. For reading multiple drafts, responding to innumerable questions, and for their general wisdom, I once again thank Ted, Annie, and Michael, and, again, PJ, Ragini, and Sunny. Joe Jeon read just about everything in this book several times and has provided me with a model of generosity and

ACKNOWLEDGMENTS

professionalism that I strive to emulate. Thanks to him, this book was supported in part by the Core University Program for Korean Studies of the Ministry of Education of the Republic of Korea and the Korean Studies Promotion Service at the Academy of Korean Studies. I rush to add that this book received support from the UCI Humanities Center. Darwin Tsen and Chih-ming Andy Wang provided crucial feedback for this book's final chapter on Taiwanese American return fiction. At a late stage in revisions, I benefited tremendously from Dan Sinykin's and Chris Suh's generosity. A few people appeared in my life at the end of this project who would have improved it tremendously had I met them at the beginning: Wendy Cheng, Ian Rowen, and Lawrence Yang.

Spending a decade writing a book requires a judicious oscillation between self-seriousness and self-ridicule. For their help with the latter, and for joy they brought into my life, I owe much to the Loud Group, the Condors, our Bay Area Legal Aid crew, Team Oakland, Denise Ho and Alex Ledin, Stephanie Tsai and Sam Appel, Jennifer Huang and Doug "Dougadougadouga" Yoshida, Darice Wong and Jason Kutch, Annie Ro and Fernando Rodriguez, Stephen Lee and Adrianne De Castro, Weihsin Huang, George Sanchez, and Alex Nishikawa. Agatha (most beautiful dog), Bao Bao (it's Bao Bao!). Thanks also to my *Hyphen* peeps. In many ways, the roots of this book and the routes it tracks sprung forth from the vision we created together more than twenty years ago.

All that said, this book is for and about my family. Growing up in the mildewy, unfriendly suburbs of Northwest Houston, I always felt like we were out of place. Writing this book has taught me about our connection to the world—our typicality and how we have never been alone. To my parents Gratia Hsieh and Timothy Fan, and my sisters Judy and Kathrine, thank you for your love, support, and patience. Li Chen, Albert Chen, Peggy Chen, Oliver Wang, Colette Wang, and Rosalie Wang have grounded me as well as provided endless hours of entertainment. Lenny, too. The extended Fan family, 阿姨, and the Kuos have made Taiwan home.

Finally, to the Chen-Fan Pack. Eliot, Casey, Shuli, and Amy . . . we did it!

NOTES

INTRODUCTION

1. Marilyn Chin and Maxine Hong Kingston, "A MELUS Interview: Maxine Hong Kingston," *MELUS* 16, no. 4 (Winter 1989): 68–69.
2. Sau-ling Wong, *Reading Asian American Literature: From Necessity to Extravagance* (Princeton, NJ: Princeton University Press, 1993), 3. Elaine Kim, Shirley Geok-lin Lim, and Amy Ling also noted the boom in Lim and Ling's *Reading the Literatures of Asian America* (Philadelphia: Temple University Press, 1992). I should caution here that we should not interpret this boom as evidence of the diversification of American fiction. Published American authors in the postwar period have been overwhelmingly white, and the institutional logics of the publishing industry have maintained this predominance. As Dan Sinykin observes, the supposed diversification of publishing that Amy Tan's success, alongside that of Toni Morrison, Sandra Cisneros, and Louise Erdrich during this period, "masked the profound whiteness of the trade publishing industry." *Big Fiction: How Conglomeration Changed Book Publishing and American Fiction* (New York: Columbia University Press, 2023), 233. See also Richard Jean So, *Redlining Culture: A Data History of Racial Inequality and Postwar Fiction* (New York: Columbia University Press, 2020), and Laura McGrath, "Comping White," *Los Angeles Review of Books* (January 21, 2019), https://lareviewofbooks.org/article/comping-white/.
3. Min Hyoung Song, *The Children of 1965: On Writing, and Not Writing, as an Asian American* (Durham, NC: Duke University Press, 2013), 8. Song's characterization relies on a sharp uptick in awards given to Asian American fiction and fiction writers, also beginning in the 1980s. On the importance of the genre of historical fiction to this uptick, as well as to the award economy and canonization of other "ethnic" American literatures, see Alexander Manshel's *Writing Backwards: Historical*

INTRODUCTION

Fiction and the Reshaping of the American Canon (New York: Columbia University Press, 2024).

4. This sustained literary boom has laid the groundwork for the recent efflorescence of Asian American film and television, much of which has adapted literary objects. Examples are ABC's 2015–2020 *Fresh off the Boat*, based on Eddie Huang's 2013 autobiography; Netflix's 2018 *To All the Boys I've Loved Before*, adapted from Jenny Han's 2014 novel; Disney+'s 2023 *American Born Chinese*, based on Gene Luen Yang's 2006 graphic novel; Hulu's 2024 *Interior Chinatown*, adapted from Charles Yu's 2020 novel; and the 2018 film *Crazy Rich Asians*, adapted from Kevin Kwan's 2013 novel.

5. World Bank, *The East Asian Miracle: Economic Growth and Public Policy* (New York: Oxford University Press, 1993), 2.

6. Wong, *Reading Asian American Literature*, 9.

7. The relation between the end of the "American Century" and the rise and revival of various forms of the "Asian Century" is a trope that I owe to Giovanni Arrighi's books *The Long Twentieth Century: Money, Power, and the Origin of Our Times* (New York: Verso, 1994), and *Adam Smith in Beijing: Lineages of the Twenty-First Century* (New York: Verso, 2007). See also "The Asian Century: Idea, Method, and Media," ed. Christopher T. Fan, Paul Nadal, Ragini Tharoor Srinivasan, and Tina Chen, *Verge: Studies in Global Asias* 11, no. 2 (forthcoming, 2025).

8. In his paraphrase of Susan Koshy's work, which makes this point, Viet Thanh Nguyen writes: "The assimilationist paradigm of descent and consent . . . and the imperative to claim an American identity found in many accounts of Asian American literature are no longer necessarily the dominant motivations of new immigrant populations." *Race and Resistance: Literature and Politics in Asian America* (New York: Oxford University Press, 2002), 21; Susan Koshy, "The Fiction of Asian American Literature," *Yale Journal of Criticism* 9, no. 2 (Fall 1996): 315–46. On the "transnational turn" in Asian American studies see Tina Chen and Eric Hayot, "Introducing *Verge*: What Does It Mean to Study Global Asias?" *Verge: Studies in Global Asias* 1, no. 1 (Spring 2015): vi–xv; Kandice Chuh and Karen Shimakawa, eds., *Orientations: Mapping Studies in the Asian Diaspora* (Durham, NC: Duke University Press, 2001); Eric Hayot, "The Asian Turns," *PMLA* 124, no. 3 (May 2009): 906–17; Shirley Geok-Lin Lim, John Gamber, Stephen Hong Sohn, and Gina Valentino, *Transnational Asian American Literature: Sites and Transits* (Philadelphia: Temple University Press, 2006); and Wong, "Denationalization Reconsidered: Asian American Cultural Criticism at a Theoretical Crossroads," *Amerasia Journal* 21, no. 1 (1995): 1–28.

9. See chapter 3 of Bruce Cumings, *Parallax Visions: Making Sense of American-East Asian Relations* (Durham, NC: Duke University Press, 2002) and Thomas B. Gold, *State and Society in the Taiwan Miracle* (Armonk, NY: M. E. Sharpe, 1986). As Robert Wade has written, the World Bank's report was in large part written by the Bank of Japan itself, which was promoting liberalization over against the Japanese government's commitment to a developmental direction. "Japan, the World Bank, and the Art of Paradigm Maintenance: *The East Asian Miracle* in Political Perspective," *New Left Review* 217 (May–June 1996): 3–36. On the role of adoption as the "commodification of children" in South Korea's industrialization, see Eleana J.

INTRODUCTION

Kim, *Adopted Territory: Transnational Korean Adoptees and the Politics of Belonging* (Durham, NC: Duke University Press, 2010).

10. Jim Glassman, *Drums of War, Drums of Development: The Formation of a Pacific Ruling Class and Industrial Transformation in East and Southeast Asia, 1945–1980* (Chicago: Haymarket Books, 2018), 3.
11. Abby Budiman and Neil G. Ruiz, "Asian Americans Are the Fastest-Growing Racial or Ethnic Group in the U.S." (Pew Research Center, April 9, 2021), https://www.pewresearch.org/fact-tank/2021/04/09/asian-americans-are-the-fastest-growing-racial-or-ethnic-group-in-the-u-s/. See also Mary Hanna and Jeanne Batalova, "Immigrants from Asia in the United States" (Migration Policy Institute, March 10, 2021), https://www.migrationpolicy.org/article/immigrants-asia-united-states-2020.
12. Other ethnic literary traditions saw their initial booms in earlier periods: for instance, the Harlem and Chicago "Renaissances" of the early twentieth century and the civil rights-era proliferation of Chicanx and Latinx literatures. In response to Henry Louis Gates Jr.'s well-known lauding of 1992's "proliferation of titles" in African American fiction, Richard So notes that Gates's anecdotal assessment "mistakes the success of a few individual authors for a transformation in the larger field." *Redlining Culture: A Data History of Racial Inequality and Postwar Fiction* (New York: Columbia University Press, 2020), 11.
13. Song, *The Children of 1965*, 8.
14. Frédéric Docquier and Hillel Rapoport, "Globalization, Brain Drain, and Development," *Journal of Economic Literature* 50, no. 3 (September 2012): 682.
15. Docquier and Rapoport, "Globalization, Brain Drain, and Development," 684.
16. On the challenges that South Korea's postwar governments faced in directing education policy towards industrial needs, see Michael J. Seth, *Education Fever: Society, Politics, and the Pursuit of Schooling in South Korea* (Honolulu: University of Hawaiʻi Press, 2002), 110–39.
17. Jennifer Lee and Min Zhou define "hyper-selection" as that circumstance in which "an immigrant group boasts not only a higher percentage of college graduates compared with nonmigrants from their country of origin but also a higher percentage of college graduates compared with the general population in the host country," "Hyper-Selectivity and the Remaking of Culture: Understanding the Asian American Achievement Paradox," *Asian American Journal of Psychology* 8, no. 1 (2017): 8.
18. Jini Kim Watson, *The New Asian City: Three-Dimensional Fictions of Space and Urban Form* (Minneapolis: University of Minnesota Press, 2011), 253. The account of Northeast Asian regionalism that I provide later in this introduction is inspired by Watson's pursuit of "the New Asian City" as what she calls a "regional material formation" rather than urban monads (8). My goal in the chapters that follow is in many ways to show how the uneasiness that Watson mentions suffuses post-65 Asian American fiction and registers the "unfinished business of developmental nationalism" in Asia (253).
19. As Guy Ortolano recounts, the arts versus sciences trope extends at least as far back as the Arnold-Huxley debates of the late nineteenth century; see *The Two Cultures Controversy: Science, Literature, and Cultural Politics* (Cambridge: Cambridge University Press, 2009). In his 1959 lecture "The Two Cultures and the

Scientific Revolution," Snow decried the antagonism between "traditional" culture (humanist disciplines), and scientific culture. For Snow, the two-cultures conflict allegorized U.S.-Soviet conflict. Advocating for greater understanding between the two cultures, Snow expressed a postwar optimism that, in addition to envisioning a technocratic rapprochement between the United States and USSR, was shared by theorists of so-called postindustrial society, who saw science and technology as the key to endless industrial expansion and often invoked Snow in their arguments. See, for example, Daniel Bell, *The Coming of Post-Industrial Society: A Venture in Social Forecasting* (New York: Basic Books, 1973), and Michael Marien, "The Two Visions of Post-Industrial Society," *Futures* 9, no. 5 (October 1977): 415–31.

20. Sau-ling Wong, "Necessity and Extravagance in Maxine Hong Kingston's *The Woman Warrior*: Art and the Ethnic Experience," *MELUS* 15, no. 1 (Spring 1988): 3–26.

21. E. D. Huntley, *Maxine Hong Kingston: A Critical Companion* (Westport, CT: Greenwood Press, 2000), 7.

22. Mark McGurl, *The Program Era: Postwar Fiction and the Rise of Creative Writing* (Cambridge, MA: Harvard University Press, 2009), 262.

23. David Ekbladh, *The Great American Mission: Modernization and the Construction of an American World Order* (Princeton, NJ: Princeton University Press, 2009), 19.

24. Maxine Hong Kingston, *The Woman Warrior: Memoirs of a Girlhood Among Ghosts* (New York: Knopf, 1976), 63.

25. Here I am inspired by Seo-young Chu's formalist account of science fiction as a mimetic rather than antimimetic genre, whose "objects of representation are nonimaginary yet cognitively estranging." *Do Metaphors Dream of Literal Sleep? A Science-Fictional Theory of Representation* (Cambridge, MA: Harvard University Press, 2011), 3.

26. Istvan Csicsery-Ronay Jr., *The Seven Beauties of Science Fiction* (Middletown, CT: Wesleyan University Press, 2008), 2; Kingston, *Woman Warrior*, 5.

27. Yoon Sun Lee, *Modern Minority: Asian American Literature and Everyday Life* (New York: Oxford University Press, 2013), 19.

28. Paraphrased in Chih-ming Wang, *Transpacific Articulations: Student Migration and the Remaking of Asian America* (Honolulu: University of Hawai'i Press, 2013), 82.

29. Glassman, *Drums of War, Drums of Development*, 4.

30. AnnaLee Saxenian, *The New Argonauts: Regional Advantage in a Global Economy* (Cambridge, MA: Harvard University Press, 2007). In addition to the post-65 Asian American PMC knowledge worker, crucial to these industries and supply chains has been the labor of Asian women: see Aihwa Ong, "Labor Arbitrage: Displacements and Betrayals in Silicon Valley," in *Neoliberalism as Exception: Mutations in Citizenship and Sovereignty* (Durham, NC: Duke University Press, 2006), 157–74; Shawn Wen, "The Ladies Vanish," *New Inquiry*, November 11, 2014, https://thenewinquiry.com/the-ladies-vanish/; and Janice Lobo Sapigao's astonishing poetry collection *Microchips for Millions* (San Francisco: Philippine American Writers and Artists, 2016). Relatedly, Lisa Nakamura has written about the early

semiconductor industry's exploitation of Navajo land and women workers in "Indigenous Circuits: Navajo Women and the Racialization of Early Electronic Manufacture," *American Quarterly* 66, no. 4 (December 2014): 919–41.

31. On this history see Diane C. Fujino's foundational and expansive body of work; see also Calvin Cheung-Miaw, "Asian Americans and the Color-Line: An Intellectual History of Asian American Studies, 1969–2000" (PhD diss., Stanford University, 2021); Rene Cruz, Cindy Domingo, and Bruce Occena, eds., *A Time to Rise: The Collective Memoirs of the Union of Democratic Filipinos (KDP)* (Seattle: University of Washington Press, 2017); Max Elbaum, *Revolution in the Air: Sixties Radicals Turn to Lenin, Mao and Che* (New York: Verso, 2002); May Chuan Fu, "Keeping Close to the Ground: Politics and Coalition in Asian American Community Organizing, 1969–1977" (PhD diss., UC San Diego, 2005); Michael Liu, Kim Geron, and Tracy Lai, *The Snake Dance of Asian American Activism: Community, Vision, and Power* (Lanham, MD: Lexington Books, 2008); Daryl Maeda, *Chains of Babylon: The Rise of Asian America* (Minneapolis: University of Minnesota Press, 2009); Glenn Omatsu, "The 'Four Prisons' and the Movements of Liberation: Asian American Activism from the 1960s to the 1990s," in *Contemporary Asian America*, ed. Min Zhou and Anthony Christian Ocampo (New York: NYU Press, 2000), 298–330; William Wei, *The Asian American Movement* (Philadelphia: Temple University Press, 1993); Judy Tzu-Chun Wu, *Radicals on the Road: Internationalism, Orientalism, and Feminism During the Vietnam Era* (Ithaca, NY: Cornell University Press, 2013).

32. Theresa Hak Hyung Cha's *DICTEE* was central to this shift, especially Elaine Kim and Norma Alarcón's 1994 edited collection on her work, *Writing Self, Writing Nation: Essays on Theresa Hak Kyung Cha's Dictée* (Berkeley: Third Woman Press, 1994).

33. Representative works include Victor Bascara, *Model Minority Imperialism* (Minneapolis: University of Minnesota Press, 2006); Takeshi Fujitani, *Race for Empire: Koreans as Japanese and Japanese as Americans during World War II* (Berkeley: University of California Press, 2011); Christine Hong, *A Violent Peace: Race, U.S. Militarism, and Cultures of Democratization in Cold War Asia and the Pacific* (Stanford, CA: Stanford University Press, 2020); Jodi Kim, *Ends of Empire: Asian American Critique and the Cold War* (Minneapolis: University of Minnesota Press, 2010); Simeon Man, *Soldiering through Empire: Race and the Making of the Decolonizing Pacific* (Berkeley: University of California Press, 2018); Sunny Xiang, *Tonal Intelligence: The Aesthetics of Asian Inscrutability During the Long Cold War* (New York: Columbia University Press, 2020); Lisa Yoneyama, *Cold War Ruins: Transpacific Critique of American Justice and Japanese War Crimes* (Durham, NC: Duke University Press, 2016).

34. Kim, *Ends of Empire*, 20.

35. In her well-known critique of liberal feminist political projects, Wendy Brown defines a "wounded attachment" as a melancholic mode in which "well-intentioned contemporary political projects and theoretical postures inadvertently redraw the very configurations and effects of power that they seek to vanquish," in *States of Injury: Power and Freedom in Late Modernity* (Princeton, NJ: Princeton University Press, 1995), ix.

36. Yogita Goyal, "Introduction: The Transnational Turn," in *The Cambridge Companion to Transnational American Literature*, ed. Yogita Goyal (New York: Cambridge University Press, 2017), 6.
37. Yoonmee Chang defines the ethnographic imperative as "explicit directives and implicit pressures to create superficially informative and exoticized 'insider's views' of Asiatic culture." *Writing the Ghetto: Class, Authorship, and the Asian American Ethnic Enclave* (New Brunswick, NJ: Rutgers University Press, 2010), 7.
38. This analytical operation becomes especially urgent as Asian- and Asian American–identified authors continue to produce more and more fiction that can be described as "racially asymmetric," which Stephen Hong Sohn defines as a mode of narrative perspective in which "the author's ethnoracial status is not easily or directly mirrored within the fictional world." *Racial Asymmetries: Asian American Fictional Worlds* (New York: NYU Press, 2014), 2. The challenges of accounting for the Asian American status of asymmetric and "postracial" fiction, in which racial markers are deliberately removed or deformed, compel us, first, to be self-reflexive about our goals in pursuing such an accounting; and, second, either to double down on avowals of reified racial categories, or, as I will be doing, to attend to the material relations that make possible the reification of racial categories in the first place. As Yoon Sun Lee writes, "The project is not simply to abolish the racial stereotype with an empirical fact but also to examine the ground of what makes any type possible." "Type, Totality, and the Realism of Asian American Literature," *Modern Language Quarterly* 73, no. 3 (September 2012): 423.
39. On periodizing Asian American history and literature aside from the canonical 1965 and 1968 delimiters, see Jinqi Ling, *Narrating Nationalisms: Ideology and Form in Asian American Literature* (New York: Oxford University Press, 1998), 3–30.
40. On U.S. identity politics' roots in Maoism, see Colleen Lye, "Identity Politics, Criticism, and Self-Criticism," *South Atlantic Quarterly* 119, no. 4 (2020), 701–14, and "Asian American 1960s," in *The Routledge Companion to Asian American and Pacific Islander Literature*, ed. Rachel C. Lee (New York: Routledge, 2014), 213–23.
41. Kevin Floyd, Jen Hedler Phillis, and Sarika Chandra, "Introduction," in *Totality Inside Out: Rethinking Crisis and Conflict Under Capital*, ed. Kevin Floyd, Jen Hedler Phillis, and Sarika Chandra (New York: Fordham University Press, 2022), 9. See also Olúfẹ́mi O. Táíwò, *Elite Capture: How the Powerful Took Over Identity Politics (And Everything Else)* (Chicago: Haymarket Books, 2022).
42. Recent accounts of model minoritization that have inspired my thinking include erin Khuê Ninh's books *Ingratitude: The Debt-Bound Daughter in Asian American Literature* (New York: NYU Press, 2011) and *Passing for Perfect: College Impostors and Other Model Minorities* (Philadelphia: Temple University Press, 2021); Jennifer Lee and Min Zhou, *The Asian American Achievement Paradox* (New York: Russell Sage Foundation, 2015); David L. Eng and Shinhee Han, *Racial Melancholia, Racial Dissociation: On the Social and Psychic Lives of Asian Americans* (Durham, NC: Duke University Press, 2019); James Kyung-jin Lee, *Pedagogies of Woundedness: Illness, Memoir, and the Ends of the Model Minority* (Philadelphia: Temple University Press, 2021); and Takeo Rivera, *Model Minority Masochism: Performing the Cultural Politics of Asian American Masculinity* (New York: Oxford University Press, 2022).

INTRODUCTION

43. Lukács draws from Friedrich Engels's famous definition of realism as a genre that depicts "typical characters under typical circumstances."
44. Yoon Sun Lee, "Type, Totality," 420.
45. Yoon Sun Lee, "Type, Totality," 418. On the spatial displacements that constitute post-65 Asian American life, see Shenglin Chang, *The Global Silicon Valley Home: Lives and Landscapes Within Taiwanese American Trans-Pacific Culture* (Stanford: Stanford University Press, 2005), Wendy Cheng, *The Changs Next Door to the Díazes: Remapping Race in Suburban California* (Minneapolis: University of Minnesota Press, 2013), Shalini Shankar, *Desi Land: Teen Culture, Class, and Success in Silicon Valley* (Durham, NC: Duke University Press, 2008), and Karen Tongson, *Relocations: Queer Suburban Imaginaries* (New York: NYU Press, 2011).
46. On *Woman Warrior* as a quintessential text of the Asian American 1960s, see Lye, "Asian American 1960s."
47. Yoon Sun Lee and Christopher Lee each make similar observations regarding the apparent irreconcilability between typicality and identity within an Asian Americanist framework. See Yoon Sun Lee, "Type, Totality," 420; and Christopher Lee's introduction to *The Semblance of Identity: Aesthetic Mediation in Asian American Literature* (Stanford, CA: Stanford University Press, 2012), 1–22.
48. In U.S. left discourse, Karen E. Fields and Barbara J. Fields's *Racecraft: The Soul of Inequality in American Life* (London: Verso, 2012) is perhaps the most high-profile and influential recent argument for class-first approaches. The best and most politically and intellectually generous account of the race/class problematic is Sarika Chandra and Christopher Chen's chapter "Remapping the Race/Class Problematic," in Floyd, Phillis, and Chandra, *Totality Inside Out*, 135–91.
49. Indeed, as Floyd, Phillis, and Chandra point out, the Combahee River Collective's famous statement from 1977, in which they coined the term "identity politics," was responding to a longstanding identity politics that predominated U.S. radical politics: a worker's identity politics that insisted at every turn on the primacy of anticapitalist critique (7). This was a position that the Collective supported, but with a caveat that has become one of the Statement's most quoted lines: "We are not convinced . . . that a socialist revolution that is not also a feminist and antiracist revolution will guarantee our liberation," Combahee River Collective, "A Black Feminist Statement," in *This Bridge Called My Back: Writings by Radical Women of Color*, eds. Cherríe Moraga and Gloria Anzaldúa (New York: Kitchen Table Press, 1983), 213.
50. Cheung-Miaw, "Asian Americans and the Color-Line," 129, 17.
51. Lisa Lowe, *Immigrant Acts: On Asian American Cultural Politics* (Durham, NC: Duke University Press, 1996).
52. Kandice Chuh, *Imagine Otherwise: On Asian Americanist Critique* (Durham, NC: Duke University Press, 2003); Lye, "Racial Form," 94.
53. Lye's example is Walter Benn Michaels, who describes Asian American cultural politics as a "kind of blackface, a performance that produces the image of racialized oppression alongside the reality of economic success," quoted in "Racial Form," 100n7.
54. Mark Chiang and Yen Le Espiritu track the institutional priorities that motivate commitments to strategic essentialism: Chiang, *The Cultural Capital of Asian American Studies: Autonomy and Representation in the University* (New York:

NYU Press, 2009), and Espiritu, *Asian American Panethnicity: Bridging Institutions and Identities* (Philadelphia: Temple University Press, 1993). To these institutional critiques, Viet Thanh Nguyen adds an account of Asian America's ideological diversity in *Race and Resistance*. Susan Koshy critiques strategic essentialism's grounding of Asian American identity in the weak soil of "catachresis." "The Fiction of Asian American Literature," 342. Jinqi Ling critiques strategic essentialism's ahistoricality in *Narrating Nationalisms: Ideology and Form in Asian American Literature* (New York: Oxford University Press, 1998). On Lye's critique via "racial form," see n65 in this chapter. erin Khûe Ninh critiques institutional incentives behind dismissals of the model minority as a myth in *Ingratitude*.

55. Ninh, *Ingratitude*, 61.
56. Yoon Sun Lee, "Type, Totality," 424.
57. Charles Yu, *How to Live Safely in a Science Fictional Universe* (New York: Vintage Books, 2010), 16.
58. Nguyen, *Race and Resistance*; Christine So, *Economic Citizens: A Narrative of Asian American Visibility* (Philadelphia: Temple University Press, 2008).
59. As Christopher Lee argues in his book *The Semblance of Identity*, critiques of strategic essentialism and of identity have been with Asian American cultural politics from its very inception.
60. Elaine Castillo, "A Stabbing in Finsbury Park," *The Rumpus*, October 30, 2013, https://therumpus.net/2013/10/30/a-stabbing-in-finsbury-park.
61. See Catherine Ceniza Choy, *Empire of Care: Nursing and Migration in Filipino American History* (Durham, NC: Duke University Press, 2003).
62. Bruce Cumings, "The Origins and Development of the Northeast Asian Political Economy: Industrial Sectors, Product Cycles, and Political Consequences," *International Organization* 38, no. 1 (1984): 3, my emphasis.
63. Christine So, *Economic Citizens*, 13.
64. Lisa Lowe, "The International within the National: American Studies and Asian American Critique," *Cultural Critique* 40 (1998): 36–37.
65. On "racial form" see Colleen Lye's foundational work in *America's Asia: Racial Form and American Literature, 1893–1945* (Princeton, NJ: Princeton University Press, 2005), and her articles "Introduction: In Dialogue with Asian American Studies," *Representations* 99, no. 1 (Summer 2007): 1–12; "Form and History in Asian American Literary Studies," *American Literary History* 20, no. 3 (Summer 2008): 548–55; and "Racial Form," *Representations* 104, no. 1 (Fall 2008): 92–101. The key distinction of "racial form" is its analytical shift away from reified forms of race (which Yoon Sun Lee calls "visuality," and that Frantz Fanon, in *Black Skin, White Masks*, relegates to an "epidermal schema") to material processes of reification that reveal the historical variability of the racial forms determining not only how race is represented, but also how racialized social relations concretize in institutions. See Yoon Sun Lee, "Racialized Bodies and Asian American Literature," *American Literary History* 30, no. 1 (Spring 2018): 166–76. Although Lye draws more directly from Raymond Williams than Marx to conceptualize race as a material relation ("Racial Form," 97), it wouldn't be inaccurate to say that the "form" of "racial form" is the "form" of Marx's "form of appearance," which is the phrase he uses across his work to describe phenomenal expressions of the value-form. "Racial

form" thus augments dominant accounts of racialization in the United States, especially Michael Omi and Howard Winant's in their enormously influential 1986 book *Racial Formation in the US* (now in its third edition), which, Lye argues, tend to rely on a transhistorical, even "tautological" account of race as a self-evident category without a robust class dimension ("In Dialogue," 2). For a similar account of race as not a reified essence but an "epistemic field that has been extended and filled with content according to specific historical imperatives of national sovereignty itself," see Nikhil Pal Singh, "Racial Formation in an Age of Permanent War," in *Racial Formation in the Twenty-First Century*, ed. Daniel Martinez HoSang, Oneka LaBennett, and Laura Pulido (Berkeley: University of California Press, 2012), 288.

66. "A History of Separation," *Endnotes* 4 (October 2015), https://endnotes.org.uk/issues/4/en/endnotes-preface.
67. Colleen Lye, "Unmarked Character and the 'Rise of Asia': Ed Park's Personal Days," *Verge* 1, no. 1 (2015): 230, my emphasis.
68. Lye, "Unmarked Character," 234, my emphasis.
69. See Jasper Bernes, *The Work of Art in the Age of Deindustrialization* (Stanford, CA: Stanford University Press, 2017).
70. Susan Koshy's "The Fiction of Asian American Literature" is the classic critique of the "additive" yet Chinese and Japanese-dominated approach to pan-ethnic Asian American literary history. See also Colleen Lye, "The Sino-Japanese Conflict of Asian American Literature," *Genre* 39 (Winter 2006): 43–63.
71. Long Le-Khac and Kate Hao, "The Asian American Literature We've Constructed," *Post45* 6, no. 2 (2021), https://culturalanalytics.org/article/22330-the-asian-american-literature-we-ve-constructed.
72. As of 2022, Northeast Asian American faculty comprise 65 percent of the sixteen largest Asian American Studies departments and programs (29% Chinese; 20% Indian; 16% Korean; 15% Japanese; 5% Filipinix; 4% Taiwanese; 4% Vietnamese; 1% other). Thanks to my research assistant Danielle Shi for collecting this data.
73. Cumings, "Origins and Development," 2.
74. Kaname Akamatsu, "A Historical Pattern of Economic Growth in Developing Countries," *The Developing Economies* 1, no. 1 (August 1962): 3–25.
75. Jeremy A. Yellen, *The Greater East Asia Co-Prosperity Sphere: When Total Empire Met Total War* (Ithaca, NY: Cornell University Press, 2019), 4.
76. Chris Suh, *The Allure of Empire: American Encounters with Asians in the Age of Transpacific Expansion and Exclusion* (New York: Oxford University Press, 2023).
77. Ho-fung Hung, *The China Boom: Why China Will Not Rule the World* (New York: Columbia University Press, 2016), 54.
78. "Vox Media Preview of The Podium: I Think You're Interesting Featuring Chang Rae Lee," *The Podium from Vox Media and NBC Sports Group*, December 14, 2017, http://art19.com/shows/the-podium-nbc-olympics/episodes/0466dd68-c1c6-43a3-a3ad-9df92a91f5ba.
79. One of my goals will be to contribute to what Yoonmee Chang has called "a hermeneutics of race and class that is specific to Asian Americans." *Writing the Ghetto*, 4.
80. See Wong, "Introduction."
81. Lee, "Type, Totality," 421.

INTRODUCTION

82. Barbara and John Ehrenreich, "The Professional-Managerial Class," *Radical America* 11, no. 2 (March 1977): 12. The Ehrenreichs' article appeared in the midst of a broad reassessment of the new middle class after the collapse of the New Left in the United States and prompted a number of responses arguing that the PMC doesn't qualify as a class in the classical Marxist two class schema of proletariat and bourgeoisie. The Ehrenreichs would later eulogize the PMC in their retrospective essay "Death of a Yuppie Dream: The Rise and Fall of the Professional-Managerial Class," *Rosa Luxemburg Stiftung*, February 12, 2013, https://rosalux.nyc/death-of-a-yuppie-dream/. For a classic critique of the PMC's status as a class, see Erik Olin Wright, "Intellectuals and the Working Class," *Critical Sociology* 8, no. 1 (1978): 5–18. A classic critique of the "middle class" as a class can be found in Harry Braverman, *Labor and Monopoly Capital: The Degradation of Work in the Twentieth Century* (New York: Monthly Review Press, 1974). For a recent attempt at recuperating the political potential of the PMC, see Gabriel Winant, "Professional-Managerial Chasm," *n+1*, October 10, 2019, https://www.nplusonemag.com/online-only/online-only/professional-managerial-chasm/.
83. In literary studies, the books that have been most valuable to me in understanding this emergence are Bernes, *The Work of Art in the Age of Deindustrialization*; Andrew Hoberek, *Twilight of the Middle Class: Post-World War II Fiction and White-Collar Work* (Princeton, NJ: Princeton University Press, 2005); Alan Liu, *Laws of Cool: Knowledge Work and the Culture of Information* (Chicago: University of Chicago Press, 2004); Michael Szalay, *New Deal Modernism: American Literature and the Invention of the Welfare State* (Durham, NC: Duke University Press, 2000); Michael Szalay, *Hip Figures: A Literary History of the Democratic Party* (Stanford, CA: Stanford University Press, 2012).
84. Bell, *The Coming of Post-Industrial Society*, 127.
85. McGurl, *The Program Era*, 4.
86. McGurl, *The Program Era*, x.
87. Tao Lin's short fiction and novel *Taipei* (2013) might be read as frontal rejections of the institutional attachments of Asian American fiction (e.g., the Asian American Writers Workshop, the United States as a locus for Asian American identity, etc.), as well as a Silicon Valley fiction that heavily incorporates Internet forms (Gchat, email, blog posts, typography, etc.) and centers "precariat" characters who, when they are working, are doing the equivalent of piecework for new media companies.
88. Chang, *Writing the Ghetto*, 5, my emphasis.
89. Always ahead of her time, Kingston in many ways established the paradigm for this mini-boom with *Woman Warrior* (1976) and its sequel, *China Men* (1980).
90. Lyndon B. Johnson, "Remarks at the Signing of the Immigration Bill," in *Public Papers of the Presidents of the United States: Lyndon B. Johnson, 1965*, vol. 2 (Washington, DC: U.S. Government Printing Office, 1966), 1037–40.
91. Madeline Hsu, *The Good Immigrants: How the Yellow Peril Became the Model Minority* (Princeton, NJ: Princeton University Press, 2015), 21.
92. Lee and Zhou, *The Asian American Achievement Paradox*, 6.
93. Jens Manuel Krogstad and Jynnah Radford, "Education Levels of U.S. Immigrants Are on the Rise" (Pew Research Center, September 14, 2018), https://www

INTRODUCTION

.pewresearch.org/fact-tank/2018/09/14/education-levels-of-u-s-immigrants-are-on-the-rise/.
94. Paul Ong and John M. Liu, "U.S. Immigration Policies and Asian Migration," in *The New Asian Immigration in Los Angeles and Global Restructuring*, ed. Edna Bonacich, Lucie Cheng, and Paul Ong (Philadelphia: Temple University Press, 1994), 58.
95. Pyong Gap Min and Sou Hyun Jang, "The Concentration of Asian Americans in STEM and Health-Care Occupations: An Intergenerational Comparison," *Ethnic and Racial Studies* 38, no. 6 (2015): 845, 848.
96. "Characteristics of H-1B Specialty Occupation Workers: Fiscal Year 2022 Annual Report to Congress October 1, 2021–September 30, 2022," U.S. Citizen and Immigration Services (March 13, 2023), 9, 14.
97. Min and Jang, "Concentration of Asian Americans in STEM," 847.
98. Lee and Zhou, *The Asian American Achievement Paradox*, 21–50, 49, 3, 6.
99. Bonacich, Cheng, and Ong, *New Asian Immigration*, 9.
100. The Chicago School of neoliberal economics, in Paul Nadal's remarkable account, embellished this legacy in its development of human capital theory, displacing "a familiar assumption of Asiatic belatedness by singling out [Meiji] Japan as emblematic of neoliberal human capital formation avant la lettre." "How Neoliberalism Remade the Model Minority Myth," *Representations* 163 (August 2023): 89.
101. Walter Adams, "The Problem," in *The Brain Drain*, ed. Walter Adams (New York: Macmillan, 1968), 1.
102. Adams, "The Problem," 1.
103. Saxenian, *The New Argonauts*, 19.
104. Alejandro Portes and Adrienne Celaya, "Modernization for Emigration: Determinants and Consequences of the Brain Drain," *Daedalus* 142, no. 3 (2013): 172.
105. Portes and Celaya, "Modernization for Emigration," 178, 174.
106. Portes and Celaya, "Modernization for Emigration," 172.
107. Alejandro Portes, "Modernization for Emigration: The Medical Brain Drain from Argentina," *Journal of Interamerican Studies and World Affairs* 18, no. 4 (November 1976): 404.
108. "Global Talent 2021: How the New Geography of Talent Will Transform Human Resource Strategies" (Oxford Economics, 2012), https://www.oxfordeconomics.com/Media/Default/Thought%20Leadership/global-talent-2021.pdf; Saxenian, *The New Argonauts*, 19; Portes and Celaya, "Modernization for Emigration," 171.
109. Saxenian, *The New Argonauts*, 198.
110. In their influential collection *Transpacific Studies: Framing an Emergent Field* (2014), Viet Thanh Nguyen and Janet Alison Hoskins outline a similar vision: "Through a transpacific framework, we can see how the American war [in Vietnam] was not simply a military or political event involving a few countries, but was actually part of larger strategies of economic maneuvering in which the future Asian powers of the Pacific Rim played a key part" (7). Where I perhaps depart from their vision is on a methodological distinction. Whereas Nguyen and Hoskins begin with the transpacific concept and then proceed to specific sites and objects—leveraging their debt to ethnic and especially Asian American studies approaches, which proceed via strategic essentialism from a "semblance" of identity (to use Christopher Lee's term) to specific subgroups—what I am attempting moves in

the opposite direction. I begin with the specificity of Northeast Asia and move outward, to examine how "Asian American literature" emerges from the itineraries of specific classes of post-65 Northeast Asian Americans. Erin Suzuki and Aimee Bahng, in an essay that should stand as a model for intellectual humility and solidarity, offer a similar critique of the "transpacific" category, but from the standpoint of indigenous, Pacific Islander studies, responding to critiques of their own past uses of "transpacific": "settler epistemologies and taxonomies tend to subsume Indigenous Pacific subjectivity within broader rubrics, even de- or postcolonial ones. Thus the burgeoning use in Asian American studies of the keyword *transpacific* might well relegate Indigenous peoples of the Pacific to a kind of flyover status." Erin Suzuki and Aimee Bahng, "The Transpacific Subject in Asian American Culture," in *The Oxford Encyclopedia of Asian American Literature and Culture*, ed. Josephine Lee (New York: Oxford University Press, 2020), https://oxfordre.com/literature/display/10.1093/acrefore/9780190201098.001.0001/acrefore-9780190201098-e-877

111. Patricia Chu, in her major study of Asian American return memoirs, argues that recent narratives of return register "a way to expand Asian American subjectivities and histories beyond the borders of the United States," *Where I Have Never Been: Migration, Melancholia, and Memory in Asian American Narratives of Return* (Philadelphia: Temple University Press, 2019), 11. Chu's primary interest is in how this expansion of subjectivity and identity is pursued by Asian American authors "in a move to reclaim or remember the Asian histories that an earlier wave of Asian American scholarship neglected" (11). She argues that return narratives primarily take the form of countermemory and postmemory, generating imaginative correctives to dominant historical narratives and the melancholic disavowals that structure them: "these accounts perform rhetorical work akin to trauma therapy" (40). Elsewhere, Chu examines return narratives in fiction from 1965 to 1996, arguing that Asian American literature "has always been deeply, inherently transnational," despite cultural nationalist disavowals of Asia and the transnational. "Rethinking Nationalistic Attachments Through Narratives of Return," in *Asian American Literature in Transition: 1965–1996*, ed. Asha Nadkarni and Cathy Schlund-Vials (Cambridge: Cambridge University Press, 2021), 280. Chih-ming Wang's account of Asian American return fiction is the one that most closely approaches mine. He shows how these fictions' depictions of transnational space are structured by U.S.-led global capitalism and end up smuggling in a U.S. exceptionalism in which "triumphant globalization may be rescripted as the prolongation of Cold War trauma." "When Asian Americans Return to Asia: Return Narratives, Transpacific Imagination, and the Post/Cold War," *Southeast Asian Review of English* 58, no. 2 (2021): 97. On recent Indian and South Asian return narratives, see Ragini Tharoor Srinivasan, "The Rhetoric of Return: Diasporic Homecoming and the New Indian City," *Room One Thousand* 3, no. 3 (2015): 308–35, and "Global India in 21st-Century Asian American Literature," *Oxford Research Encyclopedias, Literature* (July 30, 2018), https://oxfordre.com/literature/display/10.1093/acrefore/9780190201098.001.0001/acrefore-9780190201098-e-873. On Japanese American travel narratives of return, see "The Universality of Exchange: Japanese American Travel Narratives and the Emergence of the Global Citizen," in Christine So's *Economic Citizens*.

INTRODUCTION

112. More than two decades would pass before Asian Americanist scholars would acknowledge the landmark event of Chiang's award and, more generally, turn their attention to SF by Asian Americans. It is not insignificant that the first scholar to note (at least in an English-language publication) Chiang's award was not an Asian American scholar but the Chinese SF author Han Song, who wrote: "Both [Ken] Liu and Chiang write in English, but their achievements showcase the rise of science-fiction writers with Chinese backgrounds in the twenty-first century." Han Song, "Chinese Science Fiction: A Response to Modernization," *Science Fiction Studies* 40, no. 1 (March 2013): 15. Han's recognition of Liu and Chiang as SF authors "with Chinese backgrounds" speaks to the vicissitudes of ethnicity and national identity that have unfolded in the post-65 period against the backdrop of U.S.-Asia political economy. Along these lines, the recognition of Chiang's award was in a way doubly belated, given what had become a long-established scholarly discourse of "techno-orientalism" that, beginning in the late 1980s, grew out of work by scholars like Fredric Jameson, Toshiya Ueno, David Morley, and Kevin Robins, who are not Asian Americanists. As a category that responded to the proliferation of orientalist tropes in SF and mainly U.S.-based racial forms structured by U.S.-Japan economic rivalry, "techno-orientalism" would have seemed an obvious focus for the interests and commitments of Asian American studies. See Aimee Bahng, *Migrant Futures: Decolonizing Speculation in Financial Times* (Durham, NC: Duke University Press, 2017); Anne Anlin Cheng, "Dolls," in *Ornamentalism* (New York: Oxford University Press, 2019), 127–51; Fredric Jameson, *Postmodernism, or, the Cultural Logic of Late Capitalism* (Durham, NC: Duke University Press, 1991); Fredric Jameson, "The Constraints of Postmodernism," in *The Seeds of Time* (New York: Columbia University Press, 1994), 129–206; David Morley and Kevin Robins, "Techno-Orientalism: Japan Panic," in *Spaces of Identity: Global Media, Electronic Landscapes and Cultural Boundaries* (New York: Routledge, 1995), 147–73; David S. Roh, Betsy Huang, and Greta Niu, eds., *Techno-Orientalism: Imagining Asia in Speculative Fiction, History, and Media* (New Brunswick, NJ: Rutgers University Press, 2015); Stephen Hong Sohn, "Introduction: Alien/Asian: Imagining the Racialized Future," *MELUS* 33, no. 4 (2008): 5–22; Toshiya Ueno, "Techno-Orientalism and Media-Tribalism: On Japanese Animation and Rave Culture," *Third Text* 13, no. 47 (1999): 95–106.
113. See also Ellen Oh and Elsie Chapman, eds., *A Thousand Beginnings and Endings* (New York: HarperCollins, 2018).
114. On Asian American detective fiction, see Calvin McMillin, "Asian American Detective Fiction," in *Oxford Research Encyclopedia*, October 30, 2019, https://oxfordre.com/literature/display/10.1093/acrefore/9780190201098.001.0001/acrefore-9780190201098-e-813; and Monica Chiu, *Scrutinized! Surveillance in Asian North American Literature* (Honolulu: University of Hawai'i Press, 2014). Another notable post-65 genre of Asian American writing, as James Kyung-Jin Lee observes, is produced by South Asian physicians—such as Atul Gawande, Abraham Verghese, Siddhartha Mukherjee—who comprise "the public face of U.S. medicine," *Pedagogies of Woundedness: Illness, Memoir, and the Ends of the Model Minority* (Philadelphia: Temple University Press, 2022), 12.
115. An example of this would be the actor George Takei's one-off SF novel *Mirror Friend, Mirror Foe* (1979), cowritten with Robert Asprin, a space opera about a

Japanese assassin tasked with quelling a robot uprising. Laurence Yep's 1973 novel *Sweetwater* was perhaps the first SF novel published by an Asian American. Al T. Miyadi's "It Came upon a Midnight Clear," published in the Japanese American Citizen League's *Pacific Citizen* newspaper in 1950, was perhaps the first piece of SF short fiction published by an Asian American. While Miyadi doesn't appear to have published anything more, Yep would go on to produce a large body of work, but only one more SF novel: *Shadow Lord: A Star Trek Novel* (1985).

116. "Wong's Lost and Found Emporium" was adapted into an episode of *The Twilight Zone* in 1985.
117. McGurl, *The Program Era*, 34.
118. Quoted in McGurl, *The Program Era*, 12.
119. Sinykin, *Big Fiction*, 135.
120. McGurl, *The Program Era*, 33.
121. Disambiguating trends in post-65 Asian American fiction from cognate trends in US and Anglophone fiction—e.g., the "genre turn," so-called "postracial" aesthetics, postmodernism, etc.—will be a recurring move in what follows, inspired in part by Lisa Lowe's insight in *Immigrant Acts* that "national culture generates formal deviations whose significances are misread if simply assimilated as modernist or postmodernist aesthetic modes" (32).
122. Lowe, *Immigrant Acts*, 30, 31.
123. Claire Jean Kim, "The Racial Triangulation of Asian Americans," *Politics & Society* 27, no. 1 (March 1999): 105–38.
124. Patricia Chu, *Assimilating Asians: Gendered Strategies of Authorship in Asian America* (Durham, NC: Duke University Press, 2000), 16.
125. Chad Harbach, "Introduction," in *MFA vs NYC: The Two Cultures of American Fiction* (New York: n+1/Faber and Faber, 2014), 4.
126. Louis Menand, "Literature and Professionalism," in *Discovering Modernism: T. S. Eliot and His Context* (New York: Oxford University Press, 1987), 97–132. Thomas Strychacz, *Modernism, Mass Culture, and Professionalism* (Cambridge: Cambridge University Press, 1993).
127. See Szalay, *New Deal Modernism*. See also Sean McCann, "Training and Vision: Roth, DeLillo, Banks, Peck, and the Postmodern Aesthetics of Vocation," *Twentieth-Century Literature* 53, no. 3 (2007): 298–326.
128. Audrey Wu-Clark, *The Asian American Avant-Garde: Universalist Aspirations in Modernist Literature and Art* (Philadelphia: Temple University Press, 2015), 5. Here, Wu-Clark adapts Joseph Jeon's work on Asian American avant-garde poetry, *Racial Things, Racial Forms: Objecthood in Avant-Garde Asian American Poetry* (Iowa City: University of Iowa Press, 2012).
129. Phillip E. Wegner, *Shockwaves of Possibility: Essays on Science Fiction, Globalization, and Utopia* (New York: Peter Lang, 2014), 72. My thanks to Mitch Murray for pointing me to Wegner's "heuristic genres."
130. McCann, "Training and Vision," 310–11.
131. On unreliable narration as Asiatic racial form, see Sunny Xiang, "The Korean Voice of American Empire: The Democratic Spokesman and the Model Minority Narrator," *Journal of Asian American Studies* 17, no. 3 (October 2014): 273–304.
132. Hoberek, *Twilight of the Middle Class*, 25.
133. Kathy Wang, *Family Trust* (New York: William Morrow, 2018), 213.

134. Ling Ma, *Severance* (New York: Farrar, Straus and Giroux, 2018), 135.
135. McCann, "Training and Vision," 315.
136. Anticipated, perhaps, by *Woman Warrior*'s famously cryptic final sentence, "It translated well," which we can read as looking across a gap of time to the children of 1965 and Asia's rise.
137. Andrew Hoberek, "Literary Genre Fiction," in *American Literature in Transition, 2000–2010*, ed. Rachel Greenwald Smith (Cambridge: Cambridge University Press, 2017), 71–72.
138. Walt Whitman Rostow, *The Stages of Economic Growth: A Non-Communist Manifesto* (Cambridge: Cambridge University Press, 1960), 155.
139. Yu, *How to Live Safely*, 35.
140. Even allowing that no book can be totally comprehensive, I regret the absence of Yiyun Li and Min Jin Lee, whose lives and work give expression to the transnational fantasies of economic mobility described in these pages.
141. Funie Hsu, Brian Hioe, and Wen Liu, "Collective Statement on Taiwan Independence: Building Global Solidarity and Rejecting US Military Empire," *American Quarterly* 69, no. 3 (September 2017): 465–68.

1. DEEP CONDITIONS OF THE WORLD

1. David Ekbladh, *The Great American Mission: Modernization and the Construction of an American World Order* (Princeton, NJ: Princeton University Press, 2009), 21.
2. Ekbladh quotes the modernization devotee Paul Hoffman, who headed the UN's Economic Cooperation Administration and the Ford Foundation, two crucial organs for U.S. modernization projects, and who, speaking to his staff at a hotel in Seoul, once said, "we have the proof [of modernization theory] and here is the proving ground." *The Great American Mission*, 126.
3. Ekbladh, *The Great American Mission*, 19.
4. Jim Glassman, *Drums of War, Drums of Development: The Formation of a Pacific Ruling Class and Industrial Transformation in East and Southeast Asia, 1945–1980* (Chicago: Haymarket Books, 2018), 4.
5. Wendy Cheng's book *Island X* offers an account of leftist and communist Taiwanese international students in the United States who rejected, sometimes violently, the Kuomintang's authoritarian rule at home and repression of the Taiwanese diaspora in the United States. *Island X: Taiwanese Student Migrants, Campus Spies, and Cold War Activism* (Berkeley: University of California Press, 2023).
6. Lisa Yoneyama and Takeshi Fujitani both note a similar aporia in Asian area studies. Lisa Yoneyama, *Cold War Ruins: Transpacific Critique of American Justice and Japanese War Crimes* (Durham, NC: Duke University Press, 2016), 244n33; Takeshi Fujitani, *Race for Empire: Koreans as Japanese and Japanese as Americans During World War II* (Berkeley: University of California Press, 2011), 231. I use the term "transimperiality" to highlight the continuity between Japan and U.S. empires while acknowledging the relevance of "inter-imperiality," which emphasizes the coexistence of empires via competition or cooperation. For a longue durée theoretical account of inter-imperiality, see Laura Doyle, *Inter-Imperiality: Vying Empires, Gendered Labor, and the Literary Arts of Alliance* (Durham, NC: Duke

1. DEEP CONDITIONS OF THE WORLD

University Press, 2020). On the recent turn to transimperiality in history, see Setsu Shigematsu and Keith L. Camacho, eds., *Militarized Currents: Toward a Decolonized Future in Asia and the Pacific* (Minneapolis: University of Minnesota Press, 2010) and Kristin L. Hoganson and Jay Sexton, eds., *Crossing Empires: Taking U.S. History into Transimperial Terrain* (Durham, NC: Duke University Press, 2020). In Asian/American literary studies, Filipinx scholars have generally been much more attentive to transimperiality. See Johaina K. Crisostomo, "'Self-Reliance, Self-Sacrifice': Translating Ethics Across Empires in Maximo M. Kalaw's *The Filipino Rebel* (1930)," *American Quarterly* 73, no. 3 (September 2021): 535–56; Toni Hays, "Open Concept: Land and Home in Asian/America" (PhD diss., UC Irvine, 2024); and Paul Nadal, "Cold War Remittance Economy: US Creative Writing and the Importation of New Criticism into the Philippines," *American Quarterly* 73, no. 3 (September 2021).

7. Dipesh Chakrabarty, "The Legacies of Bandung: Decolonization and the Politics of Culture," in *Making a World After Empire: The Bandung Movement and Its Political Afterlives*, ed. Christopher J. Lee (Athens: Ohio University Press, 2010), 45–68.
8. See Victor Bascara, *Model Minority Imperialism* (Minneapolis: University of Minnesota Press, 2006); Leo T. S. Ching, "Beyond Nation and Empire," *American Quarterly* 73, no. 2 (June 2021): 383–88; Fujitani, *Race for Empire*; and Robert G. Lee, "The Cold War Origins of the Model Minority Myth," in *Orientals: Asian Americans in Popular Culture* (Philadelphia: Temple University Press, 1999), 145–79.
9. Ken Liu, "The Man Who Ended History: A Documentary," in *The Paper Menagerie and Other Stories* (New York: Saga Press, 2016), 399.
10. Ruth Ozeki, *A Tale for the Time Being* (New York: Penguin Books, 2013), 39.
11. Betsy Huang, *Contesting Genres in Contemporary Asian American Fiction* (New York: Palgrave Macmillan, 2010), 3.
12. Maxine Hong Kingston, *The Woman Warrior: Memoirs of a Girlhood Among Ghosts* (New York: Knopf, 1976), 205.
13. On the transnational turn in Asian American literature, see Kandice Chuh and Karen Shimakawa, eds., *Orientations: Mapping Studies in the Asian Diaspora* (Durham, NC: Duke University Press, 2001); Eric Hayot, "The Asian Turns," *PMLA* 124, no. 3 (May 2009): 907–17; Shirley Geok-Lin Lim, John Gamber, Stephen Hong Sohn, and Gina Valentino, *Transnational Asian American Literature: Sites and Transits* (Philadelphia: Temple University Press, 2006); Colleen Lye, "The Asian American 1960s," in *The Routledge Companion to Asian American and Pacific Islander Literature*, ed. Rachel C. Lee (New York: Routledge, 2014), 213–23; David Palumbo-Liu, *Asian/American: Historical Crossings of a Racial Frontier* (Stanford, CA: Stanford University Press, 1999); and Sau-ling Wong, "Denationalization Reconsidered: Asian American Cultural Criticism at a Theoretical Crossroads," *Amerasia Journal* 21, no. 1 (1995): 1–28.
14. Precursors to the transnational turn might be found in novels like Ninotchka Rosca's *State of War* (1988) and Richard Kim's two novels *The Martyred* (1964) and *The Innocent* (1968). In the 1990s, as the transnational turn was picking up steam, scholars often pointed out that the Asian American movement and its political identities had always incorporated an international dimension. What distinguishes the transnational turn of the 1990s in my estimation is not only the ontological elevation of Asia to a *presence* (rather than evaded or nostalgic past) but above all

the material rebalancing of U.S.-Asia relations. That is, Asia was now not only a source of identification and solidarity but also an inexorable manifestation of capital.
15. Min Hyoung Song, *The Children of 1965: On Writing, and Not Writing, as an Asian American* (Durham, NC: Duke University Press, 2013), 181. Song is building upon Rachel Adams's observation that writers like "Jhumpa Lahiri, Sandra Cisneros, Chang Rae Lee [sic], Junot Diaz, Ruth Ozeki, Jessica Hagedorn, Gish Jen, Bharati Mukherjee, Susan Choi, Oscar Hijuelos, Edwidge Danticat," who are either immigrants or children of immigrants, ushered in an "American Literary Globalism" in the 1990s and 2000s, "The Ends of America, the Ends of Postmodernism," *Twentieth Century Literature* 53, no. 3 (Fall 2007): 251. It is worth pointing out that seven of the eleven authors that Adams lists here are Asian American. Not on Adams's list is Karen Tei Yamashita, whose work, beginning with her 1990 debut novel *Through the Arc of the Rainforest*, is, in Jinqi Ling's estimation, paradigmatic of the transnational turn itself, and for precisely that reason, he argues that "more than any other contemporary Asian American writer, [Yamashita] has contributed to the reshaping of the Asian American literary imagination." *Across Meridians: History and Figuration in Karen Tei Yamashita's Transnational Novels* (Stanford, CA: Stanford University Press, 2012), xi.
16. Aimee Bahng, *Migrant Futures: Decolonizing Speculation in Financial Times* (Durham, NC: Duke University Press, 2018), 32.
17. Bruce Sterling, "Introduction," in *Mirrorshades: The Cyberpunk Anthology*, ed. Bruce Sterling (New York: Ace Books, 1988), xiv.
18. Toni Hays argues that recent revivals of Japan-inflected techno-orientalism register a nostalgia for a more stable Asian "other" during the era of the China threat.
19. David Morley and Kevin Robins, *Spaces of Identity: Global Media, Electronic Landscapes and Cultural Boundaries* (New York: Routledge, 1995), 168.
20. David S. Roh, Betsy Huang, and Greta Niu, eds., *Techno-Orientalism: Imagining Asia in Speculative Fiction, History, and Media* (New Brunswick, NJ: Rutgers University Press, 2015), 7.
21. Here I borrow Viet Thanh Nguyen's phrase, adapted from Aihwa Ong, for the strategies that Asian Americans partake of, beyond the reductive binary of accommodation and resistance, to make life livable under racial capitalism. *Race and Resistance: Literature and Politics in Asian America* (New York: Oxford University Press, 2002), 4.
22. William Gibson, "Burning Chrome," *Omni*, July 1982, 72–78.
23. Ching, "Beyond Nation and Empire." On the tension between Asian studies and Asian American studies, see Tina Chen and Eric Hayot, "Introducing Verge: What Does It Mean to Study Global Asias?," *Verge: Studies in Global Asias* 1, no. 1 (Spring 2015): vi–xv.
24. See Bruce Cumings, *Parallax Visions: Making Sense of American-East Asian Relations* (Durham, NC: Duke University Press, 2002), 173–204.
25. Ching, "Beyond Nation and Empire," 383.
26. Kandice Chuh, "Asians Are the New . . . What?," in *Flashpoints for Asian American Studies* (New York: Fordham University Press, 2018), 228.
27. Nguyen, *Race and Resistance*, 22, 23.
28. Chuh, "Asians Are the New . . . What?," 224.

1. DEEP CONDITIONS OF THE WORLD

29. Nils Gilman, *Mandarins of the Future: Modernization Theory in Cold War America* (Baltimore: Johns Hopkins University Press, 2003), 2
30. Gilman, *Mandarins of the Future*, 5.
31. Walt Whitman Rostow, *The Stages of Economic Growth: A Non-Communist Manifesto* (Cambridge: Cambridge University Press, 1960), 4.
32. Michael E. Latham, *The Right Kind of Revolution: Modernization, Development, and U.S. Foreign Policy from the Cold War to the Present* (Ithaca, NY: Cornell University Press, 2011), 44. Specifically, in the image of the Tennessee Valley Authority: "the conviction that the TVA represented planning without Soviet-style oppression shaped later beliefs that it could be applied universally. By adopting the TVA model... foreign societies could 'skip stages' and move more rapidly down the developmental path. What worked in the United States, he later insisted, could be directly applied in China, India, Colombia, Iran, and South Vietnam" (24).
33. David Halberstam, *The Best and the Brightest* (New York: Penguin Books, 1972), 54.
34. Latham, *The Right Kind of Revolution*, 157. Critiques of modernization and development theory can be found in Andre Gunder Frank, *Capitalism and Underdevelopment in Latin America* (New York: Monthly Review Press, 1967), and *ReORIENT: Global Economy in the Asian Age* (Berkeley: University of California Press, 1998); and in J. M. Blaut, *The Colonizer's Model of the World: Geographical Diffusionism and Eurocentric History* (New York: Guilford Press, 1993).
35. Michael Adas, *Machines as the Measure of Men: Science, Technology, and Ideologies of Western Dominance* (Ithaca, NY: Cornell University Press, 1989), 402.
36. Quoted in Gilman, *Mandarins of the Future*, 26.
37. Gilman, *Mandarins of the Future*, 26.
38. Even though, as Guy Ortolano points out, Snow avoided the term "modernization" precisely because of what he saw as its continuation by the United States of British imperialism, his thinking about development "did share common assumptions with modernization theory," *The Two Cultures Controversy: Science, Literature, and Cultural Politics* (Cambridge: Cambridge University Press, 2009), 208.
39. From Karl Marx, "The Future Results of British Rule in India," quoted in Gilman, *Mandarins of the Future*, 27.
40. Latham, *The Right Kind of Revolution*, 13.
41. Gilman, *Mandarins of the Future*, 28.
42. Edward Said, *Orientalism* (New York: Vintage Books, 1979), 155.
43. Gilman, *Mandarins of the Future*, 250.
44. Roh, Niu, and Huang, "Introduction," 1.
45. See Sigrid Schmalzer, "The Global Comrades of Mr. Democracy and Mr. Science: Placing May Fourth in a Transnational History of Science Activism," *East Asian Science, Technology and Society* 16, no. 3 (May 2021): 1–22.
46. In *Ends of Empire*, Jodi Kim demonstrates how Cold War discourse relied on a refashioned orientalism: "a great investment in rendering America's Cold War other *as* an 'Other' by racializing it (the Soviet Union) and its ideological father (Marx) as essentially oriental and Eastern, eliding the ways 'European radicalism' *qua* Marxism and what we could call American liberal pragmatism are two strains within the selfsame Western political philosophical tradition." Kim, *Ends of*

1. DEEP CONDITIONS OF THE WORLD

Empire: Asian American Critique and the Cold War (Minneapolis: University of Minnesota Press, 2010), 43.
47. Adas, *Machines as the Measure of Men*, 414.
48. As Lisa Yoneyama writes, "Area studies specialists investigated social organizations, kinship systems, religious beliefs, interpersonal behavior, and other social practices among targeted populations to identify indigenous elements that would teleologically lead them onto the next stage of universal history and help achieve a modernity paralleling that of the United States. These elements would of course vary according to the areas or nations under investigation. But they were thought to be functionally equivalent cross-culturally, and it was these elements that would enable comparisons among the people studied." *Cold War Ruins*, 62–63.
49. Odd Arne Westad, *The Global Cold War: Third World Interventions and the Making of Our Times* (Cambridge: Cambridge University Press, 2007), 35.
50. Kaname Akamatsu, "A Historical Pattern of Economic Growth in Developing Countries," *The Developing Economies* 1, no. 1 (August 1962): 3–25.
51. Bruce Cumings, "The Origins and Development of the Northeast Asian Political Economy: Industrial Sectors, Product Cycles, and Political Consequences," *International Organization* 38, no. 1 (Winter 1984): 16.
52. Cumings, "Origins and Development," 3.
53. Cumings, "Origins and Development," 3.
54. Cumings, "Origins and Development," 25.
55. Ekbladh, *The Great American Mission*, 120.
56. Chris Suh, *The Allure of Empire: American Encounters with Asians in the Age of Transpacific Expansion and Exclusion* (New York: Oxford University Press, 2023).
57. David Eng, *Racial Castration: Managing Masculinity in Asian America* (Durham, NC: Duke University Press, 2000), 213.
58. Susan Koshy, "The Fiction of Asian American Literature," *Yale Journal of Criticism* 9, no. 2 (Fall 1996): 342.
59. On the relation between militarization and modernization, see Glassman, *Drums of War, Drums of Development*.
60. Cumings, "Origins and Development," 24.
61. Cumings, "Origins and Development," 33; Glassman, *Drums of War, Drums of Development*, 404.
62. Alice H. Amsden, *Asia's Next Giant: South Korea and Late Industrialization* (New York: Oxford University Press, 1989), 39.
63. Andy Green, *Education and State Formation: Europe, East Asia and the USA* (New York: Palgrave Macmillan, 2013), 328.
64. Cumings, "Origins and Development," 17.
65. Cumings, "Origins and Development," 21, 38, 35.
66. Shelley Rigger, *The Tiger Leading the Dragon: How Taiwan Propelled China's Economic Rise* (Lanham, MD: Rowman & Littlefield, 2021).
67. Michael J. Seth, *Education Fever: Society, Politics, and the Pursuit of Schooling in South Korea* (Honolulu: University of Hawai'i Press, 2002), 119; Fujitani, *Race for Empire*, 231: "In their 'guidance' to the OWI [U.S. Office of War Information] on what we might call 'hot war modernization theory,' a group identified as 'Far Eastern Regional Specialists in N.Y. and Washington' strongly urged the OWI to desist from using the term 'Westernization,' which would associate the project of

1. DEEP CONDITIONS OF THE WORLD

liberal democracy and industrial capitalism with American propaganda, and to advance what they believed was the more neutral and world-historical term 'modernization.'"

68. Quoted in Sebastian Conrad, "'The Colonial Ties Are Liquidated': Modernization Theory, Post-war Japan and the Global Cold War," *Past & Present* 216 (August 2012): 190. See also Marius B. Jansen, ed., *Changing Japanese Attitudes toward Modernization* (Princeton, NJ: Princeton University Press, 1965).
69. H. D. Harootunian, "America's Japan/Japan's Japan," in *Japan in the World*, ed. Masao Miyoshi and H. D. Harootunian (Durham, NC: Duke University Press, 1993), 215.
70. Conrad, "The Colonial Ties Are Liquidated," 192. This apparently philosophical distinction was bolstered by a "strict" gendered distinction enforced by conference organizers. According to Conrad, organizers were "at pains" to "protect the all-male scholarly community from possible infringements by accompanying partners," going so far as to hire a "Japanese hostess" to tend to the wives, who were housed at separate hotels, and who complained that the arrangements were "unduly harsh" (190–91).
71. Quoted in Gregg Brazinsky, *Nation Building in South Korea: Koreans, Americans, and the Making of a Democracy* (Chapel Hill: University of North Carolina Press, 2007), 175.
72. Brazinsky, *Nation Building in South Korea*, 172.
73. Brazinsky, *Nation Building in South Korea*, 167. The United States Information Service teamed up with the staff of Chungang, a South Korean television network, to create a weekly news program on "Modernization in Korea," which was viewed by 70,000 to 100,000 people each week (167–68). In Taiwan, similar propaganda campaigns were launched by agencies like the Sino-American Joint Commission on Rural Reconstruction: see Lawrence Zi-Qiao Yang, "Soil and Scroll: The Agrarian Origin of a Cold War Documentary Avant Garde," *Modern Chinese Literature and Culture* 31, no. 2 (Fall 2019): 41–80.
74. Chalmers Johnson, *MITI and the Japanese Miracle: The Growth of Industrial Policy, 1925–1975* (Stanford, CA: Stanford University Press, 1982).
75. Quoted in Conrad, "The Colonial Ties Are Liquidated," 182.
76. Brazinsky, *Nation Building in South Korea*, 178. A handful of the 1965 South Korean conference attendees went on to form the Modernization Research Group in Park Chung-hee's cabinet, which shaped educational policy.
77. Quoted in Amsden, *Asia's Next Giant*, 46.
78. Brazinsky, *Nation Building in South Korea*, 154.
79. Seth, *Education Fever*, 44; Brazinsky, *Nation Building in South Korea*, 47.
80. Don Adams, *Higher Educational Reforms in the Republic of Korea* (Washington, DC: U.S. Department of Health, Education and Welfare, 1965), 14. See also Seth, *Education Fever*.
81. Seth, *Education Fever*, 118, 121. The quotation is at 125.
82. J. Megan Greene, *The Origins of the Developmental State in Taiwan: Science Policy and the Quest for Modernization* (Cambridge, MA: Harvard University Press, 2008), 2.
83. Thomas B. Gold, *State and Society in the Taiwan Miracle* (Armonk, NY: M. E. Sharpe, 1986), 68.

1. DEEP CONDITIONS OF THE WORLD

84. Greene, *Origins of the Developmental State*, 7.
85. Glassman points out that Taiwanese business leaders also grew impatient with Chiang's revanchism. *Drums of War, Drums of Development*, 394.
86. Henry F. McCusker Jr. and Harry J. Robinson, *Report on Education and Development: The Role of Educational Planning in the Economic Development of the Republic of China* (Menlo Park, CA: Stanford Research Institute, 1962).
87. Greene, *Origins of the Developmental State*, 54; quote at 96.
88. Greene, *Origins of the Developmental State*, 71.
89. Glassman, *Drums of War, Drums of Development*, 407.
90. Greene, *Origins of the Developmental State*, 18, 8.
91. Seth, *Education Fever*, 120.
92. Greene, *Origins of the Developmental State*, 113.
93. Ted Chiang, "Understand," in *Stories of Your Life and Others* (Easthampton, MA: Small Beer Press, 2010), 70.
94. U.S. Department of Labor, "Summaries of Manpower Surveys and Reports for Developing Countries, 1958–68" (June 1969), 163.
95. Greene, *Origins of the Developmental State*, 97, 47.
96. Chih-ming Wang, *Transpacific Articulations: Student Migration and the Remaking of Asian America* (Honolulu: University of Hawai'i Press, 2013), 82.
97. Cumings, "Origins and Development," 12.
98. World Bank, *The East Asian Miracle: Economic Growth and Public Policy* (New York: Oxford University Press, 1993), 82.
99. Glassman, *Drums of War, Drums of Development*, 394.
100. See Alice H. Amsden, "Why Isn't the Whole World Experimenting with the East Asian Model to Develop?: Review of *The East Asian Miracle*," *World Development* 22, no. 4 (1994): 627–33; John A. Matthews and Dong-Sung Cho, *Tiger Technology: The Creation of a Semiconductor Industry in East Asia* (London: Cambridge University Press, 2009); Jennie Hay Woo, "Education and Economic Growth in Taiwan: A Case of Successful Planning," *World Development* 19, no. 8 (August 1991): 1029–44.
101. On the historical priors of the shaping of the model minority myth by neoliberal economists, see Paul Nadal, "How Neoliberalism Remade the Model Minority Myth," *Representations* 163 (August 2023): 79–99.
102. Amsden, "Why Isn't the Whole World Experimenting," 627, 628. Amsden goes on to show how on the basis of logic alone the "miracle" narrative is "unfalsifiable" ("If it is not possible to establish statistical links 'between growth and a specific intervention,' then neither is it possible to establish statistical links between growth and *non*-intervention") and based on "extensive bibliographical references mainly to [the World Bank's and its paid consultants'] their own work" (628, 630).
103. Matthews and Cho, *Tiger Technology*.
104. Glassman, *Drums of War, Drums of Development*, 389.
105. Julian Gewirtz, "The Futurists of Beijing: Alvin Toffler, Zhao Ziyang, and China's 'New Technological Revolution,' 1979–1991," *Journal of Asian Studies* 78, no. 1 (February 2019): 9. See also Gewirtz, *Unlikely Partners: Chinese Reformers, Western Economists, and the Making of Global China* (Cambridge, MA: Harvard University Press, 2017).

1. DEEP CONDITIONS OF THE WORLD

106. Huang Ping, "Modernization: China's Path and Logic," *Chinese Social Sciences Today*, November 4, 2011, http://www.csstoday.com/Item/9527.aspx.
107. Richard Evans, *Deng Xiaoping and the Making of Modern China* (New York: Penguin Books, 1995), 201, 252.
108. Ho-fung Hung, *The China Boom: Why China Will Not Rule the World* (New York: Columbia University Press, 2016), 54.
109. Alexandra Alter, "How Chinese Sci-Fi Conquered America," *New York Times*, December 3, 2019, https://www.nytimes.com/2019/12/03/magazine/ken-liu-three-body-problem-chinese-science-fiction.html.
110. Ken Liu, "A Brief History of the Trans-Pacific Tunnel," in *The Paper Menagerie and Other Stories*, 350.
111. As Lisa Yoneyama notes, the history of Unit 731 was introduced to the Japanese public in the early 1980s by Morimura Seiichi's nonfiction novel, *Akuma no hōshoku*, and to English-speaking audiences by Sheldon H. Harris's *Factories of Death: Japanese Biological Warfare 1932–45 and the American Cover-up* (New York: Routledge, 1994).
112. On the epistemology of testimony in Liu's story, see Patricia Chu, "'Truth as Accessible as Looking Out a Window': Unit 731 and the Ethics of Virtual Postwar Testimony," *Massachusetts Review* 60, no. 4 (Winter 2019): 682–96.
113. Rostow, *Stages of Economic Growth*, 179.
114. Rocío G. Davis argues that the film is a "prelude" to *A Tale for the Time Being* in her essay "Fictional Transits and Ruth Ozeki's *A Tale for the Time Being*," *Biography* 38, no. 1 (Winter 2015): 100. Ozeki's 1998 debut novel *My Year of Meats* alternates between the perspectives of the Japanese American television producer Jane Takagi-Little and the Japanese housewife Akiko Ueno; and her 2013 novel *A Tale for the Time Being* alternates between the perspectives of Ruth, Ozeki's metafictional doppelgänger, and Naoko Yasutani, a Japanese teenager. Ozeki describes this relation as one of "sending" and "receiving," Eleanor Ty and Ruth Ozeki, "'A Universe of Many Worlds': An Interview with Ruth Ozeki," *MELUS* 38, no. 3 (Fall 2013): 166.
115. Ty and Ozeki, "A Universe of Many Worlds," 161.
116. Reminiscent of the twist in the opening pages of the final chapter of *The Woman Warrior*, which reveal that the preceding chapter, "At the Western Palace," which is written in the style of a memoir, is in fact Maxine's thirdhand confabulated assemblage of events that her brother had told her sister about (162).
117. In *Ends of Empire*, Jodi Kim makes a similar argument in regard to the novel's registration of U.S. imperialism in Japan, with a focus on the role that "gendered racial rehabilitation" plays in the "complex ways in which Japanese and Japanese American subjects—formerly enemies and 'enemy aliens,' respectively—are transformed into a Cold War junior ally in Asia and a 'model minority' in America through their interpellation by and suturing to the protocols and logics of America's Cold War imperial project" (104).
118. My claim here is a rephrasing of how Ozeki narrates her own literary output. In regard to the huge array of disparate elements and themes that characterize her novels, she remarks to Eleanor Ty: "I see them all as inseparable, a kind of interconnectedness, which I think was there in the first two books but is even more overt in [*A Tale for the Time Being*]" (161).

119. Ozeki, *A Tale for the Time Being*, 141, original emphasis.
120. John Swenson-Wright, *Unequal Allies? United States Security and Alliance Policy Toward Japan, 1945–1960* (Stanford, CA: Stanford University Press, 2005), 181.
121. Andrew (Adhy) Kim, "Japanese Melancholy and the Ethics of Concealment in Ruth Ozeki's *A Tale for the Time Being*," *Mosaic* 52, no. 4 (December 2019): 84.
122. Kim, "Japanese Melancholy," 87.
123. Ty and Ozeki, "A Universe of Many Worlds," 162.
124. Ty and Ozeki, "A Universe of Many Worlds," 166; Michelle N. Huang, "Ecologies of Entanglement in the Great Pacific Garbage Patch," *Journal of Asian American Studies* 20, no. 1 (February 2017): 99.
125. Edward Fowler, *The Rhetoric of Confession: Shishosetsu in Early Twentieth-Century Japanese Fiction* (Berkeley: University of California Press, 1992), 128. Named after but, as Edward Fowler argues, not identical to the German "Ich-Roman" (4). An article that Ruth stumbles upon in the novel also cites Fowler.
126. Fowler, *The Rhetoric of Confession*, xvi.
127. Veronika Mikulova also makes the claim about Harumi in "Embracing Western Thought: The Development of Japanese Identity in the Works by Kazuo Ishiguro and Ruth Ozeki," MA thesis, Masaryk University, 2017, 59. Quotation from Ruth Ozeki, "Confessions of a Zen Novelist," *Lion's Roar*, February 15, 2013, https://www.lionsroar.com/confessions-of-a-zen-novelist/.
128. Fowler writes: "It was not until the 1930s, when the feminist movement allied itself with the proletarian movement, that a number of influential writers, including Miyamoto Yuriko, Hayashi Fumiko, Sata Ineko, and Hirabayashi Taiko, began to make their mark on the literary scene, using the *shishōsetsu* as their principal medium." *The Rhetoric of Confession*, xxix.
129. Fowler, *The Rhetoric of Confession*, 84.
130. Fowler, *The Rhetoric of Confession*, 77.
131. Ozeki, "Confessions."
132. Ozeki, "Confessions."
133. Ty and Ozeki, "A Universe of Many Worlds," 160.

2. WRITING LIKE AN ENGINEER

1. Yoonmee Chang, *Writing the Ghetto: Class, Authorship, and the Asian American Ethnic Enclave* (New Brunswick, NJ: Rutgers University Press, 2010), 201.
2. Stephen Hong Sohn, *Racial Asymmetries: Asian American Fictional Worlds* (New York: NYU Press, 2014), 2. For an extended analysis of asymmetry in Asian American SF, particularly in Light's story and Chiang's novella *The Merchant and the Alchemist's Gate*, see esp. chap. 5.
3. Min Hyoung Song, *The Children of 1965: On Writing, and Not Writing, as an Asian American* (Durham, NC: Duke University Press, 2013).
4. Yoon Sun Lee, *Modern Minority: Asian American Literature and Everyday Life* (New York: Oxford University Press, 2013), 18.
5. Lee, *Modern Minority*, 4, 16, 185n85.
6. Lee, *Modern Minority*, 12.

2. WRITING LIKE AN ENGINEER

7. This is of course Darko Suvin's phrase for the defining characteristic of SF, from *Metamorphoses of Science Fiction* (New Haven, CT: Yale University Press, 1979), 18.
8. Dipesh Chakrabarty, "The Legacies of Bandung: Decolonization and the Politics of Culture," in *Making a World after Empire: The Bandung Movement and Its Political Afterlives*, ed. Christopher J. Lee (Athens: Ohio University Press, 2010), 53.
9. Lee, *Modern Minority*, 4.
10. Lee, *Modern Minority*, 19. In the introduction (drawing from Lee, who is drawing from Lukács) I referred to this desire as an "aspiration toward totality."
11. Lee, *Modern Minority*, 18.
12. Lee, *Modern Minority*, 176.
13. Odd Arne Westad, *The Global Cold War: Third World Interventions and the Making of Our Times* (Cambridge: Cambridge University Press, 2007), 166.
14. Jodi Melamed, *Represent and Destroy: Rationalizing Violence in the New Racial Capitalism* (Minneapolis: University of Minnesota Press, 2011), 4.
15. Michael Adas, *Machines as the Measure of Men: Science, Technology, and Ideologies of Western Dominance* (Ithaca, NY: Cornell University Press, 1989), 412.
16. Adas, *Machines as the Measure of Men*, 413.
17. Adas, *Machines as the Measure of Men*, 412.
18. Quoted in Gregg Brazinsky, *Nation Building in South Korea: Koreans, Americans, and the Making of a Democracy* (Chapel Hill: University of North Carolina Press, 2007), 175.
19. Adas, *Machines as the Measure of Men*, 412.
20. Jim Glassman, *Drums of War, Drums of Development: The Formation of a Pacific Ruling Class and Industrial Transformation in East and Southeast Asia, 1945–1980* (Chicago: Haymarket Books, 2018), 4.
21. Bruce Cumings, "The Political Economy of the Pacific Rim," in *Pacific-Asia and the Future of the World-System*, ed. Ravi Arvind Palat (Westport, CT: Greenwood Press, 1993), 26.
22. In a slightly different vein, for a Cold War ideological account of the model minority, see Robert G. Lee, "The Cold War Origins of the Model Minority Myth," in *Orientals: Asian Americans in Popular Culture* (Philadelphia: Temple University Press, 1999).
23. Takeshi Fujitani, *Race for Empire: Koreans as Japanese and Japanese as Americans During World War II* (Berkeley: University of California Press, 2011), 190.
24. Fujitani, *Race for Empire*, 233.
25. See Chang, *Writing the Ghetto*; Eduardo Bonilla-Silva, *Racism Without Racists* (Lanham, MD: Rowman & Littlefield, 2003); Ramón Saldívar, "Second Elevation of the Novel: Race, Form, and the Postrace Aesthetic in Contemporary Narrative," *Narrative* 21, no. 1 (January 2013): 1–18; Elena Machado Saez and Raphael Dalleo, *The Latino/a Canon and the Emergence of Post-Sixties Literature* (New York: Palgrave Macmillan, 2007); Song, *The Children of 1965*; Kenneth Warren, *What Was African American Literature?* (Cambridge, MA: Harvard University Press, 2011); Touré, *Who's Afraid of Post-Blackness? What It Means to Be Black Now* (New York: Free Press, 2011).

26. Saldívar, "Second Elevation of the Novel," 2.
27. Melamed, *Represent and Destroy*, x.
28. See Robert Bellah, "Cultural Vision and the Human Future," *Teachers College Record* 82, no. 3 (1981): 1–7; and Amy Borovoy's account of Bellah's work, "Robert Bellah's Search for Community and Ethical Modernity in Japan Studies," *Journal of Asian Studies* 75, no. 2 (May 2016): 467–94.
29. Borovoy, "Robert Bellah's Search," 469.
30. Fujitani, *Race for Empire*, 233–34. On the importance of Bellah's work to the scholarly justifications for modernization theory, see Sebastian Conrad, "'The Colonial Ties Are Liquidated': Modernization Theory, Post-war Japan and the Global Cold War," *Past & Present* 216 (August 2012): 181–214. As Chris Suh shows, these points of connection between Japanese and American empire were not merely rhetorical but helped each to develop their own liberal, even "progressive" rationales for imperial expansion: "the rapprochement between the United States and Japan was representative of the larger changes in racial thinking and social relations wrought by Progressive reform." *The Allure of Empire: American Encounters with Asians in the Age of Transpacific Expansion and Exclusion* (New York: Oxford University Press, 2023), 10.
31. Fujitani, *Race for Empire*, 231.
32. Conrad, "The Colonial Ties Are Liquidated," 189–90.
33. On the "uncomfortable tie between internment and the New Deal," see Lye, *America's Asia*, 141–2.
34. Chakrabarty, "The Legacies of Bandung," 63; G. L. Downey and J. C. Lucena, "Knowledge and professional identity in engineering: code-switching and the metrics of progress," *History and Technology* 20, no. 4 (December 2004): 394.
35. Lawson Inada, "Introduction," in John Okada, *No-No Boy* (Seattle: University of Washington Press, 2014), v. When Inada, Chin, and Wong visited Okada's widow Dorothy, she apologized for burning the manuscript of his only other novel, which was unpublished, and for only being able to offer them his "other work," which "were a few technical brochures for business corporations." Okada was a technical writer for Chrysler Missile Operations in Detroit from 1953 or 1954 to 1957, when he moved to Los Angeles to do tech writing for Hughes Aircraft Company. Ruth Ozeki, "Foreword," in Okada, *No-No Boy*, vii–xviii.
36. Okada, *No-No Boy*, 53.
37. Julia H. Lee, *The Racial Railroad* (New York: NYU Press, 2022), 85.
38. Sau-ling Wong, *Reading Asian American Literature: From Necessity to Extravagance* (Princeton, NJ: Princeton University Press, 1993), 210.
39. Charles Yu, *How to Live Safely in a Science Fictional Universe* (New York: Vintage Books, 2010), 35.
40. Cecelia Tichi, *Shifting Gears: Technology, Literature, Culture in Modernist America* (Berkeley: University of California Press, 1996), 98.
41. Tichi, *Shifting Gears*, 98–99.
42. Tichi, *Shifting Gears*, 122; Edwin Layton, *The Revolt of the Engineers: Social Responsibility and the American Engineering Profession* (Baltimore: Johns Hopkins University Press, 1986).
43. Tichi, *Shifting Gears*, 99.

44. Tichi, *Shifting Gears*, 16.
45. Xuan Juliana Wang and Christopher Patterson, "A Discussion with Xuan Juliana Wang and Ricco Villanueva Siasoco," *New Books in Asian American Studies*, August 24, 2021, podcast, https://newbooksnetwork.com/association-of-asian-american-studies-book-awards-2021-xuan-juliana-wang-and-ricco-villanueva-siasoco.
46. Elizabeth Tabler, "An Interview with Ken Liu," *GrimdarkMAGAZINE*, December 4, 2021, https://www.grimdarkmagazine.com/an-interview-with-ken-liu/.
47. Betsy Huang, "Interview with Ken Liu," *Asian American Literary Review*, August 16, 2012.
48. John Okada, "The Technocrats of Industry or The Trials and Tribulations of Mr. S. V. and How He Finally Became a Real Engineer . . .," in *The Life and Rediscovered Work of the Author of No-No Boy*, ed. Frank Abe, Greg Robinson, and Floyd Cheung (Seattle: University of Washington Press, 2018), 206.
49. Okada, "Technocrats of Industry," 210.
50. Andrew Hoberek, *Twilight of the Middle Class: Post-World War II Fiction and White-Collar Work* (Princeton, NJ: Princeton University Press, 2005), 71. On the Asian American–Jewish American analogy, see Iyko Day, "Introduction: The New Jews: Settler Colonialism and the Personification of Capitalism," in *Alien Capital: Asian Racialization and the Logic of Settler Colonial Capitalism* (Durham, NC: Duke University Press, 2016), 1–40, and Lye, *America's Asia*, 57–58. Both Day and Lye ground their argument in Moishe Postone's reading of Jews as abstract forms of capital in "Anti-Semitism and National Socialism," in *Germans and Jews Since the Holocaust: The Changing Situation in West Germany*, ed. Anson Rabinbach and Jack Zipes (New York: Holmes & Meier, 1986), 302–14.
51. Bernadette Longo, *Spurious Coin: A History of Science, Management, and Technical Writing* (Albany: SUNY Press, 2000), 22.
52. Jasper Bernes, *The Work of Art in the Age of Deindustrialization* (Stanford, CA: Stanford University Press, 2017), 64.
53. Matthew G. Kirschenbaum, *Track Changes: A Literary History of Word Processing* (Cambridge, MA: Harvard University Press, 2016), 63. In a biography that Chiang included with a reprint of "Understand," he notes, wryly, "Of his nonfiction, written in his capacity as a technical writer, perhaps the most popular is the C++ Tutorial packaged with certain versions of Microsoft's C++ compiler," in *The Hard SF Renaissance: An Anthology*, ed. David G. Hartwell and Kathryn Cramer (New York: Orb Books, 2003), 342.
54. Adam Israel, "Interview: Ted Chiang," *The Clarion Foundation Blog*, February 7, 2012, http://clarionfoundation.wordpress.com/2012/02/07/interview-ted-chiang/.
55. Sherryl Vint, "Notes and Correspondence: Suggested Further Readings in the Slipstream," *Science Fiction Studies* 38, no. 1 (March 2011), http://www.depauw.edu/sfs/notes/notes113/notes113.html.
56. Tichi, *Shifting Gears*, 105.
57. This story anticipates the linguistic tropes at the center of "Story of Your Life." To accommodate the bandwidth of his expanding cognition, Leon invents a new language that is "gestalt-oriented" and is transcribed not linearly but "as a giant ideogram, to be absorbed as a whole" and whose most extreme instance would be "a colossal ideogram that describes the entire universe" (51).

58. Quoted in Jinn-yuh Hsu, "State Transformation and the Evolution of Economic Nationalism in the East Asian Developmental State: The Taiwanese Semiconductor Industry as Case Study," *Transactions of the Institute of British Geographers* 42, no. 2 (June 2017): 169.
59. Chih-ming Wang, *Transpacific Articulations: Student Migration and the Remaking of Asian America* (Honolulu: University of Hawai'i Press, 2013), 82.
60. On dissident Taiwanese international students like Guo, who came to the United States during the martial law period, see Wendy Cheng's groundbreaking book *Island X: Taiwanese Student Migrants, Campus Spies, and Cold War Activism* (Berkeley: University of California Press, 2023).
61. Longo, *Spurious Coin*, 147, 84.
62. Michael E. Latham, *The Right Kind of Revolution: Modernization, Development, and U.S. Foreign Policy from the Cold War to the Present* (Ithaca, NY: Cornell University Press, 2011), 22.
63. Nils Gilman, *Mandarins of the Future: Modernization Theory in Cold War America* (Baltimore: Johns Hopkins University Press, 2003), 14. The distinctly American content of this utopian vision—Rostow's conviction, typical of other modernization theorists, that "[utopia] already existed just outside his front door in Cambridge, Massachusetts" (202)—is something that Roger Luckhurst traces to SF's very conditions of emergence in an Americanized narrative of modernity in *Science Fiction* (Cambridge: Polity Press, 2005), 25.
64. China Miéville, "Wonder Boy," *The Guardian*, April 23, 2004, http://www.theguardian.com/books/2004/apr/24/featuresreviews.guardianreview23.
65. Miéville appears to mean "melancholy" in the colloquial sense of pervasive sadness, as opposed to the pathological depression Freud contrasts with the healthier process of mourning. There is nonetheless a structural similarity between the two. A transcendence is implied when Freud narrates the process of melancholia: "Thus the shadow of the object fell across the ego, and the latter could henceforth be judged by a special agency, as though it were the object, the forsaken object." Freud, "Mourning and Melancholia" (1917), in *The Standard Edition of the Complete Psychological Works of Sigmund Freud*, vol. 14, trans. James Strachey (London: Hogarth Press, 1953), 249. Melancholia, like melancholy transcendence, is what happens when an outside becomes an inside. This is Anne Cheng's point of departure in her reconfiguration of racialized subjectivity as a mode of melancholia in which the subject's otherness to itself is mediated by racism. *The Melancholy of Race* (New York: Oxford University Press, 2000).
66. John Clute and Peter Nicholls, *The Encyclopedia of Science Fiction* (New York: Doubleday, 1979).
67. My emphasis. Quoted in Vandana Singh, "The Occasional Writer: An Interview with Science Fiction Author Ted Chiang," *The Margins, The Asian American Writers Workshop*, October 3, 2012, http://aaww.org/the-occasional-writer-an-interview-with-science-fiction-author-ted-chiang/.
68. Max Millikan and Walt Whitman Rostow, *A Proposal: Key to an Effective Foreign Policy* (Boston: Center for International Studies, MIT, 1957), quoted in Latham, *The Right Kind of Revolution*, 56.
69. Jeremy Smith, "The Absence of God, an Interview with Ted Chiang," *Interzone* 182 (September 2002), 23–27.

2. WRITING LIKE AN ENGINEER

70. Smith, "The Absence of God, an Interview with Ted Chiang." A character in Chiang's story "Liking What You See" (2002) appears to ventriloquize this position: "There's no neural pathway that specifically handles resentment toward immigrants, any more than there's one for Marxist doctrine or foot fetishism. If we ever get true mind programming, we'll be able to create 'race blindness,' but until then, education is our best hope." "Liking What You See: A Documentary," in *Stories of Your Life and Others*, 258.
71. Chiang interview with Vandana Singh.
72. Chiang interview with Betsy Huang.
73. For account of Asiatic racial form as "mode" and "salience," see Mark Jerng, *Racial Worldmaking: The Power of Popular Fiction* (New York: Fordham University Press, 2017), and "The Asiatic Modal Imagination," in *Asian American Literature in Transition, 1996–2020*, ed. Betsy Huang and Victor Román Mendoza (Cambridge: Cambridge University Press, 2021), 173–99. As "tone," see Sunny Xiang, *Tonal Intelligence: The Aesthetics of Asian Inscrutability During the Long Cold War* (New York: Columbia University Press, 2020).
74. For a reading of *Aloft* through the optic of racial form, see Mark Jerng, "Nowhere in Particular: Perceiving Race, Chang-rae Lee's *Aloft*, and the Question of Asian American Fiction," *Modern Fiction Studies* 56, no. 1 (Spring 2010): 183–204.
75. Lin's novel *Taipei* (New York: Vintage Books, 2013) includes a scene at the Asian American Writers Workshop, in which his protagonist, a semiautobiographical Taiwanese American writer named Paul, looks around and mutters to his companion, "I feel like I hate everyone" (133). Frank Chin's patrolling of the divide between "real" and "fake" Asian American literature (Chinese American in particular) has offered one of the foundational antinomies of Asian American literary studies. See the preface to Frank Chin, Jeffrey Paul Chan, Shawn Wong, and Lawson Fusao Inada, eds., *Aiiieeeee!: An Anthology of Asian American Writers* (Washington, DC: Howard University Press, 1974), and Frank Chin, "Come All Ye Asian American Writers of the Real and the Fake," in *The Big Aiiieeeee! An Anthology of Chinese American and Japanese American Literature*, ed. Frank Chin, Jeffrey Paul Chan, Shawn Wong, and Lawson Fusao Inada (New York: Meridian, 1991), 1–92.
76. Viet Thanh Nguyen, *Race and Resistance: Literature and Politics in Asian America* (New York: Oxford University Press, 2002).
77. Chiang, "Story of Your Life," 95.
78. Gilman, *Mandarins of the Future*, 202.
79. H. G. Wells, *The Time Machine* (New York: Oxford University Press, 2017), 8.
80. Chris Swoyer, "The Linguistic Relativity Hypothesis," *Stanford Encyclopedia of Philosophy* (2003), http://plato.stanford.edu/entries/relativism/supplement2.html.
81. Latham, *The Right Kind of Revolution*, 158.
82. Quoted in Gilman, *Mandarins of the Future*, 6.
83. Quoted in Chakrabarty, "The Legacies of Bandung," 53.
84. C. P. Snow, *The Two Cultures and the Scientific Revolution* (Cambridge: Cambridge University Press, 1959), 48.
85. Adas, *Machines as the Measure of Men*, 412.
86. Walt Whitman Rostow, *The Stages of Economic Growth: A Non-Communist Manifesto* (Cambridge: Cambridge University Press, 1960), 166.

87. Gilman, *Mandarins of the Future*, 202, 201.
88. Rostow, *The Stages of Economic Growth*, 149.
89. Rostow, *The Stages of Economic Growth*, 148.
90. Gilman, *Mandarins of the Future*, 202, 8.
91. Gilman, *Mandarins of the Future*, 12.
92. Claire Light, *Slightly Behind and to the Left: Four Stories and Three Drabbles* (Seattle: Aqueduct, 2009), 86.
93. See Longo, *Spurious Coin*, chap. 4.
94. Hoberek, *Twilight of the Middle Class*, 23; Bernes, *The Work of Art in the Age of Deindustrialization*, 66.
95. Bernes, *The Work of Art in the Age of Deindustrialization*, 76.

3. SHAKESPEARE WORDS

1. Sean McCann, "Training and Vision: Roth, DeLillo, Banks, Peck, and the Postmodern Aesthetics of Vocation," *Twentieth-Century Literature* 53, no. 3 (Fall 2007): 303.
2. Yoon Sun Lee, "Type, Totality, and the Realism of Asian American Literature," *Modern Language Quarterly* 73, no. 3 (September 2012): 421.
3. Daniel Hartley, *The Politics of Style: Towards a Marxist Poetics* (Boston: Brill, 2017), 95.
4. Charles McGrath, "Deep in Suburbia," *New York Times*, February 29, 2004, https://www.nytimes.com/2004/02/29/magazine/deep-in-suburbia.html.
5. Doug Henwood, *Wall Street: How It Works and for Whom* (New York: Verso, 1998), 88.
6. McGrath, "Deep in Suburbia."
7. Peter Monaghan, "A Korean-American Novelist's Impressive Debut," *Chronicle of Higher Education*, April 7, 1995, https://www.chronicle.com/article/a-korean-american-novelists-impressive-debut/.
8. Min Hyoung Song points this out in "Between Genres: On Chang-rae Lee's Realism," *Los Angeles Review of Books*, January 10, 2014, https://www.lareviewofbooks.org/article/chang-rae-lees-realism.
9. Hartley, *The Politics of Style*, 4.
10. Fredric Jameson, *Marxism and Form: 20th-Century Dialectical Theories of Literature* (Princeton, NJ: Princeton University Press, 1974), 333–34.
11. Raymond Williams, "Introduction," *The Pelican Book of English Prose: From 1780 to the Present Day*, vol. 2 (Harmondsworth, UK: Penguin Books, 1969), 55, 27.
12. Hartley, *The Politics of Style*, 230.
13. Hartley, *The Politics of Style*, 261.
14. Williams, "Introduction," 26.
15. Williams, "Introduction," 26.
16. Hartley, *The Politics of Style*, 79.
17. Gregg Brazinsky, *Nation Building in South Korea: Koreans, Americans, and the Making of a Democracy* (Chapel Hill: University of North Carolina Press, 2007), 176.

18. Underlying this point is a line that the character Chang-rae spews at his mother in Wayne Wang's 2019 film adaptation of "Coming Home Again," for which Lee wrote the screenplay: "My job is to be your son."
19. Two recent examples of this blurring are Alfonso Cuarón's film *Roma* (2018) and Alex Tizon's essay "My Family's Slave," *The Atlantic*, June 2017.
20. Chang-rae Lee, "Coming Home Again," *The New Yorker*, October 9, 1995, https://www.newyorker.com/magazine/1995/10/16/coming-home-again.
21. Lee, "Coming Home Again."
22. In a way, the slap finally materializes in *Native Speaker*, when Henry is recounting a fight with his father in which he prods his father's linguistic insecurities by "using the biggest words I knew, whether they made sense or not, school words like 'socioeconomic' and 'intangible,' anything I could lift from my dizzy burning thoughts and hurl against him, until my mother, who'd been perfectly quiet the whole time, whacked me hard across the back of the head and shouted in Korean, *Who do you think you are?*" (58).
23. Christine So, *Economic Citizens: A Narrative of Asian American Visibility* (Philadelphia: Temple University Press, 2008), 9–10.
24. Lee, "Coming Home Again."
25. Chang-rae Lee, "The Faintest Echo of Our Language," *New England Review* 15, no. 3 (Summer 1993): 89–90.
26. The significance of this modernist literary tradition in *Native Speaker* is also detectable in its narrative and characterological antecedents, the two clearest of which are Robert Penn Warren's *All the King's Men* and Don DeLillo's *The Names*. Both novels take up the conventions of the spy novel and political thriller to explore the political alignments and moral habits of the professional-managerial class, and many specific details from each novel find their way into *Native Speaker*. The similarities with DeLillo's novel are especially striking, and this is confirmed by Lee himself, who cites it as one of his main influences. While the first-person narrative of a young man nearing middle age and whose marriage is in crisis is perhaps not, because of its ubiquity, a surprising overlap, among the more specific homages are that DeLillo's narrator is employed by an apparently boring but ultimately mysterious organization (which turns out to be a front for the CIA), that the main conflict in the marriage is the narrator's job, and that the trope of language is material and potentially transcendent. Also, DeLillo's Greek setting appears to be referenced by Henry's closest friend at Glimmer & Co., the Greek operative Jack. Readings that put *Native Speaker* and *All the King's Men* in conversation include Jonathan Arac, "Violence and the Human Voice: Critique and Hope in *Native Speaker*," *boundary 2* 36, no. 2 (2009): 55–66; David Cowart, "Korean Connection: Chang-rae Lee and Company," in *Trailing Clouds: Immigrant Fiction in Contemporary America* (Ithaca, NY: Cornell University Press, 2006); and Amy Tang, "Interrupted Intertextuality in Chang-rae Lee's *Native Speaker*," *Race and Repetition: Asian American Literature After Multiculturalism* (New York: Oxford University Press, 2016). Thanks to Michael Szalay for encouraging me to pursue the connection to *All the King's Men*.
27. Lee, "The Faintest Echo," 90.
28. Christopher Lee, *The Semblance of Identity: Aesthetic Mediation in Asian American Literature* (Stanford, CA: Stanford University Press, 2012).

3. SHAKESPEARE WORDS

29. Sunny Xiang, "The Korean Voice of American Empire: The Democratic Spokesman and the Model Minority Narrator," *Journal of Asian American Studies* 17, no. 3 (October 2014): 287.
30. Tina Chen, "Impersonation and Other Disappearing Acts in *Native Speaker* by Chang-rae Lee," *Modern Fiction Studies* 48, no. 3 (Fall 2002): 637–67; James Kyung-Jin Lee, "Where the Talented Tenth Meets the Model Minority: The Price of Privilege in Wideman's 'Philadelphia Fire' and Lee's 'Native Speaker,'" *NOVEL: A Forum on Fiction* 35, nos. 2–3 (Spring–Summer 2002): 231–57; Crystal Parikh, "Ethnic America Undercover: The Intellectual and Minority Discourse," *Contemporary Literature* 43, no. 2 (Summer 2002): 249–84.
31. Chen, "Impersonation and Other Disappearing Acts," 638.
32. Xiang, "The Korean Voice of American Empire," 275.
33. Jodi Kim, "From Mee-gook to Gook: The Cold War and Racialized Undocumented Capital in Chang-rae Lee's *Native Speaker*," *MELUS* 34, no. 1 (Spring 2009): 118.
34. Kim, "From Mee-gook to Gook," 130.
35. Daniel Kim, "Do I, Too, Sing America?: Vernacular Representations and Chang-rae Lee's *Native Speaker*," *Journal of Asian American Studies* 6, no. 3 (October 2003): 259.
36. Kim, "Do I, Too, Sing America?," 235.
37. These scenes are modeled after the Family Red Apple boycott and protests in 1990. See Claire Jean Kim, *Bitter Fruit: The Politics of Black-Korean Conflict in New York City* (New Haven, CT: Yale University Press, 2003).
38. Parikh, "Ethnic America Undercover," 276.
39. Jodi Melamed, *Represent and Destroy: Rationalizing Violence in the New Racial Capitalism* (Minneapolis: University of Minnesota Press, 2011).
40. Xiang, "The Korean Voice of American Empire," 287.
41. My emphasis. Sarah Anne Johnson, "An Interview with Chang-rae Lee," *Association of Writers & Writing Programs* (May/Summer 2005), https://www.awpwriter.org/magazine_media/writers_chronicle_view/2464/an_interview_with_chang-rae_lee.
42. The irony is not lost on us that, in retrospect, *Native Speaker* inaugurated the Asian American program era.
43. Chang-rae Lee, *My Year Abroad* (New York: Riverhead, 2021), 241.
44. Chang-rae Lee, *On Such a Full Sea* (New York: Riverhead, 2014), 6.
45. Chen, "Impersonation and Other Disappearing Acts," 158.
46. Kim, "Do I, Too, Sing America?," 253.
47. Lee, *The Semblance of Identity*, 118.
48. Viet Thanh Nguyen, *Nothing Ever Dies: Vietnam and the Memory of War* (Cambridge, MA: Harvard University Press, 2017), 249. I thank Sunny Xiang for bringing this passage to my attention.
49. I have found the Accent Research Collaborative (ARC)'s work on the analytic of the "accent," understood as a *literary* mediation of linguistic difference, especially generative in thinking about questions of style. What I have called here "stylistic awkwardness" can also be understood as a "biography of migration," which is how Lawrence Abu Hamdan defines accented language. My thanks to Ragini Tharoor Srinivasan for bringing ARC's work to my attention.

3. SHAKESPEARE WORDS

50. Bernadette Longo, *Spurious Coin: A History of Science, Management, and Technical Writing* (Albany: SUNY Press, 2000), 147, 84.
51. Robert B. Reich, *The Work of Nations: Preparing Ourselves for 21st-Century Capitalism* (New York: Knopf, 1991), 177–80.
52. C. Wright Mills, *White Collar: The American Middle Classes* (New York: Oxford University Press, 2002), 65.
53. Mills, *White Collar*, xv. Think here of the scenes of Henry sifting through printouts of the *ggeh* members and doing data entry in Kwang's basement until late in the night.
54. And therein, Xiang argues, lies Lee's critique of the Cold War American project of linking "human" to "American." "The Korean Voice of American Empire," 295.
55. Kim, "Do I, Too, Sing America?," 233.
56. See Michael J. Seth, *Education Fever: Society, Politics, and the Pursuit of Schooling in South Korea* (Honolulu: University of Hawai'i Press, 2002).
57. Kyonghee Han and Gary Lee Downey, *Engineers for Korea* (Williston, VT: Morgan & Claypool, 2014), 30.
58. Han and Downey, *Engineers for Korea*, 43.
59. In 1962 South Korea passed legislation encouraging emigration as a population control measure. Ivan Light and Edna Bonacich, *Immigrant Entrepreneurs Koreans in Los Angeles, 1965–1982* (Berkeley: University of California Press, 1988), 103. I would also note that these somewhat subtle details about Henry's father offer a glimpse into how *Native Speaker* plays a salutary role in a project that Jini Kim Watson outlines in her book *Cold War Reckonings: Authoritarianism and the Genres of Decolonization* (New York: Fordham University Press, 2021) of situating "neoliberal orthodoxy within the matrix of bipolarized, twentieth-century decolonization" by tracking the representational logics and ideological legacies of Asian authoritarian states (186).
60. Seth, *Education Fever*, 129.
61. On the list as a paradigmatic form of the capitalist everyday in Asian American literature, see Yoon Sun Lee, "Lists, *Native Speaker*, and the Politics of Emergence," in *Modern Minority: Asian American Literature and Everyday Life* (New York: Oxford University Press, 2013), 135–53.
62. See also Lee, *Native Speaker*, 179 ("Some schools were spending more on metal detectors than on lab equipment") and 216 ("The public school has to farm them [students] out to Lelia because it doesn't have enough staff").
63. Alan Liu, *Laws of Cool: Knowledge Work and the Culture of Information* (Chicago: University of Chicago Press, 2004), 47.
64. Liu, *Laws of Cool*, 51.
65. *Native Speaker* in many ways anticipates the "black-market melodramas" that Michael Szalay describes in his book *Second Lives: Black-Market Melodramas and the Reinvention of Television* (Chicago: University of Chicago Press, 2023). Not least via its spy genre, the novel makes a great deal of the "secret second life" trope that, Szalay argues, is designed to contain through allegory the dawning realization among white middle-class Americans at the turn of the millennium that "work beyond the white middle-class household has become indistinct from work within it" (6). The novel also explicitly centers the structural fact of "middle class's increasing dependence on the informal labor markets [since the 1970s] that have long

defined much of the developing world" (27). From this angle, we might say that *Native Speaker* reveals how the racial form of the "white middle-class household" is structured in relation to post-65 South Korean American human capital not only through the racial desires of model minoritization, as that relation has most often been theorized, but also through its opposite: the expediency of the informal economy.

66. Mae M. Ngai, *Impossible Subjects: Illegal Aliens and the Making of Modern America* (Princeton, NJ: Princeton University Press, 2004), 269.
67. Muzaffar Chishti and Stephen Yale-Loehr, "The Immigration Act of 1990: Unfinished Business a Quarter Century Later," *Migration Policy Institute Issue Brief* (July 2016): 10.
68. On the Golden Venture tragedy, see Ko-lin Chen, *Smuggled Chinese: Clandestine Immigration to the United States* (Philadelphia: Temple University Press, 1999).

4. GENRES OF DEPROFESSIONALIZATION

1. Christine So, *Economic Citizens: A Narrative of Asian American Visibility* (Philadelphia: Temple University Press, 2007), 137. On this spate of memoirs see 161n1. Sau-ling Wong has called these "Gone with the Wind epics." Wong, "'Sugar Sisterhood': Situating the Amy Tan Phenomenon," in *Ethnic Canon: Histories, Institutions, and Interventions*, ed. David Palumbo-Liu (Minneapolis: University of Minnesota Press, 1995), 174–210.
2. E. D. Huntley, *Maxine Hong Kingston: A Critical Companion* (Westport, CT: Greenwood Press, 2001), 7.
3. Sau-ling Wong, *Reading Asian American Literature: From Necessity to Extravagance* (Princeton, NJ: Princeton University Press, 1993), 210; Marilyn Chin and Maxine Hong Kingston, "A MELUS Interview: Maxine Hong Kingston," *MELUS* 16, no. 4 (Winter 1989–1990): 69.
4. Chanel Miller, *Know My Name: A Memoir* (New York: Viking, 2019), 38.
5. Here I paraphrase Jasper Bernes, who in his study of postwar U.S. poets and their relationship with the cultures of labor in deindustrialization argues, "Whether or not artists and writers themselves worked under these new conditions . . . is beside the point. They knew someone who did, or read about those who did, or partook of the products of such work. My claims therefore have to do with social experience rather than personal experience strictly speaking." *The Work of Art in the Age of Deindustrialization* (Stanford, CA: Stanford University Press, 2017), 9.
6. Susan Koshy, "Neoliberal Family Matters," *American Literary History* 24, no. 2 (Summer 2013): 352.
7. The influence of *Woman Warrior* is all but explicit in many of these works. We see homage paid to its first chapter, "No Name Woman," in the title of Miller's memoir, for instance, and in *Chemistry*, where the narrator's father (like Maxine's father) had a sister whose death has been a family secret and whose name is never mentioned. Strong resemblances can be found throughout the plots and characterizations in *Sour Heart*.
8. For instance, Tina Chen's "imposture," King-kok Cheung's "articulate silence," Anne Anlin Cheng's "racial melancholia," and David Eng's "racial castration."

Chen, *Double Agency: Acts of Impersonation in Asian American Literature and Culture* (Stanford, CA: Stanford University Press, 2005); Cheng, *The Melancholy of Race: Psychoanalysis, Assimilation and Hidden Grief* (New York: Oxford University Press, 2000); Cheung, *Articulate Silences: Hisaye Yamamoto, Maxine Hong Kingston, Joy Kogawa* (Berkeley: University of California Press, 1993); Eng, *Racial Castration: Managing Masculinity in Asian America* (Durham, NC: Duke University Press, 2001).

9. Your mileage may vary on this point.
10. Mark McGurl, *The Program Era: Postwar Fiction and the Rise of Creative Writing* (Cambridge, MA: Harvard University Press, 2009), 3.
11. McGurl, *The Program Era*, 25.
12. Daniel Hartley, *The Politics of Style: Towards a Marxist Poetics* (Boston: Brill, 2017), 194.
13. Lisa Lowe, *Immigrant Acts: On Asian American Cultural Politics* (Durham, NC: Duke University Press, 1996), 32.
14. Hartley, *The Politics of Style*, 194.
15. Sean McCann, "Training and Vision: Roth, DeLillo, Banks, Peck, and the Postmodern Aesthetics of Vocation," *Twentieth-Century Literature* 53, no. 3 (Fall 2007): 302. McGurl's account of technomodernism locates in postmodern style the relation between the creative writer and the research university, which themselves are reflections of postwar exuberance over the coming of postindustrial society and the possibilities of a unity of scientific and traditional knowledge (a sublation, as Snow might have it, of the two cultures conflict). What post-65 Asian American literature demonstrates—especially its fiction—is how technomodernism might attach itself not only to a style but to a racialized class ideology. If hypertext literature is technomodernism's literalization, as McGurl argues, then the post-65 Asian American author is its personification.
16. Examples are Susan Choi's body of work, beginning with her 1998 novel *The Foreign Student*; Don Lee's 2012 *The Collective*; Annelise Chen's 2017 *So Many Olympic Exertions*. By "campus novel," I refer to novels in which the campus or faculty are the central rather than a peripheral focus—what Elaine Showalter calls the "academic novel." *Faculty Towers: The Academic Novel and Its Discontents* (Philadelphia: University of Pennsylvania Press, 2009).
17. Julia H. Lee, *Understanding Maxine Hong Kingston* (Columbia: University of South Carolina Press, 2018), 17.
18. What ultimately provokes Maxine to bully the girl is her anxiety over the abjection of feminine dependency and the promise of profession-led liberation. At the episode's culminating moment, Maxine implores, "Why won't you talk? . . . What are you going to do for a living? Yeah, you're going to have to work because you can't be a housewife. . . . You think somebody is going to take care of you all your stupid life? . . . Nobody's going to notice you. *And you have to talk for interviews, speak right up in front of the boss.* Don't you know that?" (180–81, my emphasis).
19. The text mistakenly refers to Ellis Island rather than Angel Island. Kingston notes the error in a later interview. See Lee, *Understanding Maxine Hong Kingston*, 3.
20. Catherine Malabou, *Changer de différence: Le féminin et la question philosophique* (Paris: Galilée, 2009), 75.
21. McGurl, *The Program Era*, 262.

4. GENRES OF DEPROFESSIONALIZATION

22. Yoon Sun Lee, "Type, Totality, and the Realism of Asian American Literature," *Modern Language Quarterly* 73, no. 3 (September 2012): 431.
23. Laura Hyun Yi Kang, *Compositional Subjects: Enfiguring Asian/American Women* (Durham, NC: Duke University Press, 2002), 282n19; Wong, *Reading Asian American Literature*, 200–201.
24. Candace's inherited aspiration to transcend secondariness is directed toward the mirage of a useful career that evacuates her of all content but her economic subjectivity. This sentiment is echoed in Weike Wang's novel *Joan Is Okay* (New York: Penguin Books, 2022), in which the title character, an affectless, workaholic doctor explains, "It wasn't glory that had drawn me to healthcare work but the chance to feel pure and complete drudgery in my pursuit of use" (35).
25. While the science fictionality of the "Shen Fever" premise, in the time of COVID-19, is undiminished, its status as a novum is. To the extent that a novum must be, in Suvin's famous phrase, an object of "cognitive estrangement," the notion of a pandemic resulting in the halting of society and the kind of isolation and social emptiness so powerfully depicted in Ma's novel, loses much of its estranging force. The literal can also be science fictional.
26. Colson Whitehead, *Zone One* (New York: Knopf, 2011), 90.
27. Theodore Martin, *Contemporary Drift: Genre, Historicism, and the Problem of the Present* (New York: Columbia University Press, 2019), 13.
28. Prompted by Min Hyoung Song's reading of the variations of realist aesthetics across Chang-rae Lee's oeuvre, Andrew Hoberek picks Lee's 1995 debut novel *Native Speaker* as one of two precursors of the genre turn, which he traces to 1999; the other being Michael Chabon's 1988 debut, *The Mysteries of Pittsburgh*. Both Song and Hoberek take up Lee's novel as evidence for a general phenomenon in the development of the novel and do not ask a version of the question I attempt to answer in this chapter: What is Asian American about the genre turn? See Hoberek, "Literary Genre Fiction," in *American Literature in Transition: 2000–2010*, ed. Rachel Greenwald Smith (Cambridge: Cambridge University Press, 2017), 61–75, esp. 62, and Min Hyoung Song, "Between Genres: On Chang-rae Lee's Realism," *Los Angeles Review of Books*, January 10, 2014, https://www.lareviewofbooks.org/article/chang-rae-lees-realism.
29. See King-Kok Cheung and Stan Yogi, *Asian American Literature: An Annotated Bibliography* (New York: Modern Language Association, 1988).
30. Elaine Kim, "Asian American Writers: A Bibliographical Review," *American Studies International* 22, no. 2 (October 1984): 50.
31. Jane Hu, "Typical Japanese: Kazuo Ishiguro and the Asian Anglophone Historical Novel," *Modern Fiction Studies* 57, no. 1 (Spring 2021): 123–48.
32. Lucy Tan, *What We Were Promised* (New York: Little, Brown, 2018), 30.
33. While "*Fuerdai* to the Max" is the story in Wang's collection that demonstrates most clearly how China's rise has shaped post-65 concerns, the most paradigmatically post-65 story is "Algorithmic Problem-Solving for Relationships," which features a Chinese American computer scientist and first-generation immigrant as its protagonist. The story's schematic depictions of the titular algorithms, reminiscent of Charles Yu's short stories, show how genre experimentation offers a tactic for negotiating the gravitational pull of science fictionality.
34. Jenny Zhang, *Sour Heart: Stories* (New York: Lenny, 2017), 133.

35. Kingston, *Woman Warrior*, 205–6.
36. Miller, *Know My Name*, 320.
37. Miller, *Know My Name*, 329. Rey Chow, *The Protestant Ethnic and the Spirit of Capitalism* (New York: Columbia University Press, 2002), 19–20.
38. Miller, *Know My Name*, 38–40.
39. So, *Economic Citizens*, 156.
40. Ling Ma, *Severance* (New York: Farrar, Straus, and Giroux, 2018), 201, 205, 206.
41. For more on the concept of "racial form," see note 65 in the introduction.
42. Frantz Fanon, *Black Skin, White Masks* (New York: Grove, 1952), 92.
43. Ma, *Severance*, 85.
44. Istvan Csicsery-Ronay Jr., "Science Fiction and Empire," *Science Fiction Studies* 30, no. 2 (July 2003): 235. Kingston makes a similar argument about an ethnic to global turn in the American novel in her oft-cited 1989 essay "The Novel's Next Step," *Mother Jones Magazine*, December 1989, 37–41.
45. Ma, *Severance*, 96.

5. ENOUGH?

1. I take inspiration from Jeehyun Choi's generative question: "Do Japan's peripheries produce a distinct kind of peripheral literature?" "Writing Manchukuo: Peripheral Realism and Awareness in Kang Kyŏngae's *Salt*," *Cross-Currents: East Asian History and Culture Review* 28 (September 2018): 51. On peripheral realism, see Colleen Lye and Jed Esty, eds., "Peripheral Realism," special issue of *Modern Language Quarterly* 73, no. 3 (September 2012) and Ericka Beckman, Oded Nir, and Emilio Sauri, eds., "Peripheral Literatures and the History of Capitalism," special issue of *Modern Fiction Studies* 68, no. 1 (Spring 2022).
2. Min Hyoung Song, *The Children of 1965: On Writing, and Not Writing, as an Asian American* (Durham, NC: Duke University Press, 2013).
3. Barbara and John Ehrenreich, "The Professional-Managerial Class," *Radical America* 11, no. 2 (March–April 1977): 14.
4. Chih-ming Wang argues that recent return fictions like Chang-rae Lee's *My Year Abroad* (2020) undermine what he calls the mode of "immigrant narration" that has for so long provided the master trope for Asian American literature: in which the United States is figured as the default horizon for racial and political subjectivity. Wang, "When Asian Americans Return to Asia: Return Narratives, Transpacific Imagination, and the Post/Cold War," *Southeast Asian Review of English* 58, no. 2 (2021): 95–112. Erin Suzuki and Aimee Bahng note that the returning narrators in R. Zamora Linmark's *Leche* (2011) and Viet Thanh Nguyen's *The Sympathizer* (2015) "confront the changes that U.S. militarization and/or neoliberal global capitalism have created in other parts of the world." "The Transpacific Subject in Asian American Culture," *Oxford Research Encyclopedias, Literature* (January 30, 2020), https://oxfordre.com/literature/view/10.1093/acrefore/9780190201098.001.0001/acrefore-9780190201098-e-877. On the immigrant narrative, see also Min Hyoung Song, "Asian American Literature within and beyond the Immigrant Narrative," in *The Cambridge Companion to Asian American Literature*, ed. Crystal Parikh and Daniel Y. Kim (Cambridge: Cambridge University Press, 2015), 3–15.

5. ENOUGH?

5. Immanuel Wallerstein, *The Capitalist World-Economy: Essays* (Cambridge: Cambridge University Press, 1979), 97.
6. Petrus Liu, *Queer Marxism in Two Chinas* (Durham, NC: Duke University Press, 2015), 114.
7. Kuan-Hsing Chen, *Asia as Method: Toward Deimperialization* (Durham, NC: Duke University Press, 2010), 18. For more on Taiwan's "imperial desire," see chapter 1, "The Imperialist Eye: The Discourse of the Southward Advance and the Subimperial Imaginary," in Chen's book *Asia as Method: Toward Deimperialization* (Durham, NC: Duke University Press, 2010). On the discourse of Taiwan's "silicon shield," see Craig Addison, *Silicon Shield: Taiwan's Protection Against Chinese Attack* (Irving, TX: Fusion Press, 2001), and Chris Miller, *Chip War: The Fight for the World's Most Critical Technology* (New York: Scribner, 2022).
8. Alejandro Portes and John Walton write, "Professional emigration is . . . a consequence of the reproduction of the technical apparatus of advanced nations in underdeveloped ones. Implanted [educational] institutions come to function more in accordance with needs and requirements of the advanced societies than those of the country that receives them." *Labor, Class, and the International System* (New York: Academic Press, 1981), 37.
9. Election Study Center, "Taiwan Independence vs. Unification with the Mainland (1994/12~2022/06)" (National Chengchi University, July 12, 2022), https://esc.nccu.edu.tw/PageDoc/Detail?fid=7801&id=6963.
10. Recent examples of equivocation include the Taiwanese American community's advocacy for a separate "Taiwanese" ethnic category on the U.S. census, and for the disambiguation to be reflected in studies on the Chinese and Taiwanese communities; and Taiwanese American former presidential candidate Andrew Yang's oft-repeated line, "My father grew up on a peanut farm in Asia [sic] with no floor." See also Catherine Chou, "Andrew Yang Is Taiwanese-American," *Popula*, December 18, 2019, https://popula.com/2019/12/18/andrew-yang-is-taiwanese-american/. These two components of the Taiwanese semiperipheral structure of feeling—revanchism and ressentiment, respectively—are perhaps attached to post-49 mainland Chinese (*wàishēngrén*) and pre-49 Han Chinese (*běnshēngrén*) subject formations.
11. Immanuel Wallerstein, *World-Systems Analysis: An Introduction* (Durham, NC: Duke University Press, 2004), 27.
12. Barbara Ehrenreich, *Fear of Falling: The Inner Life of the Middle Class* (New York: Twelve Books, 1989). On "success frames" and the puzzle of the cultural influence of post-65 Asian American model minoritization, see Jennifer Lee and Min Zhou, *The Asian American Achievement Paradox* (New York: Russell Sage, 2015).
13. Lisa Lowe and Jodi Kim have taken up "return" as a metaphor for the migration of "racialized and gendered imperial subjects" (Kim, 22) to the "imperial center" (Lowe, 16) as a result of U.S. Cold War interventions in Asia. Jodi Kim, *Ends of Empire: Asian American Critique and the Cold War* (Minneapolis: University of Minnesota Press, 2010); Lisa Lowe, *Immigrant Acts: On Asian American Cultural Politics* (Durham, NC: Duke University Press, 1996).
14. Jim Glassman, *Drums of War, Drums of Development: The Formation of a Pacific Ruling Class and Industrial Transformation in East and Southeast Asia, 1945–1980* (Chicago: Haymarket Books, 2018), 4. Cognates include Aiwha Ong's "flexible

citizens," in *Flexible Citizenship: The Cultural Logics of Transnationality* (Durham, NC: Duke University Press, 1999), and Susan Koshy's "neoliberal families," in "Neoliberal Family Matters," *American Literary History* 25, no. 2 (September 2013): 344–80.
15. On the trope of the "generic Asian," see Jane Hu, "Typical Japanese: Kazuo Ishiguro and the Asian Anglophone Historical Novel," *Modern Fiction Studies* 57, no. 1 (Spring 2021): 123–48.
16. Arif Dirlik, "Taiwan: The Land Colonialisms Made," *boundary 2* 45, no. 3 (2018): 18.
17. An extremely abridged, 150-page English version of Su Beng's original, three-volume Marxist account of this history can be found in *Taiwan's 400 Year History: Anniversary Edition* (Taipei: SMC Publishing, Inc., 2017).
18. As Bruce Cumings notes, "colonial administrators remarked that what could be done with economic incentives in Taiwan required coercion in Korea." "The Origins and Development of the Northeast Asian Political Economy: Industrial Sectors, Product Cycles, and Political Consequences," *International Organization* 38, no. 1 (Winter 1984): 11. Despite the People's Republic of China's oft-made claim that Taiwan was "returned" to it on October 25, 1945, the Japanese surrendered the island to the ROC, which was then occupying the island. The Japanese did not in fact officially relinquish its claim over Taiwan until the 1951 Treaty of San Francisco, in which, notably, it made no determination as to whether its claim would be transferred to the PRC or ROC.
19. Leo T. S. Ching, *Becoming "Japanese": Colonial Taiwan and the Politics of Identity Formation* (Berkeley: University of California Press, 2001), 8.
20. On nostalgia for Japanese colonialism, see James Lin's aptly titled and excellent article, "Nostalgia for Japanese colonialism: Historical memory and postcolonialism in contemporary Taiwan," *History Compass* 20, no. 11 (November 2022): 1–11. On the psychological, libidinal, and racial dimensions of Japan's scientific colonialism, see Wu Zhouli's 1945 novel *Orphan of Asia*, trans. Ioannis Mentzas (New York: Columbia University Press, 2006). On the complexities of sentiment about Japan in East Asia, see Leo T. S. Ching, *Anti-Japan: The Politics of Sentiment in Postcolonial East Asia* (Durham, NC: Duke University Press, 2019).
21. Cumings, "Origins and Development," 22.
22. KMT's surveillance apparatus extended to university campuses and Chinatowns, while U.S. intelligence largely turned a blind eye to its activities. Wendy Cheng recounts that in 1970, Peter Huang, "a lapsed graduate student at Cornell University," tried to assassinate Chiang Ching-kuo in New York, also noting "a series of shootings and bombings at several KMT offices and officials across the United States in 1979 and 1980, which resulted in the temporary placement of Taiwanese on the FBI's terrorist watch list." "'This Contradictory but Fantastic Thing': Student Networks and Political Activism in Cold War Taiwanese/America," *Journal of Asian American Studies* 20, no. 2 (June 2017): 163. See also Cheng's *Island X: Taiwanese Student Migrants, Campus Spies, and Cold War Activism* (Berkeley: University of California Press, 2023).
23. Shawna Yang Ryan, *Green Island: A Novel* (New York: Vintage Books, 2016), 188–89.
24. Baodiao is an abbreviation of Baowei Diaoyutai Yundong, "Protecting Diaoyutai Movement." See Chih-ming Wang, *Transpacific Articulations: Student Migration*

5. ENOUGH?

and the Remaking of Asian America (Honolulu: University of Hawai'i Press, 2013), 66–89.

25. Wang, *Transpacific Articulations*, 77–78.
26. Alice H. Amsden, "Taiwan's Economic History: A Case of *Etatisme* and a Challenge to Dependency Theory," *Modern China* 5, no. 3 (July 1979): 341–79. See also Thomas B. Gold's classic account, *State and Society in the Taiwan Miracle* (Armonk, NY: M. E. Sharpe, 1986).
27. Shu-mei Shih, "Globalisation and the (in)significance of Taiwan," *Postcolonial Studies* 6, no. 2 (2003): 143.
28. This is not least, as Wendy Cheng observes, because of the KMT's purging of the left in Taiwan: "As a result, dissenting, left, and radical politics within Taiwanese-identified communities [in the United States] have been largely ignored or forgotten. In fact, far from being neutral or benevolent, the numerous cases of Taiwanese students spied on by other Taiwanese on U.S. campuses illuminate the role of U.S. educational institutions as a key site of Cold War battles over hearts, minds, and bodies. And more than merely tragic or heroic victims of an authoritarian state, Taiwan and Taiwanese migrants were active and ideologically heterogeneous participants in the regional, national, and international power struggles of their time." "Refuting the Silences of Taiwanese/American History: The Case of Chen Yu-hsi," *American Quarterly* 73, no. 2 (June 2021): 344. On the complexities of left politics in Taiwan and the Taiwanese diaspora, see the special forum "Against Empire: Taiwan, American Studies, and the Archipelagic" edited by Cheng and Chih-ming Wang in *American Quarterly* 73, no. 2 (June 2021): 335–77. See also Wang, *Transpacific Articulations*, chapters 3 and 4, and Kuan-hsing Chen, *Asia as Method*. On the discourses and practices of civil defense, see Wen Liu, "The mundane politics of war in Taiwan: Psychological preparedness, civil defense, and permanent war," *Security Dialogue*, September 12, 2023, https://doi.org/10.1177/09670106231194908.
29. The high-risk nature of these complexities was amplified on December 2, 2016, when newly elected Donald Trump received a phone call from Taiwan's president, Tsai Ing-wen. This was the first time since the United States cut formal diplomatic ties with Taiwan in 1979 that a U.S. president had communicated with Taiwan's president. The call prompted Taiwanese Americans on the left to caution against cozy relations with the Trump administration and to reassert "a Taiwan independence movement that solidly rejects American military empire and, instead, builds steadfast alliance with marginalized communities and struggles for justice around the world." Funie Hsu, Brian Hioe, and Wen Liu, "Collective Statement on Taiwan Independence: Building Global Solidarity and Rejecting US Military Empire," *American Quarterly* 69, no. 3 (September 2017): 468.
30. That said, here in Taipei, where I am writing in the summer of 2022, just months after Russia invaded Ukraine and just weeks ahead of House Speaker Nancy Pelosi's diplomatic trip to Taiwan—the highest-profile diplomatic visit to Taiwan since strategic ambiguity began in 1979—we are perhaps seeing the first signs of strategic ambiguity's unraveling.
31. Here I am paraphrasing Yoonmee Chang, who observes: "The linear relationship between race and class inequity, that being racially different has negative class effects, is derailed for Asian Americans. For Asian Americans, the conventional

relationship between race and class inequality is *inverted.*" *Writing the Ghetto: Class, Authorship, and the Asian American Ethnic Enclave* (New Brunswick, NJ: Rutgers University Press, 2010), 5.

32. erin Khûe Ninh, *Ingratitude: The Debt-Bound Daughter in Asian American Literature* (New York: NYU Press, 2011), 61.

33. Suzanne Model, "Why Are Asian-Americans Educationally Hyper-selected? The Case of Taiwan," *Ethnic and Racial Studies* 41, no. 11 (2018).

34. Racial formation theory was codified by Michael Omi and Howard Winant, who, as Colleen Lye has argued, developed their theory at a moment in which the exigencies of the Reaganist threat compelled them to overcorrect for what hitherto had been the U.S. left's class-driven framework for understanding race. Colleen Lye, "In Dialogue with Asian American Studies," *Representations* 99, no. 1 (Summer 2007): 2. The best engagement with this crux is Sarika Chandra and Christopher Chen's chapter "Remapping the Race/Class Problematic," in *Totality Inside Out: Rethinking Crisis and Conflict Under Capital* (New York: Fordham University Press, 2022).

35. Bruce Cumings, "The Political Economy of the Pacific Rim," in *Pacific-Asia and the Future of the World-System*, ed. Ravi Arvind Palat (Westport, CT: Greenwood Press, 1993), 26.

36. Justin Rosenberg and Chris Boyle, "Understanding 2016: China, Brexit and Trump in the History of Uneven and Combined Development," *Journal of Historical Sociology* 32, no. 1 (March 2019): 37, 36.

37. Warwick Research Collective, *Combined and Uneven Development: Towards a New Theory of World-Literature* (Liverpool: Liverpool University Press, 2015), 71, 17. Leon Trotsky, *History of the Russian Revolution*, vol. 1, trans. Max Eastman (London: Sphere Books, 1967).

38. Nietzsche's clearest theorization of ressentiment is found in *The Genealogy of Morals*' parable of slave morality and its transvaluation: a parable that is thoroughly racialized in its depictions of the Jewish people as the "priestly race of *ressentiment par excellence*," and the "Roman, Arabian, Germanic, Japanese nobility, the Homeric heroes, the Scandinavian Vikings" as the "blond beasts" whose strength is the wellspring of the "good" that slave morality must transvalue into "evil" (489, 469–72). According to this parable, the origins of the dominant Christian virtues of pity and "neighbor-love" (*agape*) are found in the Jewish people's history of persecution and enslavement and the "impotence" and "passivity" imposed by that history. Rather than being authentically pitying and loving, acolytes of these "priestly" virtues are in fact acting upon "hatred" grown to "monstrous and uncanny proportions": a desire for "the *most spiritual revenge*" (469–70). Friedrich Nietzsche, *The Genealogy of Morals*, in *Basic Writings of Nietzsche*, trans. and ed. Walter Kaufmann (New York: Modern Library, 1992), 480. Critical accounts of ressentiment in minority U.S. politics can be found in Wendy Brown, *States of Injury: Power and Freedom in Late Modernity* (Princeton, NJ: Princeton University Press, 1995); Judith Butler, "Circuits of Bad Conscience: Nietzsche and Freud," in *The Psychic Life of Power: Theories in Subjection* (Stanford, CA: Stanford University Press, 1997); E. San Juan Jr., "Beyond Identity Politics: The Predicament of the Asian American Writer in Late Capitalism," *American Literary History* 3, no. 3 (Autumn 1991): 542 –65; and Rebecca Stringer, "'A Nietzschean Breed': Feminism, Victimology,

5. ENOUGH?

Ressentiment," in *Why Nietzsche Still?: Reflections on Drama, Culture, and Politics*, ed. Alan D. Schrift (Berkeley: University of California Press, 2000), 263–64.

39. The meanings and ethical demands of Asia's availability vary a great deal in how they are depicted in return fiction, ranging from the psychological and economic to revelations about the reach of U.S. empire. In Christine So's readings of two memoirs by sansei (third-generation) Japanese American writers—Lydia Minatoya's *Talking to High Monks in the Snow: An Asian American Odyssey* (1992) and David Mura's *Turning Japanese: Memoirs of a Sansei* (1991)—she observes that Japan is depicted as offering "a means of resolving alienation and achieving wholeness—one predicated on the exchangeability, tangibility, and materiality of objects." *Economic Citizens: A Narrative of Asian American Visibility* (Philadelphia: Temple University Press, 2007), 74. This resolution, importantly, is offered in stark contrast to the political and cultural limitations of the United States. According to So, for writers like these, "Asia, and not the United States, functions as the site for identity formation, resolution, and homecoming. Asia is used as a means of rescuing Asian Americans from the margins of United States politics and culture" (76).
40. These include, in chronological order, Ichiro Hori, "Hard to Choose," *The Pen* 160, Rohwer Relocation Center (1943); Kim Yong Ik, "From Here You Can See the Moon," *Texas Quarterly* 11, no. 2 (1968), 201–8; Kim Kichung, "A Homecoming," *Bridge* 2, no. 6 (1973): 27–31; and Ahn Andrew Kim, "A Homeward Journey," in *75th Anniversary of Korean Immigration to Hawai'i, 1903–1978*, ed. Samuel S. O. Lee (Honolulu: 75th Anniversary of Korean Immigration to Hawai'i Committee, 1978), 22–27.
41. Amy Tan, *The Joy Luck Club* (New York: Penguin Books, 1989).
42. Colleen Lye argues that *The Joy Luck Club*'s narrative of return and family reunification voiced in an Asian American idiom the end of history narratives about liberal capitalism's triumph that were prevalent in the late 1980s and early 1990s. Moreover, in her reading, Jing-mei's return carries a revanchist fantasy: it was "fiction's wish for the restoration of the China that had been lost to the United States in 1949, and an allegorization of the meaning of 1989 in these terms." "Asian American 1960s," in *The Routledge Companion to Asian American and Pacific Islander Literature*, ed. Rachel C. Lee (New York: Routledge, 2014), 216.
43. See Yasheng Huang, *Capitalism with Chinese Characteristics: Entrepreneurship and the State* (Cambridge: Cambridge University Press, 2008).
44. Rosenberg and Boyle, "Understanding 2016," 44.
45. Rosenberg and Boyle, "Understanding 2016," 41.
46. A sudden emergence is portrayed in *Crazy Rich Asians*' opening scene in 1986 London, in which the Young family responds to a hotel manager's racism by spitefully purchasing the hotel, then firing him. Despite its being a flashback, this scene is actually meant as a metaphor for capitalist futurity: a harbinger of the complete displacement of Western capital by Chinese capital, as well as a foreshadowing of Rachel's challenges when meeting the Young family. Kevin Kwan, *Crazy Rich Asians* (New York: Anchor, 2013).
47. Viet Thanh Nguyen, *Race and Resistance: Literature and Politics in Asian America* (Oxford: Oxford University Press, 2002), 22.
48. On China and counterfeit, see Sunny Xiang, "Global China as Genre," *Post45* 2 (16 July, 2019), https://post45.org/sections/issue/issue-2-how-to-be-now/; Winnie Won Yin Wong, *Van Gogh on Demand: China and the Readymade* (Chicago:

University of Chicago Press, 2013); Fan Yang, *Faked in China: Nation Branding, Counterfeit Culture, and Globalization* (Bloomington: Indiana University Press, 2015); and Byung Chul Han, *Shanzhai: Deconstruction in Chinese*, trans. Philippa Hurd (Cambridge, MA: MIT Press, 2017). A novel like *Crazy Rich Asians*, although it is set in and celebrates neoliberal Singapore, is at pains to specify how the real locus of wealth and pan-Asian authenticity, emblematized by the Young family, is the "Overseas Chinese . . . who left China long before the Communists came in, in many cases hundreds of years ago, and spread throughout the rest of Asia, quietly amassing great fortunes over time"—that is, definitively not the Mainland Chinese (33).

49. See Andrew Yang, "We Asian Americans Are Not the Virus, but We Can Be Part of the Cure," *Washington Post*, April 1, 2020, https://www.washingtonpost.com/opinions/2020/04/01/andrew-yang-coronavirus-discrimination/.
50. Shelley Rigger, *The Tiger Leading the Dragon: How Taiwan Propelled China's Economic Rise* (Lanham, MD: Rowman & Littlefield, 2021).
51. Yu's second novel, the National Book Award-winning *Interior Chinatown* (New York: Pantheon, 2020) continues the theme of post-65 Taiwanese American ressentiment, which this time names Taiwan, and materializes as the metafictionally framed conceit of the television show rather than a science fictional universe. The theme of ressentiment is especially pronounced in the backstory of one of the protagonists, Ming-chen Wu, whose father is killed by KMT soldiers, and who later emigrates to the United States to pursue a STEM degree at the University of Mississippi, where he joins a group of other Asian international STEM students (141–53).
52. Monika Fludernik defines "ideological unreliability" as a mode "where the narrator propounds a world view which is not shared by the reader. . . . the line between emotional and ideological unreliability is extremely vague." It is one of three major modes of unreliable narration, the other two being "factual inaccuracy" and "lack of objectivity." "Defining (In)sanity: The Narrator of 'The Yellow Wallpaper' and the Question of Unreliability," in *Grenzüberschreitungen: Narratologie im Kontext* (Transcending Boundaries: Narratology in Context), ed. W. Grunzweig and A. Solbach (Tübingen: Gunter Narr Verlag, 1999), 77.
53. On Beiyinu in the Taiwanese imagination, see Leslie Chang, *Beyond the Narrow Gate: The Journey of Four Women from the Middle Kingdom to Middle America* (New York: Plume, 2000).
54. A mini-archive of Taiwanese American losers would include Francie Lin's *The Foreigner* (New York: Macmillan, 2008); Ed Lin's novels *Waylaid* (New York: Kaya Press, 2002) and *David Tung Can't Have a Girlfriend Until He Gets Into an Ivy League College* (Los Angeles: Kaya Press, 2020); and Gene Luen Yang's *American Born Chinese* (New York: Square Fish, 2008).
55. Xiang, "Global China as Genre."
56. On the periodization of U.S. official antiracisms and distinctions between "liberal multiculturalism" and "neoliberal multiculturalism," see Jodi Melamed, *Represent and Destroy: Rationalizing Violence in the New Racial Capitalism* (Minneapolis: University of Minnesota Press, 2011).
57. Gerald Prince, *Dictionary of Narratology* (Lincoln: University of Nebraska Press, 2003), 103.

5. ENOUGH?

58. Dorrit Cohn, "Discordant Narration," *Style* 34, no. 2 (Summer 2000): 307.
59. In an adjacent context, Sunny Xiang has demonstrated how the trope of the unreliable narrator in Chang-rae Lee's 1995 novel *Native Speaker* mediates the U.S. Cold War cultivation of reliable Asian allies through the resurgent figure of the "Asian human." "The Korean Voice of American Empire: The Democratic Spokesman and the Model Minority Narrator," *Journal of Asian American Studies* 17, no. 3 (October 2014): 273–304.
60. Fludernik, "Defining (In)sanity," 93.
61. For instance, in regard to the male, gendered form of the stereotype in which labor efficiency is linked to effeminacy and asexuality, both Fred and Charles's son Andrew are portrayed as sexually irresistible yet hopelessly invisible in terms of career advancement.
62. Cheryl Naruse, "Overseas Singaporeans, Coming-of-Career Narratives, and the Corporate Nation," *Biography* 37, no. 1 (Winter 2014): 145–67.
63. Sophia reassures herself at one point: "I am going to be rich, but not just boring old rich. I'm going to be fucking rich" (247). At another she dismisses the facticity of "gender discrimination": "But aren't we past all that yet? That's so eighties!" (46).
64. Anna Yen, *Sophia of Silicon Valley* (New York: William Morrow, 2018), 326.
65. Christopher Chen, "The Limit Point of Capitalist Equality: Notes Toward an Abolitionist Antiracism," *Endnotes* 3, https://endnotes.org.uk/issues/3/en/chris-chen-the-limit-point-of-capitalist-equality.
66. Yoon Sun Lee, *Modern Minority: Asian American Literature and Everyday Life* (New York: Oxford University Press, 2013), 4, 16, 185n85.
67. Charles Yu, *How to Live Safely in a Science Fictional Universe* (New York: Vintage Books, 2010), 192.
68. As Ruth Ozeki's character Jiko might say about the relation between the person "flapping and slapping" about and the deep conditions of the world depicted in this passage: "Not same. . . . Not different, either." *A Tale for the Time Being* (New York: Penguin Books, 2013), 416.
69. The term "national allegory" is of course Fredric Jameson's. See "Third-World Literature in the Era of Multinational Capitalism," *Social Text* 15 (Autumn 1986): 65–88. Rather than the "national," however, the scope and desire behind the national allegories in Taiwanese American fiction have to do with the depiction of transnational collectivity that Jameson describes in *Allegory and Ideology* (New York: Verso, 2019), where he revisits and revises his earlier argument. For other recent recuperations of national allegory, see Christopher T. Fan, "Democratic Realism, National Allegory, and the Future of the Asian American Novel," *American Literary History* 35, no. 1 (Spring 2023): 471–79; Yogita Goyal, "National Allegory and Beyond: Postcolonial Critique Now," *PMLA* 137, no. 3 (May, 2022): 521–28; Katherine Hallemeier, "'To Be from the Country of People Who Gave': National Allegory and the United States of Adichie's *Americanah*," *Studies in the Novel* 47, no. 2 (Summer 2015): 231–45; Jini Kim Watson, "Introduction: Ruling Like a Foreigner: Theorizing 'Free World' Authoritarianism in the Asia-Pacific Cold War," in *Cold War Reckonings: Authoritarianism and the Genres of Decolonization* (New York: Fordham University Press, 2021), 1–25.
70. To this archive of Asia-wrapped U.S. spaces we might add Jing-mei's hotel room in *The Joy Luck Club*; the near-future cityscape of Spike Jonze's film *Her* (2013), which

doesn't announce itself as such but combined locations in Pudong, Shanghai, and Los Angeles; and Disney's *Big Hero 6*'s (2014) "San Fransokyo," which Toni Hays describes as a Japanese "skinned" San Francisco.
71. AnnaLee Saxenian, *The New Argonauts: Regional Advantage in a Global Economy* (Cambridge, MA: Harvard University Press, 2006). See also Aihwa Ong, "Labor Arbitrage: Displacements and Betrayals in Silicon Valley," in *Neoliberalism as Exception: Mutations in Citizenship and Sovereignty* (Durham, NC: Duke University Press, 2006).
72. Wang, *Transpacific Articulations*, 102.
73. This period of relative calm, no longer with us, is the context in which L. Ling-chi Wang wrote his well-known article, "The Structure of Dual Domination: Toward a Paradigm for the Study of the Chinese Diaspora in the United States," *Amerasia Journal* 33, no. 1 (2007): 144–66. Referring to a contemporaneous "reduction of hostility between China and Taiwan," he reflects on how Chinese and Taiwanese Americans are "dominated" by the dual forces of domestic racism and extraterritorial impositions of identity and political loyalty (146, 155). On the shaping influence of the KMT's extraterritorial murders of dissidents on Wang's conceptualization of dual domination, see Calvin Cheung-Miaw, "The Boundaries of Democracy: Transnational Political Murders in the Reagan Era," *Pacific Historical Review* 90, no. 4 (2021): 508–36.
74. E. Tammy Kim, "Transnationally Asian," *Columbia Journalism Review*, July 21, 2020, https://www.cjr.org/special_report/transnationally_asian.php.
75. Hsu, Hioe, and Liu, "Collective Statement," 468.
76. On the links and comparisons between Hong Kong's 2014 Umbrella Movement and Taiwan's 2014 Sunflower movement, see Ming-sho Ho, *Challenging Beijing's Mandate of Heaven: Taiwan's Sunflower Movement and Hong Kong's Umbrella Movement* (Philadelphia: Temple University Press, 2019).
77. "Contradictory, but fantastic" is a quote from Cheng, *Island X*, 29.

CONCLUSION

1. Iyko Day, *Alien Capital: Asian Racialization and the Logic of Settler Colonial Capitalism* (Durham, NC: Duke University Press, 2016), 165.
2. Day's emphasis on embodiment is drawn from Lye's argument that "It is the 'inorganic quality of the Asiatic body' that manifests the 'intangibly abstract' threat of finance capital." *Alien Capital*, 6. Day quotes from Lye's *America's Asia: Racial Form and American Literature, 1893–1945* (Princeton, NJ: Princeton University Press, 2005), 130. Echoing Day and Lye's point is David Palumbo-Liu, who writes, "The Body, as a somatic entity that exists within the contingencies of time and space, desire, need, gratification and denial, thus helps us maintain a sense of Asian America as imbricated in material history." *Asian/American: Historical Crossings of a Racial Frontier* (Stanford, CA: Stanford University Press, 1999), 6. On commodity fetishism, see Karl Marx, *Capital: A Critique of Political Economy, Volume 1*, trans. Ben Fowkes (New York: Penguin Books, 1990), 163–77.

CONCLUSION

3. Yoon Sun Lee, "Racialized Bodies and Asian American Literature," *American Literary History* 30, no. 1 (Spring 2018): 167. This argument somewhat recapitulates Frantz Fanon's trope of the "epidermal racial schema" in *Black Skin, White Masks* (New York: Grove, 1962), 92.
4. Day, *Alien Capital*, 6.
5. Day, *Alien Capital*, 7.
6. Madeline Hsu, *The Good Immigrants: How the Yellow Peril Became the Model Minority* (Princeton, NJ: Princeton University Press, 2015), 21.
7. As Hsu observes, a preoccupation with exclusion characterizes immigration studies as well. *The Good Immigrants*, 8.
8. Christopher Lee, *The Semblance of Identity: Aesthetic Mediation in Asian American Literature* (Stanford, CA: Stanford University Press, 2012), 9–13.
9. Viet Thanh Nguyen, *Race and Resistance: Literature and Politics in Asian America* (New York: Oxford University Press, 2002), 21.
10. Lee, "Racialized Bodies and Asian American Literature," 175.
11. Marx, *Capital*, 163.
12. Marx, *Capital*, 165, my emphasis.
13. Lee, "Racialized Bodies and Asian American Literature," 175. Here she explicitly has in mind Lye's work on racial form, which I gloss in note 65 of the introduction.
14. Lee, "Racialized Bodies and Asian American Literature," 175.
15. Day, *Alien Capital*, 195.
16. See note 54 in the introduction.
17. Takeo Rivera, *Model Minority Masochism: Performing the Cultural Politics of Asian American Masculinity* (New York: Oxford University Press, 2022), xxix.
18. I am not arguing for a strict period distinction between industrialization and deindustrialization: each process is present in each period.
19. Marx, *Capital*, 341.
20. Day, *Alien Capital*, 43.
21. See Robert Brenner, *The Economics of Global Turbulence: The Advanced Capitalist Economies from Long Boom to Long Downturn, 1945–2005* (London: Verso, 2006).
22. Jasper Bernes, *The Work of Art in the Age of Deindustrialization* (Stanford, CA: Stanford University Press, 2017), 19.
23. See Lye's *America's Asia*; Yoonmee Chang, *Writing the Ghetto: Class, Authorship, and the Asian American Ethnic Enclave* (New Brunswick, NJ: Rutgers University Press, 2010); Calvin Cheung-Miaw, "Asian Americans and the Color-Line: An Intellectual History of Asian American Studies, 1969–2000," PhD diss., Stanford University, 2021; Mark Chiang, *The Cultural Capital of Asian American Studies: Autonomy and Representation in the University* (New York: NYU Press, 2009); Paul Nadal, "How Neoliberalism Remade the Model Minority Myth," *Representations* 163 (August 2023): 79–99; Nguyen, *Race and Resistance*; Christine So, *Economic Citizens: A Narrative of Asian American Visibility* (Philadelphia: Temple University Press, 2008).
24. Mark Fisher, *Capitalist Realism: Is There No Alternative?* (London: O Books, 2009).
25. Annie McClanahan, "Piece-Rates, Poetry, and Digital Microwork" (presentation, Coast45, University of Southern California, Los Angeles, October 14, 2022), 25.

26. David S. Roh, Betsy Huang, and Greta Niu, "Technologizing Orientalism: An Introduction," in *Techno-Orientalism: Imagining Asia in Speculative Fiction, History, and Media*, ed. David S. Roh, Betsy Huang, and Greta Niu (New Brunswick, NJ: Rutgers University Press, 2015), 4.
27. Christopher T. Fan, "Andrew Yang and Post-65 Asian America," *American Literary History: Online Forum*, March 3, 2020, https://muse.jhu.edu/article/762155/pdf, e62.
28. Karl Marx, *Grundrisse: Foundations of the Critique of Political Economy (Rough Draft)*, trans. Martin Nicolaus (New York: Penguin Books, 1973), 706.
29. For a critique of what McClanahan calls "fauxtomation" narratives, see her chapter "Microwork, Automation, and the Insecurity of Contemporary Labor," in *Insecurity*, ed. Richard Grusin (Minneapolis: University of Minnesota Press, 2022), 31–64, as well as Aaron Benanav, *Automation and the Future of Work* (New York: Verso, 2022), and Jason Smith, *Smart Machines and Service Work: Automation in an Age of Stagnation* (Chicago: University of Chicago Press, 2020).
30. Wendy Cheng, *Island X: Taiwanese Student Migrants, Campus Spies, and Cold War Activism* (Berkeley: University of California Press, 2023), 15n33. L. Ling-chi Wang also notes this elision in "The Structure of Dual Domination: Toward a Paradigm for the Study of the Chinese Diaspora in the United States," *Amerasia Journal* 33, no. 1 (2007): 153.

BIBLIOGRAPHY

Adams, Don. *Higher Educational Reforms in the Republic of Korea.* Washington, DC: U.S. Department of Health, Education and Welfare, 1965.
Adams, Rachel. "The Ends of America, the Ends of Postmodernism." *Twentieth Century Literature* 53, no. 3 (Fall 2007): 248–72.
Adams, Walter. "Introduction." In *The Brain Drain*, ed. Walter Adams, 1–9. New York: Macmillan, 1968.
Adas, Michael. *Machines as the Measure of Men: Science, Technology, and Ideologies of Western Dominance.* Ithaca, NY: Cornell University Press, 1989.
Addison, Craig. *Silicon Shield: Taiwan's Protection Against Chinese Attack.* Irving, TX: Fusion Press, 2001.
Akamatsu, Kaname. "A Historical Pattern of Economic Growth in Developing Countries." *Developing Economies* 1, no. 1 (August 1962): 3–25.
Alter, Alexandra. "How Chinese Sci-Fi Conquered America." *New York Times*, December 3, 2019.
Amsden, Alice H. *Asia's Next Giant: South Korea and Late Industrialization.* New York: Oxford University Press, 1989.
——. "Taiwan's Economic History: A Case of Etatisme and a Challenge to Dependency Theory." *Modern China* 5, no. 3 (July 1979): 341–79.
——. "Why Isn't the Whole World Experimenting with the East Asian Model to Develop? Review of *The East Asian Miracle.*" *World Development* 22, no. 4 (1994): 627–33.
Arac, Jonathan. "Violence and the Human Voice: Critique and Hope in *Native Speaker.*" *boundary 2* 36, no. 2 (2009): 55–66.
Arrighi, Giovanni. *Adam Smith in Beijing: Lineages of the Twenty-First Century.* New York: Verso, 2007.

———. *The Long Twentieth Century: Money, Power, and the Origin of Our Times*. New York: Verso, 1994.
Badowski, Adam, Konrad Tomaszkiewicz, and Gabe Amatangelo. *Cyberpunk 2077*. Videogame, CD Projekt, 2020.
Bahng, Aimee. *Migrant Futures: Decolonizing Speculation in Financial Times*. Durham, NC: Duke University Press, 2018.
Bascara, Victor. *Model Minority Imperialism*. Minneapolis: University of Minnesota Press, 2006.
Bell, Daniel. *The Coming of Post-Industrial Society: A Venture in Social Forecasting*. New York: Basic Books, 1973.
Bellah, Robert. "Cultural Vision and the Human Future." *Teachers College Record* 82, no. 3 (1981): 1–7.
Benanav, Aaron. *Automation and the Future of Work*. New York: Verso, 2022.
Bernes, Jasper. *The Work of Art in the Age of Deindustrialization*. Stanford, CA: Stanford University Press, 2017.
Blaut, J. M. *The Colonizer's Model of the World: Geographical Diffusionism and Eurocentric History*. New York: Guilford Press, 1993.
Bonilla-Silva, Eduardo. *Racism Without Racists*. Lanham, MD: Rowman & Littlefield, 2003.
Borovoy, Amy. "Robert Bellah's Search for Community and Ethical Modernity in Japan Studies." *Journal of Asian Studies* 75, no. 2 (May 2016): 467–94.
Braverman, Harry. *Labor and Monopoly Capital: The Degradation of Work in the Twentieth Century*. New York: Monthly Review Press, 1974.
Brazinsky, Gregg. *Nation Building in South Korea: Koreans, Americans, and the Making of a Democracy*. Chapel Hill: University of North Carolina Press, 2007.
Brenner, Robert. *The Economics of Global Turbulence: The Advanced Capitalist Economies from Long Boom to Long Downturn, 1945–2005*. London: Verso, 2006.
Brockenbrough, Martha, Grace Lin, and Julia Kuo. *I Am an American: The Wong Kim Ark Story*. New York: HarperCollins, 2021.
Brown, Melissa J. *Is Taiwan Chinese? The Impact of Culture, Power, and Migration on Changing Identities*. Berkeley: University of California Press, 2004.
Brown, Wendy. *States of Injury: Power and Freedom in Late Modernity*. Princeton, NJ: Princeton University Press, 1995.
Budiman, Abby, and Neil G. Ruiz. "Asian Americans Are the Fastest-Growing Racial or Ethnic Group in the U.S." Pew Research Center, April 9, 2021. https://www.pewresearch.org/fact-tank/2021/04/09/asian-americans-are-the-fastest-growing-racial-or-ethnic-group-in-the-u-s/.
Butler, Judith. *The Psychic Life of Power: Theories in Subjection*. Stanford, CA: Stanford University Press, 1997.
Butler, Lyn Liao. *The Tiger Mom's Tale*. New York: Berkley, 2021.
Castillo, Elaine. *America Is Not the Heart: A Novel*. New York: Viking, 2018.
———. "A Stabbing in Finsbury Park." *The Rumpus*, October 30, 2013. https://therumpus.net/2013/10/30/a-stabbing-in-finsbury-park.
Cha, Theresa Hak Kyung. *DICTEE*. Berkeley: University of California Press, 1982.
Chakrabarty, Dipesh. "The Legacies of Bandung: Decolonization and the Politics of Culture." In *Making a World After Empire: The Bandung Movement and Its Political Afterlives*, ed. Christopher J. Lee, 49–71. Athens: Ohio University Press, 2010.

BIBLIOGRAPHY

Chandra, Sarika, and Christopher Chen. "Remapping the Race/Class Problematic." In *Totality Inside Out: Rethinking Crisis and Conflict Under Capital*, ed. Kevin Floyd, Jen Hedler Phillis, and Sarika Chandra, 135–91. New York: Fordham University Press, 2022.
Chang, Elysha. *A Quitter's Paradise*. New York: SJP Lit, 2023.
Chang, K-Ming. *Bestiary*. New York: One World, 2020.
Chang, Leslie. *Beyond the Narrow Gate: The Journey of Four Women from the Middle Kingdom to Middle America*. New York: Plume, 2000.
Chang, Shenglin. *The Global Silicon Valley Home: Lives and Landscapes Within Taiwanese American Trans-Pacific Culture*. Stanford, CA: Stanford University Press, 2005.
Chang, Yoonmee. *Writing the Ghetto: Class, Authorship, and the Asian American Ethnic Enclave*. New Brunswick, NJ: Rutgers University Press, 2010.
Chen, Christopher. "The Limit Point of Capitalist Equality: Notes Toward an Abolitionist Antiracism." *Endnotes* 3. https://libcom.org/article/limit-point-capitalist-equality-notes-toward-abolitionist-antiracism-chris-chen.
Chen, Ko-lin. *Smuggled Chinese: Clandestine Immigration to the United States*. Philadelphia: Temple University Press, 1999.
Chen, Kuan-Hsing. *Asia as Method: Toward Deimperialization*. Durham, NC: Duke University Press, 2010.
Chen, Tina. *Double Agency: Acts of Impersonation in Asian American Literature and Culture*. Stanford, CA: Stanford University Press, 2005.
——. "Impersonation and Other Disappearing Acts in *Native Speaker* by Chang-rae Lee." *Modern Fiction Studies* 48, no. 3 (Fall 2002): 637–67.
Chen, Tina, and Eric Hayot. "Introducing Verge: What Does It Mean to Study Global Asias?" *Verge: Studies in Global Asias* 1, no. 1 (Spring 2015): vi–xv.
Cheng, Anne Anlin. *The Melancholy of Race: Psychoanalysis, Assimilation and Hidden Grief*. New York: Oxford University Press, 2000.
——. *Ornamentalism*. New York: Oxford University Press, 2019.
Cheng, Wendy. *The Changs Next Door to the Díazes: Remapping Race in Suburban California*. Minneapolis: University of Minnesota Press, 2013.
——. *Island X: Taiwanese Student Migrants, Campus Spies, and Cold War Activism*. Berkeley: University of California Press, 2023.
——. "Refuting the Silences of Taiwanese/American History: The Case of Chen Yu-hsi." *American Quarterly* 73, no. 2 (June 2021): 343–48.
——. "'This Contradictory but Fantastic Thing': Student Networks and Political Activism in Cold War Taiwanese/America." *Journal of Asian American Studies* 20, no. 2 (June 2017).
Cheng, Wendy, and Chih-ming Wang. "Against Empire: Taiwan, American Studies, and the Archipelagic." *American Quarterly* 73, no. 2 (June 2021): 335–41.
Cheung, King-kok. *Articulate Silences: Hisaye Yamamoto, Maxine Hong Kingston, Joy Kogawa*. Berkeley: University of California Press, 1993.
Cheung, King-Kok, and Stan Yogi. *Asian American Literature: An Annotated Bibliography*. New York: Modern Language Association, 1988.
Cheung-Miaw, Calvin. "Asian Americans and the Color-Line: An Intellectual History of Asian American Studies, 1969–2000." PhD dissertation, Stanford University, 2021.
——. "The Boundaries of Democracy: Transnational Political Murders in the Reagan Era." *Pacific Historical Review* 90, no. 4 (2021): 508–36.

Chiang, Mark. *The Cultural Capital of Asian American Studies: Autonomy and Representation in the University.* New York: NYU Press, 2009.

Chiang, Ted. *Exhalation: Stories.* New York: Knopf, 2019.

——. *Stories of Your Life and Others.* Easthampton, MA: Small Beer Press, 2002.

——. "The Truth of Fact, the Truth of Feeling." *Subterranean* (Fall 2013).

——. "Understand." In *The Hard SF Renaissance: An Anthology,* ed. David G. Hartwell and Kathryn Cramer. New York: Orb Books, 2003.

Chiang, Ted, and Vandana Singh. "The Occasional Writer: An Interview with Science Fiction Author Ted Chiang." *The Margins: The Asian American Writers Workshop,* October 3, 2012. http://aaww.org/the-occasional-writer-an-interview-with-science-fiction-author-ted-chiang/.

Chieng, Chieh. *A Long Stay in a Distant Land.* New York: Riverhead, 2005.

Chin, Frank. "Come All Ye Asian American Writers of the Real and the Fake." In *The Big Aiiieeeee! An Anthology of Chinese American and Japanese American Literature,* ed. Frank Chin, Jeffrey Paul Chan, Shawn Wong, and Lawson Fusao Inada, 1–92. New York: Meridian, 1991.

Chin, Frank, Jeffrey Paul Chan, Shawn Wong, and Lawson Fusao Inada. "Preface." In *Aiiieeeee!: An Anthology of Asian American Writers,* ed. Frank Chin, Jeffrey Paul Chan, Shawn Wong, and Lawson Fusao Inada, xi–xxii. Washington, DC: Howard University Press, 1974.

Chin, Marilyn, and Maxine Hong Kingston. "A *MELUS* Interview: Maxine Hong Kingston." *MELUS* 16, no. 4 (Winter 1989): 57–74.

Ching, Leo T. S. *Anti-Japan: The Politics of Sentiment in Postcolonial East Asia.* Durham, NC: Duke University Press, 2019.

——. *Becoming "Japanese": Colonial Taiwan and the Politics of Identity Formation.* Berkeley: University of California Press, 2001.

——. "Beyond Nation and Empire." *American Quarterly* 73, no. 2 (June 2021): 383–88.

Chishti, Muzaffar, and Stephen Yale-Loehr. "The Immigration Act of 1990: Unfinished Business a Quarter Century Later." *Migration Policy Institute Issue Brief* (July 2016). https://www.migrationpolicy.org/research/immigration-act-1990-still-unfinished-business-quarter-century-later.

Chiu, Monica. *Scrutinized! Surveillance in Asian North American Literature.* Honolulu: University of Hawai'i Press, 2014.

Choi, Jeehyun. "Writing Manchukuo: Peripheral Realism and Awareness in Kang Kyŏngae's Salt." *Cross-Currents: East Asian History and Culture Review* 28 (September 2018): 48–68.

Choi, Susan. *The Foreign Student.* New York: HarperPerennial, 1999.

Chou, Catherine. "Andrew Yang Is Taiwanese-American." *Popula,* December 18, 2019. https://popula.com/2019/12/18/andrew-yang-is-taiwanese-american/.

Chou, Elaine Hsieh. *Disorientation.* New York: Penguin Books, 2022.

Chow, Rey. *The Protestant Ethnic and the Spirit of Capitalism.* New York: Columbia University Press, 2002.

Choy, Catherine Ceniza. *Empire of Care: Nursing and Migration in Filipino American History.* Durham, NC: Duke University Press, 2003.

Chu, Patricia. *Assimilating Asians: Gendered Strategies of Authorship in Asian America.* Durham, NC: Duke University Press, 2000.

BIBLIOGRAPHY

———. "Rethinking Nationalistic Attachments through Narratives of Return." In *Asian American Literature in Transition: 1965–1996*, ed. Asha Nadkarni and Cathy Schlund-Vials, 279–96. Cambridge: Cambridge University Press, 2021.

———. " 'Truth as Accessible as Looking Out a Window': Unit 731 and the Ethics of Virtual Postwar Testimony." *Massachusetts Review* 60, no. 4 (Winter 2019): 682–96.

———. *Where I Have Never Been: Migration, Melancholia, and Memory in Asian American Narratives of Return*. Philadelphia: Temple University Press, 2019.

Chu, Seo-young J. *Do Metaphors Dream of Literal Sleep? A Science-Fictional Theory of Representation*. Cambridge, MA: Harvard University Press, 2011.

Chuh, Kandice. "Asians Are the New . . . What?" In *Flashpoints for Asian American Studies*, ed. Cathy Schlund-Vials and Viet Thanh Nguyen, 224–42. New York: Fordham University Press, 2018.

———. *Imagine Otherwise: On Asian Americanist Critique*. Durham, NC: Duke University Press, 2003.

Chuh, Kandice, and Karen Shimakawa, eds. *Orientations: Mapping Studies in the Asian Diaspora*. Durham, NC: Duke University Press, 2001.

Clute, John, and Peter Nicholls. *The Encyclopedia of Science Fiction*. New York: Doubleday, 1979.

Cohn, Dorrit. "Discordant Narration." *Style* 34, no. 2 (Summer 2000): 305–21.

Combahee River Collective. "A Black Feminist Statement." In *This Bridge Called My Back: Writings by Radical Women of Color*, ed. Cherríe Moraga and Gloria Anzaldúa, 210–8. New York: Kitchen Table Press, 1983.

Conrad, Sebastian. " 'The Colonial Ties Are Liquidated': Modernization Theory, Postwar Japan and the Global Cold War." *Past & Present* 216 (August 2012): 181–214.

Cowart, David. *Trailing Clouds: Immigrant Fiction in Contemporary America*. Ithaca, NY: Cornell University Press, 2006.

Cretton, Destin Daniel, dir. *Shang-Chi and the Legend of the Ten Rings*. Marvel/Walt Disney Studios, 2021.

Crisostomo, Johaina K. " 'Self-Reliance, Self-Sacrifice': Translating Ethics Across Empires in Maximo M. Kalaw's *The Filipino Rebel* (1930)." *American Quarterly* 73, no. 3 (September 2021): 535–56.

Cruz, Rene, Cindy Domingo, and Bruce Occena, eds. *A Time to Rise: The Collective Memoirs of the Union of Democratic Filipinos (KDP)*. Seattle: University of Washington Press, 2017.

Csicsery-Ronay Jr., Istvan. "Science Fiction and Empire." *Science Fiction Studies* 30, no. 2 (July 2003): 231–45.

———. *The Seven Beauties of Science Fiction*. Middletown, CT: Wesleyan University Press, 2008.

Cuarón, Alfonso, dir. *Roma*. Netflix, 2018.

Cumings, Bruce. *The Korean War: A History*. New York: Modern Library, 2010.

———. "The Origins and Development of the Northeast Asian Political Economy: Industrial Sectors, Product Cycles, and Political Consequences." *International Organization* 38, no. 1 (Winter 1984): 1–40.

———. *Parallax Visions: Making Sense of American-East Asian Relations*. Durham, NC: Duke University Press, 2002.

———. "The Political Economy of the Pacific Rim." In *Pacific-Asia and the Future of the World-System*, ed. Ravi Arvind Palat, 23–37. Westport, CT: Greenwood Press, 1993.

Davies, Peter Ho. *The Fortunes*. Boston: Houghton Mifflin Harcourt, 2016.
Davis, Rocío G. "Fictional Transits and Ruth Ozeki's *A Tale for the Time Being*." *Biography* 38, no. 1 (Winter 2015): 87–103.
Day, Iyko. *Alien Capital: Asian Racialization and the Logic of Settler Colonial Capitalism*. Durham, NC: Duke University Press, 2016.
DeLillo, Don. *The Names*. New York: Knopf, 1982.
Dirlik, Arif. "Taiwan: The Land Colonialisms Made." *boundary 2* 45, no. 3 (2018): 1–24.
Docquier, Frédéric, and Hillel Rapoport. "Globalization, Brain Drain, and Development." *Journal of Economic Literature* 50, no. 3 (September 2012): 681–730.
Downey, G. L., and J. C. Lucena. "Knowledge and Professional Identity in Engineering: Code-switching and the Metrics of Progress." *History and Technology* 20, no. 4 (December 2004): 394.
Doyle, Laura. *Inter-Imperiality: Vying Empires, Gendered Labor, and the Literary Arts of Alliance*. Durham, NC: Duke University Press, 2020.
Ehrenreich, Barbara. *Fear of Falling: The Inner Life of the Middle Class*. 1989. New York: Twelve Books, 2020.
Ehrenreich, Barbara, and John Ehrenreich. "Death of a Yuppie Dream: The Rise and Fall of the Professional-Managerial Class." *Rosa Luxemburg Stiftung*, February 12, 2013. https://rosalux.nyc/death-of-a-yuppie-dream/.
———. "The Professional-Managerial Class." *Radical America* 11, no. 2 (March–April 1977): 7–32.
Ekbladh, David. *The Great American Mission: Modernization and the Construction of an American World Order*. Princeton, NJ: Princeton University Press, 2009.
Elbaum, Max. *Revolution in the Air: Sixties Radicals Turn to Lenin, Mao and Che*. New York: Verso, 2002.
Election Study Center. "Taiwan Independence vs. Unification with the Mainland (1994/12–2022/06)." National Chengchi University, July 12, 2022. https://esc.nccu.edu.tw/PageDoc/Detail?fid=7801&id=6963.
Eng, David. *Racial Castration: Managing Masculinity in Asian America*. Durham, NC: Duke University Press, 2001.
Eng, David L., and Shinhee Han. *Racial Melancholia, Racial Dissociation: On the Social and Psychic Lives of Asian Americans*. Durham, NC: Duke University Press, 2019.
Espiritu, Yen Le. *Asian American Panethnicity: Bridging Institutions and Identities*. Philadelphia: Temple University Press, 1993.
Evans, Richard. *Deng Xiaoping and the Making of Modern China*. New York: Penguin Books, 1995.
Fan, Christopher T. "Andrew Yang and Post-65 Asian America." *American Literary History: Online Forum*, March 3, 2020. https://muse.jhu.edu/article/762155/pdf.
———. "Democratic Realism, National Allegory, and the Future of the Asian American Novel." *American Literary History* 35, no. 1 (Spring 2023): 471–79.
Fan, Christopher T., Paul Nadal, Ragini Tharoor Srinivasan, and Tina Chen, eds. "The Asian Century: Idea, Method, and Media." *Verge: Studies in Global Asias* 11, no. 2 (forthcoming, 2025).
Fanon, Frantz. *Black Skin, White Masks*. New York: Grove, 1952.
Fields, Karen E., and Barbara J. Fields. *Racecraft: The Soul of Inequality in American Life*. London: Verso, 2012.
Fisher, Mark. *Capitalist Realism: Is There No Alternative?* London: Zero Books, 2009.

BIBLIOGRAPHY

Floyd, Kevin, Jen Hedler Phillis, and Sarika Chandra. "Introduction." In *Totality Inside Out: Rethinking Crisis and Conflict Under Capital*, ed. Kevin Floyd, Jen Hedler Phillis, and Sarika Chandra, 1–28. New York: Fordham University Press, 2022.

Fludernik, Monica. "Defining (In)sanity: The Narrator of 'The Yellow Wallpaper' and the Question of Unreliability." In *Grenzüberschreitungen: Narratologie im Kontext*, ed. W. Grunzweig and A. Solbach, 75–95. Tübingen: Gunter Narr Verlag, 1999.

———. *Towards a "Natural" Narratology*. London: Routledge, 1996.

Fowler, Edward. *The Rhetoric of Confession: Shishosetsu in Early Twentieth-Century Japanese Fiction*. Berkeley: University of California Press, 1992.

Frank, Andre Gunder. *Capitalism and Underdevelopment in Latin America*. New York: Monthly Review Press, 1967.

———. *ReORIENT: Global Economy in the Asian Age*. Berkeley: University of California Press, 1998.

Freud, Sigmund. "Mourning and Melancholia." 1917. *The Standard Edition of the Complete Psychological Works of Sigmund Freud*, vol. 14, trans. James Strachey. London: Hogarth Press, 1953.

Fu, May Chuan. "Keeping Close to the Ground: Politics and Coalition in Asian American Community Organizing, 1969–1977." PhD dissertation, UC San Diego, 2005.

Fujitani, Takeshi. *Race for Empire: Koreans as Japanese and Japanese as Americans During World War II*. Berkeley: University of California Press, 2011.

Gewirtz, Julian. "The Futurists of Beijing: Alvin Toffler, Zhao Ziyang, and China's 'New Technological Revolution,' 1979–1991." *Journal of Asian Studies* 78, no. 1 (February 2019): 115–40.

Gibson, William. "Burning Chrome." *Omni*, July 1982, 72–78.

Gilman, Nils. *Mandarins of the Future: Modernization Theory in Cold War America*. Baltimore: Johns Hopkins University Press, 2003.

Glassman, Jim. *Drums of War, Drums of Development: The Formation of a Pacific Ruling Class and Industrial Transformation in East and Southeast Asia, 1945–1980*. Chicago: Haymarket Books, 2018.

"Global Talent 2021: How the New Geography of Talent Will Transform Human Resource Strategies." Oxford Economics, 2012. https://www.oxfordeconomics.com/Media/Default/Thought%20Leadership/global-talent-2021.pdf.

Gold, Thomas B. *State and Society in the Taiwan Miracle*. Armonk, NY: M. E. Sharpe, 1986.

Goyal, Yogita, ed. *The Cambridge Companion to Transnational American Literature*. New York: Cambridge University Press, 2017.

———. "National Allegory and Beyond: Postcolonial Critique Now." *PMLA* 137, no. 3 (May, 2022): 521–28.

Green, Andy. *Education and State Formation: Europe, East Asia and the USA*. New York: Palgrave Macmillan, 2013.

Greene, J. Megan. *The Origins of the Developmental State in Taiwan: Science Policy and the Quest for Modernization*. Cambridge, MA: Harvard University Press, 2008.

Guillermo, Kawika. *All Flowers Bloom*. Minneapolis: Coffee House Press, 2020.

Halberstam, David. *The Best and the Brightest*. New York: Penguin Books, 1972.

Hallemeier, Katherine. " 'To Be from the Country of People Who Gave': National Allegory and the United States of Adichie's *Americanah*." *Studies in the Novel* 47, no. 2 (Summer 2015): 231–45.

Han, Byung Chul. *Shanzhai: Deconstruction in Chinese*. Trans. Philippa Hurd. Cambridge, MA: MIT Press, 2017.

Han, Kyonghee, and Gary Lee Downey. *Engineers for Korea*. Williston, VT: Morgan & Claypool, 2014.

Han, Song. "Chinese Science Fiction: A Response to Modernization." *Science Fiction Studies* 40, no. 1 (March 2013): 15–21.

Hanna, Mary, and Jeanne Batalova. "Immigrants from Asia in the United States." Migration Policy Institute, March 10, 2021. https://www.migrationpolicy.org/article/immigrants-asia-united-states-2020.

Harbach, Chad. "Introduction." In *MFA vs NYC: The Two Cultures of American Fiction*, 3–8. New York: n+1/Faber and Faber, 2014.

Harootunian, H. D. "America's Japan/Japan's Japan." In *Japan in the World*, ed. Masao Miyoshi and H. D. Harootunian. Durham, NC: Duke University Press, 1993.

Harris, Sheldon H. *Factories of Death: Japanese Biological Warfare 1932–45 and the American Cover-up*. New York: Routledge, 1994.

Hartley, Daniel. *The Politics of Style: Towards a Marxist Poetics*. Boston: Brill, 2017.

Hayot, Eric. "The Asian Turns." *PMLA* 124, no. 3 (May 2009): 907–17.

Henwood, Doug. *Wall Street: How It Works and for Whom*. New York: Verso, 1998.

"A History of Separation." *Endnotes* 4 (October 2015). https://endnotes.org.uk/issues/4/en/endnotes-preface.

Ho, Jean Chen. *Fiona and Jane*. New York: Penguin Books, 2022.

Ho, Ming-sho. *Challenging Beijing's Mandate of Heaven: Taiwan's Sunflower Movement and Hong Kong's Umbrella Movement*. Philadelphia: Temple University Press, 2019.

Hoberek, Andrew. "Literary Genre Fiction." In *American Literature in Transition: 2000–2010*, ed. Rachel Greenwald Smith, 61–75. Cambridge: Cambridge University Press, 2017.

———. *Twilight of the Middle Class: Post-World War II Fiction and White-Collar Work*. Princeton, NJ: Princeton University Press, 2005.

Hoganson, Kristin L., and Jay Sexton, eds. *Crossing Empires: Taking U.S. History into Transimperial Terrain*. Durham, NC: Duke University Press, 2020.

Hong, Christine. *A Violent Peace: Race, U.S. Militarism, and Cultures of Democratization in Cold War Asia and the Pacific*. Stanford, CA: Stanford University Press, 2020.

Hori, Ichiro. "Hard to Choose." *The Pen* 160, Rohwer Relocation Center (1943).

Hsu, Funie, Brian Hioe, and Wen Liu. "Collective Statement on Taiwan Independence: Building Global Solidarity and Rejecting US Military Empire." *American Quarterly* 69, no. 3 (September 2017): 465–68.

Hsu, Jinn-yuh. "State Transformation and the Evolution of Economic Nationalism in the East Asian Developmental State: The Taiwanese Semiconductor Industry as Case Study." *Transactions of the Institute of British Geographers* 42, no. 2 (June 2017): 166–78.

Hsu, Madeline. *The Good Immigrants: How the Yellow Peril Became the Model Minority*. Princeton, NJ: Princeton University Press, 2015.

Hu, Jane. "Typical Japanese: Kazuo Ishiguro and the Asian Anglophone Historical Novel." *Modern Fiction Studies* 57, no. 1 (Spring 2021): 123–48.

Huang, Betsy. *Contesting Genres in Contemporary Asian American Fiction*. New York: Palgrave Macmillan, 2010.

———. "Interview with Ken Liu." *Asian American Literary Review*, August 16, 2012. https://web.archive.org/web/20170201182535/http://aalr.binghamton.edu/specfictioninterviewliu/.
Huang, Michelle N. "Ecologies of Entanglement in the Great Pacific Garbage Patch." *Journal of Asian American Studies* 20, no. 1 (February 2017): 95–117.
Huang Ping. "Modernization: China's Path and Logic." *Chinese Social Sciences Today*, November 4, 2011. http://www.csstoday.com/Item/9527.aspx.
Huang, Yasheng. *Capitalism with Chinese Characteristics: Entrepreneurship and the State*. Cambridge: Cambridge University Press, 2008.
Hung, Ho-fung. *The China Boom: Why China Will Not Rule the World*. New York: Columbia University Press, 2016.
Huntley, E. D. *Maxine Hong Kingston: A Critical Companion*. Westport, CT: Greenwood Press, 2001.
Inada, Lawson. "Introduction." In John Okada, *No-No Boy*, 1–3. Seattle: University of Washington Press, 2014.
Israel, Adam. "Interview: Ted Chiang." Clarion Foundation Blog, February 7, 2012. http://clarionfoundation.wordpress.com/2012/02/07/interview-ted-chiang/.
Jameson, Fredric. *Allegory and Ideology*. New York: Verso, 2019.
———. *Marxism and Form: 20th-Century Dialectical Theories of Literature*. Princeton, NJ: Princeton University Press, 1974.
———. *Postmodernism, or, the Cultural Logic of Late Capitalism*. Durham, NC: Duke University Press, 1991.
———. *The Seeds of Time*. New York: Columbia University Press, 1994.
———. "Third-World Literature in the Era of Multinational Capitalism." *Social Text* 15 (Autumn 1986): 65–88.
Jansen, Marius B., ed. *Changing Japanese Attitudes Toward Modernization*. Princeton, NJ: Princeton University Press, 1965.
Jeon, Joseph. *Racial Things, Racial Forms: Objecthood in Avant-Garde Asian American Poetry*. Iowa City: University of Iowa Press, 2012.
Jerng, Mark. "The Asiatic Modal Imagination." In *Asian American Literature in Transition, 1996–2020*, ed. Betsy Huang and Victor Román Mendoza, 173–99. Cambridge: Cambridge University Press, 2021.
———. "Nowhere in Particular: Perceiving Race, Chang-rae Lee's *Aloft*, and the Question of Asian American Fiction." *Modern Fiction Studies* 56, no. 1 (Spring 2010): 183–204.
———. *Racial Worldmaking: The Power of Popular Fiction*. New York: Fordham University Press, 2017.
Jin, Ha. *A Song Everlasting*. New York: Pantheon Books, 2021.
Jin, Meng. *Little Gods*. New York: Custom House, 2020.
Johnson, Chalmers. *MITI and the Japanese Miracle: The Growth of Industrial Policy, 1925–1975*. Stanford, CA: Stanford University Press, 1982.
Johnson, Lyndon B. "Remarks at the Signing of the Immigration Bill." In *Public Papers of the Presidents of the United States: Lyndon B. Johnson, 1965*, vol. 2. Washington, DC: U.S. Government Printing Office, 1966.
Johnson, Sarah Anne. "An Interview with Chang-rae Lee." *Association of Writers & Writing Programs* (May/Summer 2005). https://www.awpwriter.org/magazine_media/writers_chronicle_view/2464/an_interview_with_chang-rae_lee.

BIBLIOGRAPHY

Kadohata, Cynthia. *Weedflower*. New York: Atheneum Books for Young Readers, 2006.
Kang, Laura Hyun Yi. *Compositional Subjects: Enfiguring Asian/American Women*. Durham, NC: Duke University Press, 2002.
Kang, Younghill. *East Goes West*. New York: John Day Company, 1937.
Khor, Shing Yin. *The Legend of Auntie Po*. New York: Kokila, 2021.
Kim, Ahn Andrew. "A Homeward Journey." In *75th Anniversary of Korean Immigration to Hawai'i, 1903–1978*, ed. Samuel S. O. Lee, 22–27. Honolulu: 75th Anniversary of Korean Immigration to Hawai'i Committee, 1978.
Kim, Andrew (Adhy). "Japanese Melancholy and the Ethics of Concealment in Ruth Ozeki's *A Tale for the Time Being*." *Mosaic* 52, no. 4 (December 2019): 73–90.
Kim, Claire Jean. *Bitter Fruit: The Politics of Black-Korean Conflict in New York City*. New Haven, CT: Yale University Press, 2003.
———. "The Racial Triangulation of Asian Americans." *Politics & Society* 27, no. 1 (March 1999): 105–38.
Kim, Daniel. "Do I, Too, Sing America?: Vernacular Representations and Chang-rae Lee's *Native Speaker*." *Journal of Asian American Studies* 6, no. 3 (October 2003): 231–60.
Kim, E. Tammy. "Transnationally Asian." *Columbia Journalism Review*, July 21, 2020. https://www.cjr.org/special_report/transnationally_asian.php.
Kim, Elaine. "Asian American Writers: A Bibliographical Review." *American Studies International* 22, no. 2 (October 1984): 41–78.
Kim, Elaine, and Norma Alarcón, eds. *Writing Self, Writing Nation: Essays on Theresa Hak Kyung Cha's DICTEE*. Berkeley: Third Woman Press, 1994.
Kim, Elaine, Shirley Geok-lin Lim, and Amy Ling. *Reading the Literatures of Asian America*. Philadelphia: Temple University Press, 1992.
Kim, Eleana J. *Adopted Territory: Transnational Korean Adoptees and the Politics of Belonging*. Durham, NC: Duke University Press, 2010.
Kim, Jodi. *Ends of Empire: Asian American Critique and the Cold War*. Minneapolis: University of Minnesota Press, 2010.
———. "From Mee-gook to Gook: The Cold War and Racialized Undocumented Capital in Chang-rae Lee's *Native Speaker*." *MELUS* 34, no. 1 (Spring 2009).
Kim, Kim Kichung. "A Homecoming." *Bridge* 2, no. 6 (1973): 27–31.
Kim, Kim Yong. "From Here You Can See the Moon." *Texas Quarterly* 11, no. 2 (1968): 201–8.
Kim, Richard. *The Innocent*. New York: Avon Books, 1968.
———. *The Martyred*. New York: Avon Books, 1964.
Kingston, Maxine Hong. *China Men*. New York: Vintage Books, 1981.
———. "The Novel's Next Step." *Mother Jones Magazine*, December 1989, 37–41.
———. *The Woman Warrior: Memoirs of a Girlhood Among Ghosts*. New York: Knopf, 1976.
Kirschenbaum, Matthew G. *Track Changes: A Literary History of Word Processing*. Cambridge, MA: Harvard University Press, 2016.
Ko, Lisa. *The Leavers*. New York: Algonquin Books, 2017.
Kogonada, dir. *After Yang*. Showtime, 2021.
Koshy, Susan. "The Fiction of Asian American Literature." *Yale Journal of Criticism* 9, no. 2 (Fall 1996): 331–46.
———. "Neoliberal Family Matters." *American Literary History* 25, no. 2 (September 2013): 344–80.

BIBLIOGRAPHY

Krogstad, Jens Manuel, and Jynnah Radford. "Education Levels of U.S. Immigrants Are on the Rise." Pew Research Center, September 14, 2018. https://www.pewresearch.org/fact-tank/2018/09/14/education-levels-of-u-s-immigrants-are-on-the-rise/.
Kuang, R. F. *The Poppy War*. New York: Harper Voyager, 2018.
Kwan, Daniel, and Daniel Scheinert, dir. *Everything Everywhere All at Once*. A24, 2022.
Kwan, Kevin. *Crazy Rich Asians*. New York: Anchor Books, 2013.
Latham, Michael E. *The Right Kind of Revolution: Modernization, Development, and U.S. Foreign Policy from the Cold War to the Present*. Ithaca, NY: Cornell University Press, 2011.
Layton, Edwin. *The Revolt of the Engineers: Social Responsibility and the American Engineering Profession*. Baltimore: Johns Hopkins University Press, 1986.
Le-Khac, Long, and Kate Hao. "The Asian American Literature We've Constructed." *Post45* 6, no. 2 (2021). https://culturalanalytics.org/article/22330-the-asian-american-literature-we-ve-constructed.
Lee, Chang-rae. *Aloft*. New York: Riverhead, 2004.
———. "Coming Home Again." *The New Yorker*, October 9, 1995. https://www.newyorker.com/magazine/1995/10/16/coming-home-again.
———. "The Faintest Echo of Our Language." *New England Review* 15, no. 3 (Summer 1993): 85–92.
———. *A Gesture Life*. New York: Riverhead, 1999.
———. *My Year Abroad*. New York: Riverhead, 2021.
———. *Native Speaker*. New York: Riverhead, 1995.
———. *On Such a Full Sea*. New York: Riverhead, 2014.
———. *The Surrendered*. New York: Riverhead, 2010.
———. "Vox Media Preview of The Podium: I Think You're Interesting Featuring Chang Rae Lee." *The Podium from Vox Media and NBC Sports Group*, December 14, 2017. http://art19.com/shows/the-podium-nbc-olympics/episodes/0466dd68-c1c6-43a3-a3ad-9df92a91f5ba.
Lee, Christopher. *The Semblance of Identity: Aesthetic Mediation in Asian American Literature*. Stanford, CA: Stanford University Press, 2012.
Lee, James Kyung-jin. *Pedagogies of Woundedness: Illness, Memoir, and the Ends of the Model Minority*. Philadelphia: Temple University Press, 2021.
———. "Where the Talented Tenth Meets the Model Minority: The Price of Privilege in Wideman's 'Philadelphia Fire' and Lee's 'Native Speaker.'" *NOVEL: A Forum on Fiction* 35, nos. 2/3 (Spring–Summer 2002): 231–57.
Lee, Jennifer, and Min Zhou. *The Asian American Achievement Paradox*. New York: Russell Sage, 2015.
———. "Hyper-Selectivity and the Remaking of Culture: Understanding the Asian American Achievement Paradox." *Asian American Journal of Psychology* 8, no. 1 (2017): 7–15.
Lee, Julia H. *The Racial Railroad*. New York: NYU Press, 2022.
———. *Understanding Maxine Hong Kingston*. Columbia: University of South Carolina Press, 2018.
Lee, Min Jin. *Free Food for Millionaires*. New York: Grand Central Publishing, 2007.
———. *Pachinko*. New York: Grand Central Publishing, 2017.
Lee, Robert G. *Orientals: Asian Americans in Popular Culture*. Philadelphia: Temple University Press, 1999.

Lee, Yoon Sun. *Modern Minority: Asian American Literature and Everyday Life.* New York: Oxford University Press, 2013.
——. "Racialized Bodies and Asian American Literature." *American Literary History* 30, no. 1 (Spring 2018): 166–76.
——. "Type, Totality, and the Realism of Asian American Literature." *Modern Language Quarterly* 73, no. 3 (September 2012): 415–32.
Lee-Tai, Amy. *A Place Where Sunflowers Grow.* San Francisco: Children's Book Press, 2006.
Leung, Brian. *Take Me Home.* New York: HarperCollins, 2010.
Li, Grace D. *Portrait of a Thief.* New York: Ballantine Books, 2022.
Light, Claire. *Slightly Behind and to the Left: Four Stories and Three Drabbles.* Seattle: Aqueduct, 2009.
Light, Ivan, and Edna Bonacich. *Immigrant Entrepreneurs Koreans in Los Angeles, 1965–1982.* Berkeley: University of California Press, 1988.
Lim, Adele, dir. *Joyride.* Lionsgate, 2023.
Lim, Shirley Geok-Lin, John Gamber, Stephen Hong Sohn, and Gina Valentino. *Transnational Asian American Literature: Sites and Transits.* Philadelphia: Temple University Press, 2006.
Lin, Chia-Chia. *The Unpassing.* New York: Farrar, Straus and Giroux, 2019.
Lin, Ed. *David Tung Can't Have a Girlfriend Until He Gets Into an Ivy League College.* Los Angeles: Kaya Press, 2020.
——. *Ghost Month.* New York: Soho Press, 2014.
——. *Waylaid.* New York: Kaya Press, 2002.
Lin, Francie. *The Foreigner.* New York: Picador, 2008.
Lin, James. "Nostalgia for Japanese Colonialism: Historical Memory and Postcolonialism in Contemporary Taiwan." *History Compass* 20, no. 11 (November 2022): 1–11.
Lin, Tao. *Leave Society.* New York: Vintage Books, 2021.
——. *Taipei.* New York: Vintage Books, 2013.
Lin, Tom. *The Thousand Crimes of Ming Tsu.* New York: Little, Brown, 2021.
Ling, Jinqi. *Across Meridians: History and Figuration in Karen Tei Yamashita's Transnational Novels.* Stanford, CA: Stanford University Press, 2012.
——. *Narrating Nationalisms: Ideology and Form in Asian American Literature.* New York: Oxford University Press, 1998.
Linmark, R. Zamora. *Leche.* Minneapolis: Coffee House Press, 2011.
Liu, Alan. *Laws of Cool: Knowledge Work and the Culture of Information.* Chicago: University of Chicago Press, 2004.
Liu, Ken. *The Hidden Girl and Other Stories.* New York: Saga Press, 2020.
——. *The Paper Menagerie and Other Stories.* New York: Saga Press, 2016.
Liu, Michael, Kim Geron, and Tracy Lai. *The Snake Dance of Asian American Activism: Community, Vision, and Power.* Lanham, MD: Lexington Books, 2008.
Liu, Petrus. *Queer Marxism in Two Chinas.* Durham, NC: Duke University Press, 2015.
Liu, Wen. "The Mundane Politics of War in Taiwan: Psychological Preparedness, Civil Defense, and Permanent War." *Security Dialogue,* September 12, 2023. https://doi.org/10.1177/09670106231194908.
Longo, Bernadette. *Spurious Coin: A History of Science, Management, and Technical Writing.* Albany: SUNY Press, 2000.

BIBLIOGRAPHY

Lowe, Lisa. *Immigrant Acts: On Asian American Cultural Politics.* Durham, NC: Duke University Press, 1996.

———. "The International Within the National: American Studies and Asian American Critique." *Cultural Critique* 40 (1998): 29–47.

Luckhurst, Roger. *Science Fiction.* Cambridge: Polity Press, 2005.

Lukács, Georg. *Realism in Our Time: Literature and the Class Struggle.* Trans. John Mander and Necke Mander. London: Harper & Row, 1971.

Lye, Colleen. *America's Asia: Racial Form and American Literature, 1893–1945.* Princeton, NJ: Princeton University Press, 2005.

———. "Asian American 1960s." In *The Routledge Companion to Asian American and Pacific Islander Literature*, ed. Rachel C. Lee, 213–23. New York: Routledge, 2014.

———. "Form and History in Asian American Literary Studies." *American Literary History* 20, no. 3 (Summer 2008): 548–55.

———. "Identity Politics, Criticism, and Self-Criticism." *South Atlantic Quarterly* 119, no. 4 (2020): 701–14.

———. "In Dialogue with Asian American Studies." *Representations* 99, no. 1 (Summer 2007): 1–28.

———. "Introduction: In Dialogue with Asian American Studies." *Representations* 99, no. 1 (Summer 2007): 1–12.

———. "Racial Form." *Representations* 104, no. 1 (Fall 2008): 92–101.

———. "Unmarked Character and the 'Rise of Asia': Ed Park's *Personal Days.*" *Verge* 1, no. 1 (2015): 230–54.

Lynch, Paul, dir. *Twilight Zone.* Season 1, Episode 9, "Wong's Lost and Found Emporium." Written by Alan Brennert. Aired November 22, 1985.

Ma, Ling. *Severance.* New York: Farrar, Straus, and Giroux, 2018.

Maeda, Daryl. *Chains of Babylon: The Rise of Asian America.* Minneapolis: University of Minnesota Press, 2009.

Malabou, Catherine. *Changer de différence: Le féminin et la question philosophique.* Paris: Galilée, 2009.

Man, Simeon. *Soldiering Through Empire: Race and the Making of the Decolonizing Pacific.* Berkeley: University of California Press, 2018.

Manshel, Alexander. *Writing Backwards: Historical Fiction and the Reshaping of the American Canon.* New York: Columbia University Press, 2024.

Marien, Michael. "The Two Visions of Post-Industrial Society." *Futures* 9, no. 5 (October 1977): 415–31.

Martin, Theodore. *Contemporary Drift: Genre, Historicism, and the Problem of the Present.* New York: Columbia University Press, 2019.

Marx, Karl. *Capital: A Critique of Political Economy, Volume 1.* 1867. Trans. Ben Fowkes. New York: Penguin Books, 1990.

———. *Grundrisse: Foundations of the Critique of Political Economy (Rough Draft).* Trans. Martin Nicolaus. New York: Penguin Books, 1973.

Matthews, John A., and Dong-Sung Cho. *Tiger Technology: The Creation of a Semiconductor Industry in East Asia.* London: Cambridge University Press, 2009.

McCann, Sean. "Training and Vision: Roth, DeLillo, Banks, Peck, and the Postmodern Aesthetics of Vocation." *Twentieth-Century Literature* 53, no. 3 (2007): 298–326.

McClanahan, Annie. "Microwork, Automation, and the Insecurity of Contemporary Labor." In *Insecurity*, ed. Richard Grusin, 31–64. Minneapolis: University of Minnesota Press, 2022.

———. "Piece-Rates, Poetry, and Digital Microwork." Presentation at Coast45, University of Southern California, Los Angeles, October 14, 2022.

McCusker, Henry F., and Harry J. Robinson. "Report on Education and Development: The Role of Educational Planning in the Economic Development of the Republic of China." Stanford Research Institute, 1962.

McGrath, Charles. "Deep in Suburbia." *New York Times*, February 29, 2004.

McGrath, Laura. "Comping White." *Los Angeles Review of Books*, January 21, 2019. https://lareviewofbooks.org/article/comping-white/.

McGurl, Mark. *The Program Era: Postwar Fiction and the Rise of Creative Writing*. Cambridge, MA: Harvard University Press, 2009.

McMillin, Calvin. "Asian American Detective Fiction." In *Oxford Research Encyclopedia*, October 30, 2019. https://oxfordre.com/literature/display/10.1093/acrefore/9780190201098.001.0001/acrefore-9780190201098-e-813.

Melamed, Jodi. *Represent and Destroy: Rationalizing Violence in the New Racial Capitalism*. Minneapolis: University of Minnesota Press, 2011.

Menand, Louis. *Discovering Modernism: T. S. Eliot and His Context*. New York: Oxford University Press, 1987.

Miéville, China. "Wonder Boy." *The Guardian*, April 23, 2004.

Mikulova, Veronika. "Embracing Western Thought: The Development of Japanese Identity in the Works by Kazuo Ishiguro and Ruth Ozeki." MA thesis, Masaryk University, 2017.

Miller, Chanel. *Know My Name: A Memoir*. New York: Viking, 2019.

Miller, Chris. *Chip War: The Fight for the World's Most Critical Technology*. New York: Scribner, 2022.

Millikan, Max, and Walt Whitman Rostow. *A Proposal: Key to an Effective Foreign Policy*. Cambridge, MA: Center for International Studies, MIT, 1957.

Mills, C. Wright. *White Collar: The American Middle Classes*. 1951. New York: Oxford University Press, 2002.

Min, Pyong Gap, and Sou Hyun Jang. "The Concentration of Asian Americans in STEM and Health-Care Occupations: An Intergenerational Comparison." *Ethnic and Racial Studies* 38, no. 6 (2015): 841–59.

Miyadi, Al T. "It Came Upon a Midnight Clear." *Pacific Citizen*, 1950.

Model, Suzanne. "Why Are Asian-Americans Educationally Hyper-selected? The Case of Taiwan." *Ethnic and Racial Studies* 41, no. 11 (2018): 2104–24.

Monaghan, Peter. "A Korean-American Novelist's Impressive Debut." *Chronicle of Higher Education*, April 7, 1995. https://www.chronicle.com/article/a-korean-american-novelists-impressive-debut/.

Morley, David, and Kevin Robins. *Spaces of Identity: Global Media, Electronic Landscapes and Cultural Boundaries*. New York: Routledge, 1995.

Nadal, Paul. "Cold War Remittance Economy: US Creative Writing and the Importation of New Criticism into the Philippines." *American Quarterly* 73, no. 3 (September 2021).

———. "How Neoliberalism Remade the Model Minority Myth." *Representations* 163 (August 2023): 79–99.

BIBLIOGRAPHY

Nakamura, Lisa. "Indigenous Circuits: Navajo Women and the Racialization of Early Electronic Manufacture." *American Quarterly* 66, no. 4 (December 2014): 919–41.
Naruse, Cheryl. "Overseas Singaporeans, Coming-of-Career Narratives, and the Corporate Nation." *Biography* 37, no. 1 (Winter 2014): 141–59.
Ng, Celeste. *Everything I Never Told You*. New York: Penguin Press, 2014.
Ngai, Mae M. *Impossible Subjects: Illegal Aliens and the Making of Modern America*. Princeton, NJ: Princeton University Press, 2004.
Nguyen, Kevin. *New Waves*. New York: One World, 2020.
Nguyen, Viet Thanh. *Nothing Ever Dies: Vietnam and the Memory of War*. Cambridge, MA: Harvard University Press, 2017.
———. *Race and Resistance: Literature and Politics in Asian America*. New York: Oxford University Press, 2002.
———. *The Sympathizer*. New York: Grove Press, 2015.
Nguyen, Viet Thanh, and Janet Alison Hoskins. "Introduction." *Transpacific Studies: Framing an Emergent Field*, ed. Viet Thanh Nguyen and Janet Alison Hoskins, 1–38. Honolulu: University of Hawai'i Press, 2014.
Nietzsche, Friedrich. *The Genealogy of Morals*. In *Basic Writings of Nietzsche*, trans. and ed. Walter Kaufmann, 480. New York: Modern Library, 1992.
Ninh, erin Khuê. *Ingratitude: The Debt-Bound Daughter in Asian American Literature*. New York: NYU Press, 2011.
———. *Passing for Perfect: College Impostors and Other Model Minorities*. Philadelphia: Temple University Press, 2021.
Oh, Ellen, and Elsie Chapman, eds. *A Thousand Beginnings and Endings*. New York: HarperCollins, 2018.
Okada, John. "The Technocrats of Industry or The Trials and Tribulations of Mr. S. V. and How He Finally Became a Real Engineer . . ." In *The Life and Rediscovered Work of the Author of No-No Boy*, ed. Frank Abe, Greg Robinson, and Floyd Cheung, 145–66. Seattle: University of Washington Press, 2018.
Omatsu, Glenn. "The 'Four Prisons' and the Movements of Liberation: Asian American Activism from the 1960s to the 1990s." In *Contemporary Asian America*, ed. Min Zhou and Anthony Christian Ocampo, 298–330. New York: NYU Press, 2000.
Omi, Michael, and Howard Winant. *Racial Formation in the United States: From the 1960s to the 1980s*. New York: Routledge, 1986.
Ong, Aiwha. *Flexible Citizenship: The Cultural Logics of Transnationality*. Durham, NC: Duke University Press, 1999.
———. *Neoliberalism as Exception: Mutations in Citizenship and Sovereignty*. Durham, NC: Duke University Press, 2006.
Ong, Paul, and John M. Liu. "U.S. Immigration Policies and Asian Migration." In *The New Asian Immigration in Los Angeles and Global Restructuring*, ed. Edna Bonacich, Lucie Cheng, and Paul Ong, 3–38. Philadelphia: Temple University Press, 1994.
Ortolano, Guy. *The Two Cultures Controversy: Science, Literature, and Cultural Politics*. Cambridge: Cambridge University Press, 2009.
Ozeki, Ruth. *All Over Creation*. New York, Viking, 2003.
———. "Confessions of a Zen Novelist." *Lion's Roar*, February 15, 2013. https://www.lionsroar.com/confessions-of-a-zen-novelist/.
———. "Foreword." In John Okada, *No-No Boy*, vii–xviii. Seattle: University of Washington Press, 2014.

———, dir. *Halving the Bones*. Ozeki Film, 1995.
———. *My Year of Meats*. New York: Viking, 1998.
———. *A Tale for the Time Being*. New York: Penguin Books, 2013.
Pak, Greg, dir. *Robot Stories*. Pak Film, 2003.
Palumbo-Liu, David. *Asian/American: Historical Crossings of a Racial Frontier*. Stanford, CA: Stanford University Press, 1999.
Pan, Emily X. R. *The Astonishing Color of After*. New York: Little, Brown, 2018.
Parikh, Crystal. "Ethnic America Undercover: The Intellectual and Minority Discourse." *Contemporary Literature* 43, no. 2 (Summer 2002): 249–84.
Park, Linda Sue. *Prairie Lotus*. New York: Clarion Books, 2020.
Phang, Jennifer, dir. *Advantageous*. Netflix, 2015.
Portes, Alejandro. "Modernization for Emigration: The Medical Brain Drain from Argentina." *Journal of Interamerican Studies and World Affairs* 18, no. 4 (November 1976): 395–422.
Portes, Alejandro, and Adrienne Celaya. "Modernization for Emigration: Determinants and Consequences of the Brain Drain." *Daedalus* 142, no. 3 (2013): 170–84.
Portes, Alejandro, and John Walton. *Labor, Class, and the International System*. New York: Academic Press, 1981.
Postone, Moishe. "Anti-Semitism and National Socialism." In *Germans and Jews since the Holocaust: The Changing Situation in West Germany*, ed. Anson Rabinbach and Jack Zipes, 302–14. New York: Holmes & Meier, 1986.
Prince, Gerald. *Dictionary of Narratology*. Lincoln: University of Nebraska Press, 2003.
Reich, Robert B. *The Work of Nations: Preparing Ourselves for 21st-Century Capitalism*. New York: Knopf, 1991.
Rigger, Shelley. *The Tiger Leading the Dragon: How Taiwan Propelled China's Economic Rise*. Lanham, MD: Rowman & Littlefield, 2021.
Rivera, Takeo. *Model Minority Masochism: Performing the Cultural Politics of Asian American Masculinity*. New York: Oxford University Press, 2022.
Roh, David S., Betsy Huang, and Greta Niu, eds. *Techno-Orientalism: Imagining Asia in Speculative Fiction, History, and Media*. New Brunswick, NJ: Rutgers University Press, 2015.
Rosca, Ninotchka. *State of War: A Novel of Life in the Philippines*. New York: Norton, 1988.
Rosenberg, Justin, and Chris Boyle. "Understanding 2016: China, Brexit and Trump in the History of Uneven and Combined Development." *Journal of Historical Sociology* 32, no. 1 (March 2019): 32–58.
Rostow, Walt Whitman. *The Stages of Economic Growth: A Non-Communist Manifesto*. Cambridge: Cambridge University Press, 1960.
Ryan, Shawna Yang. *Green Island: A Novel*. New York: Vintage Books, 2016.
Saez, Elena Machado, and Raphael Dalleo. *The Latino/a Canon and the Emergence of Post-Sixties Literature*. New York: Palgrave Macmillan, 2007.
Said, Edward. *Orientalism*. New York: Vintage Books, 1979.
Saldívar, Ramón. "Second Elevation of the Novel: Race, Form, and the Postrace Aesthetic in Contemporary Narrative." *Narrative* 21, no. 1 (January 2013): 1–18.
San Juan, Jr., E. "Beyond Identity Politics: The Predicament of the Asian American Writer in Late Capitalism." *American Literary History* 3, no. 3 (Autumn 1991): 542–65.

BIBLIOGRAPHY

Sapigao, Janice Lobo. *Microchips for Millions*. San Francisco: Philippine American Writers and Artists, 2016.
Saxenian, AnnaLee. *The New Argonauts: Regional Advantage in a Global Economy*. Cambridge, MA: Harvard University Press, 2007.
Say, Allen. *Home of the Brave*. Boston: Houghton Mifflin Harcourt, 2002.
Schmalzer, Sigrid. "The Global Comrades of Mr. Democracy and Mr. Science: Placing May Fourth in a Transnational History of Science Activism." *East Asian Science, Technology and Society* 16, no. 3 (May 2021): 1–22.
Scott, Ridley, dir. *Blade Runner*. Warner Bros., 1982.
Seth, Michael J. *Education Fever: Society, Politics, and the Pursuit of Schooling in South Korea*. Honolulu: University of Hawai'i Press, 2002.
Shankar, Shalini. *Desi Land: Teen Culture, Class, and Success in Silicon Valley*. Durham, NC: Duke University Press, 2008.
Shigematsu, Setsu, and Keith L. Camacho, eds. *Militarized Currents: Toward a Decolonized Future in Asia and the Pacific*. Minneapolis: University of Minnesota Press, 2010.
Shih, Shu-mei. "Globalisation and the (in)significance of Taiwan." *Postcolonial Studies* 6, no. 2 (2003): 143–53.
Showalter, Elaine. *Faculty Towers: The Academic Novel and Its Discontents*. Philadelphia: University of Pennsylvania Press, 2009.
Singh, Nikhil Pal. "Racial Formation in an Age of Permanent War." In *Racial Formation in the Twenty-First Century*, ed. Daniel Martinez HoSang, Oneka LaBennett, and Laura Pulido, 276–301. Berkeley: University of California Press, 2012.
Sinykin, Dan. *Big Fiction: How Conglomeration Changed Book Publishing and American Fiction*. New York: Columbia University Press, 2023.
Smith, Jason. *Smart Machines and Service Work: Automation in an Age of Stagnation*. Chicago: University of Chicago Press, 2020.
Smith, Jeremy. "The Absence of God, an Interview with Ted Chiang." *Interzone* 182 (September 2002): 23–27.
Snow, C. P. *The Two Cultures and the Scientific Revolution*. Cambridge: Cambridge University Press, 1959.
So, Anthony Veasna. *Afterparties: Stories*. New York: HarperCollins, 2021.
So, Christine. *Economic Citizens: A Narrative of Asian American Visibility*. Philadelphia: Temple University Press, 2008.
So, Richard Jean. *Redlining Culture: A Data History of Racial Inequality and Postwar Fiction*. New York: Columbia University Press, 2020.
Sohn, Stephen Hong. "Introduction: Alien/Asian: Imagining the Racialized Future." *MELUS* 33, no. 4 (2008): 5–22.
———. *Racial Asymmetries: Asian American Fictional Worlds*. New York: NYU Press, 2014.
Song, Min Hyoung. "Asian American Literature Within and Beyond the Immigrant Narrative." In *The Cambridge Companion to Asian American Literature*, ed. Crystal Parikh and Daniel Y. Kim, 41–57. Cambridge: Cambridge University Press, 2015.
———. "Between Genres: On Chang-rae Lee's Realism." *Los Angeles Review of Books*, January 10, 2014. https://www.lareviewofbooks.org/article/chang-rae-lees-realism.
———. *The Children of 1965: On Writing, and Not Writing, as an Asian American*. Durham, NC: Duke University Press, 2013.

Srinivasan, Ragini Tharoor. "Global India in 21st-Century Asian American Literature." *Oxford Research Encyclopedias, Literature*, July 30, 2018. https://doi.org/10.1093/acrefore/9780190201098.013.873.

——. "The Rhetoric of Return: Diasporic Homecoming and the New Indian City." *Room One Thousand* 3, no. 3 (2015): 308–35.

Stringer, Rebecca. "'A Nietzschean Breed': Feminism, Victimology, Ressentiment." In *Why Nietzsche Still? Reflections on Drama, Culture, and Politics*, ed. Alan D. Schrift, 263–84. Berkeley: University of California Press, 2000.

Strychacz, Thomas. *Modernism, Mass Culture, and Professionalism*. Cambridge: Cambridge University Press, 1993.

Su, Beng. *Taiwan's 400 Year History*. Taipei: SMC Publishing, 2017.

Suh, Chris. *The Allure of Empire: American Encounters with Asians in the Age of Transpacific Expansion and Exclusion*. New York: Oxford University Press, 2023.

Suvin, Darko. *Metamorphoses of Science Fiction: On the Poetics and History of a Literary Genre*. New Haven, CT: Yale University Press, 1979.

Suzuki, Erin, and Aimee Bahng. "The Transpacific Subject in Asian American Culture." In *The Oxford Encyclopedia of Asian American Literature and Culture*, ed. Josephine Lee. New York: Oxford University Press, 2020. https://oxfordre.com/literature/display/10.1093/acrefore/9780190201098.001.0001/acrefore-9780190201098-e-877.

Swenson-Wright, John. *Unequal Allies? United States Security and Alliance Policy Toward Japan, 1945–1960*. Stanford, CA: Stanford University Press, 2005.

Swoyer, Chris. "The Linguistic Relativity Hypothesis." *Stanford Encyclopedia of Philosophy*, 2003. http://plato.stanford.edu/entries/relativism/supplement2.html.

Szalay, Michael. *Hip Figures: A Literary History of the Democratic Party*. Stanford, CA: Stanford University Press, 2012.

——. *New Deal Modernism: American Literature and the Invention of the Welfare State*. Durham, NC: Duke University Press, 2000.

——. *Second Lives: Black-Market Melodramas and the Reinvention of Television*. Chicago: University of Chicago Press, 2023.

Tabler, Elizabeth. "An Interview with Ken Liu." *GrimdarkMAGAZINE*, December 4, 2021. https://www.grimdarkmagazine.com/an-interview-with-ken-liu/.

Táíwò, Olúfẹ́mi O. *Elite Capture: How the Powerful Took Over Identity Politics (And Everything Else)*. Chicago: Haymarket Books, 2022.

Takei, George. *They Called Us Enemy*. New York: Top Shelf Productions, 2019.

Takei, George, and Robert Asprin. *Mirror Friend, Mirror Foe*. Chicago: Playboy, 1979.

Tan, Amy. *The Joy Luck Club*. New York: Penguin Books, 1989.

Tan, Lucy. *What We Were Promised*. New York: Little, Brown, 2018.

Tang, Amy. *Race and Repetition: Asian American Literature After Multiculturalism*. New York: Oxford University Press, 2016.

Tizon, Alex. "My Family's Slave." *The Atlantic*, June 2017.

Tongson, Karen. *Relocations: Queer Suburban Imaginaries*. New York: NYU Press, 2011.

Touré. *Who's Afraid of Post-Blackness? What It Means to Be Black Now*. New York: Free Press, 2011.

Trotsky, Leon. *History of the Russian Revolution*. Trans. Max Eastman. New York: Pathfinder Books, 1980.

Tulathimutte, Tony. *Private Citizens: A Novel*. New York: One World, 2016.

BIBLIOGRAPHY

Ty, Eleanor, and Ruth Ozeki. "'A Universe of Many Worlds': An Interview with Ruth Ozeki." *MELUS* 38, no. 3 (Fall 2013): 160–71.
Ueno, Toshiya. "Techno-Orientalism and Media-Tribalism: On Japanese Animation and Rave Culture." *Third Text* 13, no. 47 (1999): 95–106.
U.S. Citizen and Immigration Services. "Characteristics of H-1B Specialty Occupation Workers: Fiscal Year 2022 Annual Report to Congress October 1, 2021–September 30, 2022." March 13, 2023.
U.S. Department of Labor. "Summaries of Manpower Surveys and Reports for Developing Countries, 1958–68." June 1969.
Vint, Sherryl. "Notes and Correspondence: Suggested Further Readings in the Slipstream." *Science Fiction Studies* 38, no. 1 (March 2011). http://www.depauw.edu/sfs/notes/notes113/notes113.html.
Wade, Robert. "Japan, the World Bank, and the Art of Paradigm Maintenance: The East Asian Miracle in Political Perspective." *New Left Review* 217 (May–June 1996): 3–36.
Wallerstein, Immanuel. *The Capitalist World-Economy: Essays*. Cambridge: Cambridge University Press, 1979.
———. *World-Systems Analysis: An Introduction*. Durham, NC: Duke University Press, 2004.
Wang, Chih-ming. *Transpacific Articulations: Student Migration and the Remaking of Asian America*. Honolulu: University of Hawai'i Press, 2013.
———. "When Asian Americans Return to Asia: Return Narratives, Transpacific Imagination, and the Post/Cold War." *Southeast Asian Review of English* 58, no. 2 (2021): 95–112.
Wang, Esme Weijun. *The Border of Paradise*. New York: Unnamed Press, 2016.
Wang, Kathy. *Family Trust*. New York: HarperCollins, 2018.
Wang, L. Ling-chi. "The Structure of Dual Domination: Toward a Paradigm for the Study of the Chinese Diaspora in the United States." *Amerasia Journal* 33, no. 1 (2007): 144–66.
Wang, Lulu, dir. *The Farewell*. A24, 2019.
Wang, Wayne, dir. *Coming Home Again*. Screenplay by Chang-rae Lee. Wang Film, 2019.
Wang, Weike. *Chemistry: A Novel*. New York: Knopf, 2017.
———. *Joan Is Okay: A Novel*. New York: Penguin Books, 2022.
Wang, Xuan Juliana, and Christopher Patterson. "A Discussion with Xuan Juliana Wang and Ricco Villanueva Siasoco." *New Books in Asian American Studies*, August 24, 2021. Podcast. https://newbooksnetwork.com/association-of-asian-american-studies-book-awards-2021-xuan-juliana-wang-and-ricco-villanueva-siasoco.
Wang, Xuan Juliana. *Home Remedies*. New York: Hogarth, 2019.
Warren, Kenneth. *What Was African American Literature?* Cambridge, MA: Harvard University Press, 2011.
Warren, Robert Penn. *All the King's Men*. New York: Harcourt, Brace, 1946.
Warwick Research Collective. *Combined and Uneven Development: Towards a New Theory of World-Literature*. Liverpool: Liverpool University Press, 2015.
Watanabe, Masao. *The Japanese and Western Science*. Trans. Otto Theodor Benfey. Philadelphia: University of Pennsylvania Press, 1988.

Watson, Jini Kim. *Cold War Reckonings: Authoritarianism and the Genres of Decolonization*. New York: Fordham University Press, 2021.
——. *The New Asian City: Three-Dimensional Fictions of Space and Urban Form*. Minneapolis: University of Minnesota Press, 2011.
Wegner, Phillip E. *Shockwaves of Possibility: Essays on Science Fiction, Globalization, and Utopia*. New York: Peter Lang, 2014.
Wei, William. *The Asian American Movement*. Philadelphia: Temple University Press, 1993.
Wells, H. G. *The Time Machine*. London: William Heinemann, 1895. Reprinted with introduction by Roger Lockhurst. New York: Oxford University Press, 2017. Page references are to the 2017 edition.
Wen, Shawn. "The Ladies Vanish." *The New Inquiry*, November 11, 2014. https://thenewinquiry.com/the-ladies-vanish/.
Westad, Odd Arne. *The Global Cold War: Third World Interventions and the Making of Our Times*. Cambridge: Cambridge University Press, 2007.
Whitehead, Colson. *Zone One*. New York: Knopf, 2011.
Williams, Raymond. "Introduction" to *The Pelican Book of English Prose: From 1780 to the Present Day*, 2:19–55. Harmondsworth, UK: Penguin Books, 1969.
Winant, Gabriel. "Professional-Managerial Chasm." *n+1*, October 10, 2019. https://www.nplusonemag.com/online-only/online-only/professional-managerial-chasm/.
Wong, Jade Snow. *Fifth Chinese Daughter*. New York: Harper & Brothers, 1945.
Wong, Sau-ling. "Denationalization Reconsidered: Asian American Cultural Criticism at a Theoretical Crossroads." *Amerasia Journal* 21, no. 1 (1995): 1–28.
——. "Necessity and Extravagance in Maxine Hong Kingston's *The Woman Warrior*: Art and the Ethnic Experience." *MELUS* 15, no. 1 (Spring 1988): 3–26.
——. *Reading Asian American Literature: From Necessity to Extravagance*. Princeton, NJ: Princeton University Press, 1993.
——. "'Sugar Sisterhood': Situating the Amy Tan Phenomenon." In *The Ethnic Canon: Histories, Institutions, and Interventions*, ed. David Palumbo-Liu, 174–210. Minneapolis: University of Minnesota Press, 1995.
Wong, Winnie Won Yin. *Van Gogh on Demand: China and the Readymade*. Chicago: University of Chicago Press, 2013.
Woo, Jennie Hay. "Education and Economic Growth in Taiwan: A Case of Successful Planning." *World Development* 19, no. 8 (August 1991): 1029–44.
World Bank. *The East Asian Miracle: Economic Growth and Public Policy*. New York: Oxford University Press, 1993.
Wright, Erik Olin. "Intellectuals and the Working Class." *Critical Sociology* 8, no. 1 (1978): 5–18.
Wu, Judy Tzu-Chun. *Radicals on the Road: Internationalism, Orientalism, and Feminism During the Vietnam Era*. Ithaca, NY: Cornell University Press, 2013.
Wu, Zhouli. *Orphan of Asia*. 1945. Trans. Ioannis Mentzas. New York: Columbia University Press, 2006.
Wu-Clark, Audrey. *The Asian American Avant-Garde: Universalist Aspirations in Modernist Literature and Art*. Philadelphia: Temple University Press, 2015.
Xiang, Sunny. "Global China as Genre." *Post45* 2 (16 July 2019). https://post45.org/sections/issue/issue-2-how-to-be-now/.

———. "The Korean Voice of American Empire: The Democratic Spokesman and the Model Minority Narrator." *Journal of Asian American Studies* 17, no. 3 (October 2014): 273–304.

———. *Tonal Intelligence: The Aesthetics of Asian Inscrutability During the Long Cold War*. New York: Columbia University Press, 2020.

Yamashita, Karen Tei. *I Hotel*. Minneapolis: Coffee House Press, 2010.

———. *Through the Arc of the Rainforest*. Minneapolis: Coffee House Press, 1990.

———. *Tropic of Orange*. Minneapolis: Coffee House Press, 1997.

Yanagihara, Hanya. *To Paradise*. New York: Doubleday, 2022.

Yang, Alan, dir. *Tigertail*. Netflix, 2020.

Yang, Andrew. "We Asian Americans Are Not the Virus, but We Can Be Part of the Cure." *Washington Post*, April 1, 2020.

Yang, Fan. *Faked in China: Nation Branding, Counterfeit Culture, and Globalization*. Bloomington: Indiana University Press, 2015.

Yang, Gene Luen. *American Born Chinese*. New York: Square Fish, 2008.

Yang, Lawrence Zi-Qiao. "Soil and Scroll: The Agrarian Origin of a Cold War Documentary Avant Garde." *Modern Chinese Literature and Culture* 31, no. 2 (Fall 2019): 41–80.

Yellen, Jeremy A. *The Greater East Asia Co-Prosperity Sphere: When Total Empire Met Total War*. Ithaca, NY: Cornell University Press, 2019.

Yen, Anna. *Sophia of Silicon Valley*. New York: William Morrow, 2018.

Yep, Laurence. *Shadow Lord: A Star Trek Novel*. New York: Pocket Books, 1985.

———. *Sweetwater*. New York: Harper & Row, 1973.

Yoneyama, Lisa. *Cold War Ruins: Transpacific Critique of American Justice and Japanese War Crimes*. Durham, NC: Duke University Press, 2016.

Yu, Charles. *How to Live Safely in a Science Fictional Universe*. New York: Vintage Books, 2010.

———. *Interior Chinatown*. New York: Vintage Books, 2020.

Zhang, C Pam. *How Much of These Hills Is Gold*. New York: Riverhead, 2020.

Zhang, Jenny. *Sour Heart: Stories*. New York: Lenny, 2017.

Zhang, Jenny Tinghui. *Four Treasures of the Sky*. New York: Ecco Press, 2022.

INDEX

"Abducted by Aliens!" (Light), 83
Accent Research Collaborative, 257n49
Adams, Walter, 23
Adas, Michael, 48–49, 51, 88–89, 109
Advantageous (film), 27
aesthetic freedom, 104–12
After Yang (film), 27
Akamatsu, Kaname, 17, 52
"Algorithmic Problem-Solving for Father-Daughter Relationships" (Wang, J.), 93
All Flowers Bloom (Guillermo), 112
All the King's Men (Warren), 256n26
Almond, Gabriel, 47
Altered Carbon (TV series), 43
American fiction: academic writing programs for, 18–19; cyberpunk genre, 43–46; economic organization trends in, 118; program era, 159; science fictionality in, 25; social organization trends in, 118
American Is Not the Heart (Castillo), 12–13
Amsden, Alice, 61
antimodernity, in *A Tale for the Time Being*, 76
Apter, David, 47

"articulate silence," 127, 162, 176, 259n8
Asian American authors: Asian American-ness in writing, 129–30; as class formation, 19; Lukács and, 19; racial representation anxiety for, 84, 119; science fiction awards for, 26; typicality for, 19, 121. *See also* Chinese-American women authors; style; *specific authors*
Asian American fiction: bildungsroman genre in, 29; economics as popular theme, 120; global capitalism in, 13; intergenerational occupation narratives in, 11–12; literary representation as political representation in, 2; methodological approach to, 29–31, 33–38; 1991 as "annus mirabilis," 1–2; pop culture boom for, 228n4; realism in, 85, 114; repetition trope in, 85; science fictionality and, 25–32, 33–35; side-by-sideness and, 85; STEM-oriented trajectories in, 4; transimperiality and, 40, 62–82; in two-cultures conflict, 4, 98, 229n19. *See also specific authors; specific genres; specific works*

Asian American realism, 85; utopian dimension of, 114
Asian Americans: Black Americans and, 95; class identity diversity among, 10; during Cold War era, 8; double consciousness and, 119; hyperracialization of, 128; model minority status of, 9, 14–15, 41, 47, 89, 186; "nerd syndrome" and, 93; Northeast Asia as emblematic of, 16; "Northeast Asian American," 13–18; population growth for, 3; during post-civil rights era, 28–29; racial formation for, 53, 89; racialization of, 131; racial melancholia and, 162; second-generation convergence and, 22; STEM fields and, 3–4, 18; structural characteristics of daily life for, 9; "yellow peril" stereotype for, 14–15, 186. *See also* Chinese Americans; Chinese American women authors; Taiwanese Americans
Asians, Western stereotypes about, 136
Astonishing Color of After, The (Pan), 191
autobiographical elements: in *Native Speaker*, 146–47; in *The Woman Warrior*, 162
autopoetic style, 28, 69, 121–22, 147, 158–59, 180; expository impulse and, 115; in *The Woman Warrior*, 5
awkwardness, 19–20, 35, 41, 84, 118, 121, 125–27, 138, 140, 150, 179, 186–87, 221, 257n49

Bacon, Francis, 100
Bahng, Aimee, 43, 237n110
Bandung Conference, 40–41
Bascara, Victor, 41
Beck, Ulrich, 28
Bellah, Robert, 91
Bernes, Jasper, 115, 217
Bestiary (Chang, K-M.), 191
betweenness: professional-managerial class and, 179; Taiwan and, 183–91
big data, in *Native Speaker*, 140

bildungsroman genre, in Asian American fiction, 29
biracial identity, in *Halving the Bones*, 69–70
Black, Cyril, 47
Black Americans: Asian Americans and, 95; "The Negro Family" report, 89; in post-civil rights era, 28–29
Black Skin, White Masks (Fanon), 234n65
Blade Runner (film), 43–44
block time, 106
block universe theory, 106
Bodard, Aliette de, 26, 94
Bonacich, Edna, 23
Border of Paradise, The (Wang, E. W.), 191
Boyle, Chris, 189, 194
brain drain: through emigration, 24; human capital and, 23; from Japan, 24; from South Korea, 24; from Taiwan, 24, 59
Brockenbrough, Martha, 21
Brontë, Emily, 202
Brown, Melissa J., 181
Brown, Wendy, 231n35
Buddhism: in I-novel genre, 79; *Lion's Roar*, 80; nonduality principle in, 78–79; in *A Tale for the Time Being*, 77–78, 80
Bulosan, Carlos, 30
Bumming in Beijing (film), 173
Burma (Myanmar), in Greater East-Asia Co-Prosperity Sphere, 17
Butler, Lyn Liao, 156, 191

Cantos (Pound), 98
capitalism: Asian, 202–3; China's economic transition to, 18; in *On Such a Full Sea*, 153; racial, 132; White, 202–3. *See also* global capitalism
Card, Orson Scott, 64
Castillo, Elaine, 12–13
Celaya, Adrienne, 24
Cha, Theresa Hak Kyung, 85
Chabon, Michael, 160, 261n28
Chakabarty, Dipesh, 40, 85, 91–92

INDEX

Chandra, Sarika, 8–9, 233n49
Chang, Elysha, 20
Chang, Glenn, 27
Chang, Iris, 112
Chang, Jade, 196–97, 199, 203–4
Chang, K-Ming, 191
Chang, Lan Samantha, 43
Chang, Yoonmee, 20, 83, 90, 265n31
Chemistry (Wang, W.), 20, 157, 171
Chen, Christopher, 204
Chen, Kuan-Hsing, 180
Chen, Tina, 131, 137
Chen-Fan Pack, 225
Cheng, Anne, 162, 253n65
Cheng, Lucie, 23
Cheng, Wendy, 213, 221, 241n5, 265n28
Chen Qiufan, 64
Cheung, King-kok, 127, 162
Cheung-Miaw, Calvin, 10
Chiang, Mark, 10
Chiang, Ted, 83, 94, 219; aesthetic freedom as theme for, 104–12; *Exhalation*, 97; "Hell Is the Absence of God," 101; "Liking What You See," 101; modernity in works of, 87–88; modernization theory and, 101–2, 104–12; postracial dimensions in works of, 103–4; race in literary works, 102–3; *Stories of Your Life and Others*, 97–98; "Story of Your Life," 103–4, 106–7, 110, 114; temporality trope for, 95, 104–12; textual hermeneutics and, 107; "Tower of Babylon," 26, 97, 101; "The Truth of Fact, The Truth of Feeling," 107–8; "Understand," 98–100
Chiang Ching-kuo, 99, 185
Chiang Kai-shek, 53, 57, 184–85
Chieng, Chieh, 191
Chin, Frank, 1, 92, 103, 254n75
Chin, Marilyn, 1
China: capitalist boom in, 18; economic formation in, 16; economic rise trope, 162, 172, 191–97; industrial dependency with U.S., 14; May Fourth movement in, 50; modernization theory and, 62; "ping-pong" diplomacy, 141–42; semiperipherality and, 180–81; "Silicon Shield" of Taiwan, 180; Taiwan and, 180–81, 184; tourism industry in, 42; transition to capitalism, 18; U.S.-China political consciousness, 172–73; U.S.-China-Taiwan relations, 182–83
Chinese Americans: racial identity for, 178; return narratives for, 182
Chinese American women authors, feminine identity for, 5, 135. *See also specific authors*
Chinese economic rise trope, 162, 172, 191–97
Chinese laborers, in U.S., racialization of, 14
"Chinese-ness," 192–93
Ching, Leo, 41, 46, 184
Choi, Susan, 43, 93, 103
Chong, Vincent, 94
Chou, Elaine Hsieh, 20
Chow, Rey, 173
Chu, John, 27, 94
Chu, Patricia, 29, 90, 238n111
Chu, Wesley, 94
Chuh, Kandice, 10, 47
Clarke, Arthur C., 97
Clarkesworld, 64
class identity, among Asian-Americans, 10. *See also* economic class; professional-managerial class
Clinton, Bill, 151
Clough, Brenda W., 27
Clute, John, 102
Cohn, Dorrit, 201
Cold War: Asian-Americans' inclusion during, 8; neoimperialism and, 40; U.S. militarism during, 17
colonialism: Japanese, 7; in Korean peninsula, 16–17; trauma as result of, 124–25
conceptual breakthrough trope, 102
Condorcet, Marquis de, 49
Conrad, Joseph, 130, 202
Conrad, Sebastian, 56, 91, 246n70
constitutive dislocation, 9

Crazy Rich Asians (Kwan, K.), 191, 267n46
Cretton, Destin Daniel, 191
Critique of the Gotha Programme (Marx), 111
Csicsery-Ronay, Istvan, Jr., 6, 177
Cuba, U.S. occupation of, 52
cultural genocide, 124–25
Cumings, Bruce, 13, 52, 54, 187–88, 264n18; on Northeast Asia industrialization patterns, 16–17; on Taiwan nationalism, 60; on transnational power elite, 89
Cyberpunk (videogame), 44
cyberpunk genre, 43, 45–46; premise of, 44

Dalleo, Raphael, 90
Davies, Peter Ho, 20
Day, Iyko, 215, 217–18
Death in Venice (Mann), 202
decoupling, 14
deglobalization, 14
deindustrialization, 217–18
DeLillo, Don, 31, 256n26
Deng Xiaoping, 62, 174, 193
deprofessionalization, 162–67
determinism. *See* technological determinism
Deutsch, Karl, 47, 109
DICTEE (Cha), 85
didacticism, 85; in technical writing, 94
Dirlik, Arif, 183
discordant narration, 201–2
Disorientation (Chou), 20
Docquier, Frédéric, 3
Dogeaters (Hagedorn), 1
domestic space, for Chang-rae Lee, 126–27
Dos Passos, John, 94
double consciousness, 119
Du Bois, W. E. B., 28; double consciousness for, 119

East Asian Miracle, The (World Bank), 2, 60–61
East Asia region: economic formation in, 16; economic relationship with U.S., 15–16; economic stereotypes about, 49–50; "Four Tigers" in, 2; massacres in, 3; "miracle" economies in, 2–3; Vietnam War and, 3; World Bank on, 2–3. *See also* immigration; Northeast Asia; *specific countries*
economic class: Asian American authors and, 19; identity among Asian-Americans and, 10; professional-managerial class, 150–51; white-collar workers and, 19, 139
economic growth: in Fordist economic frameworks, 4; global narratives of, 4; in post-Fordist economic frameworks, 4; in postwar Japan, 61; in postwar South Korea, 61; in postwar Taiwan, 61; science fictionality and, 35–36
economic modernization. *See* modernization
Ehrenreich, Barbara, 19, 179, 181–82
Ehrenreich, John, 19, 179
Ekbladh, David, 5, 39–40, 241n2
emigration: brain drain and, 24; from Hong Kong, 3; Singapore, 3; South Korea, 3; from Taiwan, 3
Empire of Dreams and Miracles (Card and Olexa), 64
Ends of Empire (Kim, J.), 244n46, 248n117
Eng, David, 53
Engels, Frederick, 214
English-language acquisition, shame over, 125–27
Espiritu, Yen Le, 10
Everett, Hugh, 78
Everything Everywhere All at Once (film), 27
Everything I Never Told You (Ng), 20, 157, 173
expository impulse, 112, 114, 116; autopoetic tendencies in, 115

fallacy of disaggregation, 13, 52–53
Family Trust (Wang, K.), 20, 183, 188; semiperiphality and, 197–204
Fanon, Frantz, 176, 234n65

INDEX

Far, Sui Sin, 30
Farewell, The (film), 191
fauxtomation narratives, 272n29
feminine identity: for Chinese-American women authors, 5, 135; for Kingston, 155, 173–74. *See also* identity politics
feminism, 7–8
fetishism, of Asian identities, 214–21
Fifth Chinese Daughter (Wong, J. S.), 9
Finnegan's Wake (Joyce), 98
Fiona and Jane (Ho, J. C.), 20
Fisher, Mark, 218
"Fish of Lijiang, The" (Qiufan), 64
Flower Drum Song (Lee, C. Y.), 196
"Flowers for Algernon" (Keyes), 98
Floyd, Kevin, 8–9, 233n49
Fludernik, Monika, 202, 268n52
Fong-Torres, Ben, 97
Fordist economic frameworks: Asian labor in, 15–16; economic growth in, 4. *See also* post-Fordist economic frameworks
Foreigner, The (Lin, F.), 191
Foreign Student, The (Choi), 43
Fortunes, The (Davies), 20
Foster, Sesshu, 26, 83
"Four Tigers," economic strength of, 2. *See also* Hong Kong; Singapore; South Korea; Taiwan
Four Treasures of the Sky (Zhang, J. T.), 20
Fowler, Edna, 79
Friedan, Betty, 162
Friedman, Milton, 62
"*Fuerdai* to the Max" (Wang, X. J.), 171, 261n33
Fujitani, Takeshi, 41, 89, 91

Genealogy of Morals (Nietzsche), 266n38
genre turn, 27, 33–34, 160–61, 170–71, 175, 177, 240n121; in *Native Speaker*, 261n28
Gerrold, David, 97
Gewirtz, Julian, 61–62
Ghost Month (Lin, E.), 191
Gibson, William: "Burning Chrome," 45–46; cyberpunk fiction genre and, 43, 45–46; *Neuromancer*, 43–44

Gilman, Nils, 48–49, 109, 110
Glassman, Jim, 2–3, 60; on Pacific ruling class, 6, 40, 89, 182–83
global capitalism: in Asian American fiction, 13; Japan Panic and, 44
Goldman, Emma, 79
Goyal, Yogita, 8
Greene, J. Megan, 57
Green Island (Ryan), 185, 191
Guillermo, Kawika, 112
Guo Songfen, 6, 99

Hagedorn, Jessica, 1
Hall, John W., 55
Hamdan, Lawrence Abu, 257n49
Hansen, Brooks, 120
Hao, Kate, 16
Harootunian, Harry, 55–56
Hart-Celler Immigration and Nationality Act, U.S. (1965), 3, 21–23, 216
Hartley, Daniel, 119–20, 122–23; on epics, 160
Hayashi Fumiko, 249n128
Heart of Darkness (Conrad, J.), 130, 202
Hegel, Georg Wilhelm Friedrich, 49
Hemingway, Ernest, 94, 102
Henwood, Doug, 120
Hideki Tojo, 79
Hioe, Brian, 179
Hirabayashi Taiko, 249n128
historical justice, transimperiality and, 63
History and Class Consciousness (Lukács), 9
Ho, Jean Chen, 20
Hoberek, Andrew, 30, 95, 115, 160, 170, 261n28
Home of the Brave (Say), 20–21
Home Remedies (Wang, X. J.), 157, 171, 191
Hong Kong: emigration from, 3; among "Four Tigers," 2
Hongo, Garrett, 121
Hoover, Herbert, 65
Hornig, Donald, 58
Hoselitz, Bert, 47
Hoskins, Janet Alison, 237

How Much of These Hills Is Gold (Zhang, C P.), 20
How to Live Safely in a Science Fictional Universe (Yu, C.), 6, 20, 44–45, 93, 112, 113–14; chronodiegetic space in, 204; ressentiment in, 204–13; semiperipherality and, 188
Hsu, Funie, 179
Hsuing, Kei, 219
Huang, Michelle N., 78
Huang, Peter, 264n22
Huang, S. L., 27, 94
Huang Chi-lu, 58
Hughes, Langston, 209
human capital, 237n100; brain drain and, 23; in STEM fields, 4
"Human Development" (So, A. V.), 13
Hung, Ho-fung, 17–18, 62, 185
hyperracialization, 128

I Am an American (Brockenbrough, Lin, G., Kuo, J.), 21
identity. *See* biracial identity; class identity; feminine identity; national identity; racial identity
identity politics, 233n49; racial, 150; racial identity politics, 150; universalism and, 8–9
immigration, immigrants and, from East Asia region: achievement paradox and, 22; Customs and Border Protection agencies, 152; education levels of, 21–22; under Hart-Celler Immigration and Nationality Act, 3, 21–23; hyper-selection of, 4, 229n17; under Immigration Act, 151–52; Immigration and Customs Enforcement, 152; in *Native Speaker*, 152; second-generation convergence and, 22; success frame for, 22–23. *See also* emigration
Immigration Act, U.S. (1990), 151–52
Immigration and Customs Enforcement, in U.S., 152
Immigration and Naturalization Service, in U.S., 152

imperialism: Japanese, 17, 52; K. Liu on, 66; neoimperialism, 40, 72; in *A Tale for the Time Being*, 76. *See also* transimperiality
Impostor Syndrome (Wang, K.), 20
Inada, Lawson, 92
income levels, by race, in U.S., 32
Indian Americans, 91–92
industrialization: deindustrialization and, 217–18; patterns in Northeast Asia, 16–17; in postwar Japan, 61; in postwar South Korea, 61, 86; in postwar Taiwan, 61
Industrial Revolution, 14
Ineko Sata, 249n128
Innocent, The (Kim, R.), 242n14
I-novel genre *(shishōsetsu)*, 63; Buddhist influences in, 79; *A Tale for the Time Being*, 76, 78–82; utopian vision as part of, 82
Ishiguro, Kazuo, 34, 160, 202
Island X (Cheng, W.), 241n5
Is Taiwan Chinese? (Brown, M.), 181

Jackson, Jesse, 132
Jameson, Fredric, 122, 160
Jang, Jadie, 26
Jang, Sou Hyun, 22
Japan: brain drain from, 24; colonial projects in, 7; economic formation in, 16; in Greater East-Asia Co-Prosperity Sphere, 17; imperialism of, 17, 52; industrial dependency with U.S., 14; I-novel genre and, 63; postwar industrialization in, 61; Taiwan and, 184; transimperiality and, 241n6; U.S. foreign aid to, 53–54; U.S.-Japan relations, 241n6; U.S.-Japan Security Treaty, 5; "wild-geese flying" economic concept and, 17, 52
Japanese and Western Science, The (Watanabe), 39
Japan Panic, 44
Jasmine (Mukherjee), 1
Jen, Gish, 1, 27
Jin, Meng, 155–56, 191
Joan Is Okay (Wang, W.), 261n24

INDEX

Johnson, Lyndon B., 21, 58, 89
Joyce, James, 98
Joyride (film), 191
Julius Caesar (Shakespeare), 122
justice. *See* historical justice

Kadohata, Cynthia, 21, 26
Kagawa, Julie, 27
Kang, Laura Hyun Yi, 167
Kang, Younghill, 94, 170
Kanna Sugako, 79
Kant, Immanuel, 49
Keyes, Daniel, 98
Khor, Shing Yin, 21
Kibuishi, Kazu, 27
Kim, Adhy, 77
Kim, Alice Sola, 27
Kim, Claire Jean, 28
Kim, Daniel, 131–32, 137; on political and literary representation, 141
Kim, Elaine, 170
Kim, E. Tammy, 213
Kim, Jodi, 8, 131–32, 143, 244n46, 248n117
Kim, Richard, 242n14
King, Maggie Shen, 26
Kingston, Maxine Hong: embrace of femininity, 155, 173–74; on STEM fields, 155. *See also* Woman Warrior, The
Know My Name (Miller), 156–57, 173
Ko, Lisa, 20
Korean peninsula: cleaving language and, 130; colonization of, 16–17; Japanese imperialism and, 52; partition of, 130; patronage networks, 146; technical institutions in, 145; UN Korea Reconstruction Agency, 56; U.S. Agency for International Development in, 56; U.S. Military Government in Korea, 56. *See also* South Korea
Koshy, Susan, 10, 53, 156, 228n8
Kuang, R. F., 26, 112
Kunzru, Hari, 13
Kuo, Julia, 21
Kwan, Daniel, 27, 191
Kwan, Kevin, 191, 267n46
Kwang, John, 135

Lahiri, Jhumpa, 13
language acquisition, shame over, 125–27
Latham, Michael, 48, 99, 109
Layton, Edwin, 93
Leavers, The (Ko), 20
Leave Society (Lin, Tao), 182, 191
Lee, Chang-rae, 18, 21, 27, 115–16, 219; *Agnew Belittlehead,* 121, 129; *Aloft,* 31, 103, 123–24, 126; Asian Americanness of writing, 129–30; colonial trauma for, 124–25; "Coming Home Again," 124, 127; cultural genocide and, 124–25; domestic space for, 126–27; early professional career, 120–21; English-language acquisition shame and, 125–27; "The Faintest Echo of Our Language," 124–26, 128; *A Gesture Life,* 43, 123, 126, 137; hyperracialization and, 128; literary style for, 119, 121–44; metafictional reflexivity for, 122; mismatch tropes, 130–44; *My Year Abroad,* 31, 124, 126, 135–36, 141, 153, 262n4; revolutionary change for, 136–37; science fictionality and, 122; "Shakespeare words" style for, 121–22, 144–45; *The Surrendered,* 31, 126; temporality for, 136–37; "work of voice" and, 124, 140–41. *See also Native Speaker; On Such a Full Sea*
Lee, Chin Yang, 196
Lee, Christopher, 131, 137, 216
Lee, James Kyung-Jin, 131
Lee, Jennifer, 4, 21, 229n17
Lee, Julia H., 20, 92–93
Lee, Marilyn, 173
Lee, Robert G., 41, 170
Lee, Yoon Ha, 26, 94
Lee, Yoon Sun, 9, 11, 19, 114, 165, 232n38, 234n65; on Asian American realism, 84–87; on typicality, 9, 119
Lee Kuo-ting, 57
Lee-Tai, Amy, 21
Legend of Auntie Po, The (Khor), 21
Le-Khac, Long, 16
Lerner, Daniel, 47
Leung, Brian, 20

Levy, Marion, 55–56, 88
Li, Grace D., 20
liberal multiculturalism, 132–33, 149
Light, Claire, 26; "Abducted by Aliens!," 83; *Slightly Behind and to the Left,* 112
Lim, Adele, 191
Lim, Eugene, 26
Lin, Chia-Chia, 191
Lin, Ed, 191
Lin, Francine, 191
Lin, Grace, 21
Lin, Tao, 103, 182, 191, 236n87, 254n75
Lin, Tom, 20
Ling, Amy, 174
Ling, Jinqi, 10
Lion's Roar, 80
literary realism: Asian American, 85, 114; science fictionality and, 96–97; technical writing as distinct from, 96–97; totality and, 9
Little Gods (Jin, M.), 156, 191
Liu, Alan, 150
Liu, Ken, 26, 40; "A Brief History of the Trans-Pacific Tunnel," 65; "Carthaginian Rose," 64; early life of, 64; "Good Hunting," 66; on imperialism, 66; "Liking What You See," 112; literary reputation of, 64–65; literary style of, 94–95; "The Literomancer," 66; "The Man Who Ended History," 67–68, 112, 114; "Maxwell's Demon," 66; modernization theory and, 41, 66; national identity and, 67–68; "The Paper Menagerie," 64; professional identity of, 94–95; transimperiality and, 41, 63
Liu, Marjorie, 26, 27
Liu, Petrus, 180
Liu Cixin, 64–65
Liu Wen, 179
Lo, Malinda, 27
Longo, Bernadette, 96
Long Stay in a Distant Land, A (Chieng), 191
Louie, David Wong, 43
Lowe, Lisa, 10, 14, 28, 160, 240n121

Lowe, Pardee, 170
Luckhurst, Roger, 253n63
Lukács, Georg, 9, 119; Asian American author and, 19
Lye, Colleen, 10, 14–15, 215, 234n65, 266n34, 267n42

Ma, Ling, 26, 33, 155–56, 160–61, 168–78, 191–93, 219
MacArthur, Douglas, 53
magical realism, 164
Malabou, Catherine, 164
Manchuria, in Greater East-Asia Co-Prosperity Sphere, 17
Mandel, Emily St. John, 160
Mann, Thomas, 202
Martin, Theodore, 170
Martyred, The (Kim, R.), 242n14
Marx, Karl, 49, 111, 214; on fetishism, 216
Marxism: modernization theory and, 111; positivism and, 110; Rostow on, 110
Marxism and Form (Jameson), 122
Matrix, The (film series), 43
McCann, Sean, 30–31, 118, 260n15; on postmodernism, 161
McCarthy, Cormac, 160
McClanahan, Annie, 218, 272n29
McCunn, Ruthanne Lum, 1
McGrath, Charles, 121
McGurl, Mark, 18–19, 28, 30, 159; on postmodernism, 161, 165; on technomodernism, 260n15
Melamed, Jodi, 88, 90; liberal multiculturalism and, 149; neoliberal multiculturalism and, 133
Menand, Louis, 30
metafictional reflexivity, 122, 138
Miéville, China, 101, 253n65
Milken, Mike, 120
Miller, Chanel, 155–57, 173
Mills, C. Wright, 19, 89; on white collar class, 139
Min, Pyong Gap, 22
Mirrorshades (Sterling), 43
mismatch tropes, 130–44
Miyamoto Yuriko, 249n128

INDEX

model minority: Asian Americans as, 9, 14–15, 41, 47, 89, 186; definition of, 187; Taiwanese Americans as, 180
mode of production, 160; in *Native Speaker*, 151
modernism, in literature: postmodernism, 161, 165, 240n121; in *A Tale for the Time Being*, 76; technomodernism, 260n15
modernization, economic, global narratives of, 4
modernization theory: acceleration of history in, 109–10; T. Chiang and, 101–2, 104–12; China and, 62; in Cold War era, 48–49, 89–90; intellectual importation of, 56; K. Liu and, 41, 66; Marxism and, 111; methodological approach to, 41–42; Northeast Asia and, 51, 53; Ozeki and, 41; positivism and, 40; race and racism in, 90–91; scientific universalism and, 40; Snow on, 109; socialism and, 62; standard approaches to, 47–48; in Taiwan, 57; technological determinism and, 91
Morley, David, 44
Moynihan, Daniel Patrick, 89
Mukherjee, Bharati, 1, 13
multiculturalism: liberal, 132–33, 149; neoliberal, 133, 149
Mysteries of Pittsburgh, The (Chabon), 261n28

Nadal, Paul, 237n100
Names (DeLillo), 256n26
narration, narrators and: discordant, 201–2; in *A Tale for the Time Being*, 75–76
national identity: K. Liu and, 67–68; in *A Tale for the Time Being*, 75–76; transimperiality and, 63
nationalism: in South Korea, 60; in Taiwan, 60, 212–13
Native Speaker (Lee, Chang-rae), 85, 256n26, 258n65, 269n59; autobiographical elements in, 146–47; big data in, 140; canonical status of, 131; as family stories, 135; genre turn in, 261n28; immigration themes in, 152; language of space and time, 143–44; liberal multiculturalism in, 132–33; literary mode of aesthetic in, 147; literary style of, 117, 123; lyrical passages in, 134; metafictional reflexivity in, 122, 138; mode of production in, 151; professional-managerial class in, 150–51; "Shakespeare words," 121–22, 144–45; in spy genre, 131, 137; teamwork as theme in, 147–53
nature themes, in *A Tale for the Time Being*, 77
"The Negro Family" Report (Moynihan), 89
Nehru, Jawaharlal, 109
neoimperialism: Cold War and, 40; conflation of race and sickness, 72
neoliberalism: globalization of, 149; stagism and, 48; Taiwan and, 60, 185–86
neoliberal multiculturalism, 133, 149
nerd syndrome, 93, 155
Nevala-Lee, Alec, 26
Never Let Me Go (Ishiguro), 34
New Atlantis (Bacon), 100
New Waves (Nguyen, K.), 13
Ng, Celeste, 20, 155–57, 173
Ngai, Mae, 152
Nguyen, Kevin, 13
Nguyen, Viet Thanh, 10, 47, 103, 137–38, 187, 195, 228n8; transpacific framework for, 237n110
Nicholls, Peter, 102
Nietzsche, Friedrich, 266n38
Night of the Living Dead (film), 169
Ninh, erin Khûe, 10, 162, 187
nonduality principle, 78–79
Northeast Asia: Asia America and, 16; Asian Americans and, 16; economic formation of, 16; industrialization patterns in, 16–17; modernization theory and, 51, 53; political economy of, 16; transimperiality and, 51–82; "wild-geese flying" economic concept and, 17, 52

"Northeast Asian Americans," 15–18; definition of term, 12; as geopolitical space, 13; role in U.S. industrial Revolution, 14

Obama, Barack, 64
Okada, John, 83
Olexa, Keith, 64
Omega Man, The (film), 169
Omi, Michael, 266n34
Ong, Aihwa, 243n21
Ong, Paul, 23
On Such a Full Sea (Lee, Chang-rae), 18, 21, 27, 122–26, 136–37, 141, 144; capitalism themes in, 153; mode of production in, 151
Ortolano, Guy, 229n19, 244n38
Ozeki, Ruth, 40, 160, 219, 248n118; *All Over Creation*, 71, 79, 81; biracial identity of, 69–70; Buddhist materialism and, 70; "Confessions of a Zen Novelist," 80; *Halving the Bones*, 69–72, 79; I-novel genre and, 63, 76, 78–82; modernization theory and, 41; *My Year of Meats*, 43, 71–72, 79, 81; transimperiality and, 41, 63. *See also Tale for the Time Being, A*

Pak, Greg, 27
Pan, Emily X. R., 191
Parikh, Crystal, 131–32
Park, Henry, 116
Park, Linda Sue, 21
Park Chung-hee, 57, 85, 185
Parson, Talcott, 49–50, 99
patronage networks, 146
Person of Interest, A (Choi), 93
Petersen, William, 59
Philippines, the: in Greater East-Asia Co-Prosperity Sphere, 17; U.S. occupation of, 52
Phillis, Jen Hedler, 8–9, 233n49
physical abuse, as theme, 73–74
"ping-pong" diplomacy, 141–42
Place Where the Sunflowers Grow, A (Lee-Tai), 21
PMC. *See* professional-managerial class

political economies, of Northeast Asia, 16
Pon, Cindy, 27
Poppy War, The (Kuang), 112
Portes, Alejandro, 24
Portrait of a Thief (Li), 20
positivism: Marxism and, 110; modernization theory and, 40
post-apocalyptic genre, 169–70; *Severance*, 170, 175
post-Fordist economic frameworks, 4; Asian labor in, 15–16
postmodernism, 161, 165, 240n121
Postone, Moishe, 215
postracial fiction, 232n38
post-racialism, 90; in T. Chiang works, 103–4
postracial literary aesthetics, 90
poststructuralism, 7–8
Pound, Ezra, 94, 98
Prairie Lotus (Park, L. S.), 21
Prince, Gerald, 201
Private Citizens (Tulathimutte), 13
professional-managerial class (PMC), 150–51; betweenness and, 179; expansion of, 161; Taiwanese Americans and, 179–80
program era fiction, 159
prose engineers, 92–97
Pye, Lucian, 47, 49, 55–56, 88–89
Pynchon, Thomas, 31

Quitter's Paradise, A (Chang, E.), 20

race, racism and: in T. Chaing works, 102–3; epidermal racial schema, 176; hyperracialization, 128; liberal multiculturalism, 149; modernization theory and, 90; "The Negro Family," 89; post-racialism and, 90; postracial literary aesthetics and, 90
race and sickness, conflation of: in *Halving the Bones*, 72; in *My Year of Meats*, 72
racial asymmetry, 83–84, 232n38
racial formation theory, 266n34

INDEX

racial identity: for Chinese Americans, 178; loss of, 177; for Taiwanese Americans, 183
racial identity politics, 150
racialization: of Asian Americans, 128, 131; of Chinese laborers in U.S., 14
racial melancholia, 162
racial representation anxiety, for Asian American authors, 84, 119
Rapoport, Hillel, 3
Reagan, Ronald, 151
realism. *See* Asian American realism; literary realism; magical realism
Reich, Robert, 139
Reischauer, Edwin O., 55, 91
Remains of the Day (Ishiguro), 202
Remembrance of Earth's Past (Liu), 64
Resisters, The (Jen), 27
ressentiment, 204–13, 266n38
return narratives, 182, 191, 267n40
Riesman, David, 19
Rigger, Shelley, 185, 197
Rivera, Takeo, 217
Robins, Kevin, 44
Robot Stories (film), 27
Romero, George, 169
Rosca, Ninotchka, 242n14
Rosen, Jeremy, 160
Rosenberg, Justin, 189, 194
Rostow, Walt, 47–48, 56, 69, 88, 253n63; economic development theories, 61; on Marxism, 110
Roth, Philip, 31
Ryan, Shawna Yang, 185, 191

Saez, Elena Machado, 90
Sagal, Boris, 169
Said, Edward, 50
Saldivar, Ramon, 90
Sapir-Whorf hypothesis, 108
Sawyer, Robert, 97
Saxenian, AnnaLee, 7, 23–24, 208
Say, Allen, 20–21
Scheinert, Daniel, 27, 191
science, technology, engineering, and math fields (STEM fields): in Asian American fiction, 4; Asian Americans and, 3–4, 18; double professionalization and, 19–20; human capital in, 4; program era fiction and, 159; skill sets for, 6–7; in South Korea, 146; in Taiwan, 58–59; in two-cultures conflict, 4; in *The Woman Warrior*, 5
science fiction: awards for Asian American authors, 26; cyberpunk genre, 43–46; science fictionality as distinct from, 25–26
science fictionality, 5; in American fiction, 25; Asian American fiction and, 25–32, 33–35; Asian economic futurity in, 35–36; definition of, 62; Chang-rae Lee and, 122; literary realism and, 96–97; in *My Year of Meats*, 71–72; occupational concentration and, 25; parameters of, 62; science fiction as distinct from, 25–26; technical writing and, 95; transimperiality in, 7, 62–82; as U.S.-Asia form, 25; in *The Woman Warrior*, 161–62, 174–75
scientific desert, Taiwan as, 59
scientific universalism, 40
Scott, Ridley, 43
second-generation convergence, 22
Seiss, Scott, 218–19
semiperipherality: central features of, 180; China role in, 180–81; Family Trust and, 197–204; in *How to Live Safely in a Science Fictional Universe*, 188; structure of feeling for, 181; of Taiwan, 179; Taiwan and, 179; Taiwanese Americans and, 179; Wallerstein on, 180–82
Seth, Micheal J., 57, 146
Severance (Ma), 26, 33, 156, 161, 168–69, 171–74; Chinese-ness in, 192–93; as epic literary history, 170; genre turn in, 170, 177; *The Joy Luck Club* and, 191; post-apocalyptic setting for, 170, 175–78
Shakespeare, William, 122
"Shakespeare words" style, 121–22, 144–45

Shang-Chi and the Legend of the Ten Rings (film), 191
Shih, Shu-mei, 186
shishōsetsu genre. *See* I-novel genre
side-by-sideness, 85
Singapore: emigration from, 3; among "Four Tigers," 2
Sinykin, Dan, 28
Sixteen Syllables (Yamamoto), 1
Slightly Behind and to the Left (Light), 112
Smith, Adam, 49
Snow, C. P., 49, 244n38; critique of modernization theory, 109; on two-cultures conflict, 4, 98, 229n19
So, Anthony Veasna, 13
So, Christine, 13, 174, 267n39
socialism, modernization theory and, 62
Sohn, Stephen Hong, 83–84, 232n38
Song, Han, 239n112
Song, Min Hyoung, 1–2, 43, 170, 227n3
Song Everlasting, A (Jin, H.), 156
Sophia of Silicon Valley (Yen), 20, 182, 191, 203
Soto Zen, 81
Sour Heart (Zhang, J. T.), 157, 172
South Korea: brain drain from, 24; cultural attitudes in, 4; economic formation in, 16; emigration rates from, 3; among "Four Tigers," 2; in Greater East-Asia Co-Prosperity Sphere, 17; Institute for Science and Technology, 58; nationalism in, 60; Park Chung-hee and, 57, 85, 145; postwar industrialization in, 61, 86; social attitudes in, 4; STEM professionals in, 146; typicality and, 119; U.S. foreign aid to, 53–54
spirituality themes, 81
spy genre, *Native Speaker*, 131, 137
Stages of Economic Growth, The (Rostow), 47–48, 56, 69
stagism, neoliberalism and, 48
State of War (Rosca), 242n14
STEM fields. *See* science, technology, engineering, and math fields

stereotypes: about East Asia region, 49–50; typicality as distinct from, 119; Western, 136; "yellow peril," 14–15, 186
Sterling, Bruce, 43
Stone, Oliver, 120
strategic essentialism, 23
Strychacz, Thomas, 30
style, literary: Asian American-ness of writing, 129–30; elements of, 123; Hartley on, 119–20, 122–23; for Chang-rae Lee, 119, 121–44; mismatch tropes, 130–44; mode of aesthetic, 147; in *Native Speaker*, 117, 123; poetic configuration and, 119; "Shakespeare words," 121–22, 144–45; transindividual subjectivity and, 123; "work of voice" and, 124, 140–41; for C. Yu, 206
success frame, for immigrants, 22–23
Suh, Chris, 17, 52, 251n30
Suzuki, Erin, 237n110
Szalay, Michael, 30, 258n65
Sze, Arthur, 94

Taipei (Lin, Tao), 182, 191, 236n87, 254n75
Taiwan: betweenness and, 183–91; brain drain from, 24, 59; China and, 180–81, 184; cultural attitudes in, 4; Dutch East India Company in, 183–84; economic formation in, 16; economic miracle in, 57; emigration from, 3; among "Four Tigers," 2; geopolitical position of, 180; in Greater East-Asia Co-Prosperity Sphere, 17; as Japanese colony, 184; modernization theory in, 57; National Council for Scientific Development, 58; nationalism in, 60, 212–13; neoliberalism and, 60, 185–86; postwar industrialization in, 61; as scientific desert, 59; semiperipherality and, 179; "Silicon Shield" from China, 180; social attitudes in, 4; STEM in, 58–59;

INDEX

U.S.-China-Taiwan relations, 182–83; U.S. foreign aid to, 53–54, *54*
Taiwanese Americans: as political model minority, 180; professional-managerial class and, 179–80; racial identity for, 183; return narratives for, 182; semiperipherality and, 179
Takei, George, 20
Take Me Home (Leung), 20
Tale for the Time Being, A (Ozeki), 27, 34, 45, 68; antimodernity and, 76; Buddhist philosophy in, 77–78, 80; historical events in, 72–73; imperialism themes in, 76; I-novel genre and, 76, 78–82; modernity and, 76; narration in, 75–76; national identity in, 75–76; nature themes in, 77; nonduality principle in, 78–79; physical abuse themes in, 73–74; repetition trope in, 72, 74; Soto Zen and, 81; spirituality themes in, 81
Tan, Amy, 94; *The Joy Luck Club*, 1, 45, 97, 192–94; *The Kitchen God's Wife*, 1
Tan, Lucy, 155–57, 171, 191
teamwork themes, in *Native Speaker*, 147–53
technical writing: didacticism in, 94; history of, 96; literary realism as distinct from, 96–97; prose engineers, 92–97; science fictionality, 95
technological determinism, 91
technomodernism, 260n15
temporality trope: for Chang-rae Lee, 136–37; in T. Chiang works, 95, 104–12
Thailand, in Greater East-Asia Co-Prosperity Sphere, 17
Thatcher, Margaret, 151
theory of omission, 102
They Called Us Enemy (Takei), 20
Thousand Crimes of Ming Tsu, The (Lin, Tom), 20
Through the Arc of the Rainforest (Yamashita), 1, 43, 242n15
Tichi, Cecelia, 93–94
Tiger Mom's Tale, The (Butler), 156
Tigertail (film), 191
Time Machine, The (Wells), 106

Toffler, Alvin, 62
Tokugawa Religion (Bellah), 91
To Paradise (Yanagihara), 20
totality, typicality and, 9
Trachtenberg, Allen, 93
transimperiality: Asian American fiction and, 40, 62–82; historical justice and, 63; in K. Liu works, 41, 63; national identity and, 63; Northeast Asia political economy and, 51–82; in Ozeki works, 41, 63; in science fictionality, 7, 62–82; temporal scale and, 63; U.S.-Japan relations and, 241n6
transitional justice, 63
Trans-Pacific Tunnel, 65
tropes, literary: Chinese economic rise trope, 162, 172, 191–97; conceptual breakthrough trope, 102; mismatch tropes, 130–44; repetition trope, 72, 74, 85; STEM trope, 5; temporality trope, 95, 104–12, 136–37
Tropic of Orange (Yamashita), 83
Trotsky, Leon, 189–90
Trump, Donald, 265n29
Trust Exercise (Choi), 103
Tulathimutte, Tony, 13
two-cultures conflict, 4, 98, 229n19
Typical American, A (Jen), 1
typicality: for Asian American authors, 121; South Korea and, 119; stereotype as distinct from, 119; totality and, 9

United States (U.S.): Chinese laborers in, 14; Cuba occupied by, 52; Customs and Border Protection agencies, 152; economic relationship with East Asia region, 15–16; foreign policy for, 48–50; Hart-Celler Immigration and Nationality Act, 3, 21–23, 216; Immigration Act, 151–52; Immigration and Customs Enforcement in, 152; Immigration and Naturalization Service in, 152; income levels by race, 32; industrial dependency with China, 14; industrial dependency with Japan, 14; Industrial Revolution in, 14; Japan

United States (U.S.) (*continued*)
  as foreign aid recipient, 53–54;
  "Northeast Asian American" in, 13–18;
  Philippines occupied by, 52; post-civil rights era in, 28–29; South Korea as foreign aid recipient, 53–54; Taiwan as foreign aid recipient, 53–54, 54; Taiwanese foreign students in, 184–85; transimperiality and, 241n6; U.S.-China political consciousness, 172–73; U.S.-Japan relations, 241n6; U.S.-Japan Security Treaty, 5; U.S. Military Government in Korea, 56; White Americans, 28–29. *See also* Asian Americans; Black Americans; Cold War; *specific works*
universalism: identity politics and, 8–9; modernization theory and, 40; scientific, 40
UN Korea Reconstruction Agency, 56
Unpassing, The (Lin, Chia-Chia), 191
U.S. *See* United States
U.S. Agency for International Development (USAID), 56
USAID. *See* U.S. Agency for International Development
USAMGIK. *See* U.S. Military Government in Korea
U.S.-China-Taiwan relations, 182–83
U.S.-Japan relations, 241n6
U.S. Military Government in Korea (USAMGIK), 56

Vietnam War, 3
Vint, Sherryl, 97–98

Wallerstein, Immanuel, 180–82
Wall Street, 120
Wang, Chih-ming, 51, 59–60, 211
Wang, Esme Weijun, 191
Wang, Kathy, 20, 31, 188, 220
Wang, Lulu, 191
Wang, Weike, 20, 155–57, 171, 261
Wang, Xuan Juliana, 26, 93–94, 155–57, 171, 191, 261n33
Wangs vs. The World, The (Chang, J.), 196–97, 199, 203–4

Warren, Robert Penn, 256n26
Watanabe Masao, 39
Watson, Jini Kim, 4
Weber, Max, 49–50, 99
Weedflower (Kadohata), 21
Wegner, Phillip E., 30
Weiner, Myron, 47
Wells, H. G., 106
Westad, Odd Arne, 51, 88
What We Were Promised (Tan, L.), 157, 171, 191
White Americans, in post-civil rights era, 28–29
White capitalism, 202–3
white-collar workers, 19; Mills on, 139
Whitehead, Colson, 33, 160, 169, 175
white supremacist racial order, 88–89
Whyte, William, 19
"wild-geese flying" economic concept, 17, 52
Williams, Raymond, 122–23, 133
Williams, William Carlos, 94
Winant, Howard, 88, 266n34
Wired, 43
Woman Warrior, The (Kingston), 42, 85; airport setting for, 163–64, 167; autobiographical elements in, 162; autopoetic style in, 5; deprofessionalization in, 162–67; fantastical elements of, 169; feminine identity themes in, 157; literary legacy of, 162, 259n7; magical realism in, 164; narrative structure of, 162–63; nerd syndrome and, 155; post-apocalyptic setting for, 169–70; postmodernism in, 165; science fictionality and, 161–62, 174–75; STEM trope in, 5; timing of publication for, 160–61
women. *See* Chinese-American women authors; feminine identity
Wong, Jade Snow, 9, 170
Wong, Sau-ling, 1, 93, 162, 167
Wong, Shawn, 92
"work of voice," 124, 140–41
World Bank, 60–61; on "miracle" economies in East Asia, 2–3
Wu, Frank, 94

INDEX

Wu, William F., 27
Wu-Clark, Audrey, 30
Wuthering Heights (Brontë), 202
Wu Wenguang, 173

Xiang, Sunny, 131, 133–34, 140, 200, 269n59

Yamamoto, Hisaye, 1
Yamashita, Karen Tei, 27; *Through the Arc of the Rainforest*, 1, 43, 243n15; *I-Hotel*, 85; *Tropic of Orange*, 83
Yanagihara, Hanya, 20
Yang, Alan, 191
Yang, Andrew, 195, 219
Yang, Gene Luen, 27

"yellow peril" stereotype, 14–15, 186
Yen, Anna, 20, 182, 191, 203
Yin, C. K., 58
Yin, K. Y., 57
Yoneyama, Lisa, 63, 245n48
Yōsuke Matsuoka, 17
Yu, Charles, 27, 31, 83; literary style for, 205; Taiwanese American identity for, 181. *See also How to Live Safely in a Science Fictional Universe*
Yu, E. Lily, 26, 83

Zhang, C Pam, 20
Zhang, Jenny Tinghui, 20, 155, 157, 172
Zhou, Min, 4, 21, 229n17
Zone One (Whitehead), 33, 169, 175

GPSR Authorized Representative: Easy Access System Europe, Mustamäe tee 50, 10621 Tallinn, Estonia, gpsr.requests@easproject.com

www.ingramcontent.com/pod-product-compliance
Lightning Source LLC
Chambersburg PA
CBHW022034290426
44109CB00014B/861